SISTERS OF GORE

A nineteenth-century satirical print of a melodrama produced at the Royal Victoria Theatre.

SISTERS OF GORE

GOTHIC MELODRAMAS BY BRITISH WOMEN

EDITED BY

JOHN FRANCESCHINA

ROUTLEDGE
A MEMBER OF THE ATAYLOR & FRANCIS GROUP
NEW YORK AND LONDON

First paperback edition published in 2000 by
Routledge
29 West 35th Street
New York, NY 10001

Published in Great Britiain by
Routledge
11 New Fetter Lane
London EC4P 4EE

Routledge is an imprint of the Taylor & Francis Group

Copyright © 1997 by John Franceschina
Previously published as vol. 2076 in the Garland Reference Library of the Humanities.

Library of Congress Cataloging-Publication-Data

Sisters of Gore : Gothic melodramas by British women / [edited with
  introductions and notes by] John Franceschina.
       p. cm.
       Includes bibliographical references.
       Contents: The ward of the castle—The mysterious marriage—The old
oak chest–Raymond de Percy—St. Clair of the Isles—The bond—Dacre of the
South.
       ISBN 0-8153-1781-6 (alk. paper)
       ISBN 0-415-92897-4 (pbk.)
       1. Horror tales, English. 2. Gothic revival (Literature)—Great Britain.
3. English fiction—Women authors. 4. English fiction—19th century. 5. English
fiction—18th century. 6. Women—Fiction. I. Franceschina, John Charles,
1947– . II. Series.
PR830.T3S57 1997
823'.08729089287—dc20   96-24213
                                                                      CIP

Printed on acid-free, 250-year-life paper
Manufactured in the United States of America

10 9 8 7 6 5 4 3 2 1

Contents

TheatreRoyal,Hay-Market.

This Evening, THURSDAY, June 18, 1835,

Will be performed, (FIFTH TIME)

A MUSICAL AND ORIGINAL COMEDY, in Two Acts, (*by the Author of MARRIED LIFE, UNCLE JOHN, RURAL FELICITY, &c.*) called

GOOD HUSBANDS
MAKE GOOD WIVES

THE WHOLE OF THE MUSIC by Mr. ALEXANDER LEE.

Captain Alfred Gay, -	Mr. BRINDAL,
Lieutenant Sidney,	Mr. ANDERSON,
Mr. William Faithful, -	Mr. BUCKSTONE,
Mr. Thomas Gadfly,	Mr. VINING,
James, Mr. ROSS,	Waiter, Mr. ELLIS,
Miss Careful,	Mrs. GLOVER,
Florence, Mrs. CRAWFORD, (late Miss ELIZA PATON.)	
Eleanor,	Miss TURPIN,
Mrs. Faithful, -	Mrs. HUMBY,
Mrs. Gadfly,	Mrs. NEWCOMBE.

After which, an entirely Original Comedy, in Three Acts, called

Married Life

Mr. Samuel Coddle, -	Mr. WEBSTER,
Mrs. Samuel Coddle, -	Mrs. GLOVER,
Mr. Lionel Lynx, -	Mr. VINING,
Mrs. Lionel Lynx, -	Miss TAYLOR,
Mr. Henry Dove, -	Mr. BUCKSTONE,
Mrs. Henry Dove, -	Mrs. W. CLIFFORD,
Mr. Frederick Younghusband,	Mr. BRINDAL,
Mrs. Frederick Younghusband,	Mrs. HUMBY,
Mr. George Dismal, -	Mr. STRICKLAND,
Mrs. George Dismal, -	Mrs. W. DALY.

To conclude with Mrs. GORE's Drama, in Two Acts, called

TheQUEEN'sCHAMPION

An interval of Five Years is supposed to pass between the Acts.

Salvoisy,	Mr. VINING,
TheDuc de Lauzun,	Mr. BRINDAL,
Marquis de Vassan,	Mr. STRICKLAND,
Doctor Bourdillac,	Mr. WEBSTER,
The Queen, (Marie Antoinette)	Miss TAYLOR,
Princess, (de Guemencè)	Miss E. PHILLIPS,
Louise, (a Peasant)	Mrs. HUMBY.

Stage-Manager, Mr. VINING.]   [VIVANT REX ET REGINA!

A playbill advertising Catherine Gore's melodrama *The Queen's Champion*, performed as an afterpiece at the Theatre Royal Haymarket in 1835.

Preface

Reversal of female fortune is a common melodramatic device. The heroine frequently comes to a point where all seems lost—she may have suffered cruelly through the actions of the evil villain and is often physically in danger. At the last minute, when rescue seems impossible, her release and triumph are assured. With the publication of these melodramas written by women authors between 1790 and 1843, scholarship has imitated art. With one bound and a two-hundred year wait, they are free.

This volume is a cause for celebration for theatre historians, for those who will now have the opportunity to stage and perform in the works, as well as for those who are involved in the reassessment of women's place in society in the late eighteenth and early nineteenth centuries. Until now melodrama of this period available in print was almost exclusively written by men, and the existence of works by these feisty ladies was little known. Theatre historians have primarily studied the work of male authors and there has been a significant lack of scholarship on women's work in the field. A reason for this has been the lack of knowledge of a representative female canon, especially of melodramas by women written before the Theatre Regulation Act of 1843.

Perhaps because of the matriarchal attitudes toward women nurtured in the age of Queen Victoria, the idealized woman of the nineteenth century seen in novels and drama was submissive and maternal. The Gothic melodramas popular at the turn of the century, however, often featured the more spirited damsel who took matters in her own hands to overcome her distress, such as James Cross's character Nancy who in *Blackbeard; or, The Captive Princess*, 1798, disguised herself as a pirate and joined enthusiastically in attacks on the high seas. The active female was indeed present in male melodrama, but how much more fascinating it then becomes to see her written by women. In Elizabeth Polack's *St. Clair of the Isles*, 1838, the more usual villain is actually replaced by a villainess whose manipulations are more than a match for the men in her way. Despite the fact that the women writers represented here were working in a predominantly male tradition, this cannot negate the fact that women must be better qualified than men to create female characters. Their characters must speak in voices that ring true, or which echo male stereotypes about women, knowingly played upon by the writers concerned. By reading and performing these texts, the fascination comes from reading behind the lines and distinguishing the truth from the stereotypes.

Familiarity often breeds contempt. With the move toward increasingly naturalistic drama from the late nineteenth century onward, melodrama suffered from a bad press. Serious efforts at production and reassessment of the various types of melodrama have been relatively recent, and yet without representation from its female writers, unbalanced. With this volume the imbalance is corrected. Melodrama is an immensely worthwhile area of study, and a rewarding if difficult genre to perform. Twentieth-century directors have on the whole fought shy of contemporary productions, perhaps because of melodrama's unbridled theatricality, the high octane level of emotions it demands from its actors, and the suspension of disbelief that needs to be encouraged in its audiences. By examining the background of the theatre which nurtured melodrama in the late eighteenth and early nineteenth century, John Franceschina gives an insight into how melodrama should be both analyzed and performed.

When these plays were originally written and enthusiastically received on stage, melodrama was fanatically popular with large audiences. The power of the taste of audiences of the day should not be underestimated. Without subsidy or sponsorship, theatres were obliged to listen to their audiences and were foolish if they did not bow to their preferences. Late Georgian and early Victorian theatre-goers saw the theatre as a participatory sport and just as they noisily showed their involvement in the popular pieces, so they frequently interrupted unsuccessful performances with comments and missiles, sometimes resorting to riot to demonstrate their displeasure. They were generally more unsophisticated than today's theatre-goers, eager to believe in the ghosts and Vampires of the Gothic melodramas, and the oleaginous fortune-hunters of the later 'gentlemanly' melodramas.

The earliest melodramas partly owed their existence to the division of theatres in England into 'major' and 'minor' theatres, or, theatres that had a royal 'patent' and could produce drama without interpolated music and those that did not and had to include five or six songs in each act, as long as the songs formed a 'natural part of the piece.' At the so-called 'minor' houses enthusiastic audiences demanded ever more exciting action and scenic spectacle and authors of melodrama were ready to supply it. Such was their popularity that before long proprietors of the patent or 'major' theatres found that their audiences were demanding similar entertainment, especially since the newly-enlarged auditoria of the patent houses including Covent Garden and Drury Lane were better suited to large-scale effects on stage and desperately needed large audiences to remain solvent. In 1843 the Theatre Regulation Act was passed to eliminate the artificial distinctions between the two types of theatre, but by then the system had become unworkable and the differences between their types of production had become minimal. The bills of fare being offered at the minor theatres did not change radically after the 1843 Act because the melodramas and burlesques that they presented were what the public wanted.

The plays by the writers represented in this anthology span the development of melodrama from the 1790s to the 1840s. Miss Burke's *The Ward of the Castle*, 1793, is an early example of Gothic melodrama, written before the romantic spectre-scattered genre really came to prominence. Harriet Lee's *The Mysterious Marriage*, written in 1793 and published in 1798, employs a ghost anticipating that of Monk Lewis's popular *The Castle Spectre*. Jane Scott's *The Old Oak Chest*, 1816, was the most popular melodrama written by a woman during the heyday of Gothic melodrama. It shamelessly appealed to vulgar tastes and was repaid by huge success and the reproduction of its scenes and characters in prints by publishers designed for performance at home in toy theatres. In contrast, Margaret Harvey's *Raymond de Percy; or, The Tenant of the Tomb*, 1822, did aspire to inject literary qualities into melodrama and based her melodrama on historical characters. More critically successful, Elizabeth Polack's *St. Clair of the Isles*, 1838, was set in Scotland and featured the evil villainess that the author so clearly relished creating. Finally this volume reprints two melodramas by Catherine Gore, the first female writer of 'gentlemanly melodrama'—*The Bond*, 1824, and *Dacre of the South*, 1840. The variety of these works is remarkable; their rescue from oblivion is a major contribution to several fields of study and a tribute to the authors' persistence, vision, and scholarship.

Catherine Haill
The Theatre Museum
Victoria and Albert Museum, London

The Grand Spectacle of ULTHONA THE SORCERESS, continuing to be Received with unbounded Applause, by an overflowing Audience will be Repeated for the 62d Time, *This present Evening.*

SCOTT WAS PROPRIETOR OF THE NEW THEATRE,
ADELPHI THEATRE
IS ALSO CALLED —
TRUE BLUE SCOTT

Sans Pareil,

STRAND, OPPOSITE THE ADELPHI.

By Authority of the Lord Chamberlain.

The New Comic Ballet of Action being received with the highest Approbation, WILL BE REPEATED,

THIS PRESENT EVENING.

Previous to which, will be performed, A New Musical Piece, written by Miss SCOTT, intitled, THE

SUCCESSFUL CRUISE;

Or, NOBODY COMING TO WOO.

The Music, with a New Overture, arranged and composed by Mr. Sanderson ——Principal Characters—
Mary Ann, Miss Harrison. Lubin, Master Flexmore. Colin, Master Leclerq. Mainstay, Mr. Moss. Fairlop, Mr. Glayre. William, Master Hodson. Dame Fairlop, Mrs. Macartney.
And Jennett, Miss SCOTT.

After which, the New serio-comic Ballet of Action, with new Scenery, Dresses, and Decorations, composed and produced by Mr. GIROUX, and executed by his Pupils, called,

MONKEY ISLAND;

Or, the Faithful Negro.

The Music, with a New Overture, by Mr. Sanderson.——Principal Characters—
Master Coste, Master Flexmore, Master Durousset; Misses Bradwell, Mosley, Hart, Harrison; as Monkeys, Master Brown, Tatton, Askews, Newman, and Leclerq.
And Maria, Miss CAROLINE GIROUX.

In the Ballet, will be introduced,

The Minuet de la Cour, and favorite Gavotte of

VESTRIS, FROM THE OPERA OF PARIS,

Burlesqued by Two Monkies,

Also, Two Negro Songs, by Master Durousset, written by Miss SCOTT.

In the Course of the Evening, between the Pieces,

The Favorite SONGS of *Tarry Awhile,* by Mrs. Macartney, and a *Character Song,* by Mr. Denham.
And Imitations and Peculiarities of celebrated Performers, by Mr. Campbell.

To which will be added, a New Grand Operatic Spectacle, interspersed with Songs, Choruses, Dances, Combat's, &c. with New Scenery, Machinery, Dresses and Decorations, written by Miss SCOTT; got up by Mr. GIROUX, with entire New Music and Overture, composed by Mr. Holst, entitled,

ULTHONA THE SORCERESS.

PRINCIPAL CHARACTERS,

Miranda, Miss CAROLINE GIROUX.

Lady Malcona, Mrs. Macartney. Lord Raymond, Master Coste. Ariella (good Spirit) Miss Sheen. Roselia, Miss Bradwell. Alric (the Freebooter) Master Flexmore. Woodman, Master Durousset.—Fairy, Miss Louisa Giroux. Strombello (principal Witch) Mr. Moss.
And Ulthona, Miss SCOTT.

The Whole of the Scenery and Machinery entirely New—designed by Mr. SCOTT,
Between the Musical Piece and the Spectacle will be introduced a brilliant Scene of

MECHANICAL FIRE WORKS,

Leader of the Band, Mr. Sanderson.

The Whole under the Direction of Messrs. Giroux's and Scott.

Doors open at Six - begin precisely at Seven—Box 4s. Pit 2s. Half Price a Quarter before Nine. Places for the Boxes to be taken from Ten in the Morning till the opening of the Theatre,—Servants cannot possibly keep them after Half-past Seven. Books of the Performance, and Refreshments of Tea and Coffee, to be had at the Theatre.

Various NEW ENTERTAINMENTS are in active Preparation.

J. Sweeting; Printer, 108, St. Martin's Lane.

A playbill for January 1808 describing the entertainments at the San Pareil Theatre. Marginal notes in pencil reveal that John Scott "was propriator [sic] of the Adelphi Theatre. He was called—True Blue Scott. He kept the dye shop next door. Miss Scott was the daughter of the propriator [sic] & wrote one or two plays of no merit. I knew his son." While the anonymous author of these notes may have been acquainted with the family, he certainly was unaware of Miss Scott's dramatic output.

Introduction

Aesthetically, melodrama is the dramatization of a dream world of absolutes "where virtue and vice coexist in pure whiteness and blackness" and where "life is uncomplicated, easy to understand, and immeasurably exciting" (Booth, *English Melodrama* 14). This world of certainty, in which character, conduct, and situation are extremely simple and clear, is realized in a dramatic form that "presented 'ordinary' people in domestic situations, strong plots, violence and broad humor, villainy confounded and happy endings" (Kilgarriff 16). In his *Prefaces to English Nineteenth-Century Theatre,* Michael R. Booth defines the characteristics of melodrama:

> [T]he concentration on externals, the emphasis on situation at the expense of motivation and characterization, the firm moral distinctions, the unchanging character stereotypes of hero, heroine, villain, comic man, comic woman, and good old man, physical sensation, spectacular effects (made possible by improvements in stage technology), marked musical accompaniment, the rewarding of virtue and punishing of vice, the rapid alternation between extremes of violence, pathos, and low comedy. (25)

The first kind of English melodrama, the Gothic, developed in the 1790s and flourished for nearly fifty years before "withering away," or, rather, yielding to the "sensation" melodramas of the second half of the nineteenth century (*English Melodrama* 67). Describing the Gothic tradition in literature, Ellen Moers concludes:

> In Gothic writings fantasy predominates over reality, the strange over the commonplace, and the supernatural over the natural, with one definite auctorial intent: to scare. Not, that is, to reach down into the depths of the soul and purge it with pity and terror (as we say tragedy does), but to get to the body itself, its glands, muscles, epidermis, and circulatory system, quickly arousing and quickly allaying the physiological reactions to fear. (90)[1]

In his anthology entitled *Seven Gothic Dramas 1789–1825*, Jeffrey Cox suggests that the Gothic species of drama resides in ruined castles, dungeons, crypts, secret caves, and dark forests where the natural world meets the supernatural in an attempt to unveil or recover "some unmediated absolute that stands outside the boundaries of the natural and social orders" (7).[2] Citing Walpole's defense of the incest at the center of his Gothic play, *The Mysterious Mother*, and that author's description of characters who are good and evil simultaneously, Cox concludes that the Gothic implies a moral ambiguity, even an amorality that renders it particularly dangerous (14). In her *Art of Darkness, A Poetics of Gothic*, Anne Williams reminds us that Robert D. Hume took a similar position, arguing that "the Gothic remains mired in an indeterminate realm of moral ambiguity" and reflects not the "transcendent romantic imagination" but the lesser realm of "fancy" with which women writers were often associated in the nineteenth century (6–7).

Yet, according to the few critics who took the form seriously, melodramas were supposed to be moral.[3] In *Theories of the Theatre*, Marvin Carlson cites Charles Nodier's introduction to the plays of the "Father of French melodrama," Guilbert de Pixérécourt, in which he stressed "the moral function of the melodrama" and "its emphasis on justice and humanity." Suggesting that melodrama has replaced the Church as the source of moral instruction, Nodier argued that the main difference between Romantic drama and melodrama was the former's amorality, and Pixérécourt himself condemned the Romantic drama for its lack of morality and interest in the lowest of vices: incest, patricide, rape, and prostitution (Carlson 214–215). There appears, then, to have been a formal distinction in the nineteenth century between Romantic drama and melodrama and between the Romantic and Gothic traditions. While critics such as Anne Williams argue against the distinction between Romantic and Gothic, the paradoxical nature of Gothic melodrama, simultaneously moral and amoral, was one of its chief attractions, and as such created the cynosure of escapist entertainment by reinscribing the contradictions of day-to-day existence into a *larger-than-life* formula of poetic justice.

Much has been written about women—both as author and audience—and the Gothic tradition.[4] In her preface to *Gothic (Re)Visions*, Susan Wolstenholme explains why literary criticism over the past quarter of a century has inferred a special relationship between *female* and *Gothic*:

> I contend that Gothic narrative has special potential to deal with the issues of writing and reading as a woman for formal reasons. Critics have often noted that Gothic-marked fiction particularly relies for its effect on the textual representation of a deliberately composed stage scene, which assumes an implied spectator, and also that these novels often allude to the theater and to individual plays. I believe that both this structure and these allusions participate in establishing "woman" as a textual position—or, to frame the issue in terms of a different discourse, that they suggest a meditation on the issue of writing as a woman—and that, recurring from text to text, they establish a pattern that becomes a recognizable symbolic code. (xi)

Wolstenholme's allusion to the theatrical resonance of the Gothic is a significant one even though it is used only to explicate Gothic narrative fiction. In her *Feminist Theories for Dramatic Criticism*, Gayle Austin complains that "drama, not to mention the entire realm of live performance, has barely been tapped as a source of material by the field of women's studies" and itemizes the reasons why drama presents many obstacles as a field of study:

> The writing of plays requires mastering to some degree a male-dominated, public production machinery, something that relatively few women have been able to do over the long history of the form, and consequently there is not as large a body of extant plays by women as there is of novels. Only a handful of plays by women have entered the canon of "approved" works that are published, anthologized, taught, and produced, so that we are not used to associating women with playwrighting. (2)[5]

Yet, the rediscovery—and eventual recanonization—of women's plays is considered central to feminist scholarship. In her *An Introduction to Feminism and Theatre*, Elaine Aston argues that "feminist theatre history no longer accepts the concept of a theatrical tradition which either excludes women or considers them 'lost'" and concludes that "bringing the 'lost' tradition of women's theatre history into view is an important political step if feminist theatre scholarship is to change the future history of the stage" (34).

It is therefore important to rescue from oblivion the work of "lost" women writers who have made significant contributions to the species of Gothic melodrama.[6] Such a recovery necessitates a reexamination both of genre and historical perspective for, as Jill Dolan argues in her book, *The Feminist Spectator as Critic,* "fitting a woman's play into any canon—male or female—implies that it is acquiescent to the ideology perpetuated by that canon. Canons, by implication, exclude not only worthy plays but worthy spectators on the basis of their ideological perspectives" (40).

The melodramas in this anthology function as a kind of history of the form between 1790 (when mixed-genre plays were anticipating the formal elements of melodrama) and 1843 when the Theatre Regulation Act abolished the patent-house monopoly over regular drama and allowed any licensed theatre to perform drama of any type (Brockett 400).[7] It must be remembered that during the first half of the nineteenth century, the melodrama was, by nature, a *dangerous* form of English theatre. It skirted the patent laws, aroused emotions through spectacular devices instead of poetry, and was unabashedly revolutionary in spirit and in practice (especially in challenging the hierarchy of dramatic types by mixing genres). Cox emphasizes the revolutionary aspect of Gothic drama (not specifically melodrama) by linking it to the fall of the Bastille and the defeat of Napoleon (8) while Nodier refers to melodrama specifically as embodying the "morality of the Revolution" (Carlson 214).

Just as women were actively involved in the storming of the Bastille, so were they major contributors to the genre of melodrama which, because of its highly structured conventions, provided them with opportunities for double-voicing, or reinscribing their ordinary experiences into romantic adventures in ways that were acceptable to a male-dominated art form.[8] Concurrent with the development of Gothic melodrama was a growth in the number of women in the work force (Anderson and Zinsser 2: 253), an increase of educational opportunities for women (Anderson and Zinsser 2: 116), the publication of Mary Wollstonecraft's *A Vindication of the Rights of Women* (1792), and the development of a new sense of respectability for the English actress (Richards 73).[9] The heroine in Gothic melodrama, incarcerated but striving to get free, becomes the paradigm for the new spirit of female activity.[10]

Ellen Moers draws a similar conclusion in her discussion of Mrs. Radcliffe's Gothic novels:

For Mrs. Radcliffe, the Gothic novel was a device to send maidens on distant and exciting journeys without offending the proprieties. In the power of villains, her heroines are forced to do what they could never do alone, whatever their ambitions: scurry up the top of pasteboard Alps, spy out exotic vistas, penetrate bandit-infested forests. And indoors, inside Mrs. Radcliffe's castles, her heroines can scuttle miles along corridors, descend into dungeons, and explore secret chambers without a chaperone, because the Gothic castle, however much in ruins, is still an indoor and therefore freely female space. (126)

While the possibility of female movement, inside and outside the castle, is highly attractive on the page, how much more effective is it when seen in a public arena, with flesh-and-blood actresses representing the romantic aspirations of the women in the audience. And how much more dangerous for the author. In his discussion of the English popular novel, J. M. S. Tompkins argues that, at the end of the eighteenth century, there were certain acceptable parameters within which a woman might exercise her "fancy." She was permitted to write to amuse her leisure hours or instruct her sex but she was not allowed to be ambitious:

The proper attitude for a female talent was diffidence; the proper field of exercise, the narrow circle of her intimate friends; and if for any of the permitted reasons she stepped outside the circle, let her sedulously avoid the disgraceful imputation of assurance. . . . Anonymity was the great resource, and only by the most prudent degrees was the veil dropped. (116–117)[11]

The authors in this volume, writing publicly in a transgressive mode,[12] shunned anonymity, employing instead a variety of other devices to render themselves accepted by the theatrical public. Perhaps the mounting popularity of the romance novel and women's increased attendance at the theatre at the end of the eighteenth century gave the women melodramatists the incentive to pursue their muse.[13]

That the melodrama was particularly popular with women is clear from a critical observation made in the March 1818 edition of *The Theatrical Inquisitor and Monthly Mirror*. Complaining about the audience that frequents the melodrama, the author concludes:

They are persons to whom any exertion of the intellect is absolute toil, and carefully to be avoided, who like to have their other faculties lulled into a slumber, whilst the imagination is excited and amused: this requires no species of exertion, and the sort of dream in which a person remains under the fascination of these amusements, is like that of an aerial castle-builder, the better half of the faculties are asleep, the imagination only in action. *Such are romance readers, such are the admirers of melo-drama* (italics mine). A world which is different from our own, characters claiming little affinity with humanity, striking, marvellous, and improbable incidents, and combinations, these are the leading features common to both. (159–160)

The association of the melodrama with romantic fiction is significant not only in its delineation of a similar audience[14] but it points to the precise approach taken in *The Ward of the Castle,* the first example of a Gothic melodrama written by a woman. Miss Burke's "comic opera" is the first example of a mixed-genre play by a woman that exhibits the characteristics of what will become Gothic melodrama.[15] Performed in 1793, the year before Anne Radcliffe published *The Mysteries of Udolpho, The Ward of the Castle* anticipates Colman the Younger's *Feudal Times,* a romantic melodrama produced at Drury Lane in 1799, that makes use of an identical plot, complete with the heroine's escape by boat.

Harriet Lee's *The Mysterious Marriage,* written in 1793 and published in 1798, characterizes the "castle-dungeon-ghost variety" of Gothic melodrama (*English Melodrama* 68), anticipating by a year the spectral effects in Boaden's *Fountainville Forest* (1794) and Monk Lewis's *The Castle Spectre* (1897), the play that popularized the melodramatic ghost, by four years.[16] In addition, calling for the abolition of slavery and the development of a noble friendship between women, *The Mysterious Marriage* expresses a number of *revolutionary* sentiments that have hitherto escaped critical attention.[17]

Jane Scott's *The Old Oak Chest,* performed at the Sans Pareil Theatre in 1816, is characteristic of the "bandit-forest-cottage sort" of Gothic melodrama (*English Melodrama* 68). The most popular of melodramas written by women in the nineteenth century, it exhibits no pretentions whatsoever to literary merit. Rather, it appeals to the vulgar tastes of an audience demanding spectacle, low-comedy, and romance. Perhaps the most formulaic of the plays here represented (which accounts somewhat for its popularity), *The Old Oak Chest* was fashioned from bits and pieces of earlier Gothic plays. From O'Keefe's *The Castle of Andalusia* (1782), Scott borrows the Spanish setting and banditti; from Murphy's *The Grecian Daughter* (1772), she borrows the cavern scene; and from Dimond's *The Foundling of the Forest*, she takes the character of Florian, the burning castle motif, a mysterious cottage-dwelling female character, and the reunion—after great suffering—with the son, long believed dead.[18] It appears that Jane Scott's method of finding acceptance in a male-dominated theatre was to borrow plots and themes from popular plays by men.

Margaret Harvey, a poet and scholar from Newcastle, turned to English history and her own epic poem, *The Lay of the Minstrel's Daughter,* to create *Raymond de Percy,* the first "historical" Gothic melodrama written by a woman to be performed. Produced at Sunderland in April 1822, at the height of melodrama's popularity, the play is typical of the "castle-dungeon-ghost variety" complete with a suit of armor that moves, an incident possibly borrowed from Jephson's *The Count of Narbonne* (1781) by way of *The Castle Spectre.* On first examination, *Raymond de Percy* may read as little more than an adaptation of Lewis's play. The characters of Percy, Motley, and Kenrick have the same names and functions in both plays.[19] The villain in both has an obsessive desire to possess the hero's beloved and is tormented by guilt made manifest by the apparition of a ghost in a tomb. The similarities are great, to be sure, but the differences are even more substantial. Where *The Castle Spectre* was accused of having licentious dialogue and violently democratic sentiments (Cox 221–222), *Raymond de Percy* is perhaps the most conservatively moral play in this volume. Written by the headmistress of a girls' boarding school in Bishopwearmouth for a provincial audience of sailors and merchants, the play presents women in their most traditional role of long-suffering heroine, unable to act without the assistance of a man.[20]

In contrast, *St. Clair of the Isles,* written by Elizabeth Polack for the Royal Victoria Theatre in 1838, portrays women as strong, active, and independent. The first Jewish woman to have melodramas produced on the London stage, Polack's play—an adaptation of the novel by Elizabeth Helme—is an example of "Scottish Gothic" which, according to Booth, "simply transplanted the usual characters and situations of melodrama, plus a dash of nationalism, to vaguely historical and strongly romantic Scottish settings" (*English Melodrama* 78). Unsatisfied with the typical heroines of melodrama, Polack found in Helme's romantic novel the opportunity to reinscribe the formula by replacing the traditional villain with a villainess whose evil machinations control the action of the play. What's more, the real hero of the play is not the leading man but a youth, played by a woman in pants. In all of her extant plays, Polack creates strong, heroic women characters who enact roles that are stereotypically male.[21]

Catherine Gore, among the most prolific writers of the nineteenth century, is represented by two plays, *The Bond* (1824), her first dramatic effort, and *Dacre of the South* (1840), her penultimate play, and last melodrama. Both are included in this volume to demonstrate the development of the author's approach to the Gothic, and to show the changes occurring in the melodrama midway through the nineteenth century when Romantic drama and melodrama appeared to merge as "Gentlemanly Melodrama" (*Prefaces to English Nineteenth-Century Theatre* 45; Brockett 402). While Edward Bulwer-Lytton is usually credited with establishing a melodrama capable of attracting "gentlemen" back into the theatre (Brockett 402; Rahill 116–119), Catherine Gore emerges as his female equivalent, bridging the gap between melodramatic form and the issues and concerns of high society.

The Bond is Catherine Gore's version of Goethe's *Faust Part I* (1808) with the occasional borrowing from a variety of popular melodramas by men. Present are the traditional Gothic techniques—the suffering heroine, the demonic villain, the brooding, Byronic hero, castles, sensational effects, songs, and spectres—in three acts of blank verse. Absent only is the comic relief. Poetic justice is served in the punishment of vice and conservative morality upheld.[22]

On the other hand, *Dacre of the South* (like Bulwer-Lytton's *The Lady of Lyons*) is typical of the "gentlemanly" variety of melodramas. Defining this type of five-act "drama," Rahill concludes:

> Though they are written in blank verse and have no specifically comic characters, these plays are essentially melodramas, with their simplified character types, their flamboyant heroics, and their happy ends; and they were adopted enthusiastically into the melodramatic repertoire everywhere. (119)[23]

There is no evidence that Mrs. Gore ever sought to have the play produced. In 1840, the year it was published, *Dacre* was reviewed in *The Athenaeum* and judged unfit for serious drama:

Mrs. Gore, yielding to her dramatic propensities, here gives us a five-act drama, in blank verse, on the sad story of Thomas Fiennes, Lord Dacre, so strangely condemned in the year 1542. She has made the accusation brought against her hero turn on a boyish frolic of deer-stealing, into which he suffered himself to be entrapped;—too slight a charge to be accepted as the master-incident of a serious play—on which, as on a scaffold, a structure of passion, and agony, and death, is to be raised. To the poetry of the serious drama Mrs. Gore is wholly unequal. (13–14)
As tragedy the play certainly fails. But as a melodrama self-consciously emphasizing the qualities of loyalty, freedom, class-distinction, family values, and conservative morality, the play stands as a significant example of the "gentlemanly" genre.[24]

The women represented in this volume are but a few of the female writers of the nineteenth century who produced melodramas or mixed-genre plays. The works presented here were chosen because they are significant "firsts" or characteristic representations of the different varieties of Gothic melodrama, and have not been re-published or anthologized in this century. All of the plays have been lost to both a reading and theatrical audience for at least a hundred years.[25] A complete list of plays by women authors who wrote at least one Gothic melodrama or mixed-genre play between 1790 and 1843 is supplied in Appendix C.[26]

The plays in this collection are, for the most part, spectacular, hyper-thyroid, popular theatrical entertainments. They are hardly literary masterpieces, but they do exemplify what Davis and Joyce have determined to be the three types of dramatic literature produced by women until 1900: professional theatre, amateur theatricals, and closet drama. Professional theatre was that written and, often, acted by women from all levels of the middle and working classes (*The Ward of the Castle, The Mysterious Marriage, The Old Oak Chest,* and *St. Clair of the Isles*). Amateur, or home entertainment, was that type of theatrical activity written by middle-class women for their families and friends (*Raymond de Percy*). Closet drama, which included dramatic poetry and translations of plays by celebrated dramatists, was the name given to plays not intended for production, and practiced primarily by aristocrats and other women who were highly educated (*The Bond, Dacre of the South*) (xi).[27]

I hope readers will relish the rediscovery of these "lost" melodramas by women and accept them, in the spirit in which they were written, not only as significant examples of nineteenth-century popular culture, but as hidden documents in the history of women.

Notes

1. In *Ghosts of the Gothic,* Judith Wilt expresses similar sentiments: "Dread is the father and mother of the Gothic. Dread begets rage and fright and cruel horror, or awe and worship and a shining standfastness—all of these have human features, but Dread has no face"(5).

2. Similarly, In his study of Gothic drama, *Terror and Pity Reign in Every Breast,* Paul Ranger defines Gothic drama as "a reflection of the dark and wild side of human nature, mirrored in an equally violent natural world or in architectural settings which, in their ruinous state, spoke of human mortality. . . . The plays were subject to Germanic influences which queried the traditional eighteenth-century concepts of social hierarchy, sympathy and respectability" (18). The mention of Germanic influences is especially important given the popularity of the plays of August von Kotzebue in England. In his *Gothic Drama from Walpole to Shelley,* Bertrand Evans suggests that "the year 1792 can be taken only as the date at which there *might* have occurred the earliest mingling of German and English horrific materials in Gothic plays"(90). If this is true, then the first two plays in this volume, both written in 1793, were quick to take advantage of the new development. See Rahill, *The World of Melodrama* passim, Ranger, Chapter 1, Booth, *English Melodrama,* Chapter 2, and Montague Summers, *The Gothic Quest,* Chapter 3, for detailed studies of the foreign influences on the Gothic tradition, both literary and theatrical, in England.

3. Evans seems to be addressing the apparent dichotomy between an amoral subject and a moral intent when he concludes that "Gothic drama—even plays like those by Lewis, which contain an elaborate diablerie—is thoroughly moral . . ."(45).

4. In her *Art of Darkness: A Poetics of Gothic,* Anne Williams provides an exhaustive retrospective of recent academic research. See Bibliography for a list of titles consulted in this anthology.

5. In their introduction to *Drama by Women to 1900,* Gwenn Davis and Beverly A. Joyce add that "there is much to be done in reevaluating women dramatists. Current critical and scholarly resources do not cover the range of their activities. . . . There are few considerations of nineteenth-century women dramatists"(ix–x).

6. While Cox argues in favor of a reexamination of the Gothic because it "provides one central set of texts that challenge the controlling preconceptions about nineteenth-century drama"(4), he only discusses the work of one woman author, Joanna Baillie. Evans's discussion of women authors is, with the exception of Joanna Baillie, usually little more than a mention and stops at 1816. Ranger lists plays by women between 1750 and 1820 but comments on few of them in his text. In their respective analyses of melodrama in general, and the Gothic species in particular, Dye, Booth, Brockett, Kilgarriff, and Rahill mention no women writers at all. Women melodramatists have been neglected even by feminist scholars researching theatre and the "Female Gothic." Case and Aston pass over the early nineteenth century in their historical surveys and Austin and Dolan focus essentially on the contemporary theatre. DeLamotte, Massé, Moers, Sedgwick, Williams and Wolstenholme have published important studies of Gothic novels written by women but have taken little notice of women's writing for the stage. Ellen Donkin's important study, *Getting into the Act,* describes the period between 1800 and 1830 as a low point in women's theatrical

writing arguing that "there are *occasional* (italics mine) plays produced by women, but no one emerges to replace Elizabeth Inchbald or Hannah Cowley as a long-term professional until Catherine Gore in the 1830s"(31). Dismissing the minor houses as "not being genteel," she concludes that "for many middle-class women, the reputations of the smaller houses precluded their serious consideration as places in which to produce"(32). While this was undoubtedly true for many women writers, it was not the case of the women who wrote melodramas for the minor theatres. Donkin fails to mention any of the women melodramatists even in passing. It is certainly time to challenge the preconception that nineteenth-century melodrama was exclusively a male form.

7. In his introduction to *The Golden Age of Melodrama*, Michael Kilgarriff cites the passage of the Theatre Regulation Act in 1843 as one of the causes of its "decline" in popularity during the second half of the nineteenth century (24). In her chapter on melodrama in *Visual and Other Pleasures*, Laura Mulvey concurs that 1843 was a turning point for melodrama because of the dissolution of the theatrical class structure brought about by the Theatre Regulation Act (66). Booth argues that Gothic melodrama continued into the 1870s (*The Lights o' London and Other Victorian Plays* xvi) but agrees that, by the middle of the century, it is "no longer profitable to conduct a separate examination of the melodramatic form" since Victorian "drama" is melodramatic to a great extent (*Prefaces to English Nineteenth-Century Theatre* 45). Once melodrama no longer had to function as the "other" in the theatre, it became part of the establishment and, therefore, no longer transgressive. In his *Recollections, J. R.* Planché is especially vocal about the function of melodrama in the years preceding the Theatre Regulation Act:

> With these exceptions [Drury Lane, Covent Garden, and the Haymarket during summer seasons], no theatre within the bills of mortality was safe from the common informer, did its company venture to enact any drama in which there was not a certain quantity of vocal or instrumental music. The Lyceum, a new establishment, was specially licensed for the performance of English opera and musical dramas, and the Adelphi and Olympic Theatres had the Lord Chamberlain's license for the performance of burlettas only, by which description, after much controversy both in and out of court, we were desired to understand dramas containing not less than five pieces of vocal music in each act, and which were also, with one or two exceptions, not to be found in the *repertoire* of the patent houses [i.e., Drury Lane, Covent Garden, and the Haymarket]. All beside the above-named six theatres were positively out of the pale of the law. There was no Act of Parliament which empowered the magistrates to license a building for dramatic performances. Astley's, the Surrey, the Victoria, Sadler's Wells etc., had, in common with Vauxhall, a license "for music and dancing" *only,* by which was originally meant public concerts and balls, gradually permitted to extend to ballets and pantomimes and equestrian performances: but no one had a legal right to open his mouth on a stage unaccompanied by music; and the next step was to evade the law by the tinkling of a piano in the orchestra throughout the interdicted performances. (2: 70–76, qtd. Kilgarriff 483–484)

8. See Elaine Showalter's important essay, "Feminist Criticism in the Wilderness" for a discussion of the nature of the female authorial voice in literature. Arguing that "all language is the language of the dominant order, and women, if they speak at all, must speak through it"(200), Showalter deduces that all women's writing is a "'double-voiced discourse' that always embodies the social, literary, and cultural heritages of both the muted and the dominant"(201). See also Jeanine Dwinell's unpublished thesis, "Gender Issues in the Plays of Catherine Gore" for a critical application of Showalter's theories. Davis and Joyce agree that the theatre, especially in the nineteenth century, was a conservative forum used by women "to express their major concerns"(xviii).

9. See *The Rise of the English Actress,* Chapters 4 and 5. See also Tracy C. Davis, *Actresses as Working Women: Their Social Identity in Victorian Britain,* passim.

10. Gothic melodrama created a new aesthetic of the sensational and explored ways of representing ideological struggles without incurring censorship. Among the ideological concerns of the day was the growing activity among women in the workplace.

11. Mary Ellmann discusses a number of feminine stereotypes that have emerged in Western civilization in her book *Thinking About Women.* These include formlessness, passivity, instability, confinement, piety, materiality, spirituality, irrationality, and compliancy—all of which support Tompkins's argument regarding attitudes toward women writers. For a complete discussion of these stereotypes, see Ellman, Chapter 3.

12. Though the melodrama was an exceptionally popular genre, it was maligned by classicists and romantics alike (Carlson 214). Even today, we tend to look upon melodrama as a highly inferior form of theatre.

13. In discussing the rise of women's dramatic writing at the end of the eighteenth century (virtually simultaneous with the rise of melodrama), Donkin credits women's attendance at plays with anchoring the idea of the woman playwright in the public imagination. She concludes:

> Everyone, but especially young women, could attend the theatre and see for themselves concrete evidence of other women's success and recognition. That had the potential for creating a momentum that made women playwrights slightly less dependent upon the chemistry or good will of any one particular manager, and more focused on taking their rightful place in the profession. (108)

14. See Blakey's *The Minerva Press 1790–1820* and Summers's *The Gothic Quest,* Chapter 2, for extensive discussions of female readership of romantic fiction.

15. In his *A Study of Melodrama in England from 1800–1840,* Dye mentions only one earlier mixed-genre play by a woman, Hannah Cowley's *A Day in Turkey; or the Russian Slaves,* produced in 1791 (35). Cowley's play, a comedy interspersed with songs, does not exhibit the characteristics of the Gothic species. In *Terror and Pity Reign in Every Breast,* Paul Ranger cites a number of earlier plays by women (175–176). While his examples exemplify the Gothic tradition, the plays themselves are bona fide tragedies, not mixed-genre pieces.

16. Bertrand Evans credits Boaden with creating the first melodramatic ghost (101). He neglects Lee's play entirely. Citing the ghost of the murdered Evelina in *The Castle Spectre* as a representative example, Booth concludes that "the frequency with which ghosts appear in Gothic melodrama also distinguishes it from the rest of its class. These ghosts are invariably on the side of goodness and often turn up at the worst possible moment for the villain; their arrival is accompanied by fitting effects" (*English Melodrama* 81). Booth fails to take notice of Lee's play.

17. No one has discussed the similarities between Figaro's famous tirade in *The Marriage of Figaro* and Rodolphus's speech: "I have somewhat here that tells me I was not born a slave, but a man—A *poor* one I must own, yet still a man: with feelings that will not be commanded, and opinions that are not to be bought"(III.iii.) Not even Janet Todd's excellent, *Women's Friendship in Literature* makes reference to the noble female relationship in this play. Given Lee's stature as a writer of fiction, such an omission is conspicuous.

18. There are a number of other thematic adaptations from earlier plays: Lewis's *Adelmorn the Outlaw* (1801) presents the rightful heir to a kingdom living as an outlaw because of an "alleged" crime; Arnold's *The Woodman's Hut* (1814) offers yet another version of the mysterious cottage-dwelling female; and Pocock's *The Miller and His Men* (1813) introduces the character of the miller who is really a bandit in disguise.

19. The hero, the fool, and the villain's henchman.

20. A comparison of the final moments of each play is indicative of their differences. In Harvey's melodrama, Conrade fights the hero, knowing that he will be defeated and thus punished for his crimes. Tormented by guilt, he welcomes the opportunity to give his life in reparation for the life he took. In Lewis's play, Osmond demonstrates no contrition whatsoever and continues his attempts at rape and murder until a ghostly apparition disarms him long enough for the heroine, Angela, to stab him in the chest. In both plays, the villain is allowed to live, but while Harvey's hero proclaims munificence ("the warrior's greatest conquest is to save"), Lewis's hero dismisses the act as unwarranted charity ("Though ill-deserved by his guilt, your generous pity is still amiable").

21. See the introduction to *St. Clair* on page 227 for a discussion of the female characters in *Esther, The Royal Jewess,* an Eastern melodrama, and *Woman's Revenge,* a burletta. In *Subjects of Slavery, Agents of Change,* Kari J. Winter argues that "in Gothic novels written by men . . . innocent heroines are routinely raped, tortured, and killed. In Gothic novels written by women, innocent heroines are usually guided by the authors into an understanding of human evil, a knowledge that in many cases empowers them to survive and escape from the severe forms of victimization that male Gothic novelists delight in depicting" (78). In her melodramas, Polack goes beyond empowering women by knowledge. She gives them authority, stature, and money.

22. Like Goethe, Gore ends the play with "End of the First Part"as if to promise a second play. While *Faust Part II* was published in 1831, no second part of Gore's play was completed.

23. See Rahill's discussion of Bulwer-Lytton's melodramas in *The World of Melodrama,* Chapter 15, "Patent House Melodrama." The plays discussed are *The Lady of Lyons* (1838) and *Richelieu* (1839).

24. In his introduction to *The Lights o' London,* Booth comments that Victorian drama, especially melodrama, is "riddled with class conflict" which provides not only a "forceful dramatic expression but also a significant aspect of Victorian society." He also suggests the presence in Victorian melodrama of issues involving the nouveau riche versus the old landed gentry (xxv)—issues which were the concern of the "gentlemanly"audience. All of these themes are found in *Dacre of the South.*

25. Even the 1996 anthology *Female Playwrights of the Nineteenth Century* fails to include a single play by any of the authors discussed here.

26. I have not chosen to include Joanna Baillie, perhaps the most illustrious Gothic dramatist of the early nineteenth century, in this volume for several reasons. Scullion includes her *The Family Legend* in the anthology *Female Playwrights of the Nineteenth Century;* Cox recently reproduced her *De Monfort* in his anthology, *Seven Gothic Dramas 1789–1825*; and a facsimile edition of her plays was issued by Garland in 1977. Even though Evans argues that "of her twenty-six dramatic works, ten may be classified as predominantly Gothic, and all reveal conspicuous marks of the tradition"(200), given the fact that Baillie's plays are hardly "lost" and that, as an author, she is considered more as a writer of "verse tragedies" than melodramas (Moers 118), she was omitted from this collection.

27. In *British Plays of the Nineteenth Century,* J. O. Bailey suggests that "closet drama" was the locus for "the most radical experimentation with the romantic verse play" and "a third contender in the struggle for survival between the verse drama and the evolving melodrama"(26). While Bailey mentions Joanna Baillie's *Orra* in his discussion of Gothic melodrama (24), he fails to note Catherine Gore's experiments in closet drama.

THE WARD OF THE CASTLE

A Comic Opera

In 2 Acts

by

Miss Burke

The Ward of the Castle

Nothing is known about Miss Burke (or Mrs. Burke as she is called in *The London Stage*)[1] but her *The Ward of the Castle* is, perhaps, the first Gothic melodrama written by a woman. Complete with subterranean passageways, incarcerated young ladies, forced marriages, narrow escapes, mistaken identities, exotic, if not spectacular, effects, and comic servants, the so-called "opera" follows in the traditions of the Gothic novel (and its various theatrical incarnations[2]) established by Walpole, Radcliffe, and Lee, as well as Pixérécourt's Parisian melodrama with its emphasis on "violence, show, moral simplicity, emotional distress, rhetoric, and music" (Booth, *Prefaces to English Nineteenth-Century Theatre* 24). Miss Burke's single dramatic effort was given three performances at Covent Garden beginning 24 October 1793 and drew generally unfavorable reviews from the press.[3] But even though only the songs and choruses were published (Nicoll 3: 378), and the play never revived, the work has more than mere curiosity value. By means of an interesting metatheatrical device in which Jacquinetta's romance novels virtually dictate her code of behavior and parallel the action of the play, Miss Burke's opera provides sensational escapist entertainment along with a brief, though significant, look into the reading habits of women at the end of the eighteenth century.

Like Polly Honeycomb, the title character of Colman's farcical "Dramatic Novel" (1760), Jacquinetta is addicted to reading. Both characters appear to escape the actual reality of their temporal situation through the virtual reality of the novel, and Polly's affection for conceit-laden domestic fare is closely related to the picaresque romance favored by Jacquinetta.[4] While the one might turn on highly ornamental prose and doggerel verse and the other on action and adventure, the author of the literary satire *The Age* (1810) suggests that the following table may be used to transform any romance into a domestic novel, or vice versa:

Where you find:

A castle	put	An house.
A cavern		A bower.
A groan		A sigh.

A giant	A father.
A blood-stained dagger	A fan.
Howling blasts	Zephyrs.
A knight	A gentleman without whiskers.
A lady who is the heroine	Need not be changed, being versatile.
Assassins	Killing glances.

. . . .

A gliding ghost	A usurer, or an attorney.
A witch	An old housekeeper.
A wound	A kiss.
A midnight murder	A marriage.

(qtd. Summers 35)

More important, perhaps, than the subject matter is the male reaction to the ladies' reading. Exclaiming "Bah, nonsense . . . Stuff, stuff, stuff!" the Duke throws Jacquinetta's book out the door and argues "How dangerous it is to suffer a Woman to read at all" (8-9). Honeycomb responds in kind to what he considers his daughter Polly's madness:

> Was ever man so heartily provoked? . . . Instead of happiness and jollity, my friends and family about me, a wedding and a dance, and every thing as it should be, here am I, left by myself;— deserted by my intended son-in-law, bullied by my attorney's clerk, affronted by my own servant, my daughter mad, my wife in the vapours, and all in confusion. This comes of cordials and novels. Zounds! . . . a man might as well turn his daughter loose in Covent Garden, as trust the cultivation of her mind to a circulating library. (16)

While circulating libraries connected to publishing houses had been in existence since the Restoration, by the second half of the eighteenth century, they had earned the reputation of pandering to the escapist fantasies of young women and were considered "vile places, indeed" (Sheridan 10). One of the more notorious of these vile places was the Minerva Press on Leadenhall Street whose proprietor, William Lane, "made a large fortune by the immense quantity of trashy novels[5] which he sent forth . . ." (qtd. in Summers 73). But irrespective of the literary merits of these novels, it was the ideas they put into women's heads that caused concern. Miss Burke reflects this attitude in the Duke's interrogation of Jacquinetta:

Duke. I make no doubt but that innocent book is full of the wickedest intrigues —
Jacquinetta *(aside, shaking her head).* Not one—
Duke. And elopements—
Jacquinetta *(aside).* O yes, eleven times—she and her maid.
Duke. Amorous billets convey'd in the bills of pigeons.
Jacquinetta *(aside).* As sure as fate he has been reading it himself. It's lucky for me I have the last nine volumes in my closet. (8)

Jacquinetta is not the first young lady in literature to be seduced by Mlle. de Scudéry's ten-volume romance, *Clélie* (1654-60), translated by John Davies (1656-71; 1678).[6] Like Jacquinetta, Arabella of Charlotte Lennox's *The Female Quixote* (1752) is obsessed with the Roman legend of Cloelia who, having been given as hostage to an Etruscan king, escaped his clutches, swam the Tiber, and returned safely to Rome. Both Jacquinetta and Arabella live in the realm of romance and their expectations of day-to-day reality are shaped by the idealized exploits of mythical heroes and heroines.[7] It is significant that Jacquinetta affirms to the Duke her belief that her little book "contains the whole duty of man" (8) and that Arabella was "taught to believe that love was the ruling principle of the world; that every other passion was subordinate to this; and that it caused all the happiness and miseries of life" (Lennox, qtd. Summers 26).

Polly, Arabella, and Jacquinetta all attempt to make real life correspond to their fantasies. But unlike Polly and Arabella, whose realities are vastly different than those portrayed in their favorite novels, Jacquinetta is living the life of a Gothic heroine. Her books describe forced marriages, incarcerations, disguises, and daring escapes, the very stuff of her day-to-day existence. Not needing to fantasize a life of adventure, Jacquinetta accepts, even rejoices in, her captivity with the knowledge that one day her hero will come for her: it says so in her book!

Through Jacquinetta, Miss Burke has created a "witty and stylish comic opera" (Blain, Clements, and Grundy 157), which simultaneously employs and satirizes Gothic conventions. In making the young lady obsessed with romanticism a romantic figure in her own right, the author has added yet another mirror to nature and created an escapist world where women's fantasies can become real.

Several Covent Garden favorites took leading roles in the original production: Johnstone played the Duke of Alberossa, Incledon acted Sir Bertram, and Munden performed the bluff role of Geoffrey. Mrs. Clendining portrayed Matilda, the incarcerated heroine, and Mrs. Martyr played Jacquinetta. The opening night playbill reports that male chorus roles were taken by Linton, Tett, Sayer, Little, Street, and Kendricks. Female chorus parts were sung by Miss Stuart, Mrs. Watts, Mrs. Follett, Mrs. Costello, Miss Kirton, Mrs. Lloyd, Miss Paye, Miss Leferve, Mrs. Bayzand, and Mrs. Blurton. Though the playbill advertised, "Books of the Songs to be had at the Theatre," neither the author nor the composer was named.

The original music was provided by Tommaso Giordani (spelled *Giardini* in the published *Songs, Duets, Choruses, &c.* and *Jiordani* in *The Times* review*)*, a celebrated composer of Italian opera in England, but many of the melodies used in the play were taken from popular *airs* of the eighteenth century. Since Giordani's compositions for *The Ward of the Castle* were never published, it is only through an examination of the familiar airs that we can appreciate the tonal texture of the piece. What we discover is a work filled with an endless variety of musical modes, rhythms, and styles, each carefully chosen to delineate dramatically the character, situation, or mood. Matilda's first song, "Joy! thou dear precarious boon!" is set to Giordani's bravura rondo, "Ah per me non v'e piu bene," popularized by Signora Sestini in Anfossi's comic opera, *Il Geloso in Cemento*.[8] Operatic in scope, the lyrical melody displays the demands placed upon leading ladies of the eighteenth-century musical stage. The published edition of the aria, in full score, calling for two horns, two clarinets, two bassoons, two separate string parts, cembalo, and bass, also demonstrates the typical orchestration of the period.

While the romantic heroine is given music of a more serious nature, the bluff character, Geoffrey, sings popular jaunty jig tunes. His "When I was apprenticed and learned my trade" is set to the bitingly satirical ballad, "The Maid of the Sky-Light; or, The Devil among the Lawyers," the original lyric of which narrates the routing of lawyers from Westminster Hall by a naïve cleaning girl. It is highly appropriate for Geoffrey to sing about his personal dexterity using a tune that would remind the audience that:

No longer let France then her Joan of Arc boast,
Of her Countries stout Foes who subdu'd a whole host,

On the Maid of the Skylight, more honor shall fall,
She routed the Lawyers from Westminster Hall.
In the second act, Geoffrey makes an odd appearance, as if to cover a change of scene and costume. Here, he sings, almost verbatim, the celebrated "Green Grow the Rushes O," advertised as "A favorite Scotch Song, now Sung in the Polite Circles." Whether or not the song was an afterthought—something forced upon the author by practical necessity—or an especially crowd-pleasing number for Mr. Munden, Miss Burke makes no apology for it. Rather, she writes Geoffrey a monologue that refers to the Scottish song specifically (as if to tantalize the audience), and he sings it, with only the slightest alterations in lyrics, happily ignoring the fact that it has little to do with anything in the plot!

The trio between the Duke, Matilda, and Jacquinetta to the tune of "Che Faro" from Gluck's, *Orpheus and Eurydice* (1762) is particularly significant as that opera had been performed at Covent Garden the previous season for Mrs. Billington's benefit and was certainly in the audience's memory. While the production itself was not a great success, Roger Fiske reports that "Che Faro" had been the rage as early as 1770 when the opera was given at the King's Theatre and ultimately popularized by the celebrated Italian singer Tenducci (547).[9] Miss Burke's use of the melody in *The Ward of the Castle* reminds the audience that Orpheus lost Eurydice forever because he glanced at her face while trying to retrieve her from the Underworld,[10] and implies that the duke's desperate desire to behold Matilda's face (to calm his jealous apprehensions) may produce the same effect.

Also noteworthy is the use of "Adieu Coeur Moi" for Bertram and Matilda's parting duet at the end of act one. Advertised as a "Negro Melody" and written in a Creole dialect, the song dramatizes a lover's farewell before departing for St. Louis in the New World. The childlike simplicity of the tune is counterbalanced by the romantic passion expressed in the lyrics:

Then love me when I leave,
Love me, or else, I'll die.

Substituting a request for "one gentle smile" in place of "one little kiss" in the original text, Miss Scott adds a certain chivalrous formality to the piece without violating either the tone or the meaning of the song. Certainly the use of an American melody—a tune based neither in European operatic conventions nor in the English ballad tradition—gave a kind of romantic exoticism to the score, and the dramatic situation—the loss of a loved one to the New World—added an important resonance to Matilda's temporary separation from Sir Bertram. Two of the concerted numbers in the play exist in their original form. The effervescent trio, "Come, Let Us All a Wooing Go" is set to Atterbury's madrigal-like "Come Let Us All a Maying go." The playful antiphony of the song is an appropriate musicalization of the previous, highly manipulative, scene and adds yet another timbre to the tonal texture of the piece. The chorus finale, "See the Peaceful Queen of Night," is based on the "much admired Glee" in three parts, "From the Fair Lavinean Shore," a stately anthem apotheosizing capitalism on the one hand, and, on the other, celebrating the glory of traveling far distances to realize one's ideal. That the ideal in the original song was a highly mercenary one gives the dramatic moment a subtle edge. Since the audiences for *The Ward of the Castle* would have known the lyrics to the popular airs, the use of such melodies not only contributed to the variety of the musical fabric, but provided a subtle social commentary as well.

The text of the play is taken from Larpent Manuscript 992 at the Henry E. Huntington Library in San Marino, California. Song lyrics are from the printed copy of *Songs, Duets, Choruses, &c. in The Ward of the Castle* at the British Library. Capitalization, spelling, and punctuation have been regularized. All annotations, additions, and deletions are noted in the text.

Notes

1. *The Feminist Companion to Literature in English* argues that she is not Anne Burke, a governess in London who published eight highly inflated melodramatic novels between 1785-1805 (157). Whether or not Miss Burke was related to the well-known Edmund or John Burke is a matter of conjecture. Mrs. Thrale rates Mrs. Edmund Burke high in the area of good humor and low in all other areas: useful and ornamental knowledge, powers of conversation, personal mien and manner (331), and ascribes no particular talents to the lady. Rather she infers that Mrs. Burke is a slovenly housekeeper:

> See Burke's bright Intelligence beam from his Face,
> To his Language give Splendor—his Action give Grace;
> Let us list to the Learning that Tongue can display,
> Let it steal all Reflexion, all Reason away;
> Lest home to his House we the Patriot pursue,

Where Scenes of another Sort rise to our View;
Where Meanness usurps sage Economy's Look,
And Humour cracks Jokes out of Ribaldry's Book;
Till no longer in Silence, Confession can lurk,
That from Chaos and Cobwebs could spring even Burke. (475- 476)
It is also unlikely that she is related to Master Burke, the celebrated child actor of the early nineteenth century.

2. Booth lists Walpole's unacted, *The Mysterious Mother* (1768), Jephson's *The Count of Narbonne* (1781), Cumberland's *The Carmelite* (1784), McDonald's *Vimonda* (1787), and Greatheed's *The Regent* (1788) (*English Melodrama* 69). Among other Gothic dramas by men, Ranger adds *Almida* (1771) by Dorothea Celesia, *Percy* (1777) and *The Fatal Falsehood* (1779) both by Hannah More, and *Albina, Countess of Raimond* (1779) by Hannah Cowley. Unlike Burke's melodrama, these Gothic plays by women belong to the tragic tradition. Celesia's play, in fact, was a translation of Voltaire's tragedy *Tancrède*.

3. *The Times* was especially critical:

> *The Ward of the Castle*, a new Comic Opera, as stated in the Bill, was performed yesterday evening after Reynold's pleasant Comedy of *How to grow Rich* . . . . The story from when the piece is taken is almost as old as the "Babes in the Wood," but the incidents and conduct of the fable have not the merit either of interesting the attention or awakening the passions. The business though artfully conducted is yet extremely simple. The whole dependence is placed on an *under*-plot, if we may be allowed the pun; for the use made of a subterraneous passage furnishes the only possible trap for applause. The language has not any thing offensive, nor have the characters any claim to novelty. Indeed the only aim at any thing like character appertains to Jeoffry and Jaquinetta—the former is a complete copy of Walter, the carpenter in the *Children of the Wood*—and the latter is but a bad *edition* of Polly Honeycomb and Miss *Biddy Tipkin*.
>
> Some very pretty music—mostly by Jiordani, delightfully executed by the Performers, who really formed a most admirable operatic Quintetto—ensured the *Ward of the Castle* a more favorable reception than her intrinsic merits, literary or dramatic, could have entitled her to have claimed. (Friday, October 25, 1793)

4. In Colman's play, Polly refuses level-headed Ledger, the man her father wishes her to marry, in favor of Scribble, a young opportunist in the guise of a doggerel poet. Even after Scribble is unmasked Polly persists in her romantic infatuation, much to the dismay of Mr. Ledger who urges that "she'd make a terrible wife for a sober citizen" (16).

5. Minerva Press along with its attached circulating library published twice as many novels by women as by men. Tompkins reports that by 1790, fly-leaves of novels from the Minerva Press advertised "Legendary Tales, Old English Tales, Historical Stories and Historical Romances" (238) all of which appear to have capitalized on the more sensational aspects of history and myth to provide highly escapist entertainment for its essentially female clientele. In 1793 alone, the year *The Ward of the Castle* was produced, the Minerva Press published fourteen novels and an opera, *Caernarvon Castle; or, The Birth of the Prince of Wales*, by John Rose.

6. Summers lists a variety of highly popular French romances which were translated into English during the seventeenth century. Notable among them (because Jacquinetta refers to it) is *Cassandre* (1642–50) which was first translated by Sir Charles Cotterel in 1652, and reprinted as late as 1738 (107).

7. In Lennox's novel, Arabella, thinking she is about to be abducted, plunges in the Thames to escape her fate like her heroine, Cloelia. After she is rescued, a sober old minister nurses her back to physical and mental health, which results in her relinquishing her romantic

ideals. Summers states that Arabella's leap into the river was suggested by de Subligny's satire, *The Mock Clelia. Being a Comical History of French Gallantrie and Novels* (1678), in which the heroine imagines she is Cloelia and throws herself into a canal (27).

8. Pasquale Anfossi's opera was first performed in London at the King's Theatre in 1777. Giordani was among a number of other composers who contributed arias to "beef up" Anfossi's work.

9. Fiske quotes the Epilogue to *She Stoops to Conquer* (1773) which describes how "Madam":

Pretends to taste, at Operas cries caro,
And quits her Nancy Dawson for Che Faro. (548)

10. In its original context, the air portrays Orpheus's grief at the loss of his beloved Eurydice and asks the question, "What will I do without her?"

THE WARD OF THE CASTLE

Dramatis Personae

Duke of Alberossa.
Sir Bertram *(A Knight)*.
Geoffrey *(Squire to Sir Bertram)*.
Sailors, etc.
Matilda *(Countess de Vergy)*.
Jacquinetta *(her maid)*.

Scene: A fortified castle in Normandy.

Act I. Scene I.

Before the castle gates. A march is played. The Duke and his attendants come out from the gates to receive Sir Bertram, who enters as from battle, accompanied by Geoffrey with guards and prisoners.

Duke. Welcome, Sir Bertram, welcome valiant youth. The success of your arms this day has been most worthy of you.
Sir Bertram. My Lord, you overrate my services.
Geoffrey. Not in the least, my lord—you cannot overrate them. The truth is, the knight, my master, bore a wonderful deal of hewing and hacking this day—But I never knew a brave man that was not rather too modest.
Duke *(to Sir Bertram)*. You have indeed brought home the true symbols of victory with you *(points to captives)*.
Geoffrey *(to the captives)*. Miscreant slaves! These chains become you.
Duke *(to the guards)*. March your prisoners round to the postern.
Sir Bert. Attend them, Geoffrey, 'til his grace has given his further orders.
Geof. Away before me there.
(Exeunt Geoffrey , Prisoners and Guards.)
Duke. This defeat will, no doubt, reduce my haughty foe to sue for peace.

Sir Bert. It has, my Lord.—I bring with me his overtures in writing: here they are, my lord—I have promised him an interview with your Grace this very evening at the hour of seven.

Duke *(aside).* At seven? That is my stated hour of visiting Matilda in the tower. *(to Sir Bertram.)* I will not fail to fulfill the promise. Meantime I will go and consider of these articles.

(Exeunt Duke and his attendants.)

Sir Bert *(alone).* How carefully the Duke excludes one ever from within those castle gates. But I think myself amply repaid for all my toils, by the Lodge he has assigned me in the Oak Court of the castle. Little did he think he was furnishing me with the means of penetrating underground to the apartment of his lovely ward.[1]

Song: Sir Bertram

To love alone each pain we owe,
    To love each fond relief,
What other Power could this bestow
    Alternate joy and grief?

To pierce with woe the feeling heart,
    Or make it spring with joy,
Thou, wicked Urchin, hast the art,
    'Tis thine, thou silly Boy.

(Enter Geoffrey.)

Geoffrey. Well, Sir, from the success of your arms this day, I think you may expect from the Duke any reward you choose to ask, either for yourself or your humble squire.

Sir Bertram. You shall not fail of your reward at least, Geoffrey.[2] Profit or reward was not the motive of my enlisting under his banners.

Geof. No, no, Sir; I know it was all a stratagem contrived to steal away from him that beauteous creature he is treasuring up there for himself—But with all his jealous precautions, I think we shall outwit him at last with our subterraneous passage!

Sir Bert. Ay, Geoffrey, if our trap-door at the other end of it were but finished.[3]

Geof. Why, Sir, there is not, I may say, above the breadth of my nail wanting to give you daylight into the Lady Matilda's apartment.

Sir Bert. O delightful! Then, my dear Geoffrey, I may depend on you completing it by seven this evening when the Duke will be absent.[4]

Geof. And is the lady within there, prepared not to scream or make an alarm at your sudden appearance?

Sir Bert. I have here a letter to apprise her of my intention; But how to convey it—?

Geof. In at the window, Sir—In at the little peep-hole window that looks from the tower towards the sea!

Sir Bert. But think of its immense height and distance.—

Geof. No matter for that, Sir; Give the letter to me. I'll ensure its falling at her feet.

Sir Bert. *(gives him the letter.)* Then I'll go in guest of the Duke; and do you watch your opportunity when I have engaged him in earnest conversation at a distance from the tower—And, here, Geoffrey *(Gives him a purse.)* perhaps a little circulation of cash may help to quicken our business.

Geof. 'Gad, Sir, it will help at least to keep the wind out of my pockets; for they were as empty as a conscientious Roman of a fast-day. *(Exeunt.)*

Scene II.

Matilda's apartment in the Tower. Matilda and Jacquinetta discovered: Matilda working at her toilette and Jacquinetta reading a book earnestly.

Song (Matilda) to the Air of "Ah, per me!" by Giordani

Joy! thou dear precarious boon!
Soon we lose thee—ah how soon!
Let one still, in Fancy's glass
Catch thy phantoms as they pass;
'Tis all of joy that I can know,
'Tis all we mortals taste below,
Bright and blushing as the thorn,

Soon thy roseate wreathes are torn.[5]

Jacquinetta. O dear Ma'am, how can you be always singing that melancholy song! *(aside.)* I can't read a word while she is singing.

Matilda. Why should you wish, Jacquinetta, to deprive me of any of my amusements when you know they are so few? And this is my favorite Air, because it was taught me by my Bertram when life was gay and love was young.

Jac. Your amusements, Ma'am, are few enough indeed; But I can't help thinking, if you would sit down and finish the nine volumes of *Cloelia,* you'd find it vastly more amusing than that melancholy ditty. I declare, Ma'am, with all your generosity to me, and the Duke's bribes to make me stay, I could never have existed here for these ten long months, shut up under eighteen strong locks, if it had not been for those four and twenty volumes of charming romances. Celia and Cloelia, and Cassandra! Oh! Such love! And such hair-breadth 'scapes! delightful. Then you know, Ma'am, one is always making some little comparison between oneself and the heroine.

Mat. So one is, Jacquinetta.

Jac. And I am so glad when I find she is not quite a regular beauty, and has blue eyes, and something below the usual size *(or whatever else is descriptive of the actress' person).*

Mat. *(resuming her tambour work.)* But as to you, Jacquinetta, Cloelia has not been your only consolation in this confinement. You have constant pleasure in tormenting the unfortunate Duke's jealousy, with conjuring up, perpetually, new alarms.

Jac. That I own has been a great solace to me—How I shou'd like to have a jealous testy lover myself, for the sake of tormenting him— But for a lover that wou'd not be jealous, but wou'd think one all lovely, all perfection, like Cloelia here—La, I cou'd be so kind to him—But Cloelia is a stiff creature.—Over head and ears in love, but wou'd rather die than own it—*(Reads on to herself.)*

Mat. I am sure I ought never to be tired of romance, for I find some quality in my Bertram in every hero that I read of.

(A noise of locks opening and doors unfolding.)

Mat. O Jacquinetta, I hear the Duke approaching.

Jac. O dear, Ma'am, don't speak to me now; I have the Prince on his knees here. *(Reads on.)*

Mat. How the sound of those Locks jars my very heart!

Jac. *(reading to herself.)* O noble! I long to know what she'll say to that. *(Peeping to the next page.)* O, now she is in her airs again! *(With emotion.)* Ah, this is carrying matters too far—Tut, tut! is that the way to behave to a Prince? And on his knees too! Now, Ma'am, I'll be judged by you—Just let me read her answer to you.

Mat. No, no, Jacquinetta, this is no time—I tell you the Duke is coming.

(The noise of locks continues increasing.)

Jac. Could not she say, "my Lord"—No, that's not right to a Prince—I should say, "Sir"—or, "please your Highness" yes, please your Highness. I mean "your royal Highness, this unlooked for condescension" *(Stammering.)* "in a person—in a Prince of your Royal Highness" *(Stammering.)* "Highness royal qualifications" *(Being unable to go on, she returns to the book.)*

(The noise without terminates in a gentle rapping at the Door.)

Mat. Answer that rapping, Jacquinetta. Tell the Duke he may enter.

Jac. *(without raising her eyes from the book.)* In a minute, Ma'am—I'll open in a minute. *(Reading eagerly.)* I' faith, he'll carry her off—Serve her right too.

Mat. How can you delay opening the door? The Duke will be offended.

Jac. *(giving a scream of joy.)* Oh there—this is the eleventh time—what men they were in those days! The eleventh time, Ma'am, she has been carried off, and her maid with her every time.

(Enter DUKE.)

Duke *(with angry impatience and looks of alarm).* What means this whispering hesitation? *(To Matilda.)* Excuse, Madame, this abrupt intrusion; your unaccountable delay excited my fears.

Jac. *(muttering.)* I beg your Grace's pardon; but indeed I could not stir while he was on his knees.

Duke. Who?—Who was on his knees? *(To Matilda.)* I insist on knowing what this means.

Mat. O dear, my Lord, only the creation of her own fancy—How could you suppose any creature cou'd gain admittance within these walls; or who wou'd wish to share the gloom which surrounds me in this close confinement?

Duke. Come, come, Matilda. I don't like to hear you so often recur to this repining strain—You should be thankful for being withdrawn from the snares of the world.

Song (Duke)

Encircled by the dazzling round,
In ev'ry look there's danger found;
But thus retired from public view,
The rose of youth retains its hue;
Nor flattery's breath, nor art deform
The beauties of that lovely form.

Jac. But consider, my Lord, how necessary a little variety is to a young person—I do believe the Lady Matilda wou'd grow tired even of your Grace, if she was to see nothing else for a few months longer.
(The Duke looks angry at Jacquinetta.)
Mat. Dear lov'd society! Alas, the walls never make answer.
Duke. Well, well, that shall be remedied—Be assured, I shall afford you much more of my society than I have done.
Mat. *(aside, looking mournfully at Jacquinetta).* Worse and worse!
Duke. And for dress, have you not every elegance you can wish?
Mat. But who is there to see it?
Duke. Sure you have Jacquinetta there to admire the beauties which your glass unfolds to you.
Jac. *(laughing.)* O no, your Grace's pardon for that. We women were never made for the purpose of admiring one another.
Duke. And what in the name of folly were you made for?

Air (Jacquinetta)

Women for higher joys were meant
    Than the smiles of each other can e'er impart,
Leave them together, they'll but lament,
    Left quite alone, they break their heart.

Then all their discourse is heigho!

Mat. *(joining in.)*—Heigho!

Duke.   —Why so? Why so?
Mat. and Jac.   —Heigho! Heigho!

Jac. Men's eyes were made for glasses bright,
    To reflect the lustre of female grace;
Take but away our proud birthright,
    And our blossoming beauties will fade apace.

      Then in vain they may cry heigho!

Mat.   — Heigho!
Duke.   —Go, go, go, go.

Mat. and Jac.   —Heigho! Heigho!
    And in vain they may cry heigho!

Duke. ⁶You, Jacquinetta, I see, are nothing the poorer for the chaste solitude you live in here—Retire to your apartment. I have private business with the Countess.

Jac. *(aside.)* I'm glad of it. I'll get another comfortable reading of my little Hero. *(Endeavoring to conceal the book as she goes out.)*

Duke *(following to shut her out).* What huge volume is that you are carrying away?

Jac. *(aside.)* O Lord. I hope he won't take it from me. *(Aloud, stammering.)* This Book? O, my Lord, this little book, it contains the whole duty of man, I assure your Grace.

Duke. Hold—I don't take all you say for gospel. Let me look into it. *(Reads.)* "The life and adventures of the incomparable"—Bah, nonsense—"With the achievements of the most magnanimous Prince of—" Stuff, stuff, stuff! *(Throws down book.)* Soh! And this contains the whole duty of man, does it?

Jac. To my way of thinking, my Lord. *(Curtsies.)*

Duke. You shall never set eyes on it again.

Jac. *(crying.)* O Ma'am. Ma'am! To take away the life, and the most innocent adventures—to take it away for ever!

Duke. Innocent? I make no doubt but that innocent book is full of the wickedest intrigues—

Jac. *(aside, shaking her head.)* Not one—

Duke. And elopements—

Jac. *(aside.)* O yes, eleven times—she and her maid.

Duke. [7]Amorous billets convey'd in the bills of pigeons.

Jac. *(aside.)* As sure as fate he has been reading it himself.[8] It's lucky for me I have the last nine volumes in my closet.

Duke. Go shut yourself in there. *(Throws the book out of the door he came in at. Exit Jacquinetta.)*

Duke. How dangerous it is to suffer a woman to read at all!

Mat. *(aside.)* What can the Duke have to say to me in private? I tremble more at the apprehension of his tenderness than even of his tyranny.

Duke. Matilda, you have no doubt discovered that I have long beheld you with eyes of fond solicitude.

Mat. You have been a very careful Guardian indeed, my Lord.

Duke. Careful? That is but a cold description of my conduct. But it is ever thus you respect my growing tenderness, by your chilling manners—[9]You know your father's will is express that you shall not marry without my consent openly declared, by my presenting you at the altar to your husband; under the penalty of forfeiting all claim to the Estate and Manors of Vergy.

Mat. Then I am sure I shall never marry.

Duke. The difficulty of that excuse I at once remove by offering myself to you.

Mat. Oh heavens!

Duke. Tomorrow then, my fair Matilda, I shall expect to find you ready to fulfill your father's will.

Mat. *(with emotion.)* Can my father's will be fulfilled without my heart declaring its consent? O impossible! *(Weeps.)*

Duke. Nay, nay, that is more than can be expected from such reserve as yours—The restraint of female modesty still imposes silence even where the heart is most gratified.[10] As a pledge of the sincerity of my passion, I here present you with a thing of inestimable value. *(Puts it on her finger.)* 'Twas a gift of friendship bestowed on me by one of the greatest potentates of the age. Farewell, beauteous Matilda.

(Exit Duke. The noise of locks and bars is repeated.)

Mat. *(alone.)* O that my Bertram were here to rescue me from this tyranny! *(Weeps.)*

(Enter Jacquinetta.)

Jac. *(peeping in.)* I'm sure I heard the rattling signal of the Duke's departure. *(Entering).* Lord. Ma'am, what has he been saying that has made such a weeping statue of you?

Mat. O, Jacquinetta, I am more to be pitied than words can express.

Jac. O me, what has he done to you? The vile Harpy!

Mat. He has declared his cruel intentions of marrying me to-morrow.

Jac. Is that all, Ma'am?[11] Dear Ma'am, don't take on so[12]—will you always persist in detesting the whole sex?

Mat. You know, Jacquinetta, I do not detest the whole sex.— There is one for whose sake—

Jac. *(interrupting.)* Yes, Ma'am. I know your old romantic attachment to that young knight, Sir Bertram—But la! You might as well be constant to the man in the moon;—He is fighting at the Holy Wars, as they call them, and will never come back 'till we are both as old and as yellow as the parchment cover of poor little Cloelia.

Mat. I have more pleasure in thinking on the virtues of my Bertram than in all the other joys this world can afford.

Jac. Very true, Ma'am—But that don't make our time pass merrily for all that.

Mat. Ah! Jacquinetta! it is alone the presence of him we love that can make time pass pleasantly away.

Air by Giordani (Matilda)

The hours were fleet,
And moments sweet,
    When gaily spent with him I loved;
    Each day still prov'd his constant flame,
    The hours return! but not the same.

Since he is vanished from my sight,
From me is fled all gay delight,
    With him I loved
Each day still prov'd his constant flame,
The hours return! but not the same.

Jac. *(surprised.)* Dear Ma'am, what beautiful thing is that on your finger?

Mat. O, 'tis a hateful pledge of affection forced on me by the Duke at parting.

Jac. Dear! what a particular shape! and what brilliancy! Well, I never saw a more beautiful sparking thing in my life—Ay, ay, at him alone—He knew what he was about—To be sure he has some shining points about him—This was a sweet love token.

(Noise of window breaking, followed by the sound of a heavy body falling on the floor)

Mat. Good heavens, what noise is that? It is quite terrifying.

Jac. Hush, Ma'am—there surely was a Pane of Glass broken.

Mat. It certainly was the window of my Dressing Closet above.

Jac. Dear Ma'am, let us run up and see what it is.

Mat. Do you so, Jacquinetta—I have no courage.

(Exit Jacquinetta.)

Mat. *(alone.)* My Spirits are so alarmed. I tremble at every sound.

Jac. *(from within.)* O Lord, O Lord!

Mat. *(with impatience.)* Well, Jacquinetta?

(Re-enter Jacquinetta.)

Jac. The window, Ma'am, sure enough, is broken all to shivers—And what's more strange—

Mat. What?

Jac. More strange—I have not breath to tell it—there's a parcel that came thro' the window, as heavy at least as a young child.

Mat. What can it contain?

Jac. Ola! Ma'am, help me to open it—I am ready to die with impatience—Where is your scissors—your knife—your tambour needle—anything—

Mat. Stay, Jacquinetta; perhaps it is dangerous to open it.

Jac. Dangerous! O dear! it's too little to do us any harm.

Mat. It may be a trial of me sent by the Duke.

Jac. La! Ma'am, he never took you for anything but a woman; he could never suppose you had not curiosity to examine it—Ola! there's no end to these covers of paper, and cords, and shavings upon shavings stuffed between—Ah, here it is at last, and a lump of lead lapped up in it.

Mat. What, what, Jacquinetta?

Jac. A letter, Ma'am, as I live.

Mat. And what's the direction?

Jac. *(reads.)* "To the Lady Matilda, Countess de Vergy."

Mat. *(snatching it.)* Give it, give it to me.

Jac. *(in great fuss.)* Make haste, and open it, Ma'am.

Mat. O enchanting! It is my Bertram's writing. *(Reads to herself.)*

Jac. O pray, Ma'am, read out—you may trust me with his secret, you may indeed. Ma'am—I have no one to tell it to.

Mat. Peace then. *(Reads with animation.)* "Loveliest of women"—

Jac. Ay, that's just like the Prince Sorismenes.

Mat. *(reading.)* "The youth you once honor'd with your regard, and who has never ceased to adore you"—

Jac. Ay; Sir Bertram—

Mat. *(continuing.)* [13] "Not being able to obtain more than a lodge in the out-court, he has from thence contrived a subterraneous *passage*"—

Jac. That's something under ground; Ma'am, is not it?

Mat. *(continuing.)* "Communicating with the tower in which you reside by a trap-door in the ground apartment"—

Jac. *(screaming with joy.)* A trap-door! O beyond my expectations—A trap-door—*(Runs and hugs Matilda.)* O, I beg your pardon, Ma'am; I shall go mad with joy—Well, a trap-door! I trust it will be big enough for me to pass thro'—! A trap-door! Lord, whereabouts?

Mat. If you will but listen—

Jac. O yes, Ma'am: tell me more.

Mat. *(reading.)* "The Duke's absence from the castle being certain at the hour of seven, the striking of the town clock shall be the propitious moment for opening the trap-door."

(They both hastily look at their watches.)

Jac. It wants but five minutes and a half of the appointed hour, Ma'am.

Mat. Not quite so much, Jacquinetta.

Jac. So much the better, Ma'am.

Duet (Matilda and Jacquinetta)

What joy to hear the tell-tale sound!
   'Twill turn this little earth to heaven;

Each toll will make our hearts rebound,
     While slowly we count seven.
(Clock strikes slowly while they sing.)
     Hark! one—hush! hush! there's two—Old Time says three;
     Alas, how slow! how even!
     Now, now, 'tis four—now five, and then comes six,
     And now my heart strikes seven.

(Sound of carpenter's work below.)
     Mat. O Jacquinetta, I hear a voice from below.
     Jac. Ay, sure enough that is the sound of the chisel—Well, I
never heard such sweet music in my life—If I cou'd but find the place.
(Searching with her hand.) It's here! It's somewhere here. *(Starts.)* O
lud! I felt the hammer.
     Mat. O dear. I am in such agitation!
     Jac. Dear Ma'am, never mind your agitation; but come here to
feel how this Board shakes.
     Mat. I can't stir; I tremble so.
     Jac. Be merry at least, Ma'am; sure you never had such mirth.
Think of your Knight, Sir Bertram, coming all the way from Jerusalem
or Jericho to release you. *(Shouting.)* O lud! he'll be up in a minute—I
suppose he'll appear in armour—I think I hear the clink of it—Sing,
Ma'am; do, pray sing to show you are merry.
(Singing from below.)
     Jac. Ola! the dear creature thinks it was him we desired to sing—
I'll listen, and tell you what he is singing.

Song (from below)

     The boards are tough, but I'll work apace,
     Tic a tac, tic, tac, too,
     For when I think of a pretty, pretty face
     The hammer goes, and the chisel too.

     Jac. *(sings.)* At every sound of the tic, tac stroke
     My heart goes pit a pat, pit, pat too,
     O may success then crown the work
     Of your tic a tac, tic, tac, too.[14]

Geoffrey *(putting up his head)*. I must have the first peep.

Mat. O heavens, who is that?

Jac. As I live, Geoffrey, the carpenter—My hero after all and not yours—My dear, dear Geoffrey!

Geof. My dear, dear Jacquinetta!

(Enter Sir Bertram from below hastily.)

Sir Bertram. Stand by there! Let me fly to my Matilda's feet. *(Pushes Geoffrey aside.)*

Mat. O Bertram; no words can express my joy.

Sir Bert. *(kneels to her.)* And has my lovely Matilda often recall'd our mutual vows of love and constancy, when, blushing she wou'd bid me hope to live for her?

Mat. O, Bertram.[15]

Duet (Matilda and Bertram)

Sir Bert. The fond impression of my early days
    Still on my memory dwells;
Matilda's figure on my fancy plays,
    And in my bosom swells.

Mat. Soft as the breath of Southern gales,
    Your gentle accents fell;
Both. And fondly I believ'd the soothing tales,
    Your flattering tongue would tell.[16]

(They walk aside in earnest conversation. Geoffrey and Jacquinetta come forward)

Geof. And to find my pretty Jacquinetta here!

Jac. Ay, but you did not kneel down to kiss my hand yet, like a hero.

Geof. Egad I must lay down the trap-door first.

Jac. O, don't lay it down, Geoffrey; perhaps you might not be able to get it up again.[17]

Geof. See how it fits, Jacquinetta? *(To Sir Bertram.)* Look, Sir;—Lord, he no more minds—That's the way with all your great men—So they get their dirty work done, they never care how, or by whom.

Jac. Dear me, Geoffrey, what a mere carpenter you are—You think of nothing but your work.

Geof. Well, and don't you like me the better for that? 'Od, since the last time you stood listening to the music of the saw, pet, what have you heard half so pleasant in this old rookery, eh?

Jac. No; but then I have quite new notions since that time, and I have thought a great deal more of myself since I read about Ladies, and Heroines, and Knights—

Geof. And 'Squires, mayhap?—Well, tho' I am not a man to be asham'd of the ladder that raised me, I am a 'Squire too, Miss Jacquinetta, as little as you think of me.

Jac. You a Squire?

Geof. Ay, 'Squire to that gallant Knight there.

Jac. *(with glee.)* To Sir Bertram?

Geof. Yes, I have been stiffen'd up into an easy Gentleman since I saw you last, and if you'll believe me, 'twas the greatest hardship I ever went thro' in my life—There was I obliged to walk like a Gentleman, to look and talk like a Gentleman.

Jac. Ay, and to eat like a Gentleman I warrant you. And was it you, Geoffrey, that made that ingenious way under ground too?

Geof. Was it me? Don't you know my dexterity?

Song (Geoffrey)
(To the air of "I'll tell you a Story that happened of late")

When I was apprenticed and learned my trade,
 With my row de dow, row de dow dero,
I took up the chisel and threw down the spade;
 Fal, lal, de ral, lal de ral, dero.

But now with a shovel, and mattock, and bill,
 With my row de dow, &c.
I work like a horse, or a thief in a mill,
 Fal, lal, de ral, lal de ral, dero.

It is very fine sport to be fighting all day,
 With my row de dow, &c.
And all night, like a mole, to be mining away;
 Fal, lal, de ral, lal de ral, dero.

But now all my art has been put to the proof,

Row de dow, &c.
When I work'd through the vault and cut through' the roof;
You repaid me with fal, lal de lal..

(Geoffrey and Jacquinetta walk aside in conversation. Sir Bertram and Matilda come forward.)

Sir Bert. Nay, but my lovely Matilda, your fears destroy our happiness—Tho' I would, without hesitation, resign all the estates and titles of Vergy, I cannot tamely submit to his usurping the honor of your father's house, which you were born to grace.

Mat. O, I was born only to be miserable!—'Twas but this very day the Duke reminded me of my father's will, which requires my being presented by his hand, to him who is to be my Lord.

Sir Bert. By his hand?

Mat. At the same time he presented me with this curious Ring— *(Takes it off her finger.)* Take it, my dear Bertram, as a pledge of my truth to you and my aversion to the Duke. *(Gives the ring to Sir Bertram, who kisses it.)*

Sir Bert. And did the Duke strongly urge the subject of his marriage with you?

Mat. He gave me only 'till tomorrow to be free—But I am resolved to resign my life before I'll consent to be his.

Sir Bert. Strange as it may appear to you, I wish to conceal from the Duke for the present, the repugnance you feel towards him, as I have a plan by which I hope to make him resign all pretentions to you.

Mat. The thought restores life to me! But how?

(Here a sound of locks, &c. as before.)

Jac. O lud, Ma'am. I heard the first lock open; What will become of us?

Sir Bert. 'Tis impossible the Duke can have return'd so quickly.

Mat. Fly, fly, I entreat you, or we shall all be discovered.

Sir Bert. To fly is death to me.

Mat. To stay is destruction to me.

Geof. Death and destruction, Sir, how can you linger?

Sir Bert. Adieu, my lovely Matilda. I'll return this evening, and apprise you fully of my plan, and concert measures with you for commuting it;—success I'm sure will depend wholly on yourself.

Geof. *(to Jacquinetta.)* Take good care of the trap-door, my dear Jacquinetta.

Duet (Sir Bertram and Matilda)
(To the French air of "Adieu coeur moi")

One gentle smile,
Before we part, my love;
One gentle smile,
To calm my fond heart.

Farewell, farewell,
Farewell, my soul's delight,
Farewell, dear maid, (dear youth,)
Adieu! till night.

(Exit Matilda. Sir Bertram through trap.)

Duet (Geoffrey and Jacquinetta)

One roguish look
Before I go, my love;
One roguish look,
So, so, so, so.

Bye, bye, bye, bye
Bye, my pretty, pretty dear;
Bye, bye, bye, bye,
Old Guardian will hear.

(Exit Geoffrey through trap.)

END OF ACT I.

Notes

1. The following line is circled in the Manuscript: "How insipid wou'd these pretty triumphs appear to me, were I not cheer'd by the thought that I am protecting my belov'd Matilda." It is often difficult to guess whether the marked passages are the result of censorship by the Lord Chamberlain's Office, or deletions by the author. In either case, they represent alterations to the play and as such will appear in notes rather than in the text.

2. "But for me, what has the Duke to bestow that I wou'd condescend to accept" is crossed out.

3. The word "opened" is deleted and the two subsequent lines are circled and crossed out:
    > Geoffrey. Opened, Sir? And so it is all one as opened—trust me for that—'Twas not for nothing so much pains were taken with my education in the best carpenter's shop in this Kingdom; I flatter myself I can turn a deal board to as many purposes as any gentleman can.
    > Sir Bertram. Well, but is the trap-door really so near being finished?

4. The following speeches that emphasize the moral justification of the hero to rescue a damsel in distress (a typical theme of Gothic melodrama) are circled and crossed out in the Manuscript:
    > Geof. But after all, Sir, bad as the Duke is, let us keep all fair and honorable on our own part—What right have you to come and steal away this Lady from the Duke? Is not he her lawful Guardian?
    > Sir Bert. He is, Geoffrey—But has he, therefore, a right to constrain her affections, of which I proudly boast myself the object; and to gratify his own interested views, compel her by the most rigorous and cruel imprisonment to marry him?
    > Geof. Nay, if your object is to rescue an injur'd Damsel, I am ready with hand and fist to assist you.
    > Sir Bert. But haste to the trap-door.

5. According to the published copy of the *Songs, Duets, Choruses, &c.* in *The Ward of the Castle*, the last four lines were omitted in performance.

6. The beginning of the Duke's speech, "Absurd, silly, diabolical—let me hear no more of it" is crossed out.

7. The beginning of the Duke's line, "These natural inventions of brothers for marrying off their sisters out of (words unintelligible)" is crossed out.

8. Between Jacquinetta's lines, there is the following speech for the Duke which is circled and crossed out: "I wonder, Matilda, you cou'd give ear to such ribald absurdity—There was the love scene that made you forget your duty when I demanded admittance—But it is the last time." The beginning of Jacquinetta's next line is crossed out completely and unintelligible.

9. The following short scene is circled and crossed out:
    > Duke. However, this may be all dissembling, the natural cloaking of a woman's mind. Tell me, Matilda, what are your real sentiments towards me?
    > Mat. My Lord, as the chosen friend of my father, I respect—
    > Duke *(interrupting)*. There again! Respect? your father's friend? Yes, and if I had been your great grandfather's friend, you would respect me still more I suppose! Is this a due return for the fondness I have lavished on you? O Matilda, you have been the subject of my dearest and my latest thoughts.
    > Mat. Your Grace is better to me than I deserve.
    > Duke. I have hitherto cautiously guarded those dangerous advantages you possess, of youth, beauty, and fortune, from the artful snares of insidious Tempters.

The Ward of the Castle   41

Mat. Heigh ho!

Duke. And I have resolved in elevating you to a situation that will give dignity and protection to those native graces.

The next two speeches are circled but not crossed out:

Mat. O my Lord, they are quite unworthy your consideration.

Duke *(aside).* Her answers are still evasive; but I will not be influenced by her inclinations.

10. The following line of the Duke is circled: "I shall leave you at present to recover your agitation at such unexpected good fortune."

11. The following two speeches are circled in the Manuscript:

Jac. Why, that is rare news I think; for you know, once he is your husband, he is no longer your Guardian, and then you may take your pleasure and go everywhere; and see everybody—and I shall be so happy to attend your Grace.

Mat. No, Jacquinetta, his jealous tyranny will only be redoubled. *(Weeps.)*

12. An illegible phrase is crossed out.

13. The following speeches are circled and crossed out in the Manuscript:

Mat. *(continuing.)* "Enlisted himself some months since under the banners of the Duke of Alberossa, to lead his troops to war, with a view of gaining admittance into the castle which encloses the most lovely of her sex."

Jac. Aye, that's your Ladyship.

14. This song is not printed with the published *Songs, Duets, Choruses, &c.* Jacquinetta's following speech, emphasizing the romantic, melodramatic nature of the piece, is circled and crossed out in the Manuscript: "He's a noisy creature, and his voice reminds me of a certain person I'd be glad to set eyes on. *(Starts.)* O Lud, it's opening—here he comes—here's your Hero.

15. The continuation of the speech, "'twas that cheering thought alone enabled me to bear this sad imprisonment" is circled in the text.

16. In the Manuscript, this duet was written as a song for Matilda, exchanging the words "My Bertram's figure" for "Matilda's figure" in the third line.

17. Geoffrey's response is circled in the Manuscript: "I must see how it fits, Jacquinetta— Come, help me to lay it down there—why, it fits you see; as exact as the teeth in a shark's mouth. Feel it, Jacquinetta." Jacquinetta's reply, "Well, so it (word illegible)" is crossed out.

Act II. Scene I.

Sir Bertram's apartment. Sir Bertram and the Duke discovered in conversation. Geoffrey waiting behind.

Sir Bertram. Your Grace's so immediate return is quite unexpected—You met the Herald at the town-gate I understand.

Duke. The same from the Count to put off our interview—I consented to a week's truce without much reluctance as it gives me time to consider what conditions I shall accede to.

Sir Bert. And very fortunately for me, my Lord, it gives me an opportunity of communicating to you a private affair of a most interesting nature relating to myself.

Duke. Pray proceed without reserve.

Sir Bert. A Turkish Lady who had honor'd me with a mutual exchange of vows, lately became a captive to the Spanish, a misfortune which I (alas!) wanted the power to remedy.

Duke. Unfortunate!

Sir Bert. This day an express has brought me the delightful intelligence of her being ransomed—She is now on her way hither with the utmost expedition; and this very evening, with your permission, I expect the happiness of presenting to you my lovely Selima.

Geoffrey *(aside).* Heavens and earth! Is my master's head turned?

Duke. Dear Sir Bertram, I share your happiness with all my heart—Every honor shall attend the Lady's arrival. I welcome her to the castle.

Sir Bert. Your offer, my Lord, is perfectly gallant,—But my Selima's retired disposition would be distressed by those attentions offered her in public—When she is arrived, and has recovered her first agitation, I'll send to acquaint your Grace.

Duke. I shall be impatient to see her. I suppose her beauty— *(Interrupts himself with emotion.)* Bless me, what ring is that?

Sir Bert. *(affecting indifference.)* Ring, my Lord?

Duke. That ring, Sir, I saw upon your finger—Is it yours?

Sir Bert. *(affecting surprise.)* Is it mine, my Lord?

Duke. Ay, Sir; Where did you get that ring?

Sir Bert. *(affecting to be offended.)* How, my Lord! Is that a question from one man of Honor to another!

Duke *(recollecting himself)*. Pardon me, Sir Bertram; my address was ungracious;—'twas my surprise—But will you indulge me with a nearer view of that ring?

Sir Bert. By all means, my Lord.—On my hand;—I have a little superstition taking it off.

Duke *(aside)*. Heavens, what a discovery! As I live, the very ring I gave this morning to Matilda.

Sir Bert. 'Tis a mere bauble in itself;—but I would not part with it for the most precious jewel—The hand that placed it here endowed it with inestimable value.

Duke *(aside)*. I'm resolved I'll know how he has obtained it—

Sir Bert. Your Grace seems disturbed;—has anything happened?

Duke. No, no, nothing:—nothing but the surprising resemblance of that ring to one I thought myself master of.—

Sir Bert. Very natural, my Lord. *(Aside.)* This succeeds to my wish.

Duke *(aside)*. But first I must have an explanation with Matilda— *(Aloud.)* Excuse, Sir Bertram, my abrupt departure—I must hasten away to some business of importance, which this moment occurs to my recollection. *(Exit Duke.)*

Geoffrey *(coming forward impatiently)*. Good heavens, Sir, was you bent on ruining all, by imprudently discovering that ring?

Sir Bert. Imprudently? Do you suppose I did it without design?[1] I must fly thro' the subterraneous passage and restore this ring to the Countess before the Duke can find his winding way into her apartment.

Geof. Shall I attend you, Sir?

Sir Bert. No, no, you would but delay me.

(Exit at door in back-scene, and in view of the audience descends rapidly into the subterraneous passage, through the trap-door.)

Scene II.

Matilda's Apartment. Matilda, Jacquinetta and Duke discovered.

Matilda. How importunate you are my Lord about such a trifle— If I could have supposed the ring was to be produced every time your

Grace was pleased to surprise me with a visit, I should have been more careful.

Duke. I see, Madam, you are trying to elude my inquiries—But I am not to be thus put off—Were it even a trifle—which, as a Pledge of my truth, you should not deem it,—still, Madam, as your Guardian, I have a right to be satisfied in the minutest particular that concerns you.

Mat. [2]Oh my Lord, I do not dispute your right to have your own present back again—But sure, you cannot doubt of its safety;—It has no magical property of vanishing, or becoming visible—The only difficulty is to recollect what I have done with it. Perhaps thrown it carelessly among jewels which I never put on.

Jacquinetta. Like enough, Ma'am;—I'll bring the black Japann'd box to his Grace to examine himself. *(Goes out.)*

Duke. No, Madam, this is but a shallow device—It is too plain my fears are all realized.

Jac.[3] *(returning)* Here, your Grace, here's the Japann'd Box, and the Shagreen Case too. *(Aside to Matilda.)* I have the ring—I got it from the trap-door.[4] *(Aloud to the Duke.)* I'm sure the contents are of no more use to my Lady than to her Grandmother that bequeathed them to her.

Duke. Open, open the box.

Jac. Here, Ma'am, are your large three-dropp'd earrings.

Duke. Mean trifling!

Jac. Your Mother of Pearl butterfly that has lost a wing.

Duke. Psha!

Jac. Gold Etui Case wanting a hinge—with your Grandmamma's picture at the back of it.

Duke. Impertinent!

Jac. Little square shoe-buckles, several times fallen out.

Duke. For shame, Matilda.

Jac. And here as I live is the ring—

Duke *(eagerly).* Hah! the ring?

Jac. The ring I have so often admired, with a wounded heart; and true lover's knot at the top.

Duke *(in a rage).* I'll be trifled with no longer. *(To Jacquinetta.)* Get out of my sight.

Mat. *(aside.)* I believe I have kept him long enough in suspense. *(Aloud.)* Give me the box, Jacquinetta.

Duke. Madam. I knew but too well the ring was not in your possession;—And I now insist on knowing by what secret communication—

Jac. Secret communication!

Mat. Pray, good Guardian, don't be intemperate.—Your passion seems quite to blind you. *(Puts the ring privately on her finger.)*

Duke *(in a fury).* The ring, Madam—the ring—

Song (Matilda)

The ring, you cry, "the ring,"
    Yet blindly shun its rays,
What is that shining thing;
(Displays the ring before his eyes.)
    Which casts such dazzling blaze.

Duke. Heavens! Is it possible! This is like Enchantment!
(Catches at the ring which she hastily withdraws.)

Duke *(sings).* Nay, snatch it not away,
    It boasts peculiar charms
Its presence brings the day,
    Its absence dire alarms.

Both. Nay, snatch it not away,
    It boasts peculiar charms
Its presence brings the day,
    Its absence, dire alarms.[5]

Duke. It is, it is the true ring—My senses deceived me.[6] Can you forgive me, Matilda? I was too hasty in thinking you had no value for that little gift of mine.

Mat. Oh, 'tis a precious ring to me, Sir.

Duke *(aside).* That looks well.

Jac. Well, I hope your Grace wont be in a hurry to suspect us again.

Duke. Oh let us talk no more of the past.[7]

Catch (Jacquinetta, Duke, and Matilda)
(To the tune of "Come let us all a maying go")

Come let us all a wooing go,
And fondly our passion show,
The wedding ring, and Parson bring,
And the Cuckoo in vain shall sing;
Tho' fools may jeer, ne'er seem to hear,
But love renew from year to year.
(Exeunt.)

Geoffrey *(alone).* What a stupid,—thick-headed fellow I must be not to understand one word of my master's design in this affair.—My fear is, that his Scheme lies too deep, and that we shall all be blown up by his hair-brained fancies.—I wish for all that he had taken me with him thro' the trap-door—I shou'd so like to have another heart-stirring glance at that little Jacquinetta—What bewitching things these Ladies are!—How I love the Scotch Ploughman for singing their praise so sweetly.

Song. (Geoffrey)
(To the air of "Green grow the Rushes O")

There's nought but care on ev'ry han'
    In ev'ry hour passes O,
What signifies the life of man,
    If 'twere not for the lasses O.

CHORUS: Then heigh for the lasses O,
        Heigh for the lasses O.
        What signifies the life of man
        If 'twere not for the lasses O.

For you, so wise, who sneer at this,
    You're nought but silly asses O,
The wisest man the world e'er saw,
    He dearly loved the lasses O.

CHORUS: He loved the lasses O,

Heigh for the lasses O.
The wisest man the world e'er saw,
He dearly loved the lasses O.

Old nature swears, the lovely dears
Her noblest work she classes O,
Her 'prentice han' she tried on man,
And then she made the lasses O.

CHORUS: Then she made the lasses O,
Heigh for the lasses O.
Her 'prentice han' she tried on man,
And then she made the lasses O.[8]

(Exit.)

Scene III.[9]

(Enter Sir Bertram conducting Matilda in a superb Turkish habit.)

Sir Bertram. Now, my lovely Matilda, all our hopes depend on your well sustaining the part you are so correctly dressed for in this trying interview with the Duke.

Matilda. Have you already prepared him to expect a Turkish Lady whom you are to espouse?

Sir Bert. I have told him a fine romantic story. The Duke believes it all and has promis'd to give you away at the altar.

Mat. O my Bertram, 'tis your influence alone cou'd bear me thro' so fearful a situation.

Sir. Bert. Fear nothing my love—Remember you are to assume a character as well as dress foreign to your own.

(Enter Geoffrey hastily.)

Geoffrey. Sir, Sir, here comes the Duke—Prepare your gravity to receive him.

Matilda. Heavens! What a part I have to act.

(Enter Duke.)

Duke. I come, Sir Bertram, to welcome the fair Stranger from the East.

Sir Bert. *(leading Matilda forward.)* I am happy in presenting to your Grace, my lovely Selima, the sole object of my love and whom, by your Grace's power, I hope soon to call my bride.

Duke. Permit me the honor of kissing that fair hand.

Mat. My Lord, as the friend and patron of my Bertram, I honor and respect you.

Duke *(aside).* Ftah! her voice seems familiar to me—Her accents to resemble those of Matilda.

Sir Bert. Pray, my Lord, be seated.

Mat. Nay, you shall sit by one, Sir—In my Country it is deem'd a special favour to sit by a Lady.

Duke. In any Country, Madam, it must be deem'd an honor. *(Aside.)* I cannot recover my astonishment.

Sir Bert. My lord, you seem rapt in thought.

Duke. I am much struck, Sir, with that Lady's voice.

Sir Bert. Her speaking voice is admirable—But how must you be charmed when you hear her sing! *(To Matilda.)* Pray, my dear Selima, let me entreat you.

Mat. You shall hear a Persian song that was often my solace in my hideous captivity. *(Sings—a Persian Air.)*

Shub e harigue, beem e modge
Girdaub e chuni hail!
Cuija danund haul e ma,
Subuch saraun e Sahil![10]

Duke. I am lost in admiration *(Aside.)* and astonishment.—I cannot bear this suspense any longer. I must require that Veil to be withdrawn. *(Aloud.)* May I not hope to see that lovely face unveil'd?

Mat. Surely, my Lord—I wish it could better repay so flattering a request. *(Sir Bertram assists in withdrawing her veil.)*

Duke *(starts).* Distraction! It is she—it is Matilda!

Sir Bert. Who, my Lord? What is it that disturbs your Grace?

Duke. What outrage is this you have dared to commit on me?

Sir Bert. Outrage, my Lord?

Duke. That Lady, whom, by some vile treachery, you have convey'd from within my castle is Matilda, Countess de Vergy—I here claim her as my ward. *(Goes to take hold of her.)*

Sir Bert *(interrupting).* Hold, my Lord;—your intemperance transports you—That Lady is under my protection: and with my life I'll shield her from insult.

Duke. Your life shall answer for your temerity in detaining her.

Sir Bert. My Lord, my Lord, recollect yourself—You know I have never been admitted within your castle, and must be a perfect stranger to what it contains—If, indeed, the Lady you name resembles my Selima so strongly, she must be a treasure; and I pity the apprehension you seem to have suffered.

Duke *(pondering).* Resemble? There are strong resemblances.

Mat. Is there a Lady in the castle whom I have the honor to resemble? Pray let me be known to her.

Duke *(aside).* Sure, sure, Matilda cou'd not assume such confidence—I'll fly and satisfy myself if she be in safety. Meantime a strong guard shall secure every passage from this Lodge. *(Aloud.)* Sir Bertram, if I am under any delusion, a few minutes shall ascertain it.

Sir Bert. I am as anxious as your Grave to prove your error. I trust you will find your ward in perfect safety.

Mat. We shall expect your return with impatience.

(Exit Duke.)

Mat. He's gone to search for me. O, let me hasten and be ready for his reception.

Sir Bert. When, where is Jacquinetta to assist you?

Mat. She waits for me at the trap-door.

Sir Bert. Haste then, haste.

(Exeunt Sir Bertram and Matilda down a trap-door.)

Geoffrey *(alone).* This is just what I foresaw—If my master had an ounce of my prudence, this cou'd never have happened—Why the deuce, when he got her uncaged, could not he fly away with her? But he must flourish and parade her before the Duke forsooth, and so get her imprison'd for life—Dungeons, chains and irons will be her portion—Sir Bertram will have the honor of losing his life in single combat; but as for me, I shall be hang'd upon the first convenient tree, as the aider and abettor of his devices—If Jacquinetta was out of the scrape, I should not tremble half so much—If it was not for her I'd secure my retreat, and not wait to hear my sentence pronounced. All this comes now, I suppose, of that crabbed Article in her father's will—Lord! Lord! how many bye-roads these great folk are obliged to take in their way to the Land of Matrimony!

Song (Geoffrey)

Papa must be ask'd, mama must consent
And Lawyers prepar'd with whole skins of parchment;
With clauses, and pauses, and villainous stuff,
Of jointure, remainder, of words full enough,
    Alas, the poor soul! Alas, the poor soul![11]
With whereas and likewise and wherefore,
Besides, as aforesaid and therefore,
    And twenty *et ceteras* to wind up the whole.

A license must then from the Archbishop come,
The neighbours invited by beat of the drum,
The parson, array'd in his cassock and band,
Joins this formal young Couple fast hand in hand.
    Alas, the poor soul! Alas, the poor soul!
You, Bertram, take Matilda to wife,
To cherish her all the days of your life
    And twenty *et ceteras* to wind up the whole.
(Exit.)

Scene IV.[12]

Matilda's Chamber: A canopied sofa stands at one side.

(Enter Matilda from a trap-door in a loose wrapping dress, and Jac-quinetta.)
    Matilda. Quick, quick, Jacquinetta, give me something to veil my face and conceal this agitation I am in, from the Duke.
(A noise of locks and bolts.)
    Jacquinetta. O lud, Ma'am, I hear him close at hand—Do lie down on the sofa, that you may seem the more composed.
    Mat. *(lying down.)* Settle my clothes, Jacquinetta.
    Jac. Ods my life, we forgot the turban.
    Mat. Here, here, tear it off, and hide it anywhere.

Jac. *(hides the turban and settles Matilda's headdress.)* Now, Ma'am, lye down and be asleep in a moment *(Closes the curtains, sits down at the table and affects to be asleep over her work.)*
(Enter the Duke, impetuously.)
Duke. The place is alarmingly quiet—Ho, Jacquinetta!
Jac. *(rubbing her eyes.)* La, oh Lord—what's this, did not I hear myself called?
Duke. Jacquinetta! Where is the Countess?
Jac. O Lord, ha' mercy, is it your Grace? I beg a thousand pardons. I never heard you coming in. The sleep came upon me so by surprise—I don't know when such a thing happened to me before.
Duke *(impatiently).* Cease your apologies, and show me to the Countess.
Jac. O my Lord, that is quite impossible.
Duke. Impossible? I knew it! She is not here then?
Jac. O yes, that she is—But sure your Grace don't expect me to show you to her after she is gone to bed—I never knew you—you that were always so polite and so gallant, and so punctilious, and so—
Duke. Impertinent trifling! Satisfy me this instant that your Lady is in these apartments, or your head shall be the forfeit.
Jac. *(affecting fright.)* O Lord! Why, where shou'd she be but there in bed, and fast asleep too. *(Withdrawing curtain.)* O dear, o dear. That she shou'd be torn in this manner out of that innocent sleep I had just humm'd her into.
Duke. Ftah! beyond my hopes she is there. Matilda herself fast locked in the arms of sleep.
Jac. Is not that what I told your Grace from the first, but I am never to be believed, but hourly threatened with racks and torture and death: and my Lady is to have her rest broke in upon, and her Bed Chamber trespassed upon.
Duke. Excuse me, Jacquinetta. A sudden distraction came across my mind—I am now fully satisfied—Don't let your Lady know I have been here—And here, take this to make amends for your fright. *(Gives her money.)* Close the curtains, and let your mistress enjoy her rest —I shan't come any more this evening to disturb her.
Jac. *(after settling the curtains.)* A very good night to your Grace—Pray shut the door softly after you *(returns to her chair and takes up her work).*

Duke. Good night, Jacquinetta. *(Going, stops and looks at his watch.)* 'Tis a very early hour for the Countess to be in bed, and so fast asleep—I suspect some artifice still—The figure may have deceived me—my mind is in so distracted a state. I almost discredit my very senses—I must see her awake and speak to her. *(Returns.)* Jacquinetta!

Jac. *(starting.)* O Lud, is your Grace there again?

Duke. Pray, how came your Lady to be so early gone to rest?

Jac. O, she was so bad, my Lord, with a headache complain'd sadly of a shooting pain in her ear.

Duke. Well, I must speak to her notwithstanding—Do you waken her?

Jac. Not for the world—I am surprised your Grace would think of it—I really won't be answerable for the consequences if you attempt to take her out of that refreshing sleep.

Duke. Answer me not—It must be so—I'll wake her myself gently.

Trio (Air: "Che faro")[13]

Duke. Matilda, dear Countess awake, let me see thee,
The scene is all illusion,
My thoughts are in confusion,
Where shall my wonder cease?

Jac. Forbear, Sir, disturb not
My Lady's soft slumbers;
Believe me, such intrusion
Will throw her in confusion;
Pray, let her rest in peace.

Duke. Soft, let me this veil displace,
No further I'll disturb her,
Nor discompose her slumber,
Than just to view her face.

Jac. There, now, Sir, the mischief's done;
You've broke my Lady's rest, Sir,
You see how she's distress'd, Sir,
You'd best at once be gone,

No, no, no further disturb her,
But haste and be gone.

Matilda. How teasing, tormenting
Such restless slumbers;
You break the dear illusion,
Make sweetest dreams confusion,
Oh! let me rest in peace.
(Exit Duke.)

Jac. *(after listening sometime.)* Now, Ma'am, we are safe on this side.

Mat. Are all the Locks fastened upon us, Jacquinetta?

Jac. I think so, Ma'am.

Mat. Then let me hasten to resume my Turkish dress and character with my Bertram.
(Exeunt down the trap-door.)

Scene V.[14]

Sir Bertram's Apartment.

(Geoffrey discovered preparing a supper table.)

Geoffrey. Now my business is to prepare the Wedding Supper—But Lord, Lord, who will there be to eat it? I am glad to see my master is alive yet, however.
(Enter Sir Bertram.)

Sir Bertram. Is everything prepared, Geoffrey?

Geof. O yes, Sir, the singers are prepared—The musicians ready tuned—The chapel too is illuminated—Nothing wanting but the bride.

Sir Bert. I trust she will not long delay—How shall I be able to account for her absence, shou'd the Duke return before her?

Geof. You, Sir? Sure you can never be at a loss in any difficulty. It has been quite past my plain comprehension how you slipt thro' any one of those cleft sticks your ingenuity has already brought you into.

Sir Bert. Past your comprehension—Yes, or that of anyone who has not felt the inspiring aid of love.

Song (Sir Bertram)

'Twas love's bright flame my bosom fir'd,
    At once my heart refin'd,
With valiant thoughts my soul inspired,
    With dangerous deeds my mind.

To gain Matilda's heart I sigh'd,
    Must be the meed of worth,
That heavenly form shou'd be allied
    To courage and to truth.

Geof. Sir, Sir, I heard a rapping at the door of the subterraneous passage.

Sir Bert. 'Tis Matilda—I fly to meet her. *(Exit.)*

Geof. *(alone.)* Sure they'll never be so hard hearted as to leave poor Jacquinetta shut up in the tower *(Looking out.)* No, not a sign of Jacquinetta—This is too provoking.

(Enter Sir Bertram and Matilda.)

Sir Bertram. And was the Duke perfectly satisfied?

Matilda. O, our success was wonderful—He returned fully convinced of his supposed mistake and made a thousand apologies for his abrupt intrusion.[15]

Sir Bert. Soft, I hear the Duke approaching.

Mat. O poor Jacquinetta, I left her in the Gallery trembling at the thoughts of appearing in her man's attire: which you prepared to disguise her to the Duke.

Geof. In the Gallery! She sha'n't long tremble there however. *(To Sir Bertram.)* Sir, if you please I'll go and reconcile her to her new dress. *(Exit Geoffrey.)*

Sir Bert. By all means, Geoffrey,[16] go and prevail on the little Turkish boy to enter.

(Enter Duke.)

Mat. I rejoice, my Lord, to see that your countenance expresses no disappointment.

Sir Bert. You found this Lady, I hope, in perfect safety.

Duke. Not an uneasy thought dwells on my mind, Sir Bertram, but from the recollection of my own impetuous and unjust conduct towards you.

Sir Bert. Every impression of it, my Lord, is effaced by your wish to remove it.

Duke. And will your Selima prove herself as forgiving as she is lovely?

Mat. Every unkind thought vanishes, my Lord, in your being satisfied.

Sir Bert. Let us then resume the festivity and harmony of our meeting. *(They seat themselves at the supper table.)*

(Enter Jacquinetta, dress'd as a Turkish Boy, conducted by Geoffrey.)

Mat. Ah, here's little Florio, my faithful page who has follow'd me thro' so many various scenes.

Duke. And did that youth suffer captivity with his fair Mistress?

Jac. Ay, noble Duke; and would have suffer'd more for a Lady's sake.

Song   (Jacquinetta)[17]

Me captive was full sixteen moons
With those vile whiskered Dons,
There work, hard work, from morn till e'en,
O 'twas worse than Quarantine.

With walls all round, so strong so high,
Me greatly tire of clear blue sky,
With work, hard work from morn 'till e'en,
O 'twas worse than Quarantine![18]

Ripe fruit like gold me dare not touch,
Nor de gold more tempting grieve me much,
But work for "blows" from morn till e'en,
O 'twas worse than Quarantine!

Till Lady come and ransom me,
Oh! how me welcom'd liberty;
For her me'll work, from morn 'till e'en,
Nor ever complain of my Quarantine.

Duke. Bravo, my little Florio—We'll all join you in that sentiment.

(Jacquinetta retires to the rear with Geoffrey conversing.)

Sir Bertram. Now, my Selima, let me lead you to the Chapel.

Duke. So soon you are to be united.

Sir Bert. Surely, my Lord: Propriety as well as love shou'd hasten our nuptials—She has here no female to matronize her and requires the protection of a husband.

Matilda. Alas, I have not a friend here to present me at the altar. Were I in my own Country, my dear brother wou'd give that sanction to our union.

Duke. I shall gladly represent your brother, Madam, in that office, if you will permit one such an honor.

Sir Bert. Your graciousness, my Lord, crowns our joy.

Duke. Let the doors be thrown open leading to the Chapel and let the musicians begin their salute to the fair Selima; while we all join in chorus.

Song (Sir Bertram)

To mirth, to friendship and to love
    Let ev'ry heart respire,
And ev'ry pulse responsive move
    To fan the sacred fire.

(CHORUS)
To Selima, the health goes round,
    To Selima the fair,
Let that sweet name the Roofs resound
    And fill the quiv'ring air.

All *(sing).* To Selima, the health goes round,
    To Selima the fair,
Let that sweet name the Roofs resound
    And fill the quiv'ring air.[19]

Duke. Your fair return'd from distant shores
    Accepts the nuptial bands;
May Love, with all his blissful stores,
    Unite your destined hands.

(CHORUS)

> To Selima, the health goes round,
> To Selima the fair,
> Let that sweet name the Roofs resound
> And fill the quiv'ring air.

All *(sing).* To Selima, the health goes round,
> To Selima the fair,
> Let that sweet name the Roofs resound
> And fill the quiv'ring air.

Scene VI.[20]

The Sea Shore. The Moon rising.

(A vessel appears ready for sailing. Sailors busy.)

Sailor. All hands to your stations—I see our noble passengers making this way.

(Enter Duke, Matilda, and Sir Bertram, followed by Geoffrey and Jacquinetta.)

Duke. All joy and happiness away my friend and his lovely Bride—I lament the necessity of your sudden departure; but hope you will soon revisit this shore.

Matilda. 'Tis an honor I shall gladly accept, my Lord.

Song (Matilda)[21]

> The terrors of the tempest o'er,
> The sea is calm again;
> How smiling looks the verdant shore,
> How smooth the azure main.

> But know, that on love's Ocean toss'd,
> 'Tis hard to gain the shore,
> The heart by dark suspicion lost,
> Can be regain'd no more.

Sir Bertram. I doubt now, my Lord, but I shall speedily return, and in a new character which you have this moment invested me with.

Duke. How, Sir Bertram?

Sir Bert. As the husband of the Countess Matilda, I claim the possessions and honors of Vergy.

Duke. O, I begin to understand your pleasantry—You allude to the hasty mistake I made this Evening, of imagining the fair Selima to be my ward Matilda—But I was not long in that error.

Matilda. You were never more in error, my Lord, than when you thought yourself secure of your prize by force of Locks and Bars.

Duke. What can this mean? Am I again to disbelieve my senses? Matilda de Vergy is now safe within the castle—I saw her there within this hour.

Mat. You did indeed, my Lord—And you as surely see her now before you released from your cruel bondage by my dear Bertram's enterprise *(Taking of her turban.)* Behold in the happy Selima, the features of your injur'd ward.

Duke. Matilda? Distraction! Rage! Witchcraft!

Sir Bert. Nay, don't reproach yourself, my Lord—You have only fulfilled the condition of the Will you were so anxious to execute.

Mat. From your hand I received my husband—'Twas the hard condition of the Will.

Duke. This is too much to believe—I will once more prove the truth of my senses. *(Exit Duke, who will return with a force sufficient to arrest their flight.)*[22]

(While they are embarking, the Duke and Guards enter.)

Duke. Seize on those Traitors—Bring them prisoners to the castle. *(The Guards endeavor to seize them, but are too late. The party escape and make signals of adieu.)*

Duke. Confusion! They are beyond my power—Darkness and danger follow them.

Glee (with double parts from the boat)
(To the air of the old Glee "From the fair Laviniah")

See the peaceful Queen of Night,
Liberal, lends her silver light,
While the trembling water's play
Guides us o'er our devious way.

Duke. Arrest the vile crew—nor let them go free!
Seize, seize on their bark!

Chorus. Blow as the winds may, here we're free,
    Then speed to our bark—
    To the boatswain's whistle hark!
For pleasure guides our helm at sea.

Guards. To the Syren's music hark!
'Tis the goddess that presides o'er the sea.

THE END.

Notes

1. The following portion of the speech, "No, no, Geoffrey, my scheme lies deeper than you are aware of, or than I have now time to explain to you; for," is circled and the words "No, no Geoffrey" are also crossed out.
2. Matilda's speech begins with an aside to Jacquinetta, "I must not let him see it, till I have proved his jealousy to the utmost—" that is circled and lightly crossed out in the Manuscript.
3. The Manuscript has the name "Jaquellin."
4. This is an interlinear addition to the Manuscript.
5. The lyrics for this song were not published.
6. The line "What a relief my mind has received by the discovery. I own I did suspect something of treachery—" is crossed out.
7. The following speech was circled, and the rest of the scene was circled and crossed out in the Manuscript:

> **Duke.** I am so harmonized by finding this ring safe that I can now think only of my approaching happiness—I trust, Matilda, no accident will delay our union beyond tomorrow—
> **Matilda.** Tomorrow? Nay, nothing so pressing—I can't give you a positive answer.
> **Jacquinetta.** Better leave my Lady to herself, your Grace—You'll see her Love will come 'round one day or another.
> **Duke.** Jacquinetta, you must not encourage her in this childish coyness—your services shall be rewarded with a handsome portion the moment I am united to Matilda.
> **Jacquinetta.** Thank your Grace.—Indeed it shan't be thrown away.

8. The Manuscript places this short scene after Act Two, Scene One. No indication of place or entrance is given. However, the printed text of the songs (available at the performance, and thus perhaps a better representation of the dramatic continuity), puts the lyrics after Act Two, Scene Two, presumably to allow for Matilda's subsequent costume change.

9. No indication of setting is given. Since the page numbers in the Manuscript copy begin again at 1, this may have been intended as a Third Act. Without the interpolation of Geoffrey's song after the last scene, Matilda would have required an interval to change her costume.

10. The text of this song was not printed.

11. This line is omitted in the printed text of the song.

12. The Manuscript designates this as "Scene Two," presumably the second scene of the Third Act.

13. No air is given in the printed version.

14. This is designated as Scene Three in the Manuscript.

15. This does not correspond with what happened in the previous scene.

16. The word "I'll" is crossed out in the Manuscript.

17. This song was not published.

18. A third verse is circled in the Manuscript. It reads:

> So closely watch'd by Master's eye,
> Like countryman or jealous spy,
> Then made to work from morn to e'en,
> O 'twas worse than Quarantine.

19. Neither this verse, nor the ensemble verse below, is included in the printed text of the songs.

20. Scene Four in the Manuscript.

21. This song was not printed.

22. A Quartetto and brief scene follow, circled and crossed out in the Manuscript. It begins:

> **Sir Bertram**. When he drew up the Will, he thought all was nice
> And to marry his Ward was a noble device;
> **Matilda**. He shut me up close under eighteen strong bars,
> And dinn'd in my ears the flame of his Wars.
> **Chorus**. 'Tis all in vain,
> 'Tis care and pain,
> And force can never move;
> The surest art
> To win a heart
> Is confidence and love.
> **Geoffrey**. I cut the trap-door up, quite to a shaving.
> **Jacquinetta**. Which has set the poor Duke a ranting and raving.
> **Geoffrey**. Now I've nothing to do but take care of my wife,
> **Jacquinetta**.Tho' your battles are o'er now commences your strife.
> **Chorus**. 'Tis all in vain,
> 'Tis care and pain,
> And force can never move;
> The surest art
> To win a heart
> Is confidence and love.
> **Geoffrey**. See, see the Duke with all his Guards approaching.
> **Matilda**. O let us embark with speed to avoid his vengeance.
> **Sir Bertram**. Haste, haste to the vessel.

THE MYSTERIOUS MARRIAGE;

or,

The Heirship of Roselva

A Play

In 3 Acts

by

Harriet Lee

The Mysterious Marriage

It is difficult to talk of Harriet Lee (1757–1851) without including her elder sister and often collaborator, Sophia (1750–1824). They were two of five daughters born to the actor-manager John Lee who played all the major theatres between 1745 and 1780. Quoting Cooke's assessment of the actor in the *Life of Macklin*, Genest paints the picture of a *more* than competent actor:

> Lee's Iago was very respectable, and showed a good judgment and thorough representation of the character—this actor was not without considerable pretensions, were they not more allayed by his vanity—he had a good person, a good voice, and a more than ordinary knowledge in his profession, which he sometimes showed without exaggeration; but he wanted to be placed in the chair of Garrick, and in attempting to reach this he often deranged his natural abilities—he was for ever, as Foote said, "doing the honours of his face"—he affected uncommon long pauses, and frequently took such out-of-the-way pains with emphasis and articulation, that the natural actor seldom appeared. (6: 165–166)

Summers reports that during his management of the theatre at Bath (1778–1779) "he sustained many important roles with great applause" (164) usually playing opposite Sarah Siddons, the "eighteenth-century's greatest English actress" (Richards 73).[1] Less successful were his attempts at play writing or, rather, adaptations of the classics which Summers calls "flat and insipid to the last degree" (164).

Inheriting their father's flair for the theatre, and attempting to supplement the household income[2] (their mother having died when Sophia was very young), Lee's daughters took to writing. Sophia was the first to pen a play and write a novel, both of which were tremendously successful. The play, *The Chapter of Accidents* (based on Diderot's *Le Père de Famille*) was performed 104 times between its premiere at the Haymarket 5 August 1780 and 1800, and the novel, a Gothic romance entitled *The Recess, or, A Tale of Other Times* (1783, 1785) went into several editions, including a translation into Portuguese. The profits from her play enabled Sophia to establish a Seminary for Young Ladies at Belvidere House in Bath,[3] where she and sister Harriet took up residence and immediately became respected members of Bath society (Summers 165).

Eager to match her sister's success, Harriet produced an anonymous epistolary novel called *The Errors of Innocence* in 1786. Its simple and sentimental plot allows the heroine a good husband while her devoted confidante gets a bad one. After much misery and moralizing, the death of the bad husband results in general rejoicing.[4] Though not a great success, the positive response to the novel encouraged Harriet to write a social comedy, *The New Peerage; or, Our Eyes May Deceive Us*, performed at Drury Lane on 10 November 1787 and published the same year. Acted nine times, the plot involves Old Vandercrab, a merchant banker, who, fourteen years before, sent his son Charles to be educated in Holland. Charles and his friend Lord Melville, returning to England at the same time, exchange places so that Charles might court Lady Charlotte, Melville's cousin. When Melville presents himself as Vandercrab's son, the old man is disgusted but ultimately allows him to marry his ward when the deception is revealed.[5]

In 1791 while Harriet and Sophia were setting up their school for young ladies at Bath, Harriet fell "painfully in love" with the Marquis Trotti who, though apparently partial to her, neglected to declare his intentions. Attempting to "precipitate a declaration," Harriet's friend, Mrs. Piozzi commissioned a letter to be intercepted by Trotti during his next visit to Bath. Unfortunately, the plan miscarried and the Marquis left England in July 1792 without ever seeing Harriet again.[6] During the courtship, Harriet wrote verses to Mrs. Piozzi which the latter deemed "strong and elegant" (Balderston 818):

> From the bright West the Orb of Day
> Far hence his dazzling Fires removes,
> While Twilight brings in sober Gray
> The pensive Hour that Sorrow loves.
>
> Tho' the dim Landschape[7] mock mine Eye
> Mine Eye its fading Charms persues,
> Oh tell me busy Fancy why
> Thro' lonely Evening wouldst thou muse?
>
> More rich Perfume does Flora yield?
> Does Zephyr blow a softer Gale?
> Do fresher Dews revive the field?
> Does sweeter Music fill the Vale?

No—idle Wand'rer—no; In vain
 For thee they blend their sweetest Powrs,
Thine Ear persues a distant Strain,
 Thy gaze still courts far distant Bow'rs.

To that lov'd Roof where Friendship's Fires
 With pure and generous Ardour burn;
Lost to whate'er this Scene inspires,
 Thy fond Affection still return.

Even now I tread the Velvet Plain,
 That spreads its graceful Curve around,
Where Pleasure bade her fairy Train
 With magic Influence bless the Ground.

Now on that more than Syren Song,
 Where Nature lends her Grace to Art;
My Sense delighted lingers long,
 And owns the Language of my heart.

And thou much lov'd! whose cultur'd Mind
 Each Muse, & every Virtue crown;
If ought to charm in mine thou find
 Ah justly deem that Charm thy own!

From thee I learn'd that Grace to seize
 Whose varying tints can gild each hour,
From thee that warm Desire to please
 Which only can supply the Pow'r.

Then let me court pale Fancy still,
 Still bid her bright Illusion last;
The present Hour She best can fill
 That kindly can recall the past.

And *Oh that Past!* fond Heart forbear,
Nor dim the Vision with a Tear.—

Following her unrequited romance, Harriet returned to the exigencies of running a school and completed a melodrama entitled *The Mysterious Marriage; or, The Heirship of Roselva*, which was eventually published in 1798, the year she declined a proposal of marriage from William Godwin, Mary Wollstonecraft's widower (Blain, Clements, and Grundy 642).[8] While the author was unsuccessful in her attempt to have the play produced on the London stage,[9] the recent success of Monk Lewis's *The Castle Spectre* played an important part in the necessity of getting it published. In Lewis's play, the ghost of the murdered Evelina makes a sensational entrance:

> *The folding-doors unclose, and the oratory is seen illuminated. In its centre stands a tall female figure, her white and flowing garments spotted with blood; her veil is thrown back and discovers a pale and melancholy countenance; her eyes are lifted upwards, her arms extended toward heaven, and a large wound appears upon her bosom.* (50)

Similarly in Miss Lee's play:

> *The Scene changes to the arched gallery as before, lighted by a lamp from the roof. Albert enters through his chamber-door, speaking to Rodolphus, whose pallet is visible from the lights within.—Thunder at intervals, with vivid flashes of lightning seen through the casements. . . .The Ghost of Constantia, shrouded in the lightest white drapery, appears before the door, passing the pallet of Rodolphus, who sleeps sweetly. . . . Vivid lightning—the Ghost glides into the chamber of the Countess.* (66–67)

While *The Mysterious Marriage* is the first play by a woman to employ the device of the ghost of the murdered heroine in a melodrama, it was perhaps equally important to Harriet Lee to affirm in print that the ghost in her play anticipated Lewis's by several years.[10]

In 1797 Harriet published *Clara Lennox,* a novel, and began collaborating with her sister on a major work, *The Canterbury Tales,* a five-volume collection of stories "striking for their satirical quality and their realistic social and psychological pictures" (Todd, *Dictionary of British Women Writers* 406). The best-known tale in the series is "The German's Tale: Kruitzner" about a strong-willed heroine caught between an ineffective husband and a proto-Byronic son.[11] Lee dramatized the story as *The Three Strangers* acted only four times beginning 10 December 1825 at Covent Garden with a cast that included Mrs. Chatterley and Charles Kemble.[12]

Nothing is known of Harriet Lee after 1825. After the death of her sister in 1824 and the failure of *The Three Strangers* in 1825, it is not unlikely that Miss Lee, now aged sixty-eight, would have gone into quiet retirement. *The Dictionary of National Biography* states that, living to the great age of ninety-four, she "was remarkable to the last for her lively conversational talents, clear judgment, powerful memory, and benevolent and kindly disposition." Summers reports that she died at Clifton "as late as August 1st, 1851" still maintaining a "fund of interesting anecdotes concerning the sister whom she so greatly loved and admired" (167). The best assessment of her personality was made my Mrs. Piozzi who considered her one of "a brilliant Constellation of agreeable Companions" (Balderston 991) and of her work, Dale Spender concludes: "She writes vigorous prose and is often prompted to express outrage as she repeatedly exposes injustice particularly as it applies to women—in her novels and plays" (234).

There were two editions of *The Mysterious Marriage* published in 1798: one in London printed for G. G. and J. Robinson, and the other in Dublin printed for P. Wogan, P. Byrne, W. Jones, J. Rice, N. Kelly, and G. Folingsby. While there are no substantial textual differences between the two editions, punctuation and layout differ significantly. The edition that follows represents the Dublin format with spelling and punctuation regularized.

Notes

1. Summers offers the following roster of Lee's characters opposite Mrs. Siddons at Bath in 1779:

> 29 September, Richard III to Siddons's Anne
> 30 October, Dumont to Jane Shore
> 18 November, Macbeth to Lady Macbeth
> 11 December, Duke to Isabella
> 16 December, Pierre to Belvidera
> 18 December, Shylock to Portia
> 19 December, Cardinal Wolsey to Queen Catherine. (164)

Lee's final stage appearance was on 14 July 1786 when he performed Macbeth at Bristol.

2. MacCarthy notes that John Lee's continued quarrels with theatre managers made it necessary for the girls to supplement the meager finances of the family (381).

3. MacCarthy reports that among their pupils was a young lady named Anne Ward who, later under the name Mrs. Radcliffe, will have a profound influence on the Gothic novel (381).

4. Referring to *The Errors of Innocence*, Tompkins suggests that "Harriet Lee, with the sympathetic knowledge of a schoolmistress still in touch with her own youth, dwells on the perpetual striving for intimacy, the craving for 'the soft enthusiasm of congenial affections' that marks the adolescent girl" (144).

5. Genest considers the play marred by the "gross caricature" of Miss Vandercrab, the old maid of the play, who, though only two or three years younger than Old Vandercrab, appears "childishly dressed in a sash, with her hair in ringlets." While he finds parts of the dialogue "tolerably good," as a whole, Genest concludes that "this is a poor play" (6: 472). Noting that the play was popular enough to merit two editions in the same year (1787), Summers finds Genest "a little severe" and suggests that "the scenes may be a little thin, but I imagine they would have been helped tremendously by the excellence of the performance" (166).

6. Balderston notes that the story of this unhappy courtship is told in Mrs. Piozzi's letters to her friend Penelope Weston, published as *The Intimate Letters of Hester Piozzi and Penelope Pennington, 1788–1821* (818).

7. The original spelling and punctuation are reproduced without comment.

8. *The Dictionary of National Biography* suggests that Godwin's egotistical behavior was displeasing to Miss Lee who also found his religious convictions unsympathetic to a happy marriage. Her last letter to him, dated 7 August 1798, suggested that they might remain friends. Godwin replied by criticizing her literary works.

9. Mrs. Piozzi's diary entry for 17 September 1793 remarks that "the Managers refuse every thing but Ballad Farces I understand, & turned the best Performers as well as the best Authors—to seek their Fortunes in other Branches of Literature—no more pickings from the Stage I am told. Harriet Lee can not get her Drama nor her Sister's forward, & judges tell me that they have very great Merit both of theme: I thought mighty well of what I saw certainly" (Balderston 866). The play referred to as "her Sister's" was probably *Almeyda; Queen of Granada* for which Harriet wrote a Prologue and Epilogue. That play was subsequently produced on 20 April 1796 at Drury Lane with Kemble and Mrs. Siddons in the major roles.

10. In *English Melodrama*, Booth argues that "the frequency with which ghosts appear in Gothic melodrama also distinguishes it from the rest of its class. These ghosts are invariably on the side of goodness and often turn up at the worst possible moment for the villain; their arrival is accompanied by fitting effects" (81). It is significant that Booth uses the ghost of the murdered Evelina as his archetype when Lee's ghost of Constantia actually anticipates it by four years.

11. See MacCarthy (386–390) for an appreciation of the story. She finds it not only the best of Lee's Gothic tales, but the finest thing she wrote.

12. Byron himself had adapted the story as *Werner* and published it in 1821. Genest recalls that "Miss H. Lee, in her advertisement prefixed to the *Three Strangers*, says, that her play had been written many years ago, and that when Lord Byron did her the honour to choose the tale of Kruitzner for the subject of his Tragedy, it became necessary to make her play known, or incur the imputation of its being a subsequent attempt—that she therefore offered it immediately (Nov. 1822) to C.G.—that it was accepted, and the ensuing Feb. fixed as the time for representation—that it was postponed wholly at her own desire" (9: 346).

The Mysterious Marriage

Dramatis Personae

The Count Roselva.
Lord Albert.
Sigismond.
Rodolphus.
Osmond.
Physician.
Uberto.
Mathias, *and other Servants.*
Prisoners.

The Countess, *daughter to the Count Roselva.*
Constantia, *her Friend.*
Theresa.

Time two days. Scene in Transylvania, within the limits of the Castle of Roselva.

ADVERTISEMENT.

It is more than two years since the manuscript from which the following play is printed was read by several literary acquaintance, among whom was Mr. Colman.[1] The difficulty that, during the present management of the theatres, attends producing any piece to advantage upon the stage, has hitherto inclined the author to consign hers to obscurity: an effort to draw it from thence by the mere circumstance of publishing, is not, she is well aware, like to be greatly successful. Yet somewhat is demanded by self-love: and as the theatre will soon probably become "a land of apparitions," she hastens to put in her claim to originality of idea, though the charm of novelty may be lost. The female spectre *she* has conjured up, was undoubtedly the offspring of her own imagination; yet by the ill-fortune of keeping the play considerably less than "nine years," she is now obliged to produce it to a disadvantage, or expose herself to the charge of being a servile imitator.[2]

In presenting to her readers scenes obviously designed for decoration, and verses intended for music, without the embellishment of either, she does herself but poor justice, and makes a very humble offering to them: yet if taste or feeling find any thing to applaud in the play, the writer will have derived as much advantage from her labours, as most dramatic writers can *at present* hope to obtain.

Act I. Scene I.

The outer wall and gate-way of a magnificent Castle, with an ascent, and distant view of the entrance.

(Osmond and Uberto meeting.)

Osmond. You come from the chase, Uberto: what's the sport?

Uberto. Sport! marry, such sport as had well nigh cost us our lives, and our friends some score of masses.

Osmond. You roused then the boar!

Uberto. I warrant you we did, and to some purpose too! An I e'er rouse another such, I'll give him leave to make a dinner of me. But for our brave guest, the Lord Sigismond, I question whether our souls had not come to tell you whereabouts they had left our bodies.—In my life shall I never forget how he churned and tore up the ground with rage! And what's most strange, methought, when his eyes glared with the greatest fury, he always looked full upon me. Yet I had not offended him either; for if some people's valour did not lie nearer the point of their lance than mine, the boar might have made his breakfast i' the forest, and we ours i' the castle, without either of us taking a fancy to a limb of the other.

Osmond. But, Sigismond!

Uberto. True! he's a hero—and your hero, I suppose, has a life or two more to spare than your commoner. Briefly, however, he advanced, brandished his spear with a determined look—as—thus!—and—I will not wrong my honesty so far as to say I saw him kill the monster—But this I will certify—I saw the monster dead, and heard our whole troop shout to the honour of Sigismond..

Osmond. 'Tis a brave youth!

Uberto. And courteous too; I warrant he's nobly born!

Osmond. At least he's nobly bred.

Uberto. And methinks love could not devise a better match of gentleness, than betwixt him and my lord's favourite, the Lady Constantia.

Osmond. Trust me, no!
Uberto, there's a secret spring of blood
That bids the obscure still soar! 'Tis Nature's touch;
Who thus would mock the avarice of Fortune,
Wooing her from her own! He'll no Constantia!
Nay much I err too, or our beauteous Countess
Beholds the young and gallant Sigismond
With more than friendly gaze. Come, come, thou'st marked it.

Uberto.
Why truly I have seen some glances pass between them, that it were worth more than my head to recount to my lord. For, despite of what nature may do in the heart of his daughter, she will never, I trow, move his into thinking that all these noble titles and princely domains should fall into the hands of a vagrant stranger—and a prisoner too.

Osmond. He had ne'er been a prisoner but in the cause of the Count. Thou knowest that on the day my lord and his daughter were ta'en captive by a band of wandering Poles—this young stranger—this valiant Sigismond, stood forth to save her from dishonour, and drew his sabre even against his countrymen.

Uberto. Yes; and his country men rewarded him for it by leaving him in our hands! — What a tale dost thou tell me, as if I was not in at the rescue; and did not with my good sword—

Osmond. Nay, good Uberto — keep but thy tongue as quiet as thy sword, and —*(Music.)* — Peace! the hunters! — 'tis the harp of Sigismond.

Uberto. And, true to the sound, see if my lady, the Countess, be not roused up to give him welcome. Well, how easily may a man perceive a thing when he's told it! Methinks I can spy out love in the very folds of her robe— and then there's a turn in her eye—-
(Music, and chorus of Hunters.)

Hail to the sprightly beams of morn!
Gaily sound the mellow horn!
Call on echo to reply,—*(Echo.)*

Hark, she answers to the cry!
(Echo repeated at intervals.)
  Sound, sound again the mellow horn!
  Echo hails the sprightly morn!

(The hunters pass in groups across the stage, and enter the castle-walls with Osmond.—the Countess descending at the same time, they salute her severally— Sigismond enters last.)

  Sigismond *(seeing the Countess).* Uberto, bear my greetings to thy lord;
I wait him on the instant. My fair hostess!
Oh how the morning brightens with the beam
That radiates from those eyes! A smile like that
Breaks from the heav'ns, when day-spring gilds the east,
And nature lives before it! Thou should'st chide
Th'uncourtly hand, that, reckless of the heart,
Lays not beneath thy feet our sylvan triumphs—
The boar's rough spoils.
  Countess. Believe me, Sigismond,
I should have deem'd the uncouth gift misplaced:
And honour more the instinctive human polish
That bade thee spare it, than the laboured courtesy
That with a bloody spoil would grace a woman.
Nay trust me, Sir,—but 'tis my father's part
To chide his guest—You have been much in danger.
E'en now I heard the tale with mingled fear—
Yet 'twas not fear — 'twas but a passing wonder!
How, rough of taste, your souls should hunt out death
And brave him e'en in scenes, which our weak sex
Shrink from the view of.
  Sigismond. Prettiness of nature! —
Who, sportive goddess, has embodied weakness
In the far form of woman, to create
Instinctive force and energy in man!
To guard such fragile loveliness as thine,
We cherish danger, my fair monitress!
And grow familiar with the forms of death.
But why of death or danger do we talk?
Hence with th'ill-omen'd words! Thy lip's rich ruby

Grows pale beneath them! While a half-drawn breath,
That quivered to a sigh, disturb'd its polish,
As summer breezes ripple the smooth stream.
    Countess. I did not sigh! Or if perchance I did,
Is it for you to weigh — You are too forward!
'Twere well to scant this aptness of remark,
And tread in narrower scope.
    Sigismond *(going).* You teach me right.
I shall remember, Madam.
    Countess. Gone so soon!
Oh, these hot spirits! What, my father waits!
Or say, the honours of our rural feast
Demand your presence! Well, Sir! we can spare you.
One word alone! Deem not, that conscious rank,
Nor all the selfish pride that waits on greatness,
Impels me thus—I lose myself again—
Begone!—
    Sigismond. Impossible! The witchery of that voice
Spreads in soft circles thro' the ambient air,
And roots me spell-bound! Witness for me heaven,
If there be cause of pride in human kind,
I deem it most in thee!—Nor aught that greatness,
Wealth, or superior power can give, e'er added
To thy attractions, or can dim their lustre!
I see the noblest in thy noble soul;
Richest in beauty; while my willing heart
Bows down to both, and owns its conqueror.
    Countess. All-gracious heaven!
    Sigismond. To tell thee that I love,
Is but to give the feeble form of words
To my soul's language! Yet I am not rash,
Save only in adoring. Proud alone
In that I deem no other of thy sex
Worthy of my thought. Nor do I to the heiress
Of these rich lands aspire—The woman only,
Shrin'd in my heart, has all its vows; its wishes
In the rude current of my fate are wrecked.
Once, and once only. *(Kisses her hand.)* Oh! that this deep sigh,
Whose forceful energy doth hake my being,

Could breathe a sacred atmosphere around!
Guard thee from sorrow, sickness, or disquiet!
And, fraught with every bliss it wafts from me,
Enrich thy fate with our united store!
I trespass—
    Countess. Oh! Too noble Sigismond!
There is a native candour at my heart,
That struggles with my sex's wonted forms
To tell thee—But it should not be! Farewell!—
Yet—If the woman claim indeed thy thought,
Oh! deem she has one virtue worthy thee;
The sense of thine.
    Sigismond *(kneeling).* Heav'ns! Did I hear aright!
    Countess. Perchance thou didst not! We may be observ'd.
Rise, gentle Sigismond — Another time —
Nay, pr'ythee rise! For see, where loved Constantia
Comes, drooping like a blossom of the spring,
That wintry gales have shook. Retire, I charge thee —
We will speak more anon.
(Exit Sigismond towards the Castle.—Constantia enters, leaning on Theresa.)
    Countess. How fares my friend?
    Constantia *(faintly).* Why, if to die be good, I should say well.
Nature, that smiles around, yet smiles not here;
(Laying her hand on her breast.)
And life but feebly flutters o'er my heart,
Ev'n as the wounded birth upon her nest.
    Countess. Oh! thou are vapourish! Trust me, I shall chide.
Is it for years like thine to talk of death?
Come, we shall mark the roses steal again
Upon thy cheek: Nay, pr'ythee look, Theresa,
Dost thou not see the wily traitors ambush'd
Ev'n mid the lilies that usurp their throne?
Your hand; Come, cheerly! This is the mere form,
The ceremony of sickness. Let me lead you
To yonder sunny border —The fresh dew
Claims cautious treading here.
(Exit Theresa.)
Now could I tell a tale—Oh! have I caught you?

Well, when a woman's heart informs her head,
How soon she may defy the schools!
'Tis a nice art, that from such premises
Can draw conclusions: I but *looked* a secret,
And you have guessed it.
    Constantia. Is Alberto come?
    Countess. Nay, pr'ythee patience! The first lord o' the court,
Without a train or courier? Cry you mercy!
The turtles of Arcadia had their wings,
And flew at will; our modern ones are clipt.
Confin'd, and tutor'd — therefore 'tis, their notes
Are oft unmusical. Yet is he *coming,*
Fast as a courtier's zeal, and great man's train,
Can convoy him!
    Constantia. Oh, wherefore comes he now?
Now, when my faded form —
    Countess. True woman still!
Come now, regret the toilette! Swear Alberto
Better at court than here; and those fair tresses,
That kiss the wanton Zephyrs as they blow,
And woo them to thy bosom, thus dishevell'd,
Were Medusean locks!
    Constantia. Oh, not for that,
Nor for the few faint graces of a form
Now crush'd to earth, do I lament!—Alberto,
If e'er he lov'd me, lov'd me not for those.
Witness, ye conscious shades! where my sick heart
Still courts the spirit of departed hours,
'Twas sympathy of thought, congenial taste,
'Twas the fair lucid web that fancy weaves
O'er yielding souls, and sensibility
Enriches with her thousand Iris hues,
That bound us to each other. — He is changed!
Changed to *himself!* The world has stepp'd between us;
Blasted with magic spell our fairy bow'rs,
Nor left ev'n Love the power to make us happy.
    Countess. Oh, we shall try its influence! True, Alberto,
No more the stripling that some two years past
Thought love supreme, now tow'rs above his equals;

Far-fam'd for valour, as for noble birth;
And boasts a monarch's favour.—Say, 'twas fortune,
A lucky chance, that bade the Turkish squadrons
Fly from his sword, and our best chieftains own him
Bravest amid the brave! He deems not so:—
But, conscious of superior power, infers
Superior merit. Yet when court cabals,
Levees, and flatterers, cease to fill the day,
When our sweet shades again shall woo to love,
And peace—But soft!—my father!—Dear Constantia,
Resume thy fortitude! I shall have much,
Much yet to tell thee.

     Count *(entering)*. Oh, you're found, my wanderers!
I sought you through the castle: sweet Constantia,
Wilt thou still play the sick one? Shame upon't!
We must call in a tribe of our young courtiers
To bid the truant blushes to their station.
We shall have feasts anon! What says my daughter?
I bring you tidings of the Lord Alberto—
He comes upon the hour.

     Countess. Indeed!

     Count. Even so!
Nay, I might tell you more, but troth you care not.
You are too much enamoured of each other
To think of revelry and sports; tho' ev'n
A brave young lord should head them.
Nay, should the king,
Devising how he may enrich a favourite,
Send him to claim a bride.

     Countess. A bride!

     Constantia. Oh heaven!

     Countess. How is't, Constantia?

     Constantia. But a sudden sickness —
Your pardon, Sir! You spoke of Lord Alberto;
Of was't the error of mine ear?

     Count. Constantia,
These sudden starts, and panic fits of tremor,
Claim heedful notice; they import a malady
Of dangerous consequence; and our true love

Bids seek a remedy. 'Twere best retire:
The air blows chill for tender frames like thine,
(The Countess leads Constantia towards the Castle.)
And tender hearts too! This fond girl disturbs me!
There is a secret in this cherished weakness
I do not wish to learn.
(To the Countess, who returns.)
Thou'rt made of tears
And soft endearments! 'Tis your sex's foible
Ever to love too little, or too much!
Of thy fair friend no more. Dear tho' I prize her,
There is a closer, softer, nearer tie,
That twines around my heart. My darling child!
With what excess of fondness I have loved thee,
Heav'n only knows! And well thy youthful grace,
Thy gentle manners, and unsullied duty,
Have justified the weakness. Can I then,
Even in the bloom and lustre of thy virtues,
Then, when my feeble age most claims their succour,
Can I consent to lose thee? Yet, my daughter,
Spite of these foolish drops that mar my speech,
It must be so! *Thou* art Lord Albert's bride.
The court, the world, demand thee! Royalty
Itself most graciously approves the union.
Fraught with remembrance of thy early charms,
Even now the favourite comes in haste to claim thee:
Mark the dispatches!

    Countess *(rejecting them).* Of *my* early charms!
Trust me, my Lord, Alberto mocks us both.

    Count. I would not have it so, nor will believe it.
There is a lurking spirit in thine eye
That leads to disobedience; mark we well!
Motives most potent and unanswerable,
That touch my honour, nay perhaps my life,
Enforce thy prompt obedience! Childish friendship,
And all the flimsy web of fine-spun feelings,
Are blown aside by the strong breath of nature.
For thy Constantia, when thou deck'st a court,
She will not want a husband. Such a dowry,

As a fond sire might give a second-born,
My love shall lavish on her.
    Countess. Vainly lavish!
A grave and winding sheet, my lov'd Constantia,
Will soon be all thy portion.
    Count. Pr'ythee, peace!
Who dies in youth, diest best; diest innocent:
Yet thou may'st love so too!
    Countess. Alas, my father!
You tremble, you are pale—some cruel secret—
Of honour and of life you spoke but late!
I marked it not; but now thick-rushing fancies
Press on my heart, and call forth all its fears.
    Count. Why should'st thou know, what knowing would afflict
thee?
Are thou not noble, rich and innocent?
    Countess. I hope I am so!
    Count. Then be sure on't quickly,
By being Albert's wife!
    Countess. Oh, tell me wherefore?
What mystery's in this? Why should I barter
A name as great, a state more rich than Albert's,
For naught that he can offer? And for virtue,
Judge me just heav'n, how scant would be its portion
In the base heart that thus could wrong itself!
    Count. Then wrong thy father! Disavow thy name!
Bring my hoar head with sorrow to the grave,
And wander forth a hopeless, helpless orphan.
    Countess. What should this mean? Heav'n shield my honour'd
sire!
Some frenzy, sure —
    Count. The worst of frenzy—Guilt!—
Yet 'twas a venial crime! Hear me, my daughter!
I will a tale unfold—
Which on thy life, thy honour, and thy duty,
I do command thee never to reveal!
—A younger brother born, and unendowed,
My youth was past in penury and arms.
I lov'd thy mother; truly, fondly loved;

Yet lived to lost her! Thee, her helpless offspring,
Unheeded by a proud and wealthy race,
I rear'd in sorrow! Till the chance of war,
On one drear night, led forth a band of Turks,
To waste the lands you seest, and spoil yon castle.
The scene was bloody; for my wealthier brother,
Heedless of danger, and unskill'd in arms,
Lodged there his wife and infants: they were twins:
Twins, as it seemed, in sorrow! To be brief,
Th' exterminating foe swept off our vassals,
And in the carnage spared nor youth nor age.
I came to claim my rights; and found yon towers,
That lift their heads so gaily o'er the landscape,
A scene of desolation! One domestic
'Scaped from the massacre; and, while he hail'd me,
Breathed unwelcome secret in mine ear —
The children —
    Countess. What of them?
    Count. *Both* were not dead!
 Hid with her nurse in the surrounding forest,
The girl survived.
    Countess. My heart divines the rest!
It was Constantia!
    Count. Pr'ythee, calm thy transports!
I saw this infant — born to princely fortunes,
Torn from great Nature's mass, and left to me:
Me, doomed henceforth her vassal, or her lord!
I *chose* my fate! The rest I need not tell.
Thou know'st with what officious care my heart
Has reared her childhood; with what tender fondness,
Next to thyself, has drawn her to my bosom.
Nor have I, like the iron-hearted villain,
Hated whom I had injured. Yet does fear,
The curse of guilt, still hangs upon my footsteps.
Her age—her form—and some surviving vassals,
Whom neither power can trace, nor wealth can silence,
May yet betray me.
    Countess. Oh! betray thyself!
Call to thy memory the glorious precept

That bids us guard the helpless and the orphan,
And boldly—

    Count. Rash, misjudging girl, beware!
Silence thy murmurs; summon all thy duty;
As Albert's wife, no voice shall dare arraign thee.
No hand of pow'r shall seize these fair domains,
Or blast me with dishonour.
(Bugle sounds without.)
Hark! the summons
That bids me greet my noble guest. Beware!
For know, the hour that tells thy father's shame,
Fixes thy father's fate!
(Lays his hand on his sword, and exit.)

Countess *(sola)*. Thou Pow'r supreme!
Gild the wild mazes of this perilous way
With thy bright star of truth!
And oh! whatever ills my fate betide,
Still let its sacred beams my footsteps guide!
Dark tho' the clouds, and black the tempest roll,
That ray is ne'er obscured that lights the *soul*.
*(Music, with an accompaniment of cymbals, &c. by Turkish slaves,
who advance with the domestics of the Count, and take their station
before the gate; they are met by the retinue of Albert: who, lastly, ap-
pears himself, and, with the procession, enters the Castle.)*

END OF THE FIRST ACT.

Notes

1. Lee notes that George Colman, the manager of the Haymarket Theatre, mentioned the
play in a letter dated October 1795.
2. Monk Lewis's popular melodrama, *The Castle Spectre,* had appeared at Drury Lane on
14 December 1797, and the first of its seven editions was published in 1798.

Act II. Scene I.

An antechamber in the Castle, with folding doors, the pillars gaily wreathed with flowers, and the niches adorned with statues, bearing baskets of flowers on their heads. (Music within.)

Osmond *(entering hastily).* What, ho! who waits there?—Quick!
More wine i' the feasting chamber! Lazy knaves!
Is this a time to stare, and shake your heels?
First let your lords be served! More wine, I say!
Let the saloon be hung with fresher flowers:
And see the ices yield not. Quick!—dispatch! *(Exit.)*
(Several servants cross the stage, bearing silver ewers of wine.)
(Uberto and Mathias.)

Uberto. Pr'ythee, good Mathias, let's have a cup of my Lord's Tokay, though it be but to drink to my Lady's health.

Mathias *(drinking).* This is rare sport, i' faith; if there be such merry days as this at court, why the devil take labour and the country, say I!

Uberto. But who, I marvel, would have thought your courtiers had been such generous fellows, Mathias?

Mathias. Nay, for the matter of that, if it be generous to eat, drink, and be merry at another man's cost, why generosity is a cheap virtue, and what few would be without.

Uberto. There thou misconceivest me, man! In the article of eating and drinking, I say not that your courtier is more kind-hearted than your clown. But if *mirth* be, as we are told, the zest of the entertainment, he must be allowed to be the most generous man alive who keeps the feast only for himself, and leaves the mirth for us, his poor servitors. Now for the instance! What think'st though of the company within?

Mathias. That my Lord is moody—the Countess hath the spleen—Sigismond is sad—and the Lady Constantia sick. For the Lord Albert, indeed —

Uberto. Oh! he hath all complaints at once! He hath the court fever; and looks at a serving-man, as though he wondered why heaven bestowed five senses on any being less magnificent than himself.

Mathias. Come, another cup of wine, and then —

Uberto. Peace, fool—We'll have more wine anon;—for see, here comes the Lord Sigismond.

(Sigismond enters from the folding doors, and passes the stage thoughtfully speaking to Uberto.—Music.)

Servant *(followed by Rodolphus).* Dispatches from the court to Lord Alberto.

(Osmond gives them to Uberto, who carries them in. Manent Osmond and Rodolphus.)

Osmond. Honest Rodolphus, welcome! Thy suit bears testimony against thee; and looks as if thou hadst seen more service than preferment at court.

Rodolphus. When I first wore this suit I was my Lord's friend; now, I am but his servant-man. I could have had a laced coat as well as the rest, had it so pleased me; but I had rather be the humble attendant of his fools, than the first fool of his attendants.

Osmond. Why what is it that hath made thee so splenetic, good Rodolphus?

Rodolphus. That, master Osmond, which might make any man splenetic—age and disappointment. I was my Lord's follower when he was an infant;—his play-fellow when he was a boy;—and now that I am grown old and grey-headed, every knave that has the wit to flatter him, steps before me.

Osmond. Yet I remember when you were here some two years ago.

Rodolphus. Aye, good Osmond, *thou* are not grown a great man, and therefore may'st reasonably have a memory of two years' standing;—yet that of a great man, I trow, is not so short, but if a service is in question, he knows where to apply. My Lord's pride left me at home; but his convenience did not forget that I should be the most faithful bearer of his dispatches. *(The folding doors are opened.)* But soft you—here he comes. He seems moved too! Why, what a fool am I to carry so green a heart under grey locks! Now could I blubber like a whipt school-boy, lest I should have been the bearer of mischief.

Albert *(with letters in his hand).* What time, Rodolphus, lost you on the road?

Rodolphus. Just two days, my Lord, four hours, and some odd minutes—the latter of which only were spent in eating and repose.

Albert *(thoughtfully).* Bear you from Arnulph aught?

Rodolphus. Nothing, my Lord.

Albert. Two days' delay! Was there no quicker convoy?

Rodolphus. None, my Lord, unless I had interest in the air, and could have borrowed a pair of wings. As far as gold or zeal could supply their place, your Lordship has no reason to complain.

Albert. 'Tis well! You may retire.

(Exit Rodolphus.)

           —My adverse star
At length hath gained th'ascendant! I am lost.
Down busy devil! *(Laying his hand on his heart.)*
Thou betray'st thyself
With fearful hushings; which, like lurid clouds,
Portend to vulgar eyes the bursting storm.
A fallen favourite! No time left to prop
My tottering fortunes with Roselva's pow'r!
Ev'n when some ready demon was at hand
To drive him to my purpose. Yet, perhaps,
All may be well yet. Once espoused, the rank,
The wealth, and numerous minions of my will,
Conjointly with my personal daring, well
Might awe ev'n royalty. 'Twere a brave deed
To crush where I have vainly strove to snare;
And with one strong, collected blow, destroy
The puny insects that would sting me thus.
It fires my hope! Who waits there? Say to the Count,
I do desire a moment's conf'rence.—Way, Sir!

(To Sigismond, whom he meets.)

Sigismond. When Albert learns to speak with courtesy,
He may have courteous hearing.

Albert. Albert, Sir,
Perhaps may want the time to scan his talk,
And deal out candied courtesies of words
By the quaint estimate of rustic breeding.

Sigismond. Civility, my Lord, 's the courtier's traffic!
I did not trespass on you for a virtue!

Albert. You are presuming!

Sigismond. Only frank, Lord Albert!
A very mirror to the passing object,
Reflecting even its blots.

Albert. Most free of speech!

This roof is privileged, or it might chance—
You're safe, Sir!

Sigismond. So I shall esteem myself,
While I do wear a sword!

(Exit. The Count enters on the other side.)

Albert. Noble Roselva,
I press upon your leisure; but the time
Is full of wayward checks. The bubble, pleasure,
Of late so sparkling to mine eye, hath burst,
And leaves my stream of fortune dark and turbid.
I must to court, my Lord.

Count. How, back so soon!

Albert. With my best speed. Some day or two, perchance,
We steal from loyalty: days which, when passed,
Like the bright lustre of a setting sun,
Shall leave a golden track. Oh! it doth move me,
Ev'n to my stretch of patience, that, or War,
Or the blind demon, Politics, should haunt us
Ev'n in the lap of Peace.

Count. 'Tis most perverse!
The cause unknown too!

Albert. Only hinted at,
And sealed to secrecy.—Oh! dared I hope —
But that were past presumption!

Count. Noble Albert
Cannot presume!

Albert. Alas! you know me not!
I do confess me proud—aspiring—rash—
Nursed in the lap of vain prosperity,
And dazzled by my fortunes! Thou, perhaps,
Wilt deem so too, if I should thus, unwooing,
Stinted the lover's offerings of sighs,
Aspire to call Roselva's heiress mine.

Count. How! Wed so suddenly!

Albert. 'Twas a rash thought!
Your pardon, Sir.

Count *(thoughtfully)*. My daughter hath a soul
Noble as duteous; and so maiden white
It hath not learnt to blush! She may be won

Beyond th' observance of her sex's rules.
And you have form and eloquence, my Lord,
To tempt a woman's will.—I will consider.

Albert. Nay, if considered—'tis half sanctified!
Come—come—it must be so! Forms and ceremonies
Are nought in honour's or in love's account.
Say, 'twere tomorrow—

Count. Well!—'tis sudden too—
It may perchance be happier!—Be it so!

Albert *(kissing his hand).* Now, by my life, this generous, frank
compliance,
Binds me your son and servant!

Count. I will leave you:
The time claims thought. A father too hath pangs,
When yielding thus the treasure of his age!
I will prepare my daughter. Gentle Albert—
When she is thine—But wherefore should I urge thee?
Thou hast a soul to feel her worth.—I'm chok'd!
(Exit abruptly.)

Albert *(solus).* Prosperous so far! Or hath my worser genius
Betrayed me to my face? A cold sick damp
Ev'n dash'd me at the moment of success,
And 'dew'd my dastard brow! Constantia too!
Oh! she came o'er me like a wintry cloud,
Blasting my noon of fortunes. She yet lives!
Th' envenomed drugs have quench'd the *flame* of life,
Yet left the *embers.*—But a single chill,
And those are cold too.—Well! it shall be weigh'd.
The demon, Pride, is busy in my soul,
Holding a thousand hideous mirrors up,
Peopled with shadowy mischiefs. One fair form
Alone stands forth, and points a bright perspective.
It must be so! Roselva's princely heiress
Shall yet be mine!
Hence then the idle fopperies of love!
Who bars my fortune, must my vengeance prove!
(Exit.)

Scene II.

A low Gothic gallery, with a range of arched doors on one side of the stage, and painted casements on the other, to correspond.

Constantia *(sola).* He bade me meet him in the western gallery:
Would he were here, or e'er my failing step
Play truant to my heart. Fain would I greet him
As in the bloom and may-day of my life!
When my light foot scarce press'd th' unconscious ground,
And health diffused a lustre o'er the day
That mock'd the paler sun-beam. I have mark'd him;
Noted each little change that time hath made
In my heart's tablet; and, with jealous glance,
Have almost chid the rude and manlier graces
That have usurp'd the primy charm of youth.
Hark!—No!—the sounding arches mock mine ear.
Ah, 'tis himself! My lord!—my love!—my Albert!
(Throws herself into his arms as he enters.)
   Albert. My sweet Constantia!—Nay, I pr'ythee check
This transport, that doth shake thy tender frame
Almost to fainting.
   Constantia. I would fain be strong,
Be rational—be calm—but 'twill not be.
My wayward heart, so long unused to joy,
Heaves with such wild convulsive throbs to meet it,
As shake the pow'rs of life! Oh, thou unkind one!
But I will not complain:—the sacred vow
That bound me to thee at the holy altar,
Binds not the heart alone; my will is thine!
Yet blame me not, if, on the verge of being
Unown'd—unhonour'd—nay, perhaps, unlov'd—
I grasp the little good that fate allows me,
With painful ecstasy!
   Albert. The *little,* say'st thou!
Oh, had Constantia still retain'd that passion
Which once shot roseate blushes o'er her cheek,
Lived in her accent, languish'd in her eye,
And gave each charm its own ethereal lustre;

Then had she met me with a joy so pure,
It had defied the feeble pow'r of fate
To dash it with a care.—Nay, pr'ythee smile!
Or I shall think thou art a very wife,
And mean'st to chide thy truant.

    Constantia. Dearest Albert!
When, deaf to gratitude's commanding voice,
And reckless of my virgin fame, I dared
To plight in secret an unsanctioned vow,
I lost that peace which is the life of virtue.
Yet thou were mine; and my idolatrous heart
Liv'd on the certitude:—till losing that,
I'd well nigh lost life too! Hours, days, and months,
Have past in sad and sober recollection
Since last we met:—and still, as they've gone by,
Some early flow'r of fancy and of youth
Hath droop'd the head and wither'd:—firmer reason
Aloe increased in vigour—spread its foliage,
Wholesome, but chilling, o'er a thankless soil.

    Albert. If this same reason makes my fair one sad,
I'll not a leaf on't—'tis a bitter plant! —
Come, come, I know this pretty self-reproach
Tends, like the veil coquetry bids you draw
O'er brightest eyes, to make the dart more sure.
But tell me, love—in those same months thou speak'st of,
Those tedious months of absence—Has thy tongue —
It were a venial trespass—Has it never —
I could not chide an 'twere so—Ne'er betray'd
The mystery of our union?

    Constantia. Never.

    Albert. How?
In the soft hours of confidence and friendship,
Ne'er hinted—smiled—or blushed away the secret?

    Constantia. Oh, never!

    Albert. The good priest too —

    Constantia. I had wrote thee,
Or I mistake, that heav'n long since had call'd him.

    Albert. 'Tis true; I had forgot.—*(Aside.)*Heav'n was most gracious

To further deeds in which heav'n has no share.
(To her.) His face was sudden too—But he was pious:
And pious minds are never unprepared
For their great audit.

    Constantia. Happy who, like him,
Have early closed the various page of life,
And lifting the dim view from hence on high,
Have traced the sacred characters of heav'n!

    Albert *(aside)*. Most beauteous saint! Now, by my life, those charms
Might warm and anchorite. An anchorite, said I?
Weak fires may thaw—She, planet-like, has spells
To rule the boundless ocean of ambition!
I shall be lost!

    Constantia. Trust me, my love, thou'rt chang'd too!
Even mid the pomp and splendour of a court,
Thy heart, perchance, is sick!

    Albert *(aside)*. My reason rather!

    Constantia. Some lovelier fair —

    Albert. I should have curs'd the tongue,
Had it been aught but thine, that dared suggest it!
Hear, and believe me, dearest, when I swear,
In all the tedious hours I've past without thee,
Ne'er hath my wandering eye encountered beauty,
But it hath breath'd a sigh for my Constantia!
And yet, my love—

    Constantia. Ah! What?

    Albert. Thou shoud'st be great,
Be noble.—Nature, when she gave thee beauty,
Matchless, imperial beauty—gave a claim
That might have bankrupt fortune's richest means;
But treacherous love has marr'd the glorious gift,
And cast thee on a beggar.

    Constantia. Are *thou* one?

    Albert. Clouded the fair perfection of that form,
That should have blaz'd, like a bright wand'ring star,
The wonder of the hemisphere—in darkness,
Obscurity, and sorrow.

    Constantia. Is it sorrow

To call thee mine? To spend my painful vigils
In dwelling on thy memory? and in pray'r
That when Constantia silent sleeps in dust
Thou may'st be happy!

    Albert. Dost thou love me, then?

    Constantia. Love you! Oh, heavens!

    Albert. Not with your sex's passion;
With jealousy, with tears, with fond endearment:
But with a flame so generous and so noble,
That it could soar beyond their feeble ken,
And aim at *manly* daring!

    Constantia. Name your proof!

    Albert. Could it renounce the selfish claims of *wife?*
Rich in my fortunes, richer in my love,
Assert its empire o'er my heart alone,
And leave the world a name?

    Constantia *(disordered).* How should I answer
To what I understand not?

    Albert. To be plain;
Thou know'st my means ill suited to my birth.—
Honour and fame are mine: but wealth—the dross,
The clay on which we build those tott'ring fabrics,
Must be acquired by art.—Roselva's heiress —

    Constantia *(faintly).* Pr'ythee no more!

    Albert. Nay shrink now!—To hear half
Were but to blast thee.

    Constantia. I *am* blasted now!
Oh heav'n!—Oh earth!—Can it be possible?
Wouldst thou thus coolly meditate destruction?
Thus spared a wide accumulating ruin?
A ruin, that would mock sweet mercy's pow'r
To raise it from the dust!

    Albert *(impatiently).*
Art mad?

    Constantia. Past cure!
Ev'n at the moment when my fleeting sense
Hung on thy image, and enfeebled life
Stood tott'ring on the precipice of fate,
Then, then to plunge me down the vast profound,

Ev'n with the outstretch'd arm that seem'd to save me!
Oh, merciless!

    Albert *(seizing her hand roughly).* Peace! Peace!

    Constantia *(wildly).* Where shall I find it?
The cherub sits in heav'n, and mocks my pray'r:
The earth is cover'd with a mist of crimes
That hides her from our view! See, how it thickens!
All's black—All's dark!—Thy hand—We're lost! Oh, mercy!
(She faints.)

    Albert. I am a devil! and have dispossest
An angel's reason!

    Constantia *(recovering).* Art thou there, my Albert?
Oh, I've had dreams. But thou art by to shield me!

    Albert. Rest then on me.

    Constantia. My brain is all confusion:
This weakness is most strange! for I have ta'en
Of those same powders, that you sent me, oft.

    Albert *(starting). Indeed!*

    Constantia. Nay, but this very morn, to cheer our meeting,
And give the name of Health to't, I had swallow'd
The cordial draught thy tender care prepared
For my worst need.

    Albert. Oh heav'n!

    Constantia. Did I not right?
Nay, trust me, love, it cheered me much; yet now,
I know not wherefore, all things swim before me.
'Tis but a moment since methought thy form
Assumed some horrid semblance.

    Albert. Rest will cheer thee.

    Constantia *(as she goes out).* When shall we meet again?

    Albert *(disturbed).* Tomorrow.

    Constantia. Here?

    Albert *(with increasing perturbation).* Yes, here.

    Constantia. 'Tis well; I shall remember.
(Exit into a chamber.)

    Albert.
Aye, indeed!
Your memory will be long then; and must reach
Ev'n to that gloom where fancy's self expires.

Constantia, thou art lost! And the black venom
That taints thy blood, has, with infectious pow'r,
Stol'n o'er my heart, and poison'd all its joys.
Away, remorse!—the deed that's past must be
As it had never been!
(Going out, he meets the Count and Countess.)

    Count. My noble guest,
You're well encounter'd—Start not thus, my daughter:
Lord Albert bears no terrors.

    Albert *(still disturbed).* Good my Lord —

    Count. Nay, gentle Albert, fathers have a privilege
To wave the forms of sex.

    Albert *(to the Countess).* Dared I believe —

    Countess. My Lord, you have a secret monitor,
Without presumption, well may bid you trust
To what you wish.—I do beseech you, spare me!
Some two hours hence my father will impart
What conscious honour, and, I hope, a sense
Of nature's rights, may dictate. Rest we thus;
Roselva's heiress cannot be unconscious
Of Lord Alberto's worth.

    Albert *(laying his hand on his breast).* My thanks are here.
(Exit.)

    Count. Why dost thou trifle thus? Why dress thy tongue
In dubious promises?

    Countess. Oh, rather, why
Must I debase truth's everlasting lustre
With vile equivocation?

    Count. Thou art chang'd.
I deem'd thee duteous: trust me I can change too!
Has then a parent's voice no pow'r to awe?
I gave thee life!

    Countess. You gave me more ev'n; virtue!
Reason, the glorious pow'r to judge of wrong;
And courage to declare. Nay, dear my father,
Look not upon me with an angry eye:
I am your daughter, tutor'd by your cares;
And can I, in one selfish hour, forget
Each nobler principle those cares have cherish'd?

You had a thousand, thousand claims to urge you:
Aspiring manhood; pride; unheeded sorrows;
The fond excesses of parental love:
All that could tempt the proud, or warm the injured.
But *I*—a creature nursed in luxury,
Whose every feeling, polished even to weakness,
Starts at the thought of wrong—shall I inflict it?
Inflict it on a helpless—suffering friend?
Bid me do this, and tremble at the future!
Tremble at the black list of nameless crimes
Such monstrous guilt may gender!
  Count. Thou perverse one!
But well I guess thy secret soul assigns
Motives more pow'rful than this fine-spun honour,
To tempt thee from thy duty.—Sigismond—
  Countess. Nay, wrong me not so far!—Tho' my heart cherish'd
A passion dearer than its vital flood;
Tho' all of happiness concentred there
Left nought to virtue but her own bright record;
I call attesting angels down to witness
That I would bid my stubborn senses yield,
And own *her* voice in yours! Yet hear me swear too
By that same heav'n whose sacred mandate bids
Not to inflict what we should grieve to suffer,
That while my lov'd Constantia lives to claim them,
Ne'er shall my treach'rous pow'r invade her rights:
Ne'er shall my secret soul conceive the wish,
Nor my base tongue pronounce th' unhallow'd vow,
That thus would sanction fraud.
  Count. Is't possible?
Away, ingrate!—Oh thou dost plant fresh thorns,
When thy soft hand alone could pluck out those
That cruel memory fixt here! Get thee hence!
I will but con a lesson of humility,
And follow thee anon.—Yes—'tis most fit
That I should learn to be an infant's vassal.
My knees are old and stubborn—but they'll bend;
At least to heav'n—and then—no matter— hence.
  Countess. I dare not leave you.

Count. You have dared do that
To which all future darings are as feathers
In the great scale of nature.

    Countess. Oh, my father!

    Count. Away, thou'lt drive me desperate!

    Theresa *(without).* Help ho! help there!

    Count. What cry was that?

    Theresa *(entering from one of the arched doors).*
The lady Constantia, Sir,
Demands your instant succour.

    Count. Say'st thou?

    Countess. Heavens!

    Theresa Half frantic—flutt'ring on the verge of being,
By fits she lives, and dies.—See —she —she's here!

    Constantia *(led in from the same door).*
Air—air—more air—Oh, you have cruel kindness!
Why do you hold me thus?—You choke—you kill me!
Aye —here I breathe more freely!

    Count. Sweet Constantia,
Give me thy hand.

    Constantia. And my pulse too, I warrant!
No—no—no more of medicine—it hath kill'd me.

    Count. Hath medicine kill'd thee?

    Constantia. Aye—a villain's, Sir?

    Count *(in disorder).* *I* gave her none!

    Physician. My Lord!

    Countess. Alas! she wanders!

    Physician. It is not strange. Exhausted nature oft,
When she hath lost her pure and healthful spring,
Genders strange meteors and wild fiery starts,
The offspring of corruption.—Yet this morn
I found her calm and temp'rate;—she's much chang'd.

    Countess. But not to death!

    Physician. Would, Madam, *I* could say so!

    Countess. Oh no—it cannot be!—the whole fair cheek
So lately shamed the morning!—whose firm pulse
Beat with the steady tone of health and virtue!

    Constantia *(drawing her hand from that of the Countess, and looking at it).* What's here? —a tear —a soft and gracious drop

From orbs of mercy—I can feel its influence —
Mark you how it hath cool'd me!

  Countess. *Cooled* thee, say'st thou?
Death's in this hand.

  Count. Her fever is most potent.

  Constantia *(gazing carelessly around).* Is there none else here?

  Count. None, dear sufferer!
Whom would'st thou?

  Constantia. Nobody—no matter—yet
Methinks there *should* be eyes, that, for each tear
You drop, should rain down torrents. Oh, that pang!
One more such, and all's past.

  Countess. Is there no aid?

  Physician. None, Madam, that my skill can minister.
The powers of life are wasted;—life itself
Hangs like a leaf upon a sapless branch,
Which the first breath may shake.

  Countess. Yet youth like hers—

  Constantia *(wildly).* Who talks of life and youth? I am wither'd—
feeble!
Grief hath struck palsies here *(Laying her hand on her heart.)*
—Feel how it trembles!
And now—Oh, agony!—You tear it from me!
(Repels the Countess.)
Spare me!—Oh, spare my heart-strings!

  Countess. Gracious heaven,
I do submit me to thy will. Oh, take her!
And with these drops of painful resignation,
May every selfish and repining thought
Be blotted from my soul!

  Physician. Repose her here. *(A small sofa is brought.)*

  Constantia *(reviving).* Why stand ye so far off?

  Count. Sweet, we are near thee.

  Constantia. Nay, nay, ye are not—and your voices too!
So low—so distant—that mine ear scarce catches —
—Light there!—*more* light—*(Starting forward.)*
—Mine eyes are dim too. Oh!— *(She dies.)*

  Countess. Too much of sorrow!

  Theresa Help there—Raise her!

Count (*dropping the lifeless hand*). No!—
'Tis past.—She's dead: and that ethereal essence
That gave the flow'r its soft and living perfume,
Is lost in air.
    Physician. Look to the Countess there!
    Count. Bear in the beauteous clay!
(*The sofa is borne off; the Count takes his daughter in his arms, and signs to the attendants, who follow the body.*)
My child—my dear one!
Nay ope thine eyes!
    Countess. They are turn'd inward, Sir!
And there have learnt a lesson of submission.
I am awe-struck, and own the voice of heav'n.
Roselva hath no heiress now but me,
And *I* no will but yours.
    Count. Still then thou'rt duteous!
Trust me, my child, I would not urge thy will,
Did I not see a train of happy days
Rise from this mournful hour.
    Countess. Perhaps they may so. One at least is rescued
From the black list, when I obey a father.
This night, with your good leave, I would devote
To pray'r for my lov'd friend.—Tomorrow's sun
Shall find a joyless, but obedient heart,
Ready, an it shall please lord Albert claim it,
To yield its plighted vow, One boon alone:
That, faithful to the business of the state,
He part o' the instant. *Our* less urgent haste
May claim some few days' respite!
    Count. At thy wish!
I will not wrong the virtue of thy sorrow
By ill-timed festivals. Yet pr'ythee cheer thee!
    Countess. Nay let me weep, my father. Dews like these
Are blasting only to the weeds of life;
The virtues bloom beneath them. Sacred tears!
How many soft and tender courtesies,
How many graces, that rapacious death
Has snatch'd from vulgar vision, new embodied,
Through your bright medium rise again to being,

Ting'd warm and high with colourings divine! *(Exeunt.)*

E<small>ND OF THE</small> S<small>ECOND</small> A<small>CT</small>.

Act III. Scene I.[1]

A garden belonging to the Castle.

(Osmond and the Physician.)

Physician. Nuptials so secret and so sudden, blending festivity as it were with tears, and mirth with mortality! By my faith, Master Osmond, but this is strange! the Lady Constantia was surely well beloved?

Osmond. By the Count most tenderly, and by the Countess to the very extremity of passion. Even now hath she past the live-long night, surrounded by her maids, in grief and meditation; interrupted only by the prayer which they chanted in unison at each running hour: till morn drew forth a requiem, whose notes swell'd with a harmony so somber and so sad, that methought it might have charm'd the disembodied spirit, and call'd it back to earth! Oh, never was love more perfect, or more true! Joy was not joy, till it was shared with Constantia; nor did sorrow ever cloud the brow of either till she sickened.

Physician. And that, as I take it, was some twelvemonth past: yet did the deadliness of her distemper never manifest itself till within the last twelve hours; and then with a suddenness!—Hinted you to the Count what we talked of, as to the manner of her death?

Osmond. I did, Sir.

Physician. And how received he it?

Osmond. At first somewhat moodily—yet with a certain strangeness that led me to bolder speech: till, on the mention of poison, he started from his seat with a petrifying frown, chid my presumption, that dar'd rashly question the decrees of heaven—enjoined my silence—and so dismissed me.

Physician. Even so!

Osmond. With no further show of zeal.

Physician. Alas! that affection should prove a still frailer flower than mortality. Yet this passes not so.—Osmond, I do once more repeat to thee, I like not the hastiness of her death. The Lord Albert stands high in the calendar of courtiers, but not of saints; and my mind hath misgivings more than my tongue dare utter. Should the workings of my fancy bear further test, thou shalt know more; in the interim, counsel with thy discretion, and obey the mandate of thy lord. Thou art moved.

Osmond. Truly, Sir, both with amazement and sorrow. There was no heart so mean that it felt not the virtues of the Lady Constantia; nor any, I trow, so base that it would not avenge the innocent.

Physician. Aye, Osmond, *there* is the test that lifts the poor man to the prince—the servant to his lord; that alone equalizes ranks, and raises up the weak to befriend the cause which the mighty abandon.—Past not the Lord Sigismond thro' yon trees?

Osmond. Rather the semblance of the Lord Sigismond—a body without a soul:—a creature so lost, that, seeing him, we might well weep over the wreck of a man; and marvel that the vehemence of one passion should so o'er-master the boasted omnipotence of reason.

Physician. There are no hearts more true than those that are touch'd with this noble energy: nor any remedy so prompt for our own sufferings, as that of righting the cause of others. Sigismond is discreet and valiant—I will unbosom myself to him.—I have yet some portion of the drugs—I will analyze them.—Theresa must again be questioned.—All shall be examined; and where the black speck is, there must we apply the caustic.—But, soft, the Count!—He seems disturb'd too—

Osmond. I cannot marvel, Sir—Our new-made bridegroom, with love that somewhat oversteps the bounds of plighted honour, sets his loyalty and speed aside; delays his purposed parting till morrow's dawn; and with a certain zeal that clothes a harsh command in gentle phrase, woos his fair bride with him to court—while she—

Physician. 'Twere best pass on!

Osmond. Have with you!

Physician. Towards the castle! *(Exeunt.)*
(Count enters, followed by Rodolphus.)

Count. I'm sick—at rest—I'll not be further mov'd—
So tell him, good Rodolphus! He doth wrong
The nobleness of his word, to press a suit,
Which in my very heat and zeal of friendship
I did deny to him. My daughter's his,
Fast as the sacred pow'r of oaths can bind her.
For her seclusion and her sequent journey
She had my license; aye, and his I trow,
Ev'n when he had no privilege to make
The law by which he bound her!
　　　　　　　　—You've my answer—

Where stays he, Sir?

    Rodolphus. I' the castle, good my Lord;
Where he hath vainly fought you.

    Count. I would have him
Still seek me vainly! We've conferr'd already;
And I do feel a hasty spleen within,
That bids me shun his presence.—If it suit
With what imports the business of the state,
That he make longer sojourn—all my means
Are at his beck—while gallant preparation
Shall wait him to the court. And for my daughter,
The treasures of her love, and of her fortune,
Will both be his—till then, my word is sacred!
I will not urge her further—So report it.
(Exit Rodolphus.)
Osmond!

    Osmond *(entering).* My Lord!

    Count *(to himself).* The heav'ns, methinks, do lour!
And guilt, that still engenders superstition,
Doth whisper that thy frown on this day's deed!
—The time is changed, good Osmond!

    Osmond. To a wonder!
The moon, so lately ris'n, is lost.—The air,
Heavy and thick, is sunk to sudden stillness:
While the streaked bosom of yon nitrous clouds
Portends intestine war—

    Distant Chorus. "Peace—
        "Peace to the lovely and the good!"

    Count. What music's that?

    Rodolphus. The villagers, my Lord, still chanting requiems
O'er fair Constantia's grave. A rustic tribute,
With which they meant to wake the silent night,
And hang on beauty's shrine a simply garland,
More wet with tears than dew; the brooding storm
I fear doth mock their humble gratitude,
And urge them homeward! Hark, my Lord, the thunder,
Ev'n now in hoarse and fearful mutterings,
Warns you to shelter! 'Tis but two months past
The rifted bolt did cleave yon solid oak,

And plough the land around.

    Count *(to himself)*. Why should I shake?—
She's dead—the ravenous grave hath swallow'd her;
Yet all's not well here; and th' offended heav'ns
Do of our granted wishes make a scourge,
To lash us into torture.—She died fairly!
But where's the voucher? A wrong'd heritage!
A nameless orphan suddenly cut off,
Ev'n at the moment—fye!—there's that i' the face on't
Would blast an angel's witness.—Well, we'll in;
There is more war than in the elements;
But where's the shelter? Would she lived again.
(Exit abruptly.)

    Osmond *(solus)*. He's deeply mov'd—nor can I wonder at it.
The potent duty that did bind my lady
To yield her hand, had yet no pow'r to quell
Her heart's wild swells:—tears—tremor—and depression,
Ev'n in the presence of the sacred altar,
Chased the bright flush of youth from off her cheek,
And stained the nuptial wreathes!

                              Good night, Rodolphus!

    Rodolphus. Good night—good night—No time for ceremony!
The storm is at our heels. Hot sulf'rous drops
Dry as they fall upon the earth's parch'd bosom,
Or else conglobe to dust! My Lord's retired!
I've borne the message of your testy Count;
The Countess mocks his suit too,—For mine own part
Having no love thoughts to disturb my slumbers,
My truckle bed is welcome.
(Chorus at a distance.)

    "Peace!"

    Rodolphus. List, I pray you!

    Chorus. "Peace to the lovely and the good!"

    Rodolphus. 'Tis heav'nly music, sure!

    Osmond. Alas! mere mortal,
Wailing mortality!

    Semi-Chorus. "Rash humanity forbear!
       "Heave not a sight, nor drop a tear!
       "When tumultuous feelings rove,

"Warm with hope, with youth, and love;
"When contending passions fly
"To blend and languish in the eye;
"When the throbbing blood bids start
"Thousand pulses from the heart;
"When the trembling senses seek
"A crimson harbour in the cheek;
"*Then* is the time to drop the tear:
"*Now* rash humanity forbear!"
Chorus. "Peace to the lovely and the good!"
Semi-Chorus. "Pain and sorrow now are o'er:
"The eye that wept shall weep no more.
"No more the anxious heart shall sigh,
"Whelm'd in doubtful ecstasy.
"Lo, where in their little cell,
"Unwak'd the tranquil senses dwell;
"Steep'd no more in sorrow's flood!
"Peace to the lovely and the good!"

(The chorus dies insensibly away, and the villagers are seen passing through the trees, strewing flowers.—Low thunder.)

Scene II.

The Countess's chamber;—a bed—Lights burning on the table.—The Countess and Theresa.

Countess. Thou'rt spent with watching, girl—get thee to bed.
Theresa. Sooth I'm not weary, Madam!
Countess. Kind Theresa!
Who thus would'st strain the offices of duty,
Till nature faint. What wonder that thine eyes
Should claim their wonted dues, when mine, ev'n mine,
With tears half glaz'd, with anxious thought, kept waking,
Feeble and dim scarce lift the heavy lid!
Theresa. Permit me, Madam, watch you!
Countess. That were cruel!
Thou'rt human, good Theresa, and dost want

Humanity's soft balm. Why dost thou tarry?
Fear'st thou the storm? Methinks th' enkindled flame,
If to the guilty it doth speak a pow'r
That in reproving shakes them,—yet in breasts,
Whose natural whiteness bears no stain of guilt,
Tho' fill'd with contrite sense of human error,
Should gender nothing, save the holy awe
That sanctifies the bosom. Courage, girl!
    Theresa. Madam, I fear it not.
    Countess. Yet somewhat fear'st thou!
    Theresa. You, and you only.
    Countess. Me! alas, vain greatness!
Hast thou then witchery enough to deck
A puny mortal like myself in terrors?
Speak thine offense!
    Theresa. Behold it, Madam!
(Pointing to Sigismond, who enters.)
    Countess *(starting).* How!—
Was this well done, my Lord?
    Sigismond. Was it well done
To bar me from thy presence?—to cut off
Ev'n the faint memory of the hours that were,
And doom me to oblivion? Oh thou false one!
Why didst thou smile to lure me to destruction?
Why did thine eyes once blend their sparkling beams
With these fond orbs; and bid my throbbing heart
Burn with a hope so ardent and so fierce,
That life itself, heav'n's own celestial flame,
Grew pale and dim before it?
    Countess *(tenderly).* Sigismond!
    Sigismond. No sight—no tear, I charge thee, lest they blast me!
Lest my responsive heart forget its wrongs,
And fondly yield thee its accustomed echo.
I come to close my great account of anguish!
To banish in one parting—deep-drawn sigh,
All the vast agonies of hopeless passion:
To bid thee live—to joy—to love—to fortune!
    Countess. I pr'ythee spare me, gentle Sigismond!
If thou would'st have my heart forbear to break,

If thou would'st have my tott'ring reason keep
Her throne secure, breathe no *kind* wish upon me!
Joy—fortune—love—Oh, they were wand'ring vapours,
My tears long since have quench'd!
    Sigismond. Thy tears—Oh heav'n!
Where is the pang should wring from thee those drops?
Hast thou e'er known the gloom of secret anguish,
Or the wild transport of a dawning joy?
Wakes not the boundless universe for thee?
Thee happy Albert leads to grace a court!
Thee, happier still, shall woo in rural shades!
While smiling fortune, and indulgent heaven,
Shall ratify the bliss!—the world is thine!
I had no world but love—no heav'n but hope!
Why didst thou steal upon the treasured store,
And rob the wretched miser while he dreamt
Of years of ecstasy?
    Countess. Away, forget me!
I would, alas, forget myself!—forget
All worldly hopes—all joys—all fleeting pleasures.
Why com'st thou then like some bright vision by me,
Startling my slumb'ring sense with transient gleams
Of unknown happiness?—the few short hours
Since last we met, a *point* to happy mortals,
Have been my round of life!
    Sigismond. Dost thou then mourn them?
    Countess. I mourn them not—they were the mark'd of fate;
And filial duty and applauding conscience
Shall bear them white to heav'n:—yet still for thee—
    Sigismond *(approaching).* For me thy tears! Oh, give the precious balm
And let me lay it to my burning heart!
    Countess. Away—
    Sigismond. Born to subdue each stormy passion,
Still thou prevail'st—and yet methinks the words
Should be more kind that bid us part for ever!
Some token too—some pledge—
    Countess *(taking a chain and ornament from her neck).*
How much I owe thee,

Honour and inborn gratitude attest!
Thou were my guardian angel—my preserver!
Oh, that my pray'rs could make this sad memorial
A precious amulet!—that it might shield thee,
Ev'n as a sacred charm, 'mid wars and dangers!
It was Constantia's—wear it at thy heart!
And sometimes, as thou sadly dost peruse it,
Recall the memory of the friends that lov'd thee,
And gem it with a tear!—*(Gives it to him.)*

Sigismond. My senses fail me!
This, said you—*this?*
Countess. The wonder!

Sigismond *(wild and fearful).* They are the same—
(Comparing it with another from his own bosom.)
The form—th'impress—the chain;
The cypher only differing.—Do not mock me!
The Turk that tore me from my native land,
Oft, in my playful hours of childish fondness,
To this sad relic drew the unconscious tear;
And bade me, should my fortunes e'er encounter
Its likeness in some wand'ring fair one's bosom,
Beware a *sister* there!

Countess *(with transport).* All righteous heav'n,
There is joy yet!—the *heirship* is restored!
Smile—smile again, Roselva!—ye wide plains
Whose princely wealth my thankless heart so oft
Hath inly mourn'd, put forth your richest treasures!
Rise, ye proud turrets, with unwonted lustre,
And grace your rightful lord!—To heav'n and him,
I bend the knee!

Sigismond *(raising her).* What means this wild emotion?

Countess *(with sudden recollection).*
My father—ruined—lost—betray'd—by me—
Oh my sick heart!
(Clap of thunder.)

Sigismond. The fierce and rending tempest
Doth shake thy constancy!

Countess. Ah no!—the storm
Is here, My Sigismond, to which I bend!—

That fortune yet reserves for thee her treasures,
I do entreat thy credence.

    Sigismond. Thou art faint!

    Countess. Joy hath its agonies! Get—get thee hence!
Of the strange mystery that veils thy fate—
We meet again—*(With embarrassment.)*

    Sigismond. Oh never!

    Countess. Trust me yes!

    Sigismond. Trust thee, thou dear one!—Oh those heavy eyes!
In sickness and in sorrow lovely still!
May some pure angel, like thyself, be near,
And guard thy slumbers.
(Kisses her hand, and exit.)

    Countess. Hear the pray'r, Constantia!
And if enfranchis'd spirits walk on earth,
Let thy fair semblance hover round my bed!
Shield from the blasting storm—the midnight ruffian,
And from the realms of sanctitude and peace
Breathe o'er my senses some celestial dream,
May soothe this mortal coil!—Methinks ev'n now
They're rapt in sweet foretaste—heavy—most heavy!
(She sleeps.)

Scene III.

*The Scene changes to the arched gallery as before, lighted by a lamp
from the roof. Albert enters through his chamber-door, speaking to
Rodolphus, whose pallet is visible from the lights within.—Thunder at
intervals, with vivid flashes of lightning seen through the casements.*

Albert. See that the tapers burn—and then to bed.
Are the heavens angry, that they chide us thus?
An 'twere their will to visit sinful heads,
I well might fear now!—Yet the forked flash
Past innocent—and feeble-minded man
Betrays himself.—It is the hour of rest!
And all the mingled sounds that swell'd of late
Thro' the low vaults and hollows of the castle,

Are sunk to stillness.

                  Thought's fantastic brood
Alone is waking:—present—past, and future,
Wild, misshaped hopes, and horrible rememb'rings,
Now rise a hideous and half viewless chaos
To fancy's vision—till the stout heart freeze
At its own retrospect.—Mem'ry, stop there!
Not a jot further!—Rather, thou bright sun,
Thou dazzling future, rise with godlike splendour,
And gild the vast horizon of ambition.
Say it be clouded by a woman's will!
Yet is she woman—therefore to be lured;
A *young* one—therefore to be bribed by gauds:
And I will tempt her with such golden glories
As her weak sex would grasp at, tho' perdition
Gaped in the gulf between!—This is her chamber!
Perchance she sleeps unguarded—at the worst,
A lover's passion, and a husband's right,
Shall justify the' intrusion!—*Who dare bar me?*
(The Ghost of Constantia, shrouded in the lightest white drapery, appears before the door, passing the pallet of Rodolphus, who sleeps sweetly.)
Ha! have my senses conjured up a phantom?
Speak, vision, if thou canst! *(Advancing.)*
(She gazes intently, and motions him from her.)
Oh horrible! *(He leans against a pillar.)*
(Vivid lightning—the Ghost glides into the chamber of the Countess.)
    Albert *(after a pause)*. I am a coward—and my fears have shaped
The thing that is not.—Yet I saw it plain—
Most manifest to view.
Nor, tho' the heav'ns had shower'd down sheets of fire,
Could it have so appall'd me.—What, Rodolphus!
Rodolphus, I say—So, Sir, you sleep sound!
    Rodolphus *(starting up)*. Aye, truly, do I my Lord—Sound sleep is the patrimony of honest poverty. My family had the trick on't, and 'twas all my father had to bequeath me.
(Thunder.)
    Albert *(starting wildly)*. Soft, Sirs!
    Rodolphus. My Lord!

Albert *(to himself)*. I've faced the deadly cannon
While its dread roaring hath mowed ranks before it:
Have danced unshrinking on the curling billows
When they have dash'd the clouds, and death beneath
Hath worn its grimmest form; and start I now?
Ev'n at the shrouded and the bloodless semblance
That fancy had embodied!

Rodolphus *(with great surprise)*. He's entranced!
Good—good my Lord.

Albert. Who's there?

Rodolphus. Heav'n and his saints have mercy on us! How wildly your Lordship looks—Do you see aught, Sir?—These dismal old arches put one in mind of nothing but murders and apparitions.

Albert. Peace, coward!

Rodolphus. Beseech you then go in, my Lord: I have some curious relics to guard us, and—hark!—No—it was only the whistling of the wind—And yet methought it was very like a groan.—*(Observing the perturbation of Albert.)* By my troth, my Lord, you're pale—i'faith you are so.

Albert *(striking him)*. Lying fool, begone!

Rodolphus. Nay, no liar, I swear—nor so much of a fool as not to know that if rank has its privileges, age and fidelity are not without theirs. I humbly wish your Lordship a good night. And when you have a follower more faithful than myself, may heaven and you reward him as he deserves!

Albert. Stay, sirrah! Mastered every way—come—come—there's gold for thee!

Rodolphus *(rejecting it)*. Ah my Lord, my Lord, thus does your grandee ever think he can purchase by wealth what he hath lost by discourtesy.—But keep your gold, Sir!—I have somewhat here that tells me I was not born a slave, but a man—A poor one I must own, yet still a man: with feelings that will not be commanded, and opinions that are not to be bought.

Albert. Thou'rt born a babbling knave, Sir! quit my sight,
Now, and for ever!—Chafed by slaves and idiots!
Begone, Sir!
(Thunder. Albert looking after Rodolphus who slowly retires.)
He may brave the thunder storm;
Darkness and midnight bring to him no spectres:

Honest and humble.—Would *I* were so too!

    Rodolphus *(still lingering).*

Has your Lordship then no further duty to enjoin me?

    Albert *(in a subdued tone).*

None—none—begone, I tell thee!

    Rodolphus. An yet, if it were not too bold, I would fain kiss your Lordship's hand before I quit your service—and—By the mass it is cold as death!—Ah, my dear Lord *(Falling on his knees.)*—My sweet Lord—My honoured Lord—tell your griefs to your poor servant!—If he be but your servant, yet hath he a heart that would break to relieve yours— and tho' this be the hand that struck me, yet many and many's the time it hath twisted its fingers in my grey locks, while, with childish fondness, you swore ever to love your poor Rodolphus.

    Albert. Thou wilt unman me! Oh, tyrannic guilt,

That dost disclaim all balm of confidence,

And leave the lacerated heart to groan

In solitary anguish!—Happy he

Who sinking on the bosom of a friend

Inhales the honied breath of sympathy,

And yields to short oblivion.

(Falls on the neck of Rodolphus.)

    Rodolphus. A murrain o' these half sentences! What signifies a man's telling himself his own griefs!

    Albert. Come—come—all's well again!—'twas but a chill.

Tell me, Rodolphus—the—the fair Constantia—

Art sure she's dead?

    Rodolphus. And buried too—You may well think of her, my Lord; she was a sweet creature; and loved you so truly—I dreamt of her ev'n now—Methought she stood as it 'twere *there,* and smiled upon me with the same rosy and kind air she was wont to have when I first followed your Lordship to the castle. Troth, her first night's lodging i' the ground is but comfortless. Well, all's one for that—the same storm beats on the grave of the prince and the peasant; and both, perhaps, sleep sweeter than he who lives to mourn them!

    Albert. Wounded by random shafts—Most subtle torture!

Well, well, enough of this.

    Rodolphus. And yet not all either, my Lord, if we could come at the truth—there's a strange muttering i' the castle, as tho' she had not been dealt fairly with—I shall know more anon!

Albert. Rather know less, Sir!
Curb this intemperate and boorish zeal
That—hark—a noise—Startled again by shadows!

Rodolphus. Shadow call you it! by my troth then it is the shadow
of a drum; and, to my thinking the voice of the Count.

(Alarm, and shouts without.)

The infidels—the Turks—arm, arm!

Albert. What should this mean?

Count *(entering)*. Havoc and desolation!
Ev'n now a savage and a fierce banditti,
Led by the Othman pow'r, invades our lands,
And drives our slaves before it!

Albert. Oh, most welcome!
Welcome thou stern and bloody front of war,
Whose very voice doth wake my lagging spirits,
And brace my unstrung sinews—trebly welcome!

Count. Call forth our vassals—let the bridge be look'd to—
Unbar the armoury, and choose—Oh, Sigismond!

Sigismond *(entering)*. My noble friend!

Count. Thou hast a valiant sword!

Sigismond. And I, be sure, will use it valiantly!
And see, th' inspiring angel comes to greet us.

(The Countess enters from her chamber.)

A thousand blushing terrors in her cheek,
All guardian spirits—sent to summon up
More than the strength of hosts in each beholder.

Albert *(interposing roughly)*. Oh unmatch'd insolence! Should I
bear this,
I were indeed a tame, convenient husband.

Count. Heav'n shield my child—these frantic fits, Lord Albert—

Sigismond. Nay, give the madman scope!—didst thou say *hus-
band?*
As soon shall soul and deep engrained guilt
Lay claim to heav'n, as thou to her:—*a husband!*
Oh Albert, I could name to thee a crime,
So deep, so dire, the fiends themselves might start,
And wonder at its blackness! Such a crime
As strikes thee from humanity's fair record,
And cancels every tie.—Let it suffice,

I do attaint thee as a *murderer!*
And when our swords have thinned yon Turkish host,
And thou return'd, flush'd with familiar conquest,
Ev'n in thy lustihood and prime of daring,
Will prove it on thy bosom! Should I wrong thee,
May the great God of battles blunt *my* steel,
And seal a bloody pardon.

    Albert. Rather *now*
Let fate decide between us! Vagrant boaster!
Think'st thou I'd enter in the listed field,
As knight to knight, with one my name might conquer?
Know as a foe I scorn thee! As an insect,
Whose buzzing noise and sting offends my sense,
I crush thee thus—
(Draws; the Count interposes.)

    Osmond *(entering).* My Lord, the foe advances!
Ev'n now the blaze of distant cottages
Gains on the view.

    Count. Good Osmond, lead our vassals
Forth by the nearer portal—
(To Albert and Sigismond.)
Have you hearts?
Myself will head them.—Have you hearts, I say?
Or are they cold, even as the steel ye bear?

    Sigismond. I do confess me guilty!

    Albert. So do I—
Our difference rest awhile upon our swords.—
Rodolphus—

    Rodolphus. My good Lord! *(They confer.)*

    Count. All-seeing heav'n,
If in this hour of painful retribution,
Some drop of mercy yet remains to mingle
In the deep draught of sorrow, save my child!
Upon this guilty and time-silver'd head
Discharge the bolt! Oh, blast the wither'd trunk,
But spare the blooming scion. Faithful Osmond,
Thy looks bespeak impatience: we will forth!
Forth! to that strife whence some of us, perhaps,
Will ne'er return! And, oh, my noble guests,

Rivals no more, but brothers of the war,
Give me your hands! And if indeed ye cherish
Aught of that gallant passion that doth lead
To guard the helpless, and avenge the injured,
Now let the flame blaze high! A last embrace!
(To his daughter.)
Perhaps indeed a last one!—I am lost
In fearful recollection!—Strike the drum!
And let the burning spirit of the war
Exhale these wat'ry vapours—Strike, I say!
(Alarm—Exeunt separately.—Long and distant drums.)

Scene IV.

Scene changes to the chapel of the Castle—a perspective view of the altar—On one side a tomb, as lately opened, hung with garlands of flowers.

(The Countess enters, followed by Osmond.)

    Countess. Dreary and desolate! The peopled castle
That late resounded with the hum of men,
Now rings harsh echoes to a single step.
Methinks the pendant banners, as I pass,
Fearful records of many a bloody field,
Wave colder blasts upon me; while the spear
And target, spoils of honourable valour,
Clang self-impelled with horrid dissonance:
The sighing winds come laden with lament,
And nothing reigns but war and devastation!
    Osmond. Beseech you, Madam, hence!—Unwholesome dews
Still hang upon the bosom of the morn,
And taint the breeze.
    Countess. Oh Osmond, night's dank dews,
Or burning noon, alike unheeded, strike
On her whole sense concentred to her heart,
Lives only there! Nay, pr'ythee tell me, Osmond,
In the vast regions of created space,
Is there one spot like this, where I could shelter?

Here the rude clangor of the distant field
Strikes feebly on my senses. Heav'n and friendship
With more than mortal influence guard the ground.
Here lie the sacred treasures of remembrance!
They fade not with yon garlands—Lost Constantia!
Devoted—murdered—Hold, my bleeding heart!
Nor burst beneath the strange, the black idea.

    Osmond. Have comfort, Madam!

    Countess. Still my burning blood,
Bid my tumultuous pulse subside to calmness;
Curb the wild swells that, mounting from my heart,
Threaten my brain! Oh, Osmond, there are crimes
Which, in a mind unversed, and new to horror,
Awake a sense so strange and turbulent,
That reason faints before it.—Ha, what noise!

    Uberto *(entering hastily)*. A messenger, an please you, from my Lord,
Craves audience.

    Countess. Oh, admit him on the instant!
Fool that thou were to dally—Well, thy tidings?
(To the Messenger who enters.)

    Messenger. Most luckless—Prest by the surrounding foe,
My Lord craves instant succour!

    Countess. Heav'n and earth!
Surrounded, say'st thou? Oh, he's lost; he's lost!
Haste, Osmond! Speed *thy* followers to my father!
Danger and death are on him.

    Osmond. Gentle Lady—

    Countess. Nay, speak not—look not as thou mean'st to dally.
While we, cool skeptics, calculate the danger,
He perishes.

    Osmond. Where doth the combat press thus?

    Messenger. Ev'n in the hollow of the left hand vale,
Where the broad umbrage gains upon the road,
The ambush'd foe rush'd on us.

    Osmond. Noble Madam,
Think of your danger, if, alone and guardless,
I violate the mandate of my Lord,

And leave—

Countess. Oh, Osmond, there's a mandate writ in heav'n,
That bids me brave all dangers for a father!
I do *command* thee hence!

Osmond. Unwillingly
I must obey.—Our last, most faithful band,
Attend me on the walls—and yet—Uberto,
Speed to their chief! Declare the Countess' will,
Back'd by my pow'r; and urge their quickest aid
To save their Lord!—*I* follow in due season.

Countess *(to Uberto).* Fly, I conjure thee!

Uberto. This way brings us nearest!

(Exit with the Messenger—Osmond, unobserved, retires another way through the chapel.)

Countess *(looking after them).*
Faithful and active! See—alive to danger,
Their fellows haste to greet them. Valiant friends!
Chieftains draw brighter swords; but yours are temper'd
By heav'n's own spirits—truth and loyalty!
Oh, that your steps were wing'd!—At length they're gone,
And my sick heart may live again to hope!
Methinks the renovating balm already
Warms and expands its pow'rs! Essence of life!
Too fine and volatile to be retained!
Spent, while inhaled; and yet so sweetly poignant,
That sense revives upon it!

(Turning, she encounters Albert.)
                              Heaven and earth!
Lord Albert here.

Albert. Trust me, a sword like Albert's
Had never left the cause till fate had fix'd it!

Countess *(faintly).* All's lost—all's gone!—My father—
Sigismond!

Albert. I dare not answer.—Thro' the postern gate
A path yet opens to us free from foes;
Lost in the spoil and plunder of the castle,
They will not heed our flight.—Nay shrink not thus;
There is no other hope.

Countess. Oh then there's none!

Albert. Nay, trust me, but there is; and safety too.
My train already hath prepar'd the means
May convoy us—
    Countess. Oh misery!
    Albert. Hark—the spoilers
Ev'n now perchance approach!—Say, darest thou brave them?
Shall this fair form, the prey of ruffian pow'r,
Grace the lewd harem? 'Tis no time for parley!
Thus with a tender violence—
    Countess. Stand off!
There's blood upon thee!
    Albert. Blood!
    Countess. Aye, guiltless blood!
Bethink you, Sir—'tis holy ground we tread on!
And the dread hand of heav'n ev'n now, perhaps,
Is stretch'd in vengeance o'er us! *Slept* you well?
Did no ill dreams molest—no thunders shake you?
Methinks the warring elements last night
Might from their graves have rous'd the sheeted dead,
And bade them haunt the guilty!—You are pale!
Oh, the dire vigils of a wounded conscience!
I shrink even at the thought on't!
    Albert. Lovely trembler!
Excess of terror hath o'erwhelmed thy reason.
Recall thy scatter'd powers! Think that thy *husband,*
Spared from the rage of war, still lives to guard thee.
Ev'n thus, all helpless, hopeless as thou stand'st,
The native rose thus blanch'd upon thy cheek,
And those bright orbs obscured with filial anguish,
Think there's a heart that beats but to protect thee;
That fondly swears—
    Countess. And innocently too!
Oh, Albert, search thy memory! Bid it trace
The black mysterious records of the past.
Question thy heart, if in yon tomb's cold bosom
No form lies hid to whom those vows were due:
No ear lies closed to which that voice was music;
Then shrink into thyself, as I shrink from thee,
With nameless horror—and determined will.

Albert. *Living,* at least, thou vainly wouldst appall me!
Nor, though the grave again should render up
Its grizzly phantoms—tho' the fire-cleft skies
Bid the blue meteors blaze again around,
And make a hell of earth—shall my firm soul
Shrink from her aim. I'm seared to recollection!
I would have sooth'd thy pride—have woo'd thy passion,
And with a baby tale of love and war,
Have won thee to my purpose—That once foil'd,
Thus I *enforce* obedience!

Countess. Help, oh help there!

Albert. Thy cries are vain—No hostile band attends
To bar my will.—Their credulous valor finds
Ample employ! I were indeed an idiot
Idly to stake upon a rapier's point,
A woman's courtesy, or greybeard's will,
That prize for which my daring soul has plunged
Ev'n to the depth of horrors.—Come—be kind,
Think of a court!

Countess *(pointing to the tomb).* A grave!

Albert. Of love!

Countess. Of murder!
Oh, monstrous sex! Have you not smiles to kill with?
Words that can stab? Deceitful sighs can wither?
But blood must crown the mischief!—Hence for ever!
Fly as thou may'st! for me, tho' thou couldst offer
Unnumber'd worlds, and every world a paradise,
I would not share them with thee!

Albert. Sayst thou so?
Nay then 'tis past thy choice. Assist me, slaves!
(To his attendants, who seize her.)

Osmond *(interposing).*
Nay, good my Lord—-

Albert. Insolent vassal, hence!

Osmond. Bethink you, Sir—Nay this then to thy heart!
(As Albert attempts to cut him down with his sabre, he draws a dagger and stabs him.)
One faithful guard may do the work of thousands.
(The Countess faints.)

Albert. It was well aimed—and bloodily enforces
Thy most pernicious precept.—Bind him fast!
(To his attendants, who seize Osmond.)
I have strength yet!
(Shout and drums at a distance.)
Victory—Victory!

    Albert. It withers at that sound!
And all the vital pow'rs, of late so firm,
Seem snapt at once!
(He falls.)

                Life—fleeting—treacherous life,
Ebb'st thou so quickly! What remains? Oh, thou
Who first hast plung'd into the world of spirits,
And tried the dark unknown—do thou expound it!
Tho' shrouded, rise! Ere from my burning blood
The strange mysterious consciousness exhale,
That makes me dust or—Fiends, stand off—
*(To Rodolphus, who enters hastily, and with other attendants offers
to raise him.)*
I live yet—
Damnation for hereafter! Hark the foe!
(Trumpet.)
Oh, how the sprightly note invigorates nature!
This tent is cold—My cloak there!
                    —To the sunshine!
Cold—cold and damp—Constantia thou'rt aveng'd!
(He dies.)
    Distant chorus of Peasants, &c.
      "Triumphant see the warriors come!
      "Strike the cymbal, strike the drum.
      "Bid the festive notes agree
      "To raise the song of victory.
      "Victory—Victory!
(Shout.)
      "Raise, raise the song of victory!"
*(A sprightly march, during which Turkish prisoners, and groups of
soldiers enter, bearing banners.)*
    Sigismond *(seeing the Countess).* Silence your drums—the flow'r
o' the war is blighted,

And victory's a name!

(The Countess recovers as the Count is led in wounded.)

    Countess. Alas, my father!

    Count. Wounded ev'n to the death! Lord Albert too!
Hath then the sword of war so quickly sever'd
The ill-starr'd knot?

    Osmond. Not so, my Lord—*his* fate—

    Count. Thy face is prologue, Osmond, to some tale,
Which my numb'd senses shrink from, tell it there.

(Pointing to the Countess.)

My dream of life is o'er—a troublous vision.
And of its mighty host of vast affections
One only lives.—My child—Nay spare this weakness.
Something I had—Bear hence the prisoners!
I yet would live to bless thee.

    Prisoner. Who is he,
That with a *master* voice thus dare to rule,
Lord of these wide domains?

    Sigismond. Old man, begone!

    Prisoner. Indeed! hast thou forget me? Did the Pole
That tore thee from me—from my memory
Blot out my name and features? Thou wert mine,
Ere yet thine ear had hail'd another tie!
How is't I find thee on thy natal lands,
A vassal, where thou should'st command? Be proud!
And bid the minions whom thou seest around,
Kneel to *Roselva!*

    Count. Gracious God—what say'st thou?

    Prisoner. I know *thee* not—yet sure thy aged head
May call to memory the blood-stained night,
When our fierce troops, like grim and angry wolves,
Assailed this castle. From the spoil I bore
Its infant heir. It was the chance of war,
And the same chance restores him!

(Pointing to Sigismond.—The Count sinks.)

    Countess. Ha, he swoons!

    Count. Th'avenging arm is o'er me! Oh my daughter,
I feel a strange and anxious flutt'ring here,
That bids me trust his words—thou know'st the tale.

Be generous *(To Sigismond.)*—Be just *(To the Countess.)*—
And may the pow'rs
Seal with my blood a long and blessed union,
Firm as your virtues—tender as your love!
(Joins their hands.)
Mysterious providence! ev'n on the spot,
Where sweetly sleeps the victim of my crimes,
Thy justice wakes to fearful *retribution!*
Oh, for a sleep like hers! Life fades apace!
No tears—No sighs *(To them.)* Young, lovely, innocent;
May parting nature find no crime to expiate!
But bear *you* pure to heav'n! Mine was the guilt;
And be it buried with me!
— One short pray'r!
(He appears to pray inwardly; then sinks into their arms and expires.)

Semi-Chorus of Peasants and Soldiers.

"The banner drop—invert the spear,
"Grace the fallen warrior's bier;
"His palm is gain'd—His race is run:
"And victory and hearts are one!
(Full chorus.)
"Yet raise the song to victory!"
(They group their banners, and incline them over the body of the Count as the curtain falls.)

THE END.

Notes

1. The published text of the play does not indicate scene breaks by number. It simply provides the description of the new scene.

The Old Oak Chest

or,

The Smuggler's Sons and the Robber's Daughter

A Melodramatic Romance

In 2 Acts

by

Jane Scott

G.Jones del.

S.Springsguth Juns.sculp.

The interior of the Sans Pareil Theatre showing a performance of *The Old Oak Chest.*

The Old Oak Chest

What we know of Jane M[arie] Scott, the young author of *The Old Oak Chest*, is intimately connected with the Adelphi Theatre, the home of melodrama in nineteenth-century London. The story begins with John Scott, an entrepreneur who made a fortune from the invention of a washing blue[1] and, in 1806, built a theatre in the Strand called the *Sans Pareil* for his stage-struck daughter (Bergan 10). A pupil of Thomas Arne, the noted English composer, Jane Scott was blessed with a "good deal of native talent" (Forman 419) if not good looks. *The Theatrical Observer* for December 1844 recalled:

> Miss Scott developed strong symptoms of [the] dramatic disease and though her extraordinary talent was undoubted by her father and friends, it was delicately hinted that the greedy public not only expected intrinsic merit for their money, but also that it must be hallowed o'er with beauty to secure the first impression. Now Miss Scott, in addition to some natural defects had the smallpox and rickets unfavorably, but as genius comes in all disguises, she really had great talent, both as an actress and a writer. (qtd. Nelson 1806–1807: 3)

After three years of performing at the back of her father's warehouse in the Strand, Jane succeeded in creating a large enough audience to convince her father to invest £10,000 in the building of a new theatre and acquire a license to perform minor entertainment.

Whether her father entirely believed in her abilities, looked upon the scheme as a good investment, or simply wanted to keep an eye on his singing actress daughter[2] (playbills indicate that he functioned as general manager of the theatre), Jane took advantage of the situation to write and perform in a number of popular entertainments until 1819 when she became a bride[3] and her father sold the theatre for £25,000 to Jones and Rodwell who refurbished it and renamed it the Adelphi. Once married, Jane Scott left the London theatre world for, after the 1819–1820 season, her name ceases to appear in playbills.

From the existing evidence, there is no doubt that Jane Scott had an especially active career between 1806 and her retirement in 1819. She began quite simply with a one-woman show (not unlike Charles Dibdin's entertainments at his own theatre, the Sans Souci,[4] or Charles Matthews's "At Homes") entitled *Miss Scott's Entertainments* where she performed songs, monologues, dances, and poetry. Also included in the evening's fare were optical illusions described as "something in the manner of the Phantasmagorias" (Nelson 1806–1807: 4) or ghostly apparitions that capitalized on the public's fascination with things Gothic.

Until the season of 1808–1809, the company of performers at the Sans Pareil consisted of Miss Scott and young amateurs. Coincidental with the burning of Covent Garden in September 1808, several adult actors from that theatre joined the Sans Pareil company, as did performers from Drury Lane when that theatre burned in February 1809. Given a new dimension of credibility because of the presence of professional actors, the Sans Pareil was enlarged the following season. As both she and her audience grew in confidence, she began to produce burlettas and melodramas, usually written to showcase her talents. While her pantomimes were usually her most popular achievements—*The Necromancer; or, The Golden Key,* for example played throughout the 1809–1810 season—her burlettas and farces proved successful enough for critics to claim that "at least two pieces by the prolific Jane Scott played every evening this year" (Nelson 1809–1810: 3). Most importantly, the season marked the author's first attempt at Gothic melodrama, *Mary, the Maid of the Inn; or, The Bough of Yew,* a verse play borrowed from Southey's poem.[5] Revived until 1816, Miss Scott's play exchanges surprise revelations for Southey's grim dénouement and thus appeals to the popular taste for complicated plots and happy endings. Catering to her audience, the author produced a number of spectacular melodramas including *Asgard, the Daemon Hunter; or, Le Diable a La Chasse* (17 November 1812), *The Forest Knight; or, The King Bewildered* (4 February 1813), *The Inscription; or, The Indian Hunters* (28 February 1814), *The Old Oak Chest; or, The Smuggler's Sons and the Robber's Daughter* (5 February 1816), *Stratagems; or, The Lost Treasure* (4 March 1816), *Camilla the Amazon; or, The Mountain Robber* (6 February 1817), *The Lord of the Castle* (13 October 1817), and *Fairy Legends; or, The Moon-light Night* (7 December 1818).

As a perusal of her titles might suggest (see Appendix C for a complete list of her plays and entertainments), Miss Scott's dramatic output embraced Gothic and exotic settings, including Turkish, Spanish, French, and Irish locales; and the objects of her subtle satire included the navy, lawyers, smugglers, and members of fashionable society. While her dramatic writing exhibited a great degree of variety, her activities as a performer did not. Miss Scott, who evidently did not appear at any other London theatre during her entire career,[6] played the soubrette role in virtually every bill. Her most popular characterizations were Sydney Nelson, a transvestite role in the melodrama, *The Inscription,* Laurette, in the burletta, *The Conjuror,* Maria Whackham, in the farce, *Whackham and Whindham,* and Roda in the melodrama, *The Old Oak Chest.* The January 1816 issue of *The Theatrical Inquisitor and Monthly Mirror* added to Miss Scott's collection of favorable reviews:

> Miss Scott deserves much praise for her exertions to render this house deservedly attractive. The interior is really fitted up in a respectable manner, and several new pieces of merit have been produced, particularly one called *The Inscription*, apparently founded on Murphy's "Desert Island." (8: 77)

Jane Scott's only published play,[7] *The Old Oak Chest; or, The Smuggler's Sons and the Robber's Daughter,* premiered as "an entire new Original Drama; or, Melo-Romantick Burletta" with "Entire New and Romantick Scenery, Dresses and Properties" at the Sans Pareil Theatre on 5 February 1816. The music, "intirely [sic] New" was composed by Mr. Jolly, the house composer; scenery designed by Mess. Scruton and Assistants; costumes and properties provided by Mr. Godbee, Miss Marchbanks and Assistants; and stage combats were under the direction of Mr. Frederick Hartland who originated the role of Count Lanfranco. The cast also included:

Almanza: James Villiers
Henrico: Joshua B. Fisher
Bruto Shabrico: Mr. Austin
Rodolph: Mr. Bishop
Nicholas de Lasso: Mr. Weston
Tinoco de Lasso: Mr. Stebbing
Paulo de Lasso: J. Jones
Rufus: Mr. Daly
Garcius: Mr. Powell
Brianthus: R. H. Widdicomb
Otho: C. Simpson
Albano: Mr. Addison
Stilleto: Richard Flexmore
Carrillo: Mr. Shaw
Wilhelm: Miss Le Brun

Florian: Miss Stebbing

Principal Hunters: Edwin Yarnold, Messrs. Powell, Sherriff, Swinney, Widdicomb, Bemetzrieder, Smith, Garcia

Principal Smugglers: Messrs. Hamblin, Baldwin, Rogers, Smith, Sherriff, Swinney, Green, Bennett

Adriana: Mrs. Riley

Roda: Miss Jane M. Scott

The play was performed 96 times at the Sans Pareil Theatre between 1816 and 1819 to generally good reviews. *The British Stage* is unyielding in its praise for the theatre, the author, and the play:

> This house is worthy of its name, since of all the theatres in London, it can claim the praise of being the prettiest. The decorations and embellishments are all new and in the best taste, and the *tout ensemble* must be allowed by every one to be uncommonly pleasing. The pieces produced, and the actors in those pieces, are of similar merit; and from the crowded audiences which are nightly assembled, we imagine the proprietor must be rapidly accumulating a fortune. His success is almost wholly to be attributed to the versatile talents of his daughter, who, both as an author and an actress, evinces remarkable ability. In the burletta of the "Old Oak Chest," which is now performing here, she is seen to great advantage in each of these capacities. (1: 31–32)

In February 1818, *The British Stage* singles out the talents of Mr. Stebbing, the actor who originated the comic role of Tinoco de Lasso:

> The Burletta of "The Old Oak Chest," and the Pantomime of "The Necromancer, or the Golden Key," have also been revived, and continue as gratifying to the audience as they are creditable to the author . . . . Amongst other performances of merit Mr. Stebbing deserves to be particularized; his personation of the fiery cook in the "Old Oak Chest" is irresistably comic. (2: 38–39)

The melodrama was published in 1828 after it was revived in a slightly altered form at the Royal Coburg Theatre on 19 July 1824. For this performance, the cast was as follows:

Count Lanfranco: Mr. Montgomery

Almanza: Mr. Gale

Henrico: Mr. Rowbotham

Nicholas de Lasso: Mr. Porteus

Paulo de Lasso: Mr. E. L. Lewis

Tinoco de Lasso: Mr. Davidge

Rodolph: Mr. Mortimer
Bruto Shabrico: Mr. Elsgood
Rufus: Mr. J. George
Conrade: Mr. Saunders
Memmo: Mr. Smith
Pietro: Mr. H. George
Adriana: Miss Waison
Roda: Mrs. Davidge
Florian: Master Meyers

A brief review in the August 1824 edition of *The Drama; or, Theatrical Pocket Magazine* reflected the continued popularity of the play:

> That clever melo-drama, "The Old Oak Chest, or the Smuggler's Sons and the Robber's Daughter," written by Miss Scott, and originally performed at the Adelphi Theatre, has been played as an after-piece during the past month, and its attraction has been such, as to crowd the theatre up to the very ceiling at half price. The acting . . . was most excellent, the scenery new, and admirably executed. (300)

As late as 1842, the play was revived (in its published format) at Sadler's Wells with the following cast:

Count Lanfranco: C. J. Smith
Almanza: Mr. Lambe
Henrico: C. J. Bird
Nicholas de Lasso: Mr. Williams
Paulo de Lasso: Mr. Aldridge
Tinoco de Lasso: John Herbert
Rodolph: Mr. Dry
Bruto Shabrico: Charles Fenton
Adriana: Miss Richardson
Roda: Mrs. Richard Barnett   (Mullin 276)

Between 1830 and 1860 scenes and characters from the Royal Coburg revival of *The Old Oak Chest* were published in three toy theatre editions by Lloyd, West, and Park.[8] Not only was the play enormously popular on the stage, but also in the home where Victorian children could entertain themselves with cut-out characters from the play much in the same way that modern children employ "action figures" from popular films or television shows. A lasting impression was left on at least one youth, the author Robert Louis Stevenson, who, writing in the April 1884 issue of *The Magazine of Art*, recalls the play by name:

And *The Old Oak Chest*, what was it all about? that postscript (1st dress), that prodigious number of banditti, that old woman with the broom, and the magnificent kitchen in the third act (was it in the third?)—they are all fallen in a deliquium, swim faintly in my brain, and mix and vanish. (*The Victoria* 6)

Given the number of revivals and toy theatre editions, *The Old Oak Chest* was clearly the most popular melodrama written by a woman before 1843, and among the most successful melodramas produced by an author of either sex in the early nineteenth century.

The edition of the melodrama printed here is based on the original Sans Pareil performance text—Larpent Manuscript 1908 at the Henry E. Huntington Library—with spelling and punctuation regularized. The significantly different published version of the play is reprinted in Appendix A.

Notes

1. W. Courthope Forman reports that Scott called the material "Old True Blue," the formula for which he had discovered on a journey through the Black Forest. The theatre opened on 27 November 1806 with "an entertainment consisting of songs, imitations, and recitations, an entertainment the whole of which was written and delivered by clever Miss Scott. A display of fireworks wound up this variety performance" (419). Nelson argues that the theatre opened on 17 November (1806–1807: 4).

2. Nelson notes that the first season was not a critical success and that attendance was not very good (1806–1807: 5).

3. In the November 1819 issue of *The British Stage*, the editor Kenrick reported that "like her theatre, we believe, Miss Scott is about to *change her name*. We have also heard the name of the happy swain, but shall want for the consummation of his bliss before we announce it to the public" (4: 35). The emphasis on the change of name refers to the recent sale of the theatre to Jones and Rodwell reported in the October 1819 edition of *The British Stage*. In his "Seasonal Summary for 1819–1820" at the newly christened Adelphi Theatre, Nelson records Miss Scott's final performance as Laura Pickle in the anonymous *Apollo Daggerwood* from 6 December 1819 through 28 February 1820 (82). It is unlikely that the Miss J. Scott appearing at the Adelphi in 1830 (as Erixene in *The Grecian Daughter*) is the author Jane Scott.

4. Charles Dibdin would appear at the Sans Pareil for one performance of his solo entertainment *Rent Day* on 19 September 1808.

5. An earlier piece called *The Red Robber; or, The Statue in the Wood* is called a melodrama in its 1812 revival. When first produced in 1808, however, it was termed a "spectacle" entertainment.

6. The Playbill for Thursday 29 October 1818 notes: "As several Ladies of the Name of Scott have appeared, and are still Performing in the various Theatres of the Metropolis—the Proprietor of the Sans Pareil, to prevent Mistakes, begs leave to inform the Public, Miss Scott, of the Sans Pareil, has never yet appeared in any other Theatre, neither is she at all related to Persons of that Name now performing Elsewhere!"

7. The February 1819 edition of *The British Stage* suggests that other of the author's plays were to have been printed: "Miss Scott writes as rapidly, and continues as beauteous as ever. She has produced several classical novelties this season, of which we have not the titles at our fingers' ends, but doubt not they will be faithfully chronicled by future editors of the 'Biographia Dramatica.' We have heard that her works are about to be printed, in twenty volumes 4to" (3: 51).

8. I am indebted to Barry Clarke of Pollock's Toy Museum in London for copies of the toy theatre editions.

The Old Oak Chest

Dramatis Personae

Lanfranco, *Governor of Andalusia*
Almanza, *a proscribed general*
Henrico, *a courier from the King*
Bruto Shabrico, *captain of banditti*
Rodolph, *a robber disguised as a woodsman*
Nicholas de Lasso, *captain of a band of smugglers*
Tinoco and Paulo, *his sons*
Wilhelm, *a goatherd boy*
Florian, *Almanza's son*
Adriana, *wife to Almanza*
Roda, *Rodolph's daughter*
Hunters, robbers, smugglers, &c.&c.

Act I. Scene I.

A Romantic view in the Spanish Mountains

Towards the back of the stage, two high craggy cliffs opposite each other with a chasm between, through which is seen the distant country and the evening sun gradually sinking. From cliff to cliff, a plank laid practicable by way of a temporary bridge. At bottom of the cliff, O.P., a cavern, the mouth of it concealed by foliage. On the side P.S. a descent from the cliff. a bush or small clump of underwood. On an elevated Pole near it, is a board on which is written "The Government offers Twenty Thousand Ducats For the apprehension of the Proscribed General Almanza. "[1]

Several Hunters are discovered resting after the toils of the chase. Some are seated in groups taking refreshment; others standing in conversation, resting on hunting spears. They come forward and sing, one after the other 'til all join.

The twilight of eve bids us home,
The twilight of eve bids us home.

And the tinkling bell
Of the monks in the dell
Seems to say to the jovial board, come boys come,
Seems to say to the jovial board, come.

1st Hunter. Well comrades the chase is done for the day. What say you to setting your faces homeward?

2nd Hunter. Truly, Signor, my face is homely enough already. If tarrying in these mountains would mend it, I would e'en stay her 'till Shrove tide.

3rd Hunter. If any man but thyself had said as much?

2nd Hunter. I would have referred him for punishment to Donna Bella my wife—and if his Face were not soon worse than mine I am no Christian.

1st Hunter. I say my Friends the wolf had the speed of us?

3rd Hunter. So has the sun. Let us be jogging.

2nd Hunter. By the mass, the lightness of the enemy's heels stood his friend. He scouted us finely.

1st Hunter. Better the enemy scout us then we scout from the enemy.

All. True. True.

3rd Hunter. By my faith, I was in hope we should have started. The proscribed General Almanza[2] —that would have been a rare day's sport for us

1st Hunter. But unluckily, sport to us would have been death to him. Therefore rejoice—we did not start the proscribed general Almanza

3rd Hunter. What! do you wish for the escape of a Traitor? I would hunt him down if I could, tho' I gain'd not a Ducat by it.

1st Hunter. And time past, thou wouldst have cried him up tho' thy gain had been a broken sconce. Go to! thou art a changeling.

3rd Hunter. Pardie! I thought better of him then he merited. Has he not lost Spain a gallant army, and surrendered one of the finest towns in Portugal? For which reason he is proscribed, his castle and rich effects destroyed, and a reward of twenty thousand ducats offered for his apprehension—that he may be dealt with according to his deeds.

1st Hunter. That he had lost some men and given up the two you name is true. But it does not follow he's a traitor. Many is the glorious victory he has gain'd for Spain. Pass on. Do ninety nine good turns and leave the hundredth undone—and all thy laurels fade, brave soldier!

3rd Hunter. Nay, I tell you, he's a traitor—an arch traitor—or I'm no sportsman.

1st Hunter. Oh, then he stands acquitted at once! If he's no more a traitor then thou art a sportsman.

3rd Hunter. Away. Thou dost ever come over me thus with this jest.

1st Hunter. Nay. If it were so easy to come over thee in jest as it is in earnest, thou wouldst not be worth breaking a jibe on. But come, Signor Jeromo, do you sound the horn as a signal to any stragglers of our party of our return.

Hunter. Not I, by the mass! Sound it thyself. I have neither right or title to the horn.

1st Hunter. How so?

Hunter. I have nothing to do with the horns. I am as yet unmarried.

1st Hunter. Therefore as the cap don't fit, thou are the fittest to sound it. Come, come, my boy, give it breath and let us pass on.

2nd Hunter. Aye, aye. Let us begone. I would not for the wealth of the king's treasury linger here after nightfall. They say Father Beelzebub holds his court every night in the ruins of our governor's old castle in the wood on the other side of the brown mountains. And, as I don't want to be introduced to his infernal majesty before my time, I shall move a speedy march from the vicinity.

1st Hunter. Which move I second. But money bags there had better stay. He may stand a chance of catching the proscribed general.

3rd Hunter. Not I. I am too liberal minded not to share the honor of such an adventure with my friends. So away!

First chorus repeated and exit hunters.

Wilhelm *(speaking off)*. Let me pass on, Signor. I am used to the steep and shall soon join the cavaliers. *(Enter Wilhelm.)* Good lack! How unlucky—they have pass'd on—and not a foot fall do I hear. They have not gone perchance the road I thought for. *(Don Henrico enters.)* Ah, Signor, are you there? Look well to your steps. The path is none of the best, I promise you. It is seldom trod except by wolves and marmots[3] in the night, and goats and sheep in the day.

Henrico. Well, boy saw you the passers by?

Boy. No Signor, worse the luck for you. They were hunters returning from the chase. They would have guided you with safety to the town.

Henrico. Yet still I'm fortunate in having thee, my little man.

Boy. Me? Guide you to the town? Sancta Maria, not me! And have to return by myself over the mountains at dark. Oh, I crave your pardon, Signor, not for my cap full of money.

Henrico. Then, out upon thee for a little coward!

Boy. Nay! Wilhelm is no coward. There's not a goatherd boy in all these mountains dare climb such crags as I, nor do I fear banditti for they would never harm poor little Wilhelm.

Henrico. What is it then you dread, boy?

Boy. I fear the troubled spirits of the dead that nightly o'er the mountains roam. Oh! you must be very great stranger indeed not to have heard the stories with which all Spain abounds.

Henrico. Why, Spain abounds with so many, lad, that I must needs ask which?

Boy. Yes. But it's a very long and very frightful story. I never tell it when the sun is going down, but go back with me to our hut, and you shall hear it all. Then your horse will be nicely rested, and you and me and grandfather can all ride upon him into town tomorrow. Oh! it will be a pure holiday for Wilhelm.

Henrico. Nay, urchin. I must to town tonight. Direct me in my way and leave me.

Boy. Well then, come up this crag and from the height you'll see the spire of the great church right before you. Then keep along yon path, close by the brow of the hill, and should the night come on, the lights in the town will guide you there in no time. Good-bye, stranger.

Henrico. Stay, boy, stay. Since we must part, hold here this cap. There's money for thee *(gives money)*. How now! art thou not satisfied?

Boy. You said there was money for me—but here is nothing but a parcel of yellow pictures.

Henrico. Go to, you simpleton. They are the king's. They will pass for money all through Spain.

The Old Oak Chest 133

Boy. I thank your goodness, but I would rather have some copper money. I know what I can buy with that. I would call in my way homeward at the vineyard of Paulo de Lasso and get a flask of his best vintage for grandfather which would make him so good humoured and so merry—I warrant he would let me ride to town with him tomorrow when he takes home your horse. I pray you, take back these fine pieces and give me some money I do know.

Henrico.[4] But unluckily, boy, I am as little acquainted with thy money as thou art with mine. However, Wilhelm, rest content. One of these pieces will procure the wished for flask. And shouldst thou come to town tomorrow, I promise to fill thy pockets to thy heart's content.

Boy. Oh! Bless your excellency. I shall give it all to grandfather. Then he will new thatch our hut against the winter and we shall be able to lodge loss travelers who cannot[5] pay for shelter in the town. Good night, kind generous stranger. Keep close to the brow of the Hill. Don't go into the forest in the night. Keep as far as ever you can from Count Lanfranco's, the Governor's frightful castle.

Henrico. Count Lanfranco's Castle?

Boy. Oh! I'd forgot—that's the Story.

Henrico. Does the governor reside there?

Boy. Oh, no, no! Nobody lives there but ghosts and hobgoblins, so don't you go near it—[6] though an angel itself should ask you. Farewell. Farewell. *(Going up the ascent.)* Yet stay, traveler, stay. Here is a little relic. It was given me by Father St. Lawrence, the mountain hermit. I never thought of it before. No harm can come to him who wears it.

Henrico. But will not Wilhelm want it?

Boy. No, no. I shall get home by daylight, for I am so happy I shall run all the way. Good-bye, Signor, good-bye. I shall see you tomorrow.

Henrico. Nay, nay, boy, keep thy relic. *(Henrico following him, Wilhelm swiftly crosses the plank.)*

Boy. Hold! Hold! do not follow. It will not bear the weight. The plank is broke in the middle. Good-bye, good-bye. *(Exit boy.)*

Henrico. Little rogue. I suspect the broken plank[7] is but an arch device to stay my steps from following. Well, well. I will not pain thy grateful[8] heart by forcing back thy gift. What a day of perplexities has this proved! Anxious to deliver the precious packet with which I am charged to Lanfranco, the governor of the town, my extreme impatience has nearly defeated the purpose I was so desirous of accomplishing. Bewildered, and astray in these vast trackless mountains, [9] my self worn out with fatigue, and my horse knocked up! Had it not been for the goatherd hut, chance, or my protecting saint placed in my way, I must have passed the night beneath some impending cliff, which, while I was buried in sleep perchance, might have buried me. However the right road[10] once more in view, I shall cast weariness behind me and, considering every moment pregnant with [11]death and danger to my beloved friend and brother-in-arms, Almanza,[12] I shall press forwards in spite of all the old goatherd and his grandson's threatened horrors from ghosts, hobgoblins and banditti. Have I got the right path now? Yes. Yes. close round by the brow of the mountain. Good. Good. 'Tis it, I remember.

Symphony. Adriana[13] *cautiously removes the boughs that cover and conceal the mouth of the cave at the foot of the cliff and comes forward looking about with anxiety and trepidation.*

Adriana. All is silent; not a breath disturbs the leaves. Even the trembling aspen is at rest. The silver grey of twilight dims each surrounding object, and gathering mists obscure the distance. Sure, my dear Almanza now may safely venture forth. It will be quite dark ere we can gain the town. Oh, what a day of horrors have we pass'd. Oft have the feet of our pursuers pressed the sod before the cave in which we lay concealed. Nay more—one paused, and plucked a blossom from the branch that shaded our retreat. Oh! how my heart died within me. But then he tuned a merry madrigal and hurried on, and Adriana breathed again—blessed forever. Blessed be the providence that screen'd us from his sight. *(Calls.)* Almanza my persecuted Love *(Sees written board.)* Ah that proscription, that dreadful proscription! That death knell to my hopes. Doubtless the whole country is placarded with the same reward, and we are at the mercy of each avaricious hind. Almanza must not see it! 'Twould urge him into madness. I must persuade him it is yet too light for him to venture forth without disguise. Yes, still must the blind, the aged mendicant conceal the brave Almanza Still as his daughter must his wretched wife bear the rude taunt of every boisterous clown.

Almanza *(Speaks from the Cave).* Adriana, is all safe, my love?

Adriana. Hush. I hear a rustling in the bushes. Ah! again, in pity to my fears, remain one little moment yet. Almanza, away. Hush. Hush. *(They retire into cavern.)*

Tinoco *(Peeps from under a bush and gets up yawning).* Well thanks to the saints, I have had an excellent nap. No thanks to the hunting party. Satan and his Imps fly away with them, I say! Here have they kept me[14] with a scorching sun on my back,[15]boiling beneath a bramble bush all day, which, every time I moved, thought proper to scratch an acquaintance with me. Zounds! I have as many marks of affection on my sweet person as a henpeck'd husband. Yet tho' I was incessantly goaded to leave my covert, there I sat like an owl in an ivy bush, watching my prey, which I expect e'er long will rally forth from yonder Cave. Well, Tinoco, honest Tinoco, thou art allow'd to be the adroitest lad at cheating the excise in all Iberia. Now if thou cannot but smuggle the prize thou hast in view into our grand depot in the mountains it will prove the richest cargo of contraband thou ever convey'd safely into port. *(A guitar sounds off.)* By the toe of his holiness here comes that saint's nightingale, my brother, Paulo, as sure as there's a windfall! That chap props in open mouth'd to catch it. However, I'll take care to make noise enough to keep my birds in their nest till he's gone. I am resolved master Paulo shall not go halves in this freight. *(He withdraws.)*

(Enter Paulo). Air

> Sweet violet of the pathless hill
> Whose modest beauties shrink from view,
> Sweet violet of the silvery rill
> My lyre I tune to love and you.
> For her who has my heart is mild,
> The tenant of a leafy glade,
> A floweret, lovely, lone, and wild,
> My gentle, blooming forest maid.
>
> Like thee, her days were pass'd unseen,
> Till Cupid, ranging through the grove,
> Delighted with her beauteous mien,
> First led me to my pensive love.
> And now I bless the happy hour
> When first I sought the leafy glade,
> And now the lone, the lovely flower

My gentle, blooming forest maid.

(Going.)

Tinoco. Hulloo, brother of mine. Whither on the wing? Come to a rest, my little crochet will you?

Paulo. What, Tinoco? Rough and rare Tinoco?

Tinoco. Thou art improved in music, faith my boy. You never stop'd in better time. But how goes it my little bird organ?

Paulo. Cheerly. Cheerly.

Tinoco. Where strole you at this late hour of eve? Came you here to meet thy gentle brother?

Paulo. No truly, I came here to meet my gentle Roda. She has been to town today, and I would fain see her through the forest to her father's cottage.

Tinoco. Found you the piece of primrose silk I left the other night in the hollow of the mulberry Tree as a present for thy intended bride? Methinks 'twill make a famous wedding garment

Paulo. But far too costly for a peasant's wife. I would rather see my Roda in the snowy garb of pure unsullied virtue; her only decorations, innocence and love.

Tinoco. That was just the wedding dress of mother Eve. But I question if the girl don't find it too cold a habit for these mountains. Talking of cold puts me in mind of the keg of brandy I dropt over your garden pails at crack of morn. Lit you in it?

Paulo. Aye, and by the same token, guess'd thou wert in the neighborhood.

Tinoco. I thought so by the by the dearness of thy piper. Brandy's a special medicine for the voice that makes mine so strong, it is a physic I'm in the habit of taking.

Paulo. I wish thou wouldst not run such risks to leave it once I have already through thy bounty stores of brandy. And I never use it.

Tinoco. Then out upon thee for a cur, a dog o'the manges! If I lived on the bleak brow of a mountain as thou dost, friend, where many a weary muleteer and careworn traveler sinks benumbed with cold, I should blush to say I had stores of Brandy and I never used it!

Paulo. Give me thy hand, Tinoco. Thou art the same generous fellow thou ever wert. But when I reflect each drop is gain'd at the hazard of a brother's—perhaps a Father's Life—I shudder at the very sight of it.

Tinoco. Ah, that's the way with all true dram drinkers. How be it? Trouble not thy self about thy worthy brother. You prefer the peaceful vocation of a vine dresser; I glory in the hair breadth 'scapes attached to smuggling. Good gain everyone to his calling.

Duet

Paulo.	Give me a cottage in a vale.
Tinoco.	Give me a Vessel in full sail
Paulo.	Give me a calm and tranquil soul.
Tinoco.	Give me a breeze and flowing bowl.
Paulo.	With a tink a ting ting, when at evening I stray
	And Philomel warbles—her dove —from the
spray	

Tinoco *(Producing a flask).*

With a tink, a ting ting, when the flocks are at rest,
This, this is the warbler that pleases me best.[16]

Well one more word, and I'm off. Wilt thou meet us at our headquarters in the forest tonight?

Paulo. The cavern near Lanfranco's castle?

Tinoco. Rightly divined.

Paulo. That I would joyfully could I persuade thee and thy father to return with me and leave the dangerous trade you follow.

Tinoco. Agreed. I like to make folks happy when I can, so to let you into a secret, if the efforts of[17] honest Tinoco prove successful this night, we meet the band to part forever.

Paulo. Heaven receive my thanks! What has brought about this blessed resolution?

Tinoco. The *blessed resolution* of the government hastens to give ten thousand ducats to the fortunate holder of the prize, General Almanza, whom the saints have inspired with resolution to break prison on purpose to afford thy worthy relatives an opportunity of complying with thy pious wishes.

Paulo. Perish the thought.

Tinoco. Zounds! does not that please you?

Paulo. Please me? Recollect yourself, Tinoco. Wouldst thou be such a monster of ingratitude to close the gates of a prison on him who set thy father free from one? Never! Never can it be erased from Paulo's memory.

Tinoco. Ah you were young and tender; your head was softer than mine so took the impression better.

Paulo. Say! Is Almanza in your Power?

Tinoco. No. But I trust he will e'er midnight. For this purpose have I toil'd like a horse ever since the burning of his castle at which, if I mistake not, thou wert present, and without offering the least assistance, ran away by the light of the flames as fast as thy legs would carry thee. Where was thy gratitude then, little Paulo?

Paulo. My deeds will speak for themselves.

Tinoco. So will mine, for I swore to exert every nerve, use every stratagem to secure the person of Almanza. Let me see—in the last twenty-four hours I have been a Jew, a juggler, a fat friar, and an old woman,[18] and shall at last trap him in my own proper person. However to silence your scruples, we will let you in for a share of the booty.

Paulo. Never! Rather would I beg, starve, bear the torture, lose liberty. Life itself I would resign to serve—to save him.

Tinoco. Well, well, we will settle that anon. Wilt thou meet us at the cave tonight, boy, for I must be gone.

Paulo. Meet? Aye! By my soul, in such a cause I would meet—

Tinoco. The Devil! I must help you out at a dead lift.

Paulo. Adieu till midnight. Hold! the password.

Tinoco. Almanza! *(They exit.)*

(Adriana comes from the cavern.)

Adriana. The voices have ceased: the prattlers bend their steps afar, and we may now pursue our way. Come forth, Almanza, no one's nigh. Give me thy hand and let thy Adriana guide thee. *(Almanza comes forward disguised as Blind Mendicant.)*

Almanza. Is it not yet dark, my love?

Adriana. No, though the clouds of night are gathering fast. I pray ye, keep the bandage o'er thine eyes. We are near the town and many folks abound. Be mindful, I entreat you, of your safety. *(Tinoco appears on the bridge.)* Hark what is that?

Almanza. Nought but the snowy beetle, buzzing on the wing of eve.

Adriana. Ah me! Everything alarms the persecuted wanderer!

Almanza. Persecuted! Basely persecuted! For what was it for, yielding many a crimson current from my veins to serve my country?

Adriana. Nay. Nay. Call not up such thoughts as these. They will unnerve thee.

Almanza. Yet, for one failure—one only failure—the fault of chance, of circumstance—perhaps of treachery—have torrents of disgrace poured like a flood on my devoted head!

Adriana. Think of it no more. Conscious rectitude must bear thee up till we escape the malice of our foes.

Almanza. Escape! fly! Justify the calumny my enemies have raised—wretch that I used to cherish such a thought—sure madness ruled the hour when I fled prison. Well may I wear a bandage o'er my face to hide the crimson blush that shame has planted there. Yet, hold! it is not even now too late—e'en to my sovereign will I take my way, surrender up my person at his feet and from his throne find justice and protection. That resolution form'd, Almanza is himself again. *(Removes the Bandage from his eyes.)*

Adriana *(Pointing to the proscription).* Nay, then[19] behold the malice of thy foes: long e'er thou gainst the presence of thy king, thy enemies will shroud thee in the iron grasp of death and triumph in thy Ruin. Then supplicate for justice at the throne of heaven. For there the prayers of innocence were never offered yet in vain. On earth there is no throne for thee to fly to.

Almanza. And must Almanza, late the idol of the throng, skulk day by day in caves and darksome holes, as if he dared not meet the glorious light? For what has he to[20] live? His name disgraced, his treasures riffled, his Castle burnt! His child, his precious little one—first dear pledge of love—a victim to the flames!

Adriana. And Almanza I have endeavor'd to inspired thee with fortitude and thou hast ruin'd mine. My child, my Florian—I saw him on a burning beam, his little arms were stretch'd toward me—he scream'd for help. The monsters tore me shrieking from the flames. They would not let his mother save or perish with him.

Almanza. Forgive me, sainted sufferer. Oh! Oh, forgive me. Misery has born so hard upon my heart that I'd forgot my sorrows were thy own.

Adriana. For thee alone, Almanza have I dosed my words with cheerfulness. The bandage o'er thine eyes absorbed thy tears, but mine have flow'd unceasing. Yet, still my heart is raised with gratitude to heaven that thou my best beloved was spared me. But go, surrender to thine enemies. Thy Adriana, then, will find a peaceful refuge in the grass for she cannot survive thee.

Almanza. Thou darling of my aching heart, pardon my wayward murmurings. Thou—Thou art all to me—for thee alone I'll try to live, till time shall blunt the keenness of my woes.

Adriana. Well then, let me place the bandage on thy brow. Our caution now must be extreme. Remember, love, the town we have to pass is governed by our mortal foe, Lanfranco. Come, come. 'Twere time that we were on our way. Lean on thy Adriana, cheerily, Almanza, cheerily.[21] *(Tinoco sings off.)*

Adriana. Ah someone is advancing. Were it not best we should retreat?

Almanza. Fear not. The rudeness of the song speaks it some muleteer or market peasant, returning from the town.

Adriana. Fear! Oh, it were sin for us to doubt. Hither most wonderful has been our preservation.

Almanza. Most wonderful indeed! A poor illiterate smuggler first beguiled my guards and freed me from my prison. Scarce had he left me when a traveling Jew came by, by whom I instantly was furnish'd with the garb I wear.

Adriana. And then the good old friar who found thy Adriana in the convent where she had hid her wretched head. Oh, with what care and kindness did he lead me to thy irons.

Almanza. Nay, too, the hospitable hostess of last night who deck'd my Adriana in the neat disguise she wears.

Adriana. And told us of the cave where we escaped of fell pursuers. Surely the hand of Providence directed all, or we had never thus passed safely on, amid so many dangers! *(Enter Tinoco singing.)* Pray you, Signor.

Tinoco. Pray? ah! marry that do I on saints' days, though I have not damaged my doublet with kneeling.

Almanza. Wilt set an old man and his daughter on the road for Valencia?

Tinoco. Nay, if setting be thy fancy, I would recommend the green sword here. The road is full of flints. You will perhaps set there, you may depend.

Adriana. You trifle with us, friend. For pity's sake, direct us.

Almanza. We are weary travelers and would fain seek a lodging in the town.

Tinoco. Then I should feign were I to tell thee thou wouldst find one.

Almanza. How is—

Tinoco. The town is full of troops. Lanfranco himself is there. Each avenue is guarded by a band most faithful to his interest.

Almanza. What means all this?

Tinoco. Lanfranco has a suspicion the proscribed Almanza will attempt to pass the town tonight.

Almanza. Needs there such precaution for a man alone, defenseless, and unarmed?

Tinoco. Go to. You know but little of him or thou would not propound that question. The whole nation, if they dared, would rise in his defense. No one doubts his innocence seeing Lanfranco, his known inveterate enemy, has been his chief accuser. However, the governor will take care there shall be no rescue. So if Almanza pops his head into the town tonight, I'll wager mine, they pop it off tomorrow.

(Adriana faints)

Almanza. My Adriana, my wife, my child. She faints from weariness and want. In yonder crag I know is water. Fetch it, stranger, in mercy, fetch it.

Tinoco. Pshaw[22] Signor, water won't fetch her. Give her a drop out of this flask—special good brandy.

Almanza. No. No. Water would be better.

Tinoco. Mix'd with brandy. That is what I always take when I feel myself faint.

Almanza. Ah! she revives.

Adriana. Which way are we to turn? Whither can we go? Ah, cruel thoughtless man, you have removed the bandage.

Tinoco. What—is the signor trouble with a weakness of the eyes?[23] Mores the pity I am near-sighted now for all. I stand so near you. I swear, I cannot see one single feature of thy father's face.

Adriana. Then we are safe!

Tinoco. Safe! I don't think anyone's safe at night in these mountains. It is Old Nick's own wolf walk, my little lamb. However if you will share my humble resting place, I can promise you a safe a certain shelter till the morning. Come. Come. You shall be heartily welcome. Follow me.

Adriana *(to Almanza).* Oh do not, do not trust him; mark you those dreadful weapons in his belt?

Tinoco. What! do you hesitate? Why you could not be more alarmed were you the proscribed general. Alarm'd? Hold. Hold. I do him wrong. Almanza never felt Alarm. Were he here, thus would he argue—I may be better off by following this honest lad's advice. If I go further, I shall perchance fare worse. Then I should say to him, just as I now say to you—Brave Almanza, there are hearts in Spain so devoted to thy service, they would yield their best blood to protect you. Follow me, general, I should say, and I will lead you to a place in which you may deride pursuit and bid defiance to your enemies. Then I should present him with a brace of pistols, just in this manner. Beware they are double barrel'd and loaded with ball. And I should conclude by saying—Almanza, if I betray you or fail in ought I have promised, shoot me through the head at once and rid the world of a deceitful villain!

Almanza. Enough! Lead on. *(They exit.)*

Scene II.

A Dark Forest. Enter Paulo and Roda

Roda. I pray you Paulo, what detained my father at thy vineyard yester eve so late? Was it thee lad, or the produce of thy vintage?

Paulo. Both had claims on his good company. We were discoursing.

Roda. On what, pray, ran thy conversation?

Paulo. Love and marriage. Shall I repeat it, Roda?

Roda. Nay; as for love, I've heard that theme full long. What said he now of marriage?

Paulo. Thus he said: when a young man like me had a neat snug cottage to shelter a wife and means to support her in it, he was either a fool or a knave not to seek one.

Roda. Well, how liked you his advice?

Paulo. So well that I set out thus: I've resolved to marry the first female I should meet an' she'd have me.

Roda. The first female you should meet with Paulo?

Paulo. Yes! But had I seen one coming that I liked not, I should have turned me to the right or left, or e'en gone home again and not sprang forward as I did to meet my Roda. Come. Come you needs must guess my meaning: your father names an early day, and Roda sure will not refuse me.

Roda. You know my heart so well that should I say thee nay, still thou wouldst not believe me. Yet e'en I yield a full consent, I have something to impart that hangs with trembling fear upon my life. But thou shalt never have to say that Roda has deceived thee.

Paulo. [24]And I have something to impart which much I fear to name, so we're on equal terms. Yet, mark! Should what I now confess cause me the misery of losing thee, swear the secret never shall escape thy lips.

Roda. I claim an equal oath. The life of one far dearer than my own hangs on it.

Paulo. Roda, you suppose me the son of the deceased peasant, Luko, but, alas, my father is a smuggler, a most notorious smuggler.

Roda. And you take my father for a simple honest woodman but, alas, he is a robber, a most notorious robber.

Paulo. Heavens and earth, a robber?

Roda. Oh, Paulo, do not cast me from you. I am no partner in my parent's crimes. Brought up by my dear grandmother far o'er the mountains, I scarcely knew my father till her death. 'Twas then he brought me to the forest hut—nor could I mourn the day. for but for that, I'd never known my Paulo!

Paulo. Come to my heart, dear girl. Alike in sorrow as in joy, henceforth our fates are one. We own the task to lure our parents from the path of guilt and lead them back to innocence and peace. Yes! we will weary heaven with our prayers till it shall smile on our endeavours. But come. Do not weep thus bitterly.

Roda. Oh! they are tears of joy—to think that you will pray with me for my poor, poor Father! And I am happy, quite happy, to think the smuggler's son still loves the robber's daughter. But now 'tis time that we should part. The gathering clouds forebode a coming storm. 'Twould make me wretched to hear the tempest rage before I thought thee sheltered.

Paulo. A few steps further?

Roda. Nay if you love me, hasten home. You know I cannot ask you to the cottage. My father is so harsh and stern, he would not bid thee welcome.

Paulo. Well! Well! I know he likes not company. One parting kiss and I will leave thee. Good night.

Roda. May heaven guard thy slumbers. *(Exit both.)*

(Enter Shabrico and Rufus.)

Shabrico. Who was it pass'd us even now? This is the second time he's cross'd me near this spot. Methought we had wove a coil of horrors so completely round this forest that none had dared to enter it at nightfall.

Rufus. 'Tis the peasant, Paulo, a harmless hind who courts the woodman Rodolpho's daughter.

Shabrico. And why, pray, is that daughter hither brought? I will have no women here except what's wanted for the castle. Those we silence when we list.

Rufus. She'll not stay long. Rodolpho means to marry her and send her hence directly.

Shabrico. She never shall go hence.

Rufus. Pshaw! Captain, she is a mere child.

Shabrico. I will not trust to that. Children oft put wise men off their guard. Her doom is fix'd. She must to the castle and, as her person pleases me, she lives or dies.

Rufus. As you like, Captain. But, mark ,it must be done unknown to Rodolph. For tho' a very savage to all nature else, he loves his daughter as the apple of his eye. And terrible would be his wrath should he suspect us.

Shabrico. Right. Is he acquainted with the subterranean way passing from his cottage to the castle?

Rufus. No—it has not been opened since he joined us.

Shabrico. Thro' that the first time Rodolph is abroad, the girl shall be conveyed. See to it quickly.

Rufus. I hope it will prove a pleasanter job then the last of the kind you gave. I shall never forget the worst: I had to drag that screaming kicking old hobgoblin, our cook, to the castle. She—who Lanani knock'd o'the head for spoiling his porridge.

Shabrico. True. True. But now to business. Guess you the hour?

Rufus. As yet it is not late.

Shabrico. The gloomy livery of the sky looks more like storm than coming night. Lanfranco will not venture here till darkness veils the earth.

Rufus. 'Tis night with these woods long e'er the sunbeams leave the mountains.

Shabrico. Are the disguises ready?

Rufus. Hard by.

Shabrico. Good. Tonight we must not move with peculiar caution. Many hunters are abroad. Some may straggle through the forest.

Rufus. Well, what then? Curse on the disguises, say I! Fitter for monks than hardy souls like us. The dagger point should silence all for me.

Shabrico. Fool! Idiot! Would not the cry of blood so frequent spilt call forth the cognizance of government? Would it not guide them to the safe retreat where we have lurked for years, feasting on human misery, sanction'd by Count Lanfranco whose sole inheritance it is— and while we aid his daring acts of villainy and let him share our plunder, safely may we live, rob whom we list, murder whom we list. Now, should we wrap the world in flames, so he found benefit, he'd laugh amidst the universal pain. Footsteps draw nigh. Give the signal. *(Rufus whistles)*

Lanfranco *(speaks off)*. Shabrico

Shabrico.[25] Here.

Lanfranco. Anyone else?

Shabrico. Yes. Rufus.

Lanfranco. All's right. *(He enters.)*

Shabrico. You are late, my Lord.

Lanfranco. I was detain'd in town by information most unwelcome.

Shabrico. How so?

Lanfranco. Almanza's friends have gain'd a pardon for him which every moment is expected to arrive. But, mark. Almanza, or the pardon, must be mine tonight. They shall not wrest him from my vengeance. He still is lurking in the mountains—it is impossible for him to 'scape me.

Shabrico. It is most wonderful he has escaped so long. Repeatedly we've had him in our very grasp, yet still he has eluded us.

Rufus. It strikes me that audacious smuggler, Nicolas de Lasso, favors him

Shabrico. I have thought so too. The night Almanza's castle was in flames, many of his band were there.

Rufus. And when we sought for plunder, all worth taking had been carried off.

Shabrico. Except his wife and her I seized—when lo! a hand of iron fell me to the earth and cried—thus! thus! I pay my debt of gratitude to brave Almanza!

Lanfranco. And have you suffer'd this and yet not seized on them?

Shabrico. You know not whom we have to deal with. They are men of desperate means and manners like ourselves. Lawless and bold, we hold intercourse but fear each other. They have a secret place of meeting in the forest, as yet unknown to us. But we will ferret out the General if he burrows with the smugglers. Trust me, Count, this night we will about it.

Lanfranco. Hark! hear you not distant voices? Let us disperse and at the castle settle our proceedings.

Shabrico. Hold! We must not separate without disguise. This eve, my Lord, you shall be one of us and play a forest spectre. Rufus, bring forth our midnight habits.

Rufus. They are here.

(They put on terrific dresses)

Shabrico. Oh, now you may pass on in safety. The very bats will fly us. You take the lamp. We know each path way to the castle blindfold. *(Exit all.)*

(Enter Henrico)

Henrico.[26] Sure, fortune will never be weary of persecuting me. After wandering all day over sun-scorch'd mountains, hungry and astray, here am I bewildered a second time in the endless mazes of an impervious wood, where every step I take seems to plunge me into further difficulties. Much as I was warned too—to avoid this forest. Yet lost in thought I hurried on till I had lost myself. Which way shall I turn? How extricate myself from these dark wilds? Must I remain here till the Morning? Hark! Did I not here a distant growl of thunder? There wants nothing but a storm to add to my felicity. Ah, surely yonder gleams a light. Some cottage in the wood. No. Now it moves: it advances nearer, now it again retreats. Some husbandman returning from the labours of the day. Halloo! It stops—and now again 'tis lost amongst the trees. May it not be some wandering vapour of the night engendered over marshy grounds, luring the ill-fated traveler to a sure destruction. It must be so. I'll not pursue it. Ah, now I see it plainer then before and, through an opening in the wood, perceive a figure wrap'd in black which bears a lamp—doubtless a holy man on a midnight visit to some sick or dying wretch. Holloo! Reverend Father, stay thy speed. In charity, assist a lost, a care-worn[27] traveler to regain his way. Holloo! Holloo!   *(Exit.)*

Scene III.

A Cottage or Woodman's Hut. Quite dark. Storm occasionally

(Enter Lanfranco, still disguised with Lamp.)

Lanfranco. Still am I pursued—closely pursued. Eternal curses light upon the wretch who dares to track my footsteps. 'Tis none of the Castle Gang; they would have answered when I gave the Signal—nor can it be a Peasant hind, for he had fled affrighted from the Path. But this intruder presses boldly on and calls on me, aloud, to wait his coming. I dare not enter Rodolph's cottage, lest he should haunt me there. He is here again.[28]
(Enter Henrico.)

Henrico. At length I have overtaken you. Ah—
(Lanfranco blows out the lamp and exits.)

Henrico. Gone, vanished, melted into Air. I am the victim of some magical delusion—sure 'twas no human form I follow'd. Nay! Nay! I must not now give way to thoughts of so much horror, for they would quite unman me. My weary limbs refuse to bear me further on. Here must I pass the night. Yet, Heavenly powers, should Almanza's pardon come too late—[29] No! No! impossible. The eye of morning shall see me on my way. Daylight will prove a safe and certain guide.[30] Beneath this spreading tree I'll wait its coming—*(Reclines beneath a tree.)*

Roda *(sings in the cottage).*   And the Lilies still grow in the valley.

Henrico. Ah, a female voice. Some cottage must be near.

Roda *(within).* Listen I go—aye,[31] indeed it is not long.
(Henrico, guided by the voice, finds the door of the cottage.)

Henrico.[32] Chance has at length befriended me. *(Henrico knocks at Cottage door. Voices cease Henrico Listens.)*

Henrico. All is still. Not a breath do I hear within the cottage. They fear to open the door at this lone hour. Perhaps some solitary female—*(Knocks again.)* Open the door, for pity sake, I do beseech you, give shelter to a luckless stranger benighted in this vast dreary forest.

(Rodolph speaking within the cottage.[33]*)*

Rodolph. From whence come you?—

Henrico. From the mountains.

Rodolph. You are of the hunting party I surmise.[34]

Henrico *(aside).* Yes, faith, I have been hunting all day long.

Rodolph. Are your companions near?—

Henrico *(aside).* Why that Question? No. Many miles behind.

Rodolph. Stop a moment till I unbar the door.

(The door opens slowly. A ruffian looking man in the habit of a woodman peeps cautiously out as if to convince himself Henrico is alone.)

Rodolph. Roda, bring hither a light—

(Enter Roda from the cottage with a lamp. Rodolph takes it and examines Henrico earnestly.)

Rodolph. I believe you may come in—'tis well you found this cottage. It is the only one in the forest. It seems inclined to be a stormy night.—Come in. Come in.

Henrico. You shall not, Friend, repent your courtesy.

Rodolph. That's as it may happen—

(They enter the cottage.)

Roda. What evil star could send this stranger here to plunge my wretched father deeper still in guilt? His habit speaks him rich—and Rodolph viewed him with a greedy eye. Ye Saints above, should danger threaten, inspire the humble Roda with the means—the fortitude—to save him.

Rodolph *(from the door).* Roda, what do you in the forest at this late hour? Come in and make the door fast, wench.

(She Exits into cottage. Enter Lanfranco.)

Lanfranco. So my pursuer has obtained a lodging for the night in Rodolph's hut. He might well have rested in a lion's den!—*(Peeps through door cracks.)* What do I see? Henrico de Rosalva, the messenger who bears Almanza's pardon from the court. Was ever bird snared more completely! Ha! Ha! Ha! I'll wait till he's at rest, then, with my daggers point, obtain his papers. Yes! the hated pardon shall be my reward. Rosalva's death!

Scene IV.

Inside of Rodolph's cottage, a wretched looking hovel. A lighted fire on the hearth. Henrico, with looks of fear and suspicion on the listen at the door. Roda preparing supper. On one side the room, an antique chest.

Henrico. I tell you, I heard someone at the door.

Rodolph. I tell you I know better. No one inhabits this forest but myself.

Henrico. Say was you abroad tonight?

Rodolph. Ha! ha! Me abroad? *(Puts his hand on a weapon concealed in his bosom.)*

Roda *(suddenly catching his arm, with apprehension)*. Father—will you tell the Stranger Supper's ready—

Rodolph. Tell him yourself. Me out in the forest?—No. Never after night fall

Roda. Will it please you to partake, sir, of our homely fare?

Rodolph. Homely fare? The Cavalier cannot expect dainties in a woodman's cottage—

Henrico. Nor would I wish it. Hunger makes the homeliest fare a banquet!

Rodolph. Roda, sing the ballad you was chanting when the Cavalier first knocked. She wants no supper. She's seen her sweetheart tonight. That's enough for her!

Ballad (Roda)[35]

The lilies quite content remained
And blessed the peaceful valley.

(At the end of ballad, a noise without. They all start from their seats.)

Roda. What noise is that without?

Henrico. Why do you tremble? What have you to fear?

Rodolph. Nothing but her own shadow—

(Rodolph walks agitated towards the door and listens.)

Roda. If it should be—

Henrico. Who?—What?—

Rodolph. Who? What? Why a bat. They see the light in the cottage and flit against the windows. The foolish wench is scared out of her senses at a bat.

Roda. In very truth, I am, father, for the bats of our forest seldom fasten on a traveler. But he bleeds to death—[36]

Henrico. If that's the case, I e'en must guard against such visitors should anything approach me in the night. I have firearms—and I shall use them.

Roda. [37]Cavalier you needs must want repose. Shall I show you to your bed?—

Rodolph. No—give me the lamp. *(Takes it from her.)* Now, Cavalier, to bed. It is nought but straw, but it is the best I have to offer—so excuse is needless.

(Symphony. Rodolph ascends a ladder into a kind of loft, turns and holds a light for Henrico, who follows with trepidation and suspicion.)[38]

Roda. I trust my presence in the cottage will protect the traveler. Nay! Of himself, methinks, my Father ne'er would harm him. But should any of his dreadful companions call, I would not answer for the stranger's life. Pray Heaven the storm may keep them far away. *(The lid of oak chest opens and a robber with lamp peeps out)* The Saints protect me, how it lightens! I wish my father would descend—for I am weary and would fain seek rest. It is very strange. I am always dreaming of the old oak chest. Last night methought I had raised the lid, when from a yawning gulf beneath, a skeleton arose and cried "Avenge my murder!"—Oh dear! I do not like to be alone at this dreer hour. The oaken chest is just at hand, and I could almost fancy I heard a noise within it. Father, I wish you would descend—*(She turns and sees the robber coming from the chest.)* Save me, a spectre—just so! I saw it in my dream.—Save me. Father, save me.

Robber. Another word, and I plunge this dagger in your heart.

Roda. Oh!

Robber. Silence! Descend. *(They descend together through the chest.)*

(Rodolph comes from above.)

Rodolph. [39]Silly wench what means these cries?—The storm is passing fast away. Here, take the light to bed.—She is not here. My heart misgives me. The door is fast—all must be safe within.— Another shriek! Where art thou child?—Speak. Answer me.—*(Exit.)*

(Lanfranco enters, getting in from the window.)

Lanfranco.—At length, I have gain'd admittance. Rodolph either would or could not hear me. I much suspect that cur's fidelity. No matter to him alone I will not trust. I have iron souls without that will effect my purpose. Here comes the woodman—

(Enter Rodolph.)

Rodolph. In vain I search. She's nowhere to be found. Ah! Lanfranco here? The mystery stands confessed.

Lanfranco. How now, Woodman Rodolph?

Rodolph. How now, Governor Lanfranco?

Lanfranco. Methinks you come full slowly to my bidding.

Rodolph. Methinks you come too quick without a bidding.

Lanfranco. Hound! Art thou mad?

Rodolph. Yes, and beware, lest I should bite. I'll not be trifled with. Restore my child, or yield thy life.

Lanfranco. What means the ruffian?

Rodolph. Evasion is in vain I know you have forced her hence. Restore her—restore her innocent, or I will bring thee and thy fell associates to the scaffold.

Lanfranco. Villain!—outlaw!—assassin!—Dare you threaten? Meet thy death from me.

(Tinoco de Rosalva, during the combat, descends.)

Tinoco. [40]Hold! Murderer, stop thy hand. What do I see? Lanfranco, Governor of Valencia!

Lanfranco. Yes, 'tis the Governor Lanfranco. Ill-stared stripling, thou hadst better ne'er been born then lived to see this day

Rodolph. Fly youth whilst yet 'tis in thy power. *(Lanfranco sounds a bugle.)* Ah! 'tis too late.

Henrico. We are lost!—We are lost!—The cottage is surrounded.

Rodolph. Then hope is at an end and thus I meet my fate.

(Attacks the Governor. Several armed ruffians enter. Henrico and Rodolph are seized.)

Lanfranco. Away with them to the dungeon of the castle. There let them die in torture. Away![41]

Notes

1. The name "DeLamora" is crossed out in the Manuscript.
2. The name "DeLamora" is again crossed out in the Manuscript here and in the reference to Almanza below.
3. The word "goats" is crossed out in the Manuscript.
4. "I thank you good [sir]" is crossed out.
5. The fragment "get a lod[ging]" is crossed out.
6. "But do not go near it" is crossed out.
7. The word "now" is crossed out.
8. The word "little" is begun but crossed out.
9. The word "has" is crossed out
10. The word "Path" is crossed out
11. The following extended passage is deleted: "death and danger [the interlinear word 'disarray' is crossed out] to my beloved brother-in-arms Laxangano, I shall pass on—fearless of danger, [interlinear passage, 'spite of all the threatened dangers from ghosts, hobgoblins, and banditti' is deleted] guided by perseverance, supported by friendship and affection."
12. The name "Laxangano" is again deleted.
13. The name "Antoinette" is replaced by "Adriana" here and in the first speech below.
14. The word "boiling" is deleted here for use later in the line.
15. The phrase "all day" is deleted.
16. The published edition adds a verse not in the Manuscript copy.
17. The adjective "thy" is crossed out.
18. A phrase at the top of the page, "whilst thou be such a Monster after" is crossed out.
19. A word evidently in error, "behohold"(sic) is deleted.
20. The word "life" is crossed out.
21. The rest of the page has the following dialogue written upside down crossed out:

   [Tinoco]: Brother, you prefer the peaceful life of a vine dresser. Good. I glory in the hair-breath scapes and dangers attached to the vocation of a smuggler. Good again. Every one to his calling. One word and I am off. Wilt thou meet me and thy father at our headquarters in the forest tonight?

   Paulo. The cavern under Count Lanfranco's castle?

   Tino. Rightly divined.
22. The word "stranger" is deleted.
23. The word "sight" is replaced.
24. The word "Then" is crossed out.
25. The Manuscript omits Shabrico's name. Instead it reads "Answer—Here."
26. No speaker is given in the Manuscript.
27. The original reads "way worn" but the "way" is scratched out.
28. The following is crossed out: "Ah Perhaps 'tis one [replacing the word "some"] of Nicholas de Lasso Band—if so I'll hunt them from the Earth—For tho' I torment all the World I will not be tormented—"
29. The remainder of the line, "on Earth I never shall know Peace or Happiness again" is deleted.
30. The word "Here" is crossed out.
31. The word "Father" is scratched out.
32. No speaker is given in the Manuscript.
33. The word "Forest" is crossed out.
34. What appears to be the beginning of the word "suppose" is crossed out.

35. No text is given for this song in the Manuscript. The printed text gives no direction for a song here, but does provide the couplet in the earlier scene.

36. Rodolph's line, "Silence thy incessant—" is crossed out.

37. The speaker is altered from Rodolph to Roda. What would have been the beginning of Rodolph's line, "Come Roda—light the Cavelier. *(To Roda.)* Give me the lamp. Come" is deleted.

38. The direction, "Roda kneels—and scene closes" is crossed out.

39. Again no speaker is named in the Manuscript, here and for Rodolph's line, on his entrance below..

40. No speaker is given.

41. While this situation corresponds to the end of the first act in the published version of the play, the Manuscript does not indicate an act break at this point.

Act II. Scene I.

Smugglers' Cavern. Nicolas DeLasso at the head of the table surrounded by his band. On one side in front—Almanza and Adriana, on the other side, Paulo and Tinoco.[1]

Chorus. Round, round, round—round pass the juice of the vine.[2]
    Round, round, round—round pass the Liquor divine.
    Since trouble's a bubble—then let the word be:
    Success to old Neptune's brave Sons of the Sea—

    A Fig for dull care—with his scythe and grey hair,
    His maxims, the Bottle shan't save.
    Then drink Lads with Glee—the Trade that is free,
    And the Smuggler that's Daring and brave;
        Toast Success to the Free Trade.
    Round, round, round &c. *(Chorus repeated.)*

(After chorus, Nicolas addressing Almanza.)
    Nicolas. Cheerly, my guests,—give reins to merriment nor look upon us with a doubtful eye.
    Adriana. Alas, my Father's blind!
    Tinoco. Humph!—None so blind as those who wont see.
    Nicolas. Silence Tinoco. Again I say fear not: we are no midnight plunderers.
    Tinoco. Stick to truth, good father, we are midnight plunders. Ergo, of the Revenue. What then?—The Revenue plunders the Subject, and the Subject plunders one another.—All the world lives more or less by Plunder.
    Paulo. Now stay thy clapper if thou canst; be more respectful to thy father's theme.
    Nicolas. It ever is his guise—thus to be prating like a magpie.
    Tinoco. Why thou wouldst not have calves head at table without tongue, father o'mine.
    Nicolas. No—but there's a want of brains on this occasion, son o'mine!
    Tinoco. There! I'm dished—
    Nicolas. Go to for a merry knave. Our habitation, stranger, it is rude and niggard, our manners rough and blunt. But here you will find

sincerity and that's a treasure seldom met with in the smooth and smiling surface of a treacherous world. But come, Tinoco. Look to our guests. Play not the careless host. Fill up his cup with Muscadine—here's choice Lucina for the damsel. You, Paulo, boast the Minstrel Art. Display at once thy skill—and with some martial story charm the listening ear.

Song (Paulo)[3]

The Soldier hears the glorious rattle,
Of War's dire summons to the Battle.
He bids adieu to beauty's charms
And cries "to arms, to arms, to arms!"

Yet when the Martial strife is o'er,
Love Fires his bosom as before;
At Cupid's shrine he soon lays down
His sword, his spear, and laurel crown.

But should he die in Glorious Battle,
Amidst dire war's destructive rattle,
His Country's tears enshrine the brave
And laurels deck the hero's grave.

Nicolas. Well sung, my boy.
Tinoco. Yes, it will be well if it alarm not our neighbours in Lanfranco's castle.
Almanza. Lanfranco's Castle
Adriana. Are we then so near?—
Nicolas. Yes by my troth. Our cavern west extends beneath it. But we have nought to fear from those who make it their retreat. They are on their nightly prowl, I ween. Come. Come. Fill to the brim and let our toast be echoed standing—
Smugglers. Name it.
Nicolas. Our password—
Smugglers. Almanza.
Almanza *(aside).* What does this mean—
(Gong sounds.)
Nicolas. Ah, that sound speaks danger nigh.

(Enter Smuggler.)

Smuggler. Captain and comrades be on your guard—

Smugglers. How now?

Smuggler. The entrance to our cavern in the forest is discovered. A band of ruffians keep the way. E'en now they are debating which shall search the cave.

Nicolas. Know you the object of their search, my friend?

Smuggler. To secure the person of the proscribed Almanza.

Nicolas. The person of Almanza is secure!

Almanza. Caught in the toil betrayed. Nay! Then away disguise. *(Throws off his mendicant's dress and appears as a Spanish Nobleman.)* Behold the man they seek, fearless and firm, resolved to die as he has lived—unconquered, but in Death. Why do you stand at bay? The sword was my inheritance. By the sword I lived, and by the sword I'll die. Come on, I say! The man who takes me gains ten thousand ducats! But I will have ten thousand drops of blood first. Come on, I say! Come on—

Adriana. First thro' thy Adriana's bleeding bosom must they strike at thine. Hear the pleading of a wretched wife: save him, in mercy.

Nicolas. Which is the man of de Lasso's Band that would betray the brave Almanza for twice ten thousand ducats? Who is the man that would not fight, or die in his defense?

Smugglers. All. All.

Almanza. Generous fellows, to what do I owe this zeal?

Nicolas. Gratitude. Remember you, the hardy smugglers thy father doomed to death when Judge of Aragon?

Almanza. Well?

Nicolas. Remember that, in pity to his wretched family, you bribed his jailer, open'd his dungeon door, and gave him life and liberty?

Almanza. 'Tis fix'd in my memory.

Nicolas. And mine—

Tinoco. Engraven on my heart—

Paulo. Entwined with my existence.

Nicolas. From that eventful hour, my self, my sons—nay more! the Band I lead, have been devoted to thy service. Thy castle, when in flames, we rifled but to secure the treasures for thy use.

Adriana. Ah me! Our richest treasure on that fatal night was lost for ever.

Paulo. Hope for the best, dear Lady. Hear a tale of joy.

Tinoco. Stay thy clapper, if thou canst. Be more respectful to thy father's theme.

Nicolas. On board a vessel which now waits thy coming on a Lake hard by, thy riches are conveyed. The closing night shall see thee safe on board. Myself and these trustworthy fellows, selected from the band as staunch and true, will pilot you afar and leave you in what ever clime best suits thy wishes.

(Enter Man.)

Man. Captain the intruders press upon us—

Nicolas. Mislead them for a few minutes. Gain us time. *(Going in the secret escape.)* Lady, you must not dare the dangers of the day. Be at hand, boys, heave up your stone—open the store house. *(They open a concealed way.)* You and the General shall remain conceal'd till the intruders have departed. Descend.

Adriana. Heaven and Earth! Not into that dark abyss—

Nicolas. Hesitation is destruction. Ascend with my men, or descend with me. My life I pledge for thine.

Almanza. Lead on. Our fate is in thy keeping.

Nicolas. Paulo and you, my lads, to thy vessel. There wait our coming. You, Tinoco, must remain. Take yon old disguise. But mark: raise the stone and free us when the storm is pass'd.

Tinoco. Mark me if I don't. There. They are snug, as a toad in a hole. Bring out my bag with the disguises.

Paulo. To Leave you thus to face so many dangers—

Tinoco. Pshaw! I have face enough for anything. My gown! My gown! Zounds! This is my old woman's gown—I meant my hermit's gown.

Man. I've found it.

Tinoco. Help me in—no matter over all. Now, off, my lads, in a whiff. When you're all clear of the cavern, I give you a signal by a whistle. Why do you linger, Paulo?

Paulo. I tremble for you.

Tinoco. That's more than I do for my self. There's nothing on earth I fear.

Paulo. But an Exciseman!

Tinoco. Don't mention it. Away with you!—

Paulo. Well then, I'll leave you, for I've a treasure of Almanza to restore to him that he will prize beyond all thou hast saved for him.

Tinoco *(whistles).* Whew—what's that?

Paulo. Distraction! the escaped gone?

Tinoco. I forgot and gave the signal.

Paulo. What's to be done? The Enemy advances—

Tinoco. Step aside and think for thy self. I cannot now think for thee. But remember, if your question'd, I am Father Lorenzo, a mountain hermit.

Paulo. Good. I shall not forget. *(Exit.)*

(Enter Shabrico, Robbers, &c.)

Robber. By the light, we're right.

Shabrico. Nay by the light, we are wrong. This seems the habitation of some holy man. Behold him, even now, at his devotions.

Robber. Let us examine him. The cloak of sanctity hides many a knave.

Shabrico. True! We crave your blessing, Father.

Tinoco. The blessing of the power you serve Light on thee sons. *(Aside.)* And that's old Nick!—Come ye thus early to confession?

Shabrico. No, but we shall bring you to confession before we part. Old grey beard, who are you? What are you?

Tinoco. O the unrighteous sinners! not to know Father Lorenzo, the mountain hermit.

Shabrico. Well then, Father Lorenzo, answer truly or we'll broil you on a gridiron, like thy namesake. Who were those we heard conversing as we entered?

Tinoco. Bless thy ears. 'Twas my poor feeble voice reading an homily.

Shabrico. Nay we heard voices many.

Tinoco. Like enough. There's echoes all around.

Shabrico *(to men).* Search the interior of the cave. So you live alone?

Tinoco. Alone? Heaven forbid! I trust I am at all times surrounded by good spirits.

Shabrico. Give us proof, Father.

Tinoco. Proof?—The Spirits here are above proof, son—they float around invisible to sinful[4] eye.

Shabrico. Nay. Cease your canting. *(Enter Robbers with Paulo.)* Who' have you there?

Robber. A bird we have shot flying. Paulo the vinedresser, if I mistake not.

Shabrico. Right many a flask I have taken of his vintage. How came you here, Paulo?

Paulo. I came—I came—

Shabrico. Yes, we know you came—but for what?

Paulo. To solicit Father Lorenzo to unite me in the band of Holy Wedlock to Roda, the Woodman's daughter.

Tinoco *(aside).* My own brother at a lie!

Shabrico. Why were you not here when we entered?

Paulo. Seeing the good Father at his prayers, I retired to the interior of the cave to offer mine.

Shabrico. Then now you retire to the interior of the cave—

Robber. And pray till you're black in the face—

Shabrico. But never let a breath escape you of this meeting or mark, thy bride shall be a Mourning Bride. Conduct him out. *(Exit Paulo.)* Found you ought to justify suspicion besides the peasant, Paulo?

Robber. Nothing, Captain.

Shabrico. No outlet from the cavern overturned?

Robber. Not the smallest.

Shabrico. We may as well retire.

Tinoco. A good riddance say I—

Shabrico. Yet, I would swear amongst the sounds that drew us hither, I heard a woman s voice.

Robber. I thought so too.

Tinoco. A woman's voice? *(Aside.)* It was the Lady Adriana's.— A woman's voice.

Shabrico. Yes a woman's—

Robber. Out with the truth at once, or you shall frizzle—

Tinoco. Well, you did hear a woman tongue, but 'twas an ancient woman at confession.

Shabrico. Produce her and we are satisfied.

Tinoco. 'Twas poor Old Jugget, the peddler's wife of Astroga. She only step'd to yonder fire to make a little broth to comfort me.

Robber. There's an old hypocrite—can't do without an old woman to comfort him.

One of the Robbers that searched the Cavern. We saw her not as we passed by. Bid her hither.

Shabrico. Aye. Bid her hither.

Tinoco. I will, my worthy masters—she has crept into some mouse hole or other. But don't frighten her. She's a poor[5] timid creature. Jugget, step here. Why, Jugget—*(Exit calling.)*

Robbers *(mimicking).* Jugget, step here. Why Jugget—*(They laugh.)*

Shabrico. What say you, my lads?—Suppose we make old Jugget *jugg it* to the castle? We want a cook in place of her Zanani sent past to the other world before her time—

Robber. The thought is excellent. We are all weary of being lick spits.

2 Robber. Besides, 'twere a shame to return to the castle empty handed.

All. Right! Right! *(They call.)* Why, Jugget—I say, Jugget—*(Answered off— "Coming, noble Cavaliers, coming.")*[6]

Robber. Cooks oft—A brawny looking old Bedlam i' faith. Here she is.

(Enter Tinoco dressed as an old woman, hobbling with a stick.)

Shabrico. Come along, old Jugget. Put your best leg[7] foremost.

Tinoco. What's your pleasure with Jugget, worthy sirs? But don't flurry me for I am a poor weak old woman.

Shabrico. Father Lorenzo says you are a famous cook, Jugget.

Tinoco. Aye, by my troth, for Prince or peasant, from a beef steak to a whole ox.

Shabrico. The very woman that we want. Away with her to the castle.

Tinoco. Keep off, or I may chance to crack a knave's sconce.

Shabrico. At her, my boys. Don't be conquered by an old woman Stick to her.

Robber. Damn her, she sticks to us.

1 Robber. Here we have her.

2 Robber. Now we have got her.

3 Robber. Off with her.

(All Hurrah.)

(They exit hurrahing.)

Scene II.[8]

A gloomy dungeon in Lanfranco's Castle. Stage dark. Henrico De Rosalva enters in chains. He paces the stage with extreme agitation. His looks are pale and horror struck; he examines the walls but desists, hopeless of escaping.

Henrico. In vain, I pace my dungeon; in vain, examine the walls. No outlet offers. Hope itself expires. My guards I have tried to bribe but they remain inflexible. Accursed Lanfranco! Unhappy Henrico, thus to be treacherously cut off in the prime of manhood by dark assassins. And thou, too, lost, ill-stared Almanza, thy fate depends on mine. *(Heavy Chains fall as though a door was opening.)* Ah! they come.—The Bloodhounds come.—They warned me to prepare. Henrico, thy final hour is come. Then Heaven have mercy on earth. I hope for none.

(Enter 2 Assassins.)

Assassins. You know our errand

Henrico. I read at once my doom—

1 Assassin. We wish to act like Gentlemen choose your weapons: sword or pistol?

2 Assassin. Aye. Whichever you fancy most—take which you please and die contented.

Henrico. Can nothing move your flinty heart?

Both. Nothing!

1 Assassin. Had you not known Lanfranco you might have lived, but as it is you die.

Henrico. Not without a struggle—

2 Assassins. Oh, then a leaden pill must settle all.[9]

(Nicolas and Almanza rush in. Nicolas exclaims, true fires at the Assassin who falls.)

Adriana *(rushes in)*. Almanza, my husband.

Almanza. Fear not, my love, all's well.

Henrico. Almanza here? Astonishment!

Almanza. Henrico de Rosalva. *(Unchains him.)*

Adriana. This is no time for explanation. Let us fly these accursed walls.

Nicolas. Believe me, Lady, I knew not my storehouse was connected with these dungeons.

Henrico. Whatever is the mystery, it has saved my life.

(The Assassin thrown down is stealing off but is stopped by Nicolas.)

Nicolas. Hold, my friend, we must not part. We have settled your comrade, now we must settle you.

Assassin. Spare my life.

Nicolas. On one condition. Know you of any secret passage by which we may escape these vaults?

Assassin. I do—a subterranean one, leading through the cottage of Rhodolph the woodman.

Nicolas. Conduct us thither in safety and you are free. *(Man takes the torch and is going.)* Hold! we move together. *(Takes the chain, fastens one end to the arm of the man, the other to his own.)* Now proceed.

Scene III.

Ancient Hall.

(Enter Shabrico. Enter several Robbers, all speaking together.)

1 Robber. Captain, there's no enduring that old fury Jugget.

1 Robber. A swinging scourge we have brought for our own backs, I trow. She has nearly knocked my eyes out.

2 Robber. My nose is drove to the other side of my face.

3 Robber. I got a punch in the bread basket that made me cry "Twang ho!"

1 Robber. By your leave, Captain, we must cut her throat.

All. We must; we must; we must.

Shabrico. At your perils, rascals, touch her. A valiant old trot i'faith! Well suited for our service, if she dresses a dinner as well as she has dressed thee. I shall find no fault with her.

Robbers *(all).* Stand clear here she comes.

(Enter Tinoco as Dame Jugget.)

Shabrico. Well, Beldam, know you your vocation?

Tinoco. Yes and, please your greatness, I am to cook for you?

Robbers. Yes, you are to cook for us all.

Tinoco. I'll do my best endeavor *(Aside.)* to cook you all.

Shabrico. Yonder's a young doe to dress for supper. See that it pleases me.

Tinoco. I pray you, my Prince, where may be the wood to roast it by?

Robber. In the forest.

Tinoco. Him! Balaam could not speak so his Ass spoke for him!

Shabrico. Go to! a shrewd old Beldam.

Tinoco. So 'tis in the forest, Sir Jackanapes? Good. Then I can help myself *(Going.)*

Robber. No you don't.

Shabrico. Stay where you are. You never quit this castle, till the day of death.

Tinoco *(half aside).* That's a day you will not live to see, Goodman Bellswagger. You'll be dancing on nothing long before.

Robber. What's that you say?

Tinoco. What's that I say? Why you have spared me a dance for nothing, had I gone to the forest. Dame Jugget's no woodcutter.

Robber. O there's plenty ready cut.

Shabrico. Begone. See that the woman has whatever she needs. Begone, I say. Away!

(Exit 2 Robbers grumbling.)

Shabrico *(to Robber).* Where is Lanfranco?

Robber. In the west tower, examining the prisoner de Rosalva's papers.

Shabrico. I shall join him, bring thither a flagon of the best wine the Castle affords.

Robber. We have some excellent abroach. 'Twas borrowed from the cellar of a Priest.

Shabrico. Ha! ha! ha! Right. Let the church alone for good living. *(Exit laughing.)*

(Tinoco solo.)[10]

(Enter the 2 Robbers with an hand discovered with green boughs.)

Robber. There. There's fuel in plenty. Now let us have a little peace.

Tinoco. Peace—Peace quotha? Nobody's any peace where I am.

Robber. I believe you.

Tinoco. Fuel! Fuel call you this stuff?—Bark, green boughs and rubbish.

Robber *(aside).* Damn her, we've worked her now. Let her make a fire with it if she can.

Tinoco. Full of sap, like your own stupid heads. Take it away.

Robber. May we be roasted over green boughs if we do.

Tinoco *(flies at them with the spit; they fly from her).* You won't, rascals. *(They evade Tinoco, who encounters Rufus in his spectre's dress, bearing Roda. Tinoco in his turn retreats, terrified, roaring.)* Murder. Fire.

Rufus. How now! Has Tartarus broke loose ? *(Places Roda on the couch.)* What means this infernal yelling? Don't you know me, comrades? *(Takes off his mask.)*

Robber. Know you? We scarcely know ourselves.

Rufus. Who's this new comer? *(Pointing to Tinoco.)* She seems a rare one.

Robber. Oh, a tidbit of the Captain's own choosing shall let you know who she is anon.

Rufus. And here's another tidbit of the Captain's own choosing. Hark ye, old fiery faces, look to this damsel.

Tinoco. I can't for looking at you.

Robber. You had better keep at arms length.

Rufus. O belike you are swayed at my appearance, but heed it not. We travel in these masks at night to scare away intruders.

Tinoco. Thou needst not wear a mask for that purpose, Friend! Thy face is ugly enough to scare the Devil.

(Rufus flies at her with his dagger.)

Rufus. What do you mean by that, you old polecat?

Tinoco *(catches him by the throat; Rufus appears almost strangled).* How do you take advantage of my weakness, villain?

Rufus. Damn your weakness. It does not lie in your grip, I'll swear.

Robber. You've got it—I told you to keep at arms length.

Rufus. I shall never be able to sing again. By the Lord, she's cracked my windpipe.

Robber. Come. Come. For the present pass it by. When time shall serve. we'll pay her off.

Rufus. You speak my mind, hey! *(Makes a motion to cut her throat.)* Well I must to Shabrico and inform him of our prize. *(To Tinoco.)* Harridan! See to that wench. Mark she eats her supper with the Captain tonight.

Roda. The Saints protect me. No, no, no!—

Rufus. Zounds! girl. Don't look like a corpse. I said you was to eat your supper with the Captain. I did not say he was to eat you for supper. Good-bye, old iron fist.

Tinoco. Farewell , Master Scarebabe.

(Exit Rufus.)

Roda *(aside).* She seems a terrible old woman, but I must solicit her compassion, 'tis the only chance that's left. *(Roda advances and kneels.)* A poor unhappy girl, thus, humbly at thy feet, implores thy pity and protection. Perhaps you have a child.

Tinoco.[11]

Roda. Then you can feel for me, torn from my parent's arms, torn from my innocent and peaceful home, just too as I was going to be married.

Tinoco. Now I do feel for you.

Roda. Oh, Paulo, Paulo, what will become of Paulo?

Tinoco *(for the first time regarding her earnestly; aside).* No! yes! As I live, my brother's destined bride. Here's a pretty addition to the work already cut out. Oh dear! oh dear!

Roda. Ah! I see you mourn for me. Have mercy, O have mercy. Save me from the dreadful captain and his gang. Let them not separate us. Keep close to me all day, and sleep with me all night.

Tinoco. I have endured nothing but fiery trials ever since I entered this kitchen.

Roda. Oh! Paulo Paulo, why art thou not here to protect me?

Tinoco. Pshaw! Don't make such a fuss about Paulo. He could do nothing more for you than I can do. He protect you—a silken lackey?

Roda. How?

Tinoco. A twanger of catgut.

Roda. What?

Tinoco. A little, dirty, scrubby, sniveling knave!

Roda. 'Tis false. 'Tis false. And you are?

Tinoco *(pulling off his cap and hat).* His brother.

Roda. Tinoco! Let me look again. It is Tinoco. Then is Roda safe.

Tinoco. O yes! as safe as a lamb in the den of a wolf.

Roda. What is to be done?

(Tinoco observes the green boughs.)

Tinoco. By the mass, a thought strikes me. I think there is a chance for thy escape directly.

Roda. Name it. Name it!

Tinoco. Should I find means to get thee conveyed out of the castle, hast thou the courage to make thy way to the lake amongst the mountains, and, sounding on its banks this whistle, hither lead those that answer it?

Roda. I have! Put me to the trial.

Tinoco. Enough. Help me with yon doe. *(They place it on the couch.)* Give me your hat. *(He puts it on the doe.)* Now your outside garment.

Roda. There, there.

(He covers the doe with it and throws a cloak over the couch. The effect is that of Roda sleeping)

Robbers *(calling at a distance).* Jugget! Dame Jugget.

Tinoco. I can't come now—I'm dressing the doe.

Roda. They come this way. For Heaven's sake! What am I to do, Tinoco?

Tinoco. Creep in among these green boughs and lie as still as an owl in day light.

(Roda gets in amongst the boughs. Noise of singing without.)

Tinoco *(calls off).* Cease your villainous noise. Don't you see the child is sleeping? *(Enter Shabrico, several Robbers, and Rufus.)* I crave thy pardon, noble Captain, I knew not it was thee.

(Shabrico, rather merry seeing the doe, supposing it Roda.)

Shabrico. A beauty. By my soul, a sleeping beauty! *(Going towards her.)*

Tinoco *(stops him).* Nay, don't disturb the maiden. Terror and fatigue weigh down her eyelids. Let her rest awhile, I pray, and be ye witness all: I swear the female form on yonder couch shall grace my noble Master's table, nay his bed, if he think fit, before the coming light.

Shabrico. Your hand to that bargain. That bell rings sweetly Dame, be it as you say.—But how is it the fire sickly gleams upon the hearth? Where are the preparations for the revel?

Tinoco *(aside).* Now's my time or never.—Let yonder pile of reeking boughs answer at once thy question. The knaves have brought it here in pure despite to gain me thy displeasure. Think ye I can raise a fire with wet grass, dress venison by a waterfall? If thou art disappointed of thy dainty fare, lay not the blame to Jugget.

Shabrico. Away with it. Bear it hence to the forest. Bring dry and proper fuel; let not thy paltry enmities disturb my peace. *(They hesitate.)* Do as I command. I'll not be trifled with. Away with it to the forest.

(Exit 2 Robbers bearing off Roda amongst the boughs.)

Tinoco. Bravely said, most gallant Captain. Ha! Ha! Ha! I can't help laughing to think you have made the varlets do exactly what I wanted ha, ha, ha—*(Exit Tinoco.)*

Shabrico *(laughing).* And thou hast done exactly what I wanted— left me Master of the hall, and of yon sleeping Fair. They say stolen fruit is most delicious. I'll put the saying to the proof. *(Advances to the couch but is prevented by Lanfranco's rushing in.)*

Lanfranco. Be on thy guard, Shabrico, be on thy guard. Rodolph has broke his dungeon, and like a furious tiger, foaming mad with rage, ranges the castle calling for his child.

Rhodolph *(without).* Where are the fiends of darkness?

Lanfranco. Ah! He comes.

Rodolph *(enter).* Restore my child—restore her to her father. I'll raise the earth—nay hell itself to find her.

Shabrico. Behold her.

Rhodolph. My fears are realized, and I am cursed indeed. O Roda, my child, my Roda *(Going to her.)*

Shabrico. Approach her not, presumptuous minion. She's my Roda. Count Lanfranco's Roda. Any man's Roda, when I am weary of her.

Rhodolph. Never! Thou knowest not the heart of Rhodolph. She lived innocent, and innocent she dies. *(He suddenly rushes to the doe and stabs it several times.)* Now, Monster, for thy heated blood— *(Rodolph fights with Shabrico and Lanfranco. Others rush in. Enter Tinoco.)*

Tinoco. What! Ten to one? O then, have at you. *(Catches the poker—a general battle. Scene closes.)*

Scene IV.

Outside of Rhodolph's cottage.

(Enter Tinoco, running.)

Tinoco. O Curse these petticoats! I could have maintained a running fight, till I had limbed all the rascals, but these infernal trammels will not let me move. If ever I command an army, I'll put all my soldiers in petticoats. Then they must fight. I'll be burnt if they can run.—If Rhodolph had done as much execution with his spit as I did with my poker, the whole gang of rogues had been in Satan's Paradise by this time. *(Clashing of swords is heard.)* Ah! Here they come and here I go. *(Attempts to run.)* O these damned petticoats!—Some one coming this way. I am beset on both sides. *(Sees the cottage.)* Ah, a cottage, the door open. In I go, without a permit—
(Enter Paulo leading the Infant Florian.)

Paulo. A little farther, boy; and thy long suffering parents will embrace their darling. What! So very weary, Florian? Rest on the bark awhile, my blossom. *(Lays Florian on the bark.)* Here I can watch the cave, yet linger near my Roda—
(Loud clashing of swords, off.)

Paulo. What do I hear? Clashing swords as if in mortal strife. They come this way; Rhodolph's cottage must afford us shelter till the whirlwinds past *(Goes into cottage.)*
(Enter Rhodolph with a sword in each hand.)

Rhodolph. I have disarmed the villains—despair has made me more than man, yet still they press upon me. My own cottage is the first place they will search; the forest best will yield me a concealment. I cannot—will not—die till I have brought those Hellhounds to the scaffold. *(Exit Rhodolph.)*
(Enter Lanfranco, Shabrico, Rufus, and others.)

Lanfranco. They have taken refuge in the cottage. Force the door.

Rufus and **others.** 'Tis firmly barred within.

Shabrico. Round to the back of the cottage: there we shall find an easy entrance. *(Exit all.)*

Scene V.

Inside of Rhodolph's cottage. Paulo discovered with Florian

Paulo. Surely the voice was dread. Lanfranco's Almanza's mortal foe. If so, this infant's lost. Rhodolph, Roda, where art thou love? Help me to conceal this hapless innocent. *(Runs upstairs with it.)*
(The chest opens. Tinoco peeps out, but shuts the chest again, on hearing the return of Paulo. Paulo descends again with the child.)

Paulo. Horror and confusion! The cottage is deserted. I hear the ruffians breaking in. Where shall I hide the child? Ah, yon chest— *(Opens it. Tinoco looks out.)*

Tinoco. Is occupied already, my good brother.

Paulo. Tinoco!

Tinoco. Stay thy surprise.—What is thy purpose here?

Paulo. To save this child, Almanza's child.

Tinoco. What! Florian?

(A crash without.)

Paulo. Ah, that crash—they come. The murderers come. Hast thou not one idea, Tinoco?

Tinoco. No, by the Lord! They're all scared away. O Providence, Providence, help us this once, tho' thou shouldst forsake us ever more. *(The cottage clock calls cuckoo.)* There's a friend in need. Thank ye, Mr. Cuckoo, for the kind. Stow him in the clock case.

Paulo *(opens the case puts in the child)*. There—there, my darling. Speak not a word till Paulo calls thee.

Tinoco. I shall have a respect for a cuckoo as long as I live, even tho' I should marry.

Paulo. Down. Down. *(Tinoco shuts himself into the chest.)*[12]
(Enter Lanfranco, Shabrico, Rufus, and others.)

Shabrico. Ah! Paulo here again? Say, where is Rodolph?

Paulo. That's more than I can tell.

Shabrico. Or more than thou wilt tell.

Lanfranco. We know he has concealed him in the cottage.

Shabrico. Fire it,—then he must come forth or perish in the flames.
(Lanfranco takes a torch to fire the gallery.)

Paulo *(seizes him)*. Barbarian!—stay thy hand.

(Shabrico, hurls Paulo from Lanfranco.)

Lanfranco. Who shall prevent me now?*(Tinoco jumps out of the chest, extinguishes the torch.)* Tinoco.

Rufus. What! Tinoco de Lasso, the Smuggler's son?

Paulo. Yes, and Paulo DeLasso, the Smugglers son.

Lanfranco. Let them die.

(They are seized. Chest opens—Nicholas de Lasso rises from it.)

Nicholas. Not while their father's able to defend them.

(Almanza, Henrico, Adriana follow from the chest.)

Lanfranco. Without there, treachery.—Without, I say,—this horn breathes death to thee, abhorred Almanza. *(Sounds a horn.)*

(A loud whistle from without. Cottage door bursts open. Enter Rhodolph, Roda, smugglers men)

Tinoco. Huzzah—we're safe. Our own signal.

Nicolas. And that breathes death to thee, *(Aside.)* accursed Lanfranco.

Lanfranco. My Friends whoe'er you are, obey the orders of your King. Seize yonder traitor, seize Almanza.

Henrico *(holding up a paper).* Behold the Sovereign's pardon for Almanza.

Rhodolph. And now seize yonder traitor; behold in me his condemnation, a witness of his correspondence with the enemy—which led to the defeat for which Almanza suffered.

Lanfranco. Ah, say you. *(Attempts to stab himself.)*

Tinoco *(prevents him).* Hold, that won't do. Give me leave, I pray, to bind his Countship to yon post. I should glory to see this proud pillar of the state propping a cottage. I say, Shabrico, Dame Jugget's an excellent cook. If they will allow me to fire the place, I'll Devil you both in no time.

Almanza. Forbear, my friend. Let Victory wear the robe of Mercy. The Law shall punish them. Restored to Honour, Wealth, and Fame. no wish remains, but that de Lasso and his sons, should share my happy fortune.

Tinoco. Then I should thank you, General, to get me a snug place in the excise. And I think my friend, Rhodolph, here will make an excellent Police Officer; two honest fellows together.

Almanza. But what says Nicolas?

Nicolas. My fate's connected with the band I lead.

Almanza. Then lead them still—but let it be to Glory. Their Country will, with open arms, receive them.

Smugglers *(all).* We wish no better.

Almanza. Be it as you say. And mark—the treasure thou hast saved for me shall be dispersed amongst your families—as earnest of the future.

Tinoco. What, all? O that I had known this, what a family I'd had.

Almanza. Yes all.

Paulo. But one, and that's a treasure hid within this cottage.

Almanza and Adriana. Name it

Paulo. Florian.

(The child opens the clock case and exclaims.)

Florian. Here I am, Paulo. Mamma, Mamma!

Almanza. My child!

Adriana. My Florian!

(He flies to his parents' arms.)

Almanza. We now are blessed indeed!

(They Kneel. Curtain Falls.)

Notes

1. This scene is called "Scene the 5th" in the Larpent Manuscript. It corresponds to the first scene of Act II in the printed text of the play.
2. In the manuscript, the lyrics to this chorus are written on the page following the end of the scene under the heading "Chorus of Smugglers omitted at beginning of scene."
3. The words for this song follow the lyrics to the Smuggler's Song in the Manuscript under the heading, "song Paulo."
4. The word "human" is crossed out in the Manuscript.
5. The word "weak" is crossed out.
6. In the Manuscript, the continuation of the line is crossed out. It reads: "I'm a poor weak old woman. Don't hurry me."
7. The word "foot" is crossed out, as are the next three lines:
    Tinoco. Alack they're both sore.
    Shabrico *(aside).* So much the better. She won't be able to run from us.
    Robber. That won't be the fault of her legs.
8. The Manuscript identifies this scene as "Act 2, Scene the second."
9. From this point on, the Manuscript is in a different hand, and punctuation is regularized.
10. Following this stage direction, a full half-page of manuscript is left blank. Evidently Tinoco had a song or extensive business at this point.
11. Tinoco's reply is missing in the Manuscript. In the printed text, he replies, "Perhaps I have—twenty—aye, and a great many more."
12. The Manuscript reads "He shuts himself into the chest."

RAYMOND DE PERCY;

or,

The Tenant of the Tomb

A Romantic Melo Drama

by

Margaret Harvey

A holograph letter to Hugh Percy, Duke and Earl of Northumberland from Margaret Harvey, the author of *Raymond de Percy*. Reprinted by permission of The British Library, shelfmark 11642.e.17.

Raymond de Percy

The little that is known of Margaret Harvey, the melodramatist of Northumberland, is derived from her published works and correspondence. The date and place of her birth are unknown but, by 1814, when her epic poem, *The Lay of the Minstrel's Daughter*, was published, she was living at 12 Newgate Street in Newcastle, not far from her mother and sisters who resided at Strawberry Place.[1] The fact that she was living away from home implies that she was on her own, working perhaps as a teacher.[2] Since no father is mentioned in the subscription list for her poem, it is assumed that he was either dead or absent from the household. Furthermore, the officers' names on the subscription list imply that Mr. Harvey may have had military connections, or served in the foreign service.[3]

It is likely that Margaret was educated at Dame Allen's School where she developed her interest in local history, intensified, undoubtedly, by the presence of a bona fide Gothic castle a short distance away. The "New" castle for which the town was named is said to have been built by William the Conqueror's eldest son, Robert, in 1060 and refortified between 1168–1178 (*Northumberland* 435–436). In the early nineteenth century, with its towers, battlements, and gatehouses, the castle stood as the embodiment of the Gothic spirit that had overtaken art and literature throughout England.

Inspired by the fortress in her own back yard, Margaret Harvey set out to create an epic poem about the Percy family, dukes of Northumberland who resided at Alnwick Castle, the great monument to Gothic architecture north of Newcastle. Dedicated to Hugh Percy, then duke and earl of Northumberland, and published for a subscription readership, the poem was an attempt to enlist the patronage of royalty and supplement her income.[4] The work is divided into six cantos of rhymed iambic pentameter, preceded by an introduction that explains why the minstrel's daughter, Ellen, rather than the minstrel himself, is the narrator of the story. It turns out that Edwin, the minstrel, had the misfortune to be struck by lightning during a storm. Northumbria's muse appears to Ellen (who is lamenting the loss of her father) and tells her to continue his work, using the harp belonging to her father that had been rescued from the flames. Inspired by the muse, Ellen begins to sing.

Canto 1 is set at Alnwick Castle in the sixteenth century and begins with Gwynilda's mourning over Raymond de Percy's grave.[5] We learn that Percy and Gwynilda were betrothed and that Percy's rival, Conrade, has designs on her. He interrupts her reverie and attempts to force himself on her when a threatening voice from the tomb diverts his attention and allows Gwynilda the opportunity to flee.

Canto 2 is divided into two parts. The first part is devoted to Gwynilda's conversation with her stepfather where she expresses her desire to enter a convent; the second depicts Conrade's dialogue, with his servant, Kenrick, in which he describes his experiences at Percy's tomb.

Canto 3 narrates the mysterious apparition of a knight in "sable guise" to Conrade who is, understandably, terrified. Later the same spectre appears to Kenrick and spirits him away.

Canto 4 is set in the convent where Gwynilda is joined by Bertha Umfranville who describes her recent escape (disguised as a boy) from Angus's tower, with the assistance of Duncan, her betrothed Hubert's faithful servant.

Canto 5 describes the visit of Anselmo, a mute hermit, to Conrade who is now gripped by fear and guilt. We learn that Conrade had poisoned Percy and, in an attempt to atone for his crime, plans to sacrifice himself at the impending tournament. He begs the hermit not to dissuade him but to pray for his soul. At the tournament arrive Lord Hubert and an unknown, mysterious knight who had saved Hubert's life during the Crusades. Duncan sings a song recapitulating Hubert's adventures.

Canto 6 begins with the arrival of the stranger dressed as the Red Cross Knight (reminiscent of Spenser's *The Fairy Queen*) who defeats Sir Conrade, his opponent. Father Anselmo appears to console the dying Conrade and reveals himself to be the servant, Kenrick. He goes on to say that Percy was not, in fact, poisoned but off fighting in the Crusades (and later, in hiding as the mysterious subterranean spectre). Raymond de Percy at last is reunited to Gwynilda who upbraids him for putting her through so much mental anguish:

Ungenerous Raymond! Cruel didst thou prove,
By such hard means to try Gwynilda's love?
To thee unknown the pangs that swell'd my breast
Excluded hope, and robb'd my soul of rest.
Replete with anguish that no tongue can tell,

And only known to those who love so well;
Thro' the dull range of each revolving day
Slow pass'd my melancholy life away;
Retracing, as the ebbing hours pass'd on,
Scenes of delight I deem'd for ever gone.
Yet thou unkind, unconscious of the smart,
Left the dark venom festering in my heart! (200)

Percy evades her accusations by enumerating Conrade's various attempts upon his life. Given the opportunity of killing Conrade in retribution, Percy responds like Shakespeare's Hamlet and claims the incapacity of killing a sleeping man.

The poem is followed by 24 pages of notes in which the historical and geographical context of the poem is discussed in great detail. While it is clear that Margaret Harvey was an authority on local history, she must also be credited with at least a reading knowledge of classical literature, exemplified in her dedicatory verses, imitated from Horace's lines, "Ego laudo ruris amoeni / Rivos, et musco circumlita saxa, nemusque":

Well pleas'd I sing Northumbria's old domains,
Her woods where sport, where plenty crowns her plains;
By moss-grown rocks where limpid currents glide,
And seek in peaceful state our eastern tide;
Once ting'd with hostile blood, whilst clashing arms
O'er vales and mountains spread their dire alarms.[6]

While the poem was of local interest, it did not propel the author on a literary career. Instead, at some point between 1814 and 1822 when she produced the melodrama based on the premise of her poem, Margaret Harvey moved to Bishopwearmouth to assume the post of headmistress at the Ladies' Academy.[7] In his *Sunderland: A Short History*, Tom Corfe describes the community south of the Wear River as a "relatively sleepy country town" (53) but notes its wealth during the first quarter of the nineteenth century:

By the end of the eighteenth century 12,000 people were crowded into the compact area of Sunderland, compared with Bishopwearmouth's relatively widespread 6,000 and the 5,000 who lived on the northern side of the river. But Sunderland itself no longer held the houses of the gentry or wealthy merchants. Those who could afford it moved into elegant mansions scattered through the fields between the port and Bishopwearmouth . . . so that those who profited from the busy activity of the port enjoyed their wealth in the neighbouring parish. By 1823 Bishopwearmouth, with less than two-thirds of Sunderland's population, was worth three times as much in rateable value; and as Bishopwearmouth donned an air of satisfied prosperity so Sunderland seemed ever more crowded, dirty and slummy.

(53–54)

Sunderland, however, was the seat for theatrical entertainment. From 1778 a theatre was fashioned out of a disused chapel on a street that was quickly renamed "Drury Lane." Needing to appeal to visiting sailors as well as local mercantile and professional people, the actors of the so-called "Sunderland Circuit" gave a variety of offerings ranging from Shakespeare to melodrama (Corfe 70). In addition, child stars and local prodigies were especially popular with the public. Among those who received particular mention were Miss Clark, a six-year-old tightrope performer and Miss Clara Fisher, a Shylock and Falstaff of great repute.[8]

While we cannot be certain of the reasons why Margaret Harvey chose to adapt her epic poem for the stage and produce it in April 1822, the dedication of the work to Mrs. Coutts hints at a possible explanation:

Though I have not the honor of being personally known to you, yet I cannot deny myself the pleasure of inscribing this, my first dramatic effort, to you, as *un petit temoignage* of the high gratification I have so often derived at the sight of your name, accompanied by deeds that need no eulogy to enhance their value. The widow and the orphan, the maimed, and those that have none to help them, exist as monuments of your worth, far beyond my capabilities to express; and administer to your benevolent heart, feelings, that preclude the humble offering of all sublunary praise.

Mrs. Coutts, better known on the London stage as Harriot Mellon, had given up her career at Drury Lane when she married the wealthy banker Thomas Coutts who was more than twice her age. Seven years later, on 2 March 1822, Coutts died, leaving his entire fortune to his wife. Now, aged forty-four and in the possession of vast amounts of money, Harriet was besieged by requests drawing upon her celebrated generosity (clearly registered in Harvey's dedication). It is not unlikely that Margaret Harvey, who published the play five months after the announcement of Mrs. Coutts's inheritance, was hoping to benefit her school. The result of Harvey's strategy is unknown, but, given Harriot Mellon's munificent personality, it is difficult to believe that any such gesture would go unrewarded.[9]

While the production of *Raymond de Percy* may have been designed to benefit Harvey's school, attracting friends and parents rather than the typical theatregoer, the performance was, by no means, amateur. Instead, it was designed to appeal to the most discerning tastes. At Sunderland, from 1816 on, melodrama was the preferred entertainment, and many of the actors appearing in her play were experienced melodrama performers and six-year veterans of the Sunderland Circuit who had an established rapport with the local audiences. According to the published text, the cast was as follows:

Richard, *Earl of Northumberland*: Mr. Foster.

Lord Raymond de Percy: Mr. Prior.

Lord Hubert de Umfranville: Mr. Dearlove.

Sir Conrade de Valmonte: Mr. Hillington.

Kenrick, *Chief of Sir Conrade's Vassals*: Mr. Vining.

Motley, *Northumberland's Fool*: Mr. Stanley.

Goliah, *Northumberland's Dwarf*: Miss Young.

Duncan, *Northumberland's Harper*: Mr. Young.

Clifford, *Chief of Northumberland's Vassals*: Mr. Monk.

Gwynilda de Porte: Mrs. Stanley.

Bertha de Umfranville: Miss Anderson.

Ursula, *Governante in Alnwick Castle*: Miss Craven.

The play follows the action of *The Lay of the Minstrel's Daughter*, often exactly quoting dialogue from the poem. Notable is the introduction of comic characters, so important to melodrama, but characteristically absent in epic poetry. Also noteworthy is the omission of Gwynilda's tirade against Raymond at the climax of the poem. Perhaps due to her position as headmistress Margaret felt that such a public censure would exemplify feminine behavior antithetical to what was being taught in the classroom, or to what was considered acceptable by an audience of itinerant sailors and merchants. The strength and autonomy of the women characters in the *Lay* demonstrate that Margaret Harvey was certainly capable of creating women of noble stature, independent of their reliance upon men. The fact that these same characters appear in the more stereotypical guise of the tortured heroine and incarcerated maiden in the melodrama is most likely due to her position in society and audience expectations.[10]

After the publication of the melodrama, her first—and last—play,[11] Margaret Harvey falls into oblivion. While her literary aspirations might have been purely practical extensions of necessity, she does emerge historically as the first woman to earn a performance of a Gothic melodrama based on a historical subject.[12]

The text of the play is derived from the edition published 1 August 1822 at Bishopwearmouth by G. Garbutt.

Notes

1. The authors of *The Feminist Companion to Literature in English* suggest that Margaret was related to Jane Harvey, the Minerva Press novelist and poet who was the daughter of Elizabeth and Lawrance Harvey of Barnard Castle, southwest of Durham (497).

2. This assumption is made based on her later career as headmistress of the Ladies' Academy at Bishopwearmouth.

3. Captains Barber, Reed, and Ward of the Northumberland militia are among those represented as are Major and Mrs. Loftie, of the foreign service in Surinam.

4. The duke and duchess of Northumberland had a history of supporting educational institutions. It is conceivable that Margaret Harvey had used her poem to enlist the patronage of Earl Percy for her school.

5. It is tempting to associate the female mourners in the poem with the author and infer that the epic might have been written soon after the death of her father.

6. Taken from Horace's *Epistulae* (1.10.6–7), the lines are literally translated: "I praise my lovely rural / Rivers, and tress, and moss-grown rocks."

7. The parishes of Sunderland and Bishopwearmouth were especially renowned for their schools. The Quakers and Freemasons had established charity schools in the district earlier in the eighteenth century and a school for poverty-stricken young women between the ages of seven and sixteen had been founded in 1778 as the result of a bequest by Mrs. Donnison, the widow of a well-to-do butcher. Here, young ladies were instructed in the arts of spinning and knitting as well as the fundamentals of English grammar. Both the Methodist and Episcopal churches began to sponsor schools based on the principles of Lancaster and Bell from about 1808 and these offered more rigorous academic instruction. What would become the Bishopwearmouth National School was opened in Low Row in 1808, and the Parochial School in Sunderland was founded in the same year. By the middle of the nineteenth century, there were 140 schools in the area, catering to at least half of the children who lived there (Corfe 70).

8. In a letter dated 15 August 1819 to the *Theatrical Inquisitor*, Clara Fisher is described as a "little prodigy" capable of enacting "more wonders than a man."

9. See Macqueen-Pope, Chapter 21, for an appreciation of Harriot Mellon who "did a great deal of good in her lifetime and harmed nobody" (315).

10. It is tempting to compare Margaret Harvey with the other schoolmistress who wrote about the Percy Family, Hannah More. While B. G. MacCarthy dismisses More as not having "contributed anything to the art of fiction" because her stories are "nearer to direct pedagogy than to literature," she does suggest that "Hannah More was another of the women writers who strove by means of fiction to inculcate morality and to counteract subversive Jacobin doctrines" (445). As an administrator, responsible for both the conduct and

education of young women, Miss Harvey possibly found herself forced to adopt conservative measures.

11. In the "Preface" to the printed edition of the play, Harvey writes:

> The following little attempt is, with all due deference, offered to the notice of the public. The leading inducement for its publication was, a wish that the friends of the author might see it as it was written; as, from the trifling charge attached to it, all idea of pecuniary recompense being totally out of the question.
>
> As a first dramatic effort, the author is induced to hope, that too severe a censure will not be passed upon her temerity and pleads in part of extenuation, its being composed in the little leisure attainable after the arduous and imperative duties of an extensive seminary.

The line "see it as it was written" suggests that the performance at Sunderland was not entirely true to the text. It is also important to note Harvey's suggestion that the publication of the play was not due to purely mercenary interests. In *English Melodrama*, Booth argues that a melodrama might earn the author fifty pounds at the minor theatres (48) and even less from the publishers who "paid very small sums for the copyright" (49). Seen in this light, Harvey's dedication to a woman of means would have been the chief source of any financial return from the play and, as I have suggested above, was possibly the catalyst for the project in the first place.

12. This is, of course, history romanticized, but Harvey's cast of characters and use of local color lend a certain historical integrity to the play. See the general Introduction for a comparison between Harvey's "historical" characters and those in Monk Lewis's *Castle Spectre*.

RAYMOND DE PERCY

Dramatis Personae

Richard, *Earl of Northumberland.*
Lord Raymond de Percy.
Lord Hubert de Umfranville.
Sir Conrade de Valmonte.
Kenrick, *Chief of Sir Conrade's Vassals.*
Motley, *Northumberland's Fool.*
Goliah, *Northumberland's Dwarf.*
Duncan, *Northumberland's Harper.*
Clifford, *Chief of Northumberland's Vassals.*
Gwynilda de Porte.
Bertha de Umfranville.
Ursula, *Governante in Alnwick Castle.*
Knights, Squires, Vassals, &c.&c.

Scenes laid at Alnwick Castle, in Northumberland, and at Castle Angus, on the Banks of the Tweed. Music selected from the Scotch.

Prologue.

It is no easy task, in this bright age,
To scribble rhyme, though it be but for the stage—
The poor deserted stage! which now no more
Boasts its deep phalanx, as in days of yore;
When thickly wedg'd in pyramidic piles,
The muses held command o'er tears and smiles;
And in conjunction with the loves and graces,
Twisted, just as they lik'd, our pretty faces.
    But as all tyrants who despotic rule,
For gentle manners, ought to go to school;
So we, the corps-dramatic beaux and wenches,
Are drilling now to live on empty benches:
Light, wholesome food it must be, without question,
And very, very, easy of digestion!
    "O la! dear me!" says Lady Grizzy Grange,

"I vonders oft vat causes this here change,
That never none now to the play repair,
T'amuse, and kill the time, and all that there."
          Yawning, my Lord replies, "'tis monstrous shocking,
T'encourage these vile drabs, that live by mocking."
          While Dandy Dick vociferates, with a roar,
"O cut the playhouse, 'tis a horrid bore!
I hate the very mention of the elves
For having dared to imitate ourselves."
          "Eh, man!" says Sawney Oats, with caustic smile,
"I'm really thinking that was scarce worth while;
Besides, I canna see ought varra funny,
For sic a sackless sight, to tak our money;
It's really waur than parting wi' oat siller
For Mother Goose, and Jack, the Giant Killer,
Wi' a' their ither feckless kickmaleries
Of ghosts, hobgoblins, exquisites and fairies."
          Oh! could thy spirit, *Garrick,* come again,
And see the skeleton of Drury Lane!
How would thy spectre lungs, with keen remorse,
Bellow aloud, "My kingdom for a horse,
Fleet as the winds, to speed my airy flight,
And shield my vision from the sick'ning sight!"
          But true it is, that time's revolving range,
Brings in its circling round a ceaseless change;
For what was yesterday the rage all o'er,
To-day can please the fickle taste no more:
Thus fashion governs with despotic sway,
And each caprice, in turn, will have its day.

Act I. Scene I.

Banqueting Hall, with proper Ornaments, appropriate Music, &c.

(Enter Northumberland, Lords, Knights, Fool, Dwarf, and Attendants, on one Side, receiving Sir Conrade, who enters on the other, followed by Kendrick.)

Northd. Welcome, Sir Conrade, welcome once more to Alnwick's towers. But wherefore so estranged of late, that much our wonder and regret was raised, ever to find you absent.

Con. Thanks brave Northumberland, thy courtesy keeps pace and honors the rich means with which thou art blest. So much I feel indebted, noble Percy, to thy generous care, that I have resolved to fix my dwelling near thee; and this morning have taken full power and possession of the Marble Hall.

Omnes. The Marble Hall!!!

Con. Yes, noble chieftains, the Marble Hall henceforth is Conrade's dwelling place. But say, why does that excite such strange emotions?

Northd. Know you not the tales that rumour spreads? 'Tis said that wicked spirits hold their revels there; and from the dark and dreary vaults beneath, strange and unhallowed sounds, at midnight hour, have often struck the lonely traveler's ear.

Con. I am no stranger to those idle tales, the mere delusions of a sickly brain, well fitted to the coward's puny ear. Much, my good lord, I would rejoice to meet those airy inmates; if once we should encounter, I'll wager no second interview with them breaks my repose.

Northd. Waving these wild reports as of light import, nor worthy of regard, yet I would warn against existing evils; the castle totters on its mouldering base, nor shelter can afford, save in the western tower, at whose lone foot the Marble Hall extends; and more, Sir Knight, than airy inmates hold their revels there.

Con. I fear them not. My shield and sword, oft tried, are yet untaught to yield; and they and I have long held fellowship.

Northd. An open generous foe no warrior dreads; but courage is ill matched, poised against the base insidious knave *(Conrade starts.)* that stabs you in the dark. But see, the banquet waits. *(They seat themselves.)* Come, fill the goblets. *(The attendants fill and hand them round.)* Health to Sir Conrade, of the Marble Hall.

Omnes. Health to Sir Conrade, of the Marble Hall.

Con. Thanks, noble Friends: my warmest thanks are poor to what I feel.

(A bugle is heard at a distance, and answered by one from the castle.)

Knight. Hark, my lord Northumberland! some one approaches; and, by the signal, I should deem the laurel bough waves o'er his helmet's plume.

(A noise without, and flourish of trumpets. Enter a warrior in armour, his visor close clasped. As he advances, Northumberland quits his seat, and embraces him.)

Northd. Welcome, my son! thrice welcome to thy native towers: so soon returned, and safe, will give a double zest to this convivial hour. I need not ask if Raymond's arms have been victorious.

Ray. The brightest honors grace the little band committed to my care. Firm as the rocks that guard my native shore, they stood unmoved amidst a host of foes; and shattered corslets, helms, and splintered shields, shew in what guise they won their laurel crowns.

Northd. My brave Northumberland, and thou their gallant leader, how every trial proves your worth beyond my utmost hopes. But see, my son, our guests await us; yet ere we charge the goblet to thy next encounter, I will present thee to a stranger knight, of noble port he seems, though pensive mood.

(Northumberland leads Raymond towards Sir Conrade, who looking at him, starts aside, and hastily unclasping his visor, and drawing his sword, advances close to Conrade, gazing him into a state of mysterious horror. Conrade springs from his seat violently agitated.)

Ray. Fly mysterious villain! coward, hence, ere hospitality's fair bond be broken, and the strong arm of vengeance due, inflicts the fate thy miscreant deeds demand. *(Conrade sullenly retires, beckoning Kendrick, who follows him.)*

Northd. Stay thy uplifted hand; and calm this passion that unmans thy soul. Say, whence this strange alarm?

Ray. Anon I will inform—my agitated spirits now forbid the task; and see, here is one approaching, whose magic charms expel e'en the dread recollections yon arch fiend had raised. *(Enter Gwynilda.)* How fares my love?

(Upon the entrance of Gwynilda, the guests take off their helmets. At the time these scenes are laid, it was the custom never to remove them, except upon the taking of an oath, at their devotions, or in the presence of Ladies.

> *"They carv'd at the meal*
> *In gloves of steel;*
> *And drank the red wine through the helmet barred."*
> Scott.)

Gwy. Overjoyed to meet them, Raymond, safe again in Alnwick's trophied hall. Pardon me, noble chieftains, this intrusion; but as I, musing, watched the day's decline; and, from my tower, marked the fair empress of the silent night by slow gradations mount her silver throne, soft on mine ear arose the bugle's sound: hope, on the instant, and her fairy train, fed the gay vision that my fancy reared; when bounding o'er the sword, fleet as the wind, with helmets glittering in the silvery ray, I saw my soul's fond wishes realized. Soon through the castle the glad tidings spread; and in a moment so replete with bliss, say, could Gwynilda fail to greet her lord, her benefactor, her preserver?

Ray. No more, my love, of this, all, all, is due to thee, and thou art my preserver; for without thee, wealth, power, and titles, would be empty sounds. Here then, in presence of our noble friends, I claim the promise given ere we parted—thyself, the rich reward of all my toils. To-morrow then we'll bid the minstrel band prepare to hail the dawn of that auspicious day.

Northd. That pleasing charge be mine. O Gwynilda! how my heart beats to own thee as a daughter; and in that name, restore the rich inheritance the chance of war bereft thee of, and loaded me withal. But for the coming joy to give thee back thy own, the conqueror's boon had been bestowed in vain.

Gwy. O generous Percy! how thy noble deeds transcend my grateful, my most ardent prayers. With all submission I will now retire; and till we meet again, warriors farewell. (Raymond hands her off, and returns. They all sit to the banquet. Re-enter Kenrick, in the back ground.)

Knight. My Lord Northumberland, has no intelligence been received of young Umfranville, Angus's noble heir?

Northd. His presence here is hourly expected.

Knight. 'Tis said he sighs in secret for the lady Bertha, who in his bosom holds a double claim, as being his kinswoman and affianced bride.

Northd. But the old Earl forbids the tender claim; and threatens Hubert with the stern resolve never to see him more, if he persists in wedding his fair cousin.

Ray. Cruel resolve! but Hubert heeds it not, his generous soul rises superior to the little views, that limit Angus in this harsh decree. Replenish to the brim; to Bertha and to Hubert raise the rosy draught.
(Kenrick in much trepidation empties a phial into Raymond's goblet, then fills it up with wine.)

Omnes. To Bertha and to Hubert. *(They raise their goblets with one hand, and their helmets with the other.)*

Ray. O may the pledge in full completion greet his glowing heart! alike alive to love and friendship's charms.

Knight. Where tarries now that northern youth, so skilled in music's lore? My memory misgives, or I have heard he strikes his harp beneath these lofty towers.

Ray. Duncan, from Yarrow Streens, if such you mean, 'tis true he tarries here. Call in the harper, bid him straight attend his office at the banquet.

(Exit an attendant, and re-enter with Duncan, who plays and sings.)

> Flattering fancy told a tale,
>   That love bade me believe;
> Soft as the sighings of the gale,
>   That fann'd my cot at eve.
>
> Deceptive hope! delusive dream!
>   That led my peace astray;
> More transient than the fickle beam,
>   That gilds a wint'ry day.
>
> Why did the fairy fabric rise,
>   Bedeck'd with blossoms rare,
> To swell my heart with bitter sighs,
>   And ripen into care!
>
> Adieu! thou false unfeeling maid,
>   Whom truth could never move;
> Whose charms my simple heart betray'd,
>   To hope thou e'er could'st love.

(During the song, Raymond appears agitated by illness.)

Ray. Duncan, that melancholy lay ill suits this festive hour. Come try a blither melody, to banish—*(He hastily rises.)* Oh! what a sudden stupor overpowers me, a strange and wild confusion presses on my brain—what can this be—mercy—aid me my friends—my sight recedes—my very soul's convulsed with agony inexpressible! *(He faints in the arms of his attendants.)*

Northd. O Raymond! O my son! speak to thy father, and dispel this dread suspense, this horrid apprehension! Bear him gentle to his couch, that every aid may quickly be applied. *(Exeunt Omnes.)*

Scene II

A Gothic Apartment in Alnwick Castle.

(Enter Goliah, followed by Motley.)

Mot. Master Goliah, I say, master Goliah, wont you speak to a body?

Gol. Vel, vat voud you say a me, monsieur Motley.

Mot. Any thing you please, just to talk a bit; for I am afraid my tongue takes the cramp with lying so long in one position—I declare it's almost stuck to the top of my mouth—bless my heart! I wish I may ever recover the proper use of it again.

Gol. No fear of dat monsieur Mote-ly, no fear.

Mot. I wish I had a little wine just to oil the hinges of it. I say, there's nobody to see us, don't you think one might venture to try the effect of a little of this? *(He draws a bottle out of one pocket, and a goblet out of the other.)* Perhaps gargling the throat may help to remove the stiffness, and soreness, and all that kind of thing.

Gol. Very goot, very goot, you better try den. *(He pours some into the goblet and drinks.)*

Mot. Well, I do declare, I am better already. Only see, I can turn my head to this side and to that side. My tongue too feels quite glib. Aye, aye, there is nothing washes the mouth like wine. I'll e'en gargle again. *(Drinks.)* I declare it's quite delightful. If the doctors sent such physic as this, bless us, what trade they would have! Come, do you take a little.

Gol. Tank you, tank you, my troat is not stiff, *(Looking earnestly at the goblet.)* beside I voud not choose to drink out of dat cup.

Mot. You would not drink out of this cup,—Why?

Gol. My Lord Raymond drunk out of it, and I do tink he is poison.

Mot. No, no, this is not it. Do you really think he is poisoned though?

Gol. Do I really tink? Yes, to be sure, I do tink he is poison. Monsieur Mote-ly you look very ill, let a me feel your pulse—one, two, tree, seven, ten, sixteen, twenty,—Oh dear! Oh dear! how it gallopa, gallopa, like de horse in de full decanter, quick, quick, quick.

Mot. I look ill, do I? Oh dear! Oh dear! if this really should be the cup my Lord Raymond drank out of—yes, I do think it is—Oh! what shall I do? what shall I do?

Gol. Compose yourself, and die like a gentleman.

Mot. Die!—Why do you in good earnest think I shall die?

Gol. Certainment! most certainly you vill; but do not be uneasy about dat; you vill go like de little pistoli-pop, and you vill be gon—you know my Lor vent just so in a moment.

Mot. Oh! what will become of me? what shall I do? Bless me! how ill I am—my head turns quite round—I am all in a mist, and my heart has made but one jump up to my throat—Oh! I shall be choked—I am sick, sick, sick.

Gol. Go along you nasty fellow, go along, you must be sick in dis place—get out vid you I say, go a your own apartment, and be sick like a gentleman, go, go, I say. *(Pushes him off.)* Ha! ha! ha! I tink I have settle your noise, monsieur Mote-ly, for little while. I often vonder vat my Lor see in dat foolish fellow to amuse him, he do noting but talk foolish alway. But I go see how my Lord Raymond is—dat vas a strange illness of his, and strange rencontre vid Sir Conrade, very strange indeed. *(Exit.)*

Scene III.

An old Apartment in Conrade's Castle, the Floor chequered in large Squares of black and white, to represent Marble. Conrade solus, seated at a Table.

Con. Kenrick, ere this, no doubt, has done the deed. Yet methinks less time were requisite; and this delay seems to portend no good. Down busy thought!—wherefore should Conrade fear—the caitiff sure durst not betray thee. *(Rises.)* No, no, his life he knows would pay the forfeiture, and promises of large reward I gave him to insure success. Self-interest in the double tie, will, therefore, bind him fast. That is the spur fixed to the heel of half mankind to speed their varied views: and shall the phantom fair to lure the base-born knave, when I have followed in the tempting train.—Perish the thought! Hence from my soul chill apprehension! 'tis a coward feeling, and the wild inmates of my stormy bosom disown its puny dictates. Distraction to my hopes! why comes he not? This torturing delay consumes me, racks my brain, and maddens into fury. Dastard loiterer, wert thou within my reach I'd—but soft, he comes. *(Enter Kenrick.)* Say, my good Kenrick, sleeps the stripling with his ancestors?

Ken. As sound he sleeps, as those who wake no more.

Con. Indeed!—Then well thy errand sped. But tell me, how thy purpose did proceed?

Ken. Even in the midst of merriment, the deadly potion stay'd his buoyant soul. "Go, call the harper," quick he cried, when lo! the latent fiend within him rose. Scarce had the minstrel sung his plaintive lay, when fiercer flamed the burning shaft within, bedimmed his sight, and parched his trembling frame, even to dissolution.

Con. Sayest thou so, good Kenrick! Then Conrade thanks thee.

Ken. Nay, thank me not; but say what further service thou wouldst claim, the night is waning fast.

Con. Yet pause a moment.—How bore Northumberland this sudden blow? and fair Gwynilda too?

Ken. But that I am not apt at tales of woe, and words were wanting to express their grief, or I might feed thy soul with food it revels on,—the speechless anguish of a parent's woe, and blighted love's wild visage of despair.

Con. 'Tis as I wish'd.—But tell me, Kenrick, whence are the bonds that bind De Percy to this Saxon maid?

Ken. When William, Duke of Normandy, assailed our shores, her father, a rich Saxon lord, De Port, by name, sternly refused to aid the conqueror's cause, and, with ill-fated Harold, fell in the battle of Hastings. His large domains, William bestowed upon our noble earl; and of her birth-right, 'reft the orphan maid. But brave De Percy would not hold the gift, save as a trust to be restored to fair Gwynilda; and straightway brought her here to Alnwick Castle.

Con. And proposed to have married her to his son—was it not so?

Ken. True, he did intend it.

Con. And that gay airy vision we have broken. O man! how futile are thy plans of bliss! when thy frail fellow mortal can dissolve the bubble into air! Now leave me Kenrick—thou and I both lack repose.

Ken. Farewell! *(Exit.)*

Con. Oh! that thy slumbers were as sound as Raymond's! then too might I repose; for, bondlike, thine and mine boasts little faith; but that I need some farther service of thee, or thou should'st wake no more. How now De Percy—how beats thy generous bosom now?—Oh! how I hate thee—for thy virtues hate thee! which set me at strong variance with myself. But what have I to do with the cold recompense of self-approval?—fantastic, visionary, scheme of bliss, I own you not! *(The bell tolls one.)* 'Tis now past midnight; and the infant hour proclaims the morn's approach; yet ere it dawns, I will renew my search to find this secret outlet from the castle; so far, I have explored in vain, *(Takes the lamp off the table.)*   perchance this effort may prove more successful. *(Exit.)*

Scene IV.

Sun-rise. Outside of Conrade's Castle, from which Kenrick enters, in a disordered state. Moat, Drawbridge, &c.

Ken. Oh! what a night of agonizing fear has been the last! my weary eyes in vain have sought repose, and even the day's return is hateful to me. How one atrocious deed widens the beaten track of guilt! and more must yet be done, ere this day closes o'er my aching head.— Unhappy Kenrick! fool to league thee with a fiend like this. *(Enter Motley.)*

Mot. Good day to you, Kenrick, you have risen with the larks this morning. What makes you so soon astir?

Ken. Why to listen to the larks, Motley. Now what called you abroad so soon?

Mot. Nay nothing called me, they only sent me an errand. You look shockingly ill this morning, Kenrick, have you seen any thing in the old castle there? for every body says it is haunted; or, perhaps, you drank some of the wine that was left at the banquet last night? I just dipped the tip of my tongue into it, and that little monster, my Lord's Dwarf, persuaded me I was poisoned.

Ken. Nothing but nonsense, you had been in your cups, Motley, that has been all.

Mot. Wherefore thou sayest unwisely, meaning, I ween, that the cups were in me: in truth, a little of the wine was; and having drunk out of Lord Raymond's goblet—*(Kenrick starts.)* Why what's the matter?— Don't be alarmed; I guessed by your looks you had been a little free last night; but the wine was in good condition, and so am I— you see I am alive and merry still. But you don't know how glad I am to see you, to get a bit of talk, for they are all as dumb as dumplings at the castle now.

Ken. That wont suit you, Motley.—But where are you going?

Mot. I am going to bid the neighbouring chiefs attend the funeral of Lord Raymond, that's all.

Ken. When do they move him?

Mot. Heaven bless that wise head of thine! Move him! why he is as dead as a herring, and as stiff and as cold as the stone images over the castle gateway.—No, no, he'll never move more, that's certain.

Ken. I mean, when and where is he to be buried?

Mot. Oh! when and where is he to be buried!—To-night, in the valley, east of the chapel.

Ken. There lie the relics of his noble ancestors.

Mot. His noble aunts and sisters!—I never heard of them, Kenrick; but I very well remember a story about the old Baron, his grandfather, and Lady Blanch, his grandmother, who were buried there; and their ghosts used to take a walk, arm in arm, on the first night of every new moon, all along the water side, and back again.

Ken. Indeed!—And did you ever see their ghosts, Motley?

Mot. O yes! Once I saw them. Poor dear Lady Blanch! she was all over as white as a large snow-ball; and my Lord the Baron, he looked, for all the world, as dark and as fuzzy as a clump of heather on the side of Cheviot, yonder. Mercy on us! how I did shiver and shake! There I stood, stock still, trembling all the time like an aspen leaf.— But it was not them after all, Kenrick.

Ken. Not them!—Who was it then?

Mot. Why guess now—But no, you'll never guess. It was Robin the miller, leading his ass for father Ambrose to go and confess his wife before she died: you know, it would have been of no use confessing her afterwards; for I heard Sir Conrade say to himself, as he left the banquet last night, "dead men tell no tales"; and I suppose the women will then be obliged to hold their tongues too.

Ken. Undoubtedly!—The day advances fast, are you not afraid of being late with your orders?

Mot. O no! There is no need to hurry, my Lord cannot go without them. May I not call as I come back? for I am sure I shall get a lock'd jaw, if I stop much longer among the dumbys at our castle.—Good day, Kenrick, good day. *(Exit.)*

Ken. Good speed to thee, Motley. So, so, "dead men tell no tales"—true, Sir Conrade; and I guess your meaning. To-night, east of the chapel, they bury Raymond—Now to my post; and, in this hour of trial, I must guard against the vigilance of Conrade, whose suspicious eye will track me wheresoever I go. *(Exit.)*

Scene V.

Castle Angus. Tower overhanging the Moat, parapet, Wall, &c.&c. Two casements in the Tower. A Light in the upper one. A Storm of Thunder, &c.&c. The lower casement opens, and an old Minstrel descends from it: looks cautiously about.

Duncan *(disguised as an old Minstrel).* So far, all is well, save this unruly storm. Now for my harp; and then to see if Philip is in readiness. *(A Noise without.)* Sure I heard the trampling of feet. *(He listens. Noise increases.)* It seems to advance this way—I must retreat—no friends of mine come from the land-ward quarter to-night. *(He retreats into the Tower again.)*
(Enter three or four of Angus' Vassals, looking cautiously about.)

First Vas. No, no, I told thee it was all thy own fears that conjured up the sound of voices, no one is here thou seest, all is safe and silent below, *(Thunder.)* though not quite so over-head.—But how wears the night?

Second Vas. The castle bell has toll'd the eleventh hour.

First Vas. Is it so far advanced? *(Thunder.)* What a dirdum is overhead.—Hast thou pass'd the guard to-night? are all on duty?

Second Vas. Oliver himself went round, and all was well. *(Thunder receding.)*

First Vas. Then get thee to rest, the noisy elements themselves seem sinking to repose.—But stop, who guards the sally port tonight?

Second Vas. Walter and Morris.

First Vas. What both?

Second Vas. Aye, both: my Lord gave special orders that a double watch be set; he seems to fear some evil near that quarter.

First Vas. Methinks the evil is not quite so distant: thou knowest the hapless inmate of this lonely tower—

Second Vas. Peace!—Art thou mad? the very winds may bear thy words to our proud master's ears, and then thou knowest thy meed. *(Thunder very distant.)* Good night, the watch-word, caution. *(Exeunt severally.)*

(Duncan again quits the tower, and after reconnoitering a little, takes his harp out of the window, and seating himself upon the parapet, plays and sings.)

> Soft falls the dew of night;
> Mild o'er the turret's height,
> Rises in lucid light,
>   The star of eve.
>
> Where the soft waters play,
> There beams the silver ray;
> And on the liquid way
>   Valiant hearts heave.
>
> Then ere the coming light
> Chases the fav'ring night,
> Seize the time fit for flight—
>   Quick! gain the tide!
>
> Who then our course shall stay,
> Whilst the strong rowers play,
> And down the wat'ry way
>   Swiftly we glide?

(During the song, the light in the upper casement flits backward and forward,—the window is opened, and Bertha speaks.)

Ber. Hubert! Hubert!

Dun. Lady, prepare! the day will soon arise, the boat is ready, and your friends await you.

Ber. Where is the Earl, my uncle?

Dun. In the castle, Lady, nor dreams of your escape.

Ber. How gained you access here?—'Tis Duncan that I speak to, is it not?

Dun. The same, my gentle mistress, at your service; but the time permits no longer parley, dispatch I pray you. *(Bertha shuts the casement. Duncan blows a whistle at the side opposite the tower. Enter a man in a boat.)*

Dun. Is all well?

Boatman. All's well.

Dun. I hope the signal has not alarmed them in the castle. Take hold, and place my harp near the stern of the boat—there, that will do very well. *(Duncan enters the boat.)* Now push through the arch, to a small iron grating you will see just by the base of the tower. *(Exeunt through the arch.)*

Scene VI.

A Hall in Earl Angus' Castle. Servants preparing for a journey; one of them arranging a suit of Armour.

First Serv. Well, well, you may say what you will about valour, and honour, and courage, and all that, but I tell you, for my part, I don't like it. You see, the old fashion suits me best, I like a pair of legs, a pair of hands and arms, and a head upon my shoulders.

Second Serv. O what a precious coward thou art!—Why if all men were like thee, the fiercest freebooter would be chief in Angus' castle here, for there would be none to defend the right.—But I say, Rowland, when do you set out?

First Serv. Why that question may be easily answered.—But I say, Rowland, when do you return?

Row. Peace, thou dastard!—I believe my Lord said he would depart the day after to-morrow; but after all, I do think this fighting the Turks but a foolish business at the best.

First Serv. O it must be delightful to gentlemen of your valour! why they will hang, draw, and quarter you, then pepper your gizzard, and make a devil on't, by way of dessert to the feast. *(All laugh.)*

Second Serv. This is charming encouragement, I must confess.— But what hast thou done with the old minstrel, that sought shelter in the castle from the storm last night?

First Serv. Done with him!—why I suppose he is fast asleep in the little tower over the moat, where I spread a couch for him—Poor old devil! he looked as if the Turks had had hold of him, for he was in a sad plight.

Row. But how durst you admit him, after the strong and positive orders of the Earl to exclude all strangers whatsoever?

Second Serv. Aye, how durst you?—I would not stand in your shoes for something, my old buck; and what is still worse, how came you to place him in the apartment below the Lady Bertha?

First Serv. I could not put him in an apartment above the Lady Bertha, because she is placed at the top of the tower.

Second Serv. By-the-bye, it's but unfair to case her up in that solitary manner, with no living soul to speak to; but if Lord Hubert sat chief in Angus's Hall, I know what I know.

Row. I'll tell thee what he knows, that should the Earl, our master, discover thy lodger, the old minstrel, in the moat tower, he'll lodge thee in the dungeon, and then good bye to light and liberty.

First Serv. By my valour, thou art right, and I'll go even this instant and dismiss him.

Second Serv. Stop, stop, I believe he has done that job himself, and if he could swim the moat, he is off without bidding you good morrow; for as I relieved guard at the sally-port, a little before midnight, I heard the sweetest strains come from that part of the castle, that ever struck my ear.—The time, the scene, all conspired to charm—the cloudless moon silvered the surface of the silent moat— the dawn had not yet tinged the highest peak in view—and not the slightest murmur remained of the storm, that last night roared around these battlements. I paused, as the night breeze gently bore the sound—so soft, so sweet, the strain, that if it was not your old harper, Oliver, it must have been the Brownie of the Tweed, warbling its vesper hymn to the queen of the night.

Row. It has been the Lady Bertha herself, she often plays and sings.

First Serv. Aye, aye, to be sure it has, she cannot sleep, poor Lady, she is in love; and I remember when the tender passion enthralled me, I never slept till after midnight. *(They all laugh.)*

Second Serv. Thou in love!—O impossible! why thou art such a notorious coward, that there is not a girl in all Northumberland would deign to look at thee. This, however, I tell thee for a truth, that the music I heard, was not in the tower, but on the outside of it; therefore, the warder will know best who was the musician.—I can only tell you, I could have listened to his melody till now.

First Serv. Outside of the castle, sayest thou?—By the valour of a knight, I like it not, for as the lattice was unbarred, and opens immediately upon the parapet of the moat, he might as easily play on the outside as within—But no, no, it could not be, he is so old and infirm, that I don't think he could jump half a yard over a straw for the earldom of Angus—Yet methinks I had better go and see if all be safe. *(Exit.)*

Second Serv. There now, do you take this armour to my Lord Hubert, whilst I go and see if all are prepared below. *(Exeunt severally.)*

END OF ACT I.

Act II. Scene I.

Alnwick Castle in the back ground; in the front, a Tomb ornamented with a warrior's trophies. Lance inverted, Helmet unlaced, Gauntlets, Spurs, and Shield, hung round the Tomb. Sword crossed with its Scabbard upon the top of the Bier. Moon rising in the distance. Gwynilda, in mourning, kneeling at the Tomb. Curtain rises to slow Music.

Gwy. Hail! hallowed scene! sacred to lost repose! where on this lonely bier my Raymond rests, nor hears the anguish that Gwynilda pours. Be calm, my heart! whilst at this dreary hour I breathe my sorrows o'er his silent shade—*(A noise without of some one approaching, Gwynilda starts.)* It was the night breeze rustling through the dell, for all again is silent—*(The noise gradually increases, Gwynilda much alarmed.)* Protect me heaven!
(Enter Sir Conrade, splendidly attired; he affects surprise at finding Gwynilda there, then courteously advances towards her.)

Con. As I supposed; and alone too. *(Aside.)* Pardon me, fair Gwynilda! this rash intrusion to thy lone retreat: thy heavenly orisons are most to blame, whose magic sounds seduced my wandering steps; for who can hear thy voice, and heedless stray, when every accent tunes the soul to love. Rise, gentle Lady! shame it were, to see so fair a suppliant press the chilling soil—Rise, and attend—*(He attempts to raise her: she suddenly rises, and starts from him.)*
       A bower I'll deck for thee,
Where spring unfading round thy steps shall bloom:
Each fragrant flower that scents the summer breeze
I'll cull, to dress, sweet maid! thy hallowed vale.

Gwy. Hence from my sight! thou miscreant, hence! nor dare with thy unhallowed feet, to invade the sacred precincts of a grief like mine—Fly! ere the retributive power in triple vengeance armed blasts thy detested sight—The thunder sleeps not when such fiends draw near.

Con. Peace, haughty maid!—who now can aid thee in this lonely glen?—Dos't thou not know the place and hour consign thee to Sir Conrade, who laughs thy pride to scorn?—Within that marble tomb thy champion rests, whose stripling passion dared to thwart my fixed designs.—But see, the herald of the morn has tipt yon eastern battlements with gold—Say, shall I lead—Come, my coy dame, I'll guard thee with a lover's arm—Come, Lady, quick!—prepare!

A Voice from the Tomb replies, Villain, forbear!!!

Con *(drawing his sword)*. Take back the villain, thou ill-manner'd slave! By the deep insult, here I swear my ready sword awaits thee—In sooth, I guess, my melancholy dame, not unattended here you sigh, and this your mystic slave.—Stand forth, thou champion of the night! whoe'er thou art, Sir Conrade fain would know.

Voice. Thine everlasting foe!!!

Charge, charge, the goblet o'er again:
Still deeper strike the dye,
That crimson'd Serra Valta's plain,
Where mouldering relics lie.
The evening star, from Pont la Trave,
Will guide thee to a lonely grave,
Where deadly breezes blew—
Say, would Sir Conrade further know,
Or wish to see his latent foe?
He straight shall rise to view!!

Con. Shield me, ye powers, from that prophetic sound! *(He falls.)*

Gwy. Merciful heaven, preserve me! *(Exit.)*

Scene II.

A Hall in Alnwick Castle. Enter Motley, running, pursued by Clifford, horse-whipping him.

Mot. Enough, enough, I tell you! Why will you give a body what they don't like to take? It is vastly ungenteel to force your favours this way.

Cliff. You don't like it, don't you? so much the better, that is one of the reasons why you get it, you rascal! *(Whipping him round the stage.)*

Mot. Poh! pshaw! be done! cannot you be quiet now? I declare I shall be all black and blue.

Cliff. Black and blue!—you shall be all the colours of the rainbow. I'll make your skin as variegated as your jacket, you mischievous villain, the next time you play such a trick, remember that!

Mot. Why I am sure I did no harm; the fen was as soft as a hasty-pudding, it would not have broken the wing of a fly. If you don't believe me, you can just take a walk in and try yourself.

Cliff *(whipping him).* What, you want to suffocate me too, do you? there, take that, and that, you rascal!

Mot. Murder! murder! murder!

(Enter Goliah.)

Gol. Bless my art! vat is de matter vid you, monsieur Mote-ly? vat monstrous large noise you make, I hear you all over de castle.

Cliff. I tell you what, Mister Goliah, there will be no peace in the castle, unless my Lord will discharge that fellow. Why do you know he has almost been the death of some of the chiefs last night, in their way hither.

Gol. Bless me, dat vas monsrous vicket!—But how? Vitch vay? I declare I quite shock.

Cliff. Shocked!—Aye so you may; had you been in their place, you would never have been seen more.

Mot. Ha, ha, ha! *(Laughs heartily.)* Had he been in their place!—Now that is a good one—why he would have been gone head and heels, before he was half as far as they were.

Gol. O fie! monsieur Mote-ly, O fie!—But, monsieur Clayfort, you not tell a me how he did de murder.

Cliff. In trying to gain the castle, last night, before sun-set, these chieftains had left the beaten track, and crossed the heath: a deep swamp, with which they were unacquainted, lay between them and the ford; and wishing to take the shortest way, they inquired of that rascal there, if the swamp was passable—

Mot. No, they did not say so; they asked if it had a good bottom, and I said, yes, it had.

Cliff. And how durst you say so?

Mot. Why it has a good one, when you get at it; and they never asked me how far that was from the top.

Cliff. O you stupid blockhead!—Well, in they went, man and horse; and it was with the greatest difficulty they were got out alive, all covered with mud and dirt.

Gol. O fie! Motely, O fie! I never tink you so bad man, indeed.

Cliff. He will be hanged some of these days, for certain. Come, Mister Goliah, we will leave him to himself, it is not honourable to hold converse with him any longer. *(Exeunt.)*

Mot. Well, what a nice dish of talk we have had! but Clifford's whip was not very sweet sauce to it though.—I wish I could see any body else coming this way, to have a little more conversation with. *(Looks out at the sides.)* No, I don't see any one coming this way. I will e'en sing a song to amuse myself; and it will be better than saying nothing at all.

There went to a feast a jolly old priest,
      He'd a face like the moon at the full,
As red and as rosy as midsummer poesy,
      And as thick as a post was his skull, his skull.
      And as thick as a post was his skull.

He was fond of a glass, and it there came to pass,
      That a monstrous potion he got;
For as he respir'd, the liquor it fir'd,
      And heated his noddle red hot, red hot.
      And heated his noddle red hot.

The guests in amaze to see his nose blaze,
      Upset all their cups and their dishes,
In the pond popp'd his phiz, which made such a whiz,
      It frighten'd to death all the fishes, the fishes,
      It frightened to death all the fishes.

The flame thus put out, at the end of his snout,
      The convent bells they set a ringing,
That old Friar Mosis had sav'd his proboscis,
      And that makes an end of my singing, my singing.
      And that makes an end of my singing.

(Exit.)

Scene III.

The Marble Hall. Conrade laid on a couch, his looks wild and haggard. An Attendant in waiting.

Con. Quick, get thee hence, and straightway order Kenrick to attend me! *(Exit Attendant. Conrade rises.)* Still on mine ear the horrid accents ring, and like the death knell to the dying wretch, strike terror to my soul.—Inexplicable, how or whence the knowledge it bespoke—I cannot fathom it. No witness to the deed now lives to tell the tale. Death stamp'd the whole with his dark signet; and who can break his adamantine seal!—All, save one, ere the next morning dawned, slept soundly: it was a cross grained chance that favoured him; but the next aim hit surer. *(Enter Kenrick.)* Kenrick, 'tis well thou art come! for by my soul the horrors of last night have so appalled me, I thought in yonder glen I should have died.

Ken *(much agitated).* In yonder glen!—Say, what the cause, Sir Knight?

Con. Full well thou knowest I last night sought the glade, with fixed intent to seize the fair Gwynilda; and, as my hopes foretold, I found her there, breathing her sorrows o'er her lover's tomb. In vain I sued, for the reluctant maid repulsed with pride my well dissembled flame. Impatient of control, I straight essayed to bear her to these towers, when, lo! a threatening voice resounded from the tomb!

Ken *(violently agitated).* Whose voice resounded?

Con. Thy question lies beyond my keen research. Startled at first by such strange interruption, a moment's recollection seemed to explain the cause: in truth, I guessed some new formed love had followed to the glen this fickle maid. Stung to the soul, I bade the dastard wight stand forth at once, and meet my ready blade—But do I live, while yet the words vibrate upon mine ear? Slow on the hollow blast they rose, and sternly threatened to present the spectre to my view.

Ken *(agitated).* What was the dreadful import of its speech?—Spoke it of Raymond ought?—Did it bewail that stripling's shortened date.

Con. I heard what yet I must not name. Kenrick, thou knowest my soul unapt to fear! yet such the important of the dreadful warning, that all my frame confessed a coward's feeling.

Ken. How fared the Lady in so dread an hour?

Con. I cannot tell; for o'er my 'wildered eyes the shade of death its sable mantle drew. In stupor bound, all sense of feeling lost, some lengthened space relieved my burning brain, and stretched me powerless on the dewy ground. At last, with doubtful gaze, I saw the day's returning light, and found Gwynilda fled.

Ken. Beshrew me! but I fear the midnight gloom has reared this phantom, that betrayed thy courage.

Con. No, Kenrick, no! nought but a hell-born shade could have purloined the record it unfolded. Now, tell me, canst thou guess who is the seer possessed of wizard spells to overpower me?

Ken. By my good sooth, Sir Knight, I cannot say: I nor deny, nor own the power of magic spells and charms; but might I counsel, thus I would advise: tread not again that lonely glade, for through the shelter that its shades afford, may spring the assassin's knife.

Con. Thy counsel to my wishes yields but scant relief; anon, we will discuss this matter more at large. Now hence; and see ere eventide that every watch is set—Double the guards; and when the sun westward of Cheviot casts his sloping rays, I charge thee, fail not to meet me in this hall.—Faint and exhausted with conflicting thoughts, I now repair me to the western tower; should ought of need require, thou wilt find me there. *(Exeunt.)*

Scene IV.

An Apartment in Alnwick Castle. Gwynilda seated at a Table.

Gwy. Still o'er my senses the horrific scene holds its strong empire with resistless sway. Bewildered and amazed, in vain I seek to solve the hidden cause, for all is wrapt in sullen mystery. The voice was like to that, whose melting numbers were wont to charm mine ear, when hope in festive mood led on the smiling hours.
(Enter an Attendant.)

Attend. The bearer of a message begs admittance.

Gwy. Did he say from whence?

Attend. From Angus' Lady.

Gwy. Admit him straight.
(Re-enter Attendant, with Bertha, in Boy's Clothes: she ought to be in a Highland Dress, with Plaid, Bonnet, and Plume of grass-green Feather, the Angus' colour.)

Ber. Lady, to you alone my errand speeds; may I crave an audience without a witness?

Gwy *(signs to Attendant to retire).* Wait without. *(Exit Attendant.)* Now freely speak the purport of thy message.

Ber. And dost thou know me not?—Can ought disguise these well known features from thee, beloved Gwynilda? *(They embrace.)*

Gwy. May my torn heart long banished bliss believe? or does some magic spell again my senses bind? Oh! say, my first, my best beloved friend! I say, from what cause, so unexpected, I behold you here? and wherefore, Bertha, wrapt in this disguise?

Ber. From the same cause, by adverse fortune driven, we seek a shelter here; for I have heard of all thy sad calamities, and, next my own, feel the dark record rankle in my heart:

Gwy. Sad! sad, indeed! the wayward destiny that now awaits me.—O Bertha! vain were words to tell thee what I feel! *(Weeps.)*

Ber. I own no common sorrow presses on thee, yet let me urge to bear thy trials firmly. The cup of life is ever blended thus—bitter and sweet, in strange commixture joined. So goodly fair is this world's tempting form, that mercy thus the salutary draught composed, to wean us from its joys.

Gwy. Then aid me heaven to bear me as I ought!—But tell me, wherefore art thou thus attired?

Ber. Short space is pass'd since from the moated tower of cruel Angus, veiled in this disguise, aided by that young northern bard, De Percy's harper, I escaped my bondage. Soon we reached the northern banks of Tyne, but tarried not, for much I feared my uncle's stern revenge, and straightway gained these towers, where suppliant ne'er in vain sought refuge.

Gwy. How then fares thy cousin Hubert? for I have learnt, Pembroke, by envious hate impelled, betrayed thee to Earl Angus.

Ber. O, ill enough he brooked that traitor's base designs! and vows his sword shall pay the forfeit, should they meet again. But now he journeys hence to Palestine; and change of scene may make his humour change.

Attend. Madam, the Earl.

(Enter Northumberland.)

Northd. My gentle daughter, for by that tender name I hold thee mine, how fares it with thee now?

Gwy. O, ill at ease, my Lord! my aching heart knows little respite from its recent woes. *(Hands Bertha to Northumberland.)* Bertha Umfranville, escaped from her uncle's bondage, craves your protection here.

Northd.   Thrice welcome! *(Embraces her.)*   Never were Alnwick's portals closed against the children of affliction. I knew thy noble father in his morn of life, when smiling fortune blest his happy hours; but ere his noon had pass'd, a sad reverse closed on the glowing scene—Thy mother too, of noble lineage sprung, in unrepining resignation bore her fortune's change. Methinks, in thee, I see them both before me; and if a stronger tie could bind me to my heart, it is that keen affliction pierces thine. *(To Gwynilda.)*   Secure within these towers, the ruthless robber of thy peace dares not assail thee. Come then, my children, let not despair too thickly veil the hope of better days: I feel a strong presentiment within, that all will yet be well.   *(Exeunt.)*

Scene V.

The Tomb.

(Enter Conrade.)

Con.   Scarce has the sun one revolution made, since on this spot my coward limbs betray'd me. But I have pondered well; and from my sickly brain the mist recedes—'Twas fell deceit, and fabricated by some caitiff to alarm me.—Shame on the feelings that unnerv'd my arm.—Yet the words convey'd no common meaning, nor blended falsehood with the curs'd recital—Perplexing doubts fever my very soul!—The secret outlet from the castle, for which my ardent search has yet been vain, may lead to this sequestered vale.—Yet that cannot be; the cavern'd vaults, 'tis said, lead to the beach.—Then how to reconcile these strong contending doubts, I know not.—But I will search it out, though every fiend should rise to bar my purpose. *(He draws his sword, and strikes the tomb with great violence.)*   Come forth, thou tenant of the tomb! if yet thy icy habitation holds thee.—*(He pauses in evident agitation; but gradually seems to gain confidence.)*   What! darest thou not appear, villain, dastard, coward?—Substance or shadow! I again invoke thee—*(He strikes again.)*—Silent still!—Sound is thy sleep, Lord Raymond; 'tis Conrade calls, and yet thou heed'st him not.—Now if thy spirit hovers near me, and ought of mortal passions doth retain, list to my fix'd resolve: No earthly power shall save thy widowed love from Conrade's arms; and ere tomorrow's sun shall shed its last faint lingering beams across thy grave, she shall be mine—irrevocably mine.—*(He pauses, and turns to the front of the* *stage. The spectre then slowly rises to the top of the tomb, clad in black armour, his visor barred with gold, and close clasped; and his helmet surmounted by a large plume of white feathers: his shield on his left arm, with a silver crescent in the centre, and a drawn sword in his right hand. He stands fixed. Conrade sheaths his sword.)*—'Tis all in vain: thy dormant spirit is for ever laid, if this hath failed to rouse thee. Now fare thee well, thou shapeless spectre of the midnight gloom! thy visionary threats I here despise.—'Twas all the fabrication of a dream. *(He turns to go off, and discovers the Spectre.)* Whence, and what art thou, detested form! that blasts my 'wildered sight?— Speak! and break the spell that rivets my strain'd eyes upon thee; or by my soul I'll cleave thee to the earth! *(The spectre slowly descends, and advances towards Conrade, who recedes as it advances.)* Avaunt! and touch me not, detested semblance!—Avaunt! *(Exit backwards, followed by the Spectre.)*

Scene VI.

A Corridor in Alnwick Castle, with galleries, stairs, and passages, branching off in different directions.

(Enter Fool.)

Mot. O dear, dear! I don't know what to do with myself—not one soul to speak to—from the highest to the lowest all glide about like so many ghosts: even old Ursula, whose tongue used to go from morn to night like the mill-clapper, is now as silent as the rest of them.—The creaking of the doors disturbs my Lady; the creaking of my shoes disturbs my Lord; and here am I, obliged to steal through the apartments, like a thief in the night, with my tongue tied, and my feet shod in pantoufles.

(Enter Ursula, upon tip-toe, with great caution, from a door in the back scene; she advances close to Motley, without his perceiving her, and taps him on the shoulder.)

Mot *(screams aloud, and drops on his knees)*. O dear! O dear! what is that? Help! murder! murder!

Urs. Get up, you great vociferatious fellow! I vow you are enough to set the whole castle in a conflagration with your volatility.

Mot *(Rising).* With my what? I declare, dame Ursula, I don't understand you; but you have almost frightened me to death.—My nerves have got such a shock, that I shan't be myself again for some time to come.

Urs. I am glad of it. Nerves indeed!—Merry comes up!—What have you to do with such superfluities? I never had any such useless companions in all my life; and I am all the better for it now.—But why don't you get to bed, the family have respired to rest some time since.

Mot. I cannot rest, Ursula, indeed I cannot.

Urs. What ails you? Are you ill? or have you seen any thing to disturb your muscles, and arrange your intellects?—but I cannot stay to talk with you now, so good night; go and discompose yourself to rest, go, go. *(He detains her by the arm.)*

Mot. Don't leave me yet! I declare this is the first time I have been able to speak to-day—I assure you it is; and I have something of consequence to impart to you.

Urs. Then depart it quickly; for I am going to the Lady Gwynilda's chamber immediately.

Mot. That is the very thing of consequence I wish to tell you, for between you and I, I think you had better not go there to-night; for *(He looks cautiously about.)* I saw such a sight there, as I passed along the gallery in my way hither, as I shall never forget.

Urs. Preserve us all! what did you see? I hope it was not the phantom of Lord Raymond come to visit her, poor Lady!

Mot. No, no, it was no more like Lord Raymond, than you are like Lady Gwynilda.—It was a shocking sight, Ursula!

Urs. Why, what in the name of all that is soporific, has the fool seen? why don't you speak out at once? and not keep me in this debilitating state of suspension.

Mot. O Ursula! this is a sad wicked world; full of falsehood; no such thing as true love left in it; it's all a hum; and I never will believe womankind any more.

Urs. I tell you what, Motley, you are a fastidious fellow, for dispersing womankind that way; but I shall take care and tell my Lord, the consternation you put upon our characters.

Mot. First of all, let me tell you what I saw. About half an hour ago, as I was creeping along the gallery in my pantoufles, as you see here, for you know it is at our peril to make a noise, I chanced to observe the door of the cedar chamber standing a little open; I knew the

Lady Gwynilda slept there, and was fain to retreat, for fear she should see me; but somehow or other, I felt a strong inclination to go on: I advanced slowly and silently along, and just as I got to the door, fully intending to shut my eyes in passing in, something unluckily compelled me to peep in, and there I beheld—O Ursula! I beheld such a sight.

Urs. Well, fool, and what didst thou behold?

Mot. As sure as you are standing there, I saw that little Scotch macaroni, that arrived here to-day with my Lord's harper, sitting by her in her chamber.

Urs *(pretending to be much surprised)*. Indeed!—You have put me quite into a flusteration.—Are you sure, you positively saw him?

Mot. Yes, positively sure! and what is still more, I actually saw both my Lady and he unrobing themselves. The youth had doff'd his bonnet and plaid, unbuckled his sword belt, and rose for the purpose of removing his jerkin, when, for fear of being discovered, I made the best of my way hither.

Urs *(bursts into a fit of laughter)*. Poor fellow! thou hast, indeed, seen a most putrefying sight!—"The little Scotch macaroni!" Ha, ha, ha!—But thou art a fool, Motley; and, therefore, I excuse thy want of concernment, and tell thee, that the man thou sawest in my Lady's chamber is a woman.

Mot. "The man that I saw in my Lady's chamber, is a woman!" Well, that's a good one to be sure; but I am not quite such a fool as to believe that a man is a woman, after all.

(A whistle is sounded within. Before the introduction of bells into the houses of the gentry, silver whistles were used for the purpose of summoning their attendants.)

Urs. There, I knew how it would be, that is the Lady Gwynilda's silver call; she has, no doubt, heard your voluminous tongue, and wants to know what all this noise is about. Get along this instant, without any more prognostication, or I will send Clifford to you in two minutes. *(Exit Ursula, by the door she entered at.)*

Mot. Well, if I must, I must; so good night, Ursula. "The man I saw was a woman!" after that, one may believe any thing. *(Exit Motley, at a side door.)*

Scene VII.

The Marble Hall. A Table, with a Lamp burning upon it. The Footlights down. The Castle bell tolls twelve. Kenrick, solus.

Ken. Twelve knells have rung; and yet he comes not!—Strange apprehensions flit across my mind!—If he has sought again De Percy's tomb, Kenrick, thy life's last hour is on the wane! *(He rises.)* Oh! for some fair pretext to lull his keen surmise! and then I'd quite these hated walls for ever, ere the full open blaze of truth bursts through the mystery that hovers round.—*(He pauses.)*—Well, be it as it may!—My soul is free from deeds so foul—My hands unstained with murder—In all the wanderings of my devious track, I could not, dared not, stoop to such atrocities.—He comes!—Now conscience, unwelcome monitor, be still!

(Enter Conrade, his arms folded, his whole appearance abstracted and sullen: he does not perceive Kenrick, who steps back as he enters.)

Con. My brain is turned!—Curse on the wild delusions that pursue me! *(Kenrick advances; Conrade starts, and puts himself in a posture of defense.)* Caitiff! how darest thou steal upon my privacy? and, like a coward creeping at my heels, catch my unguarded thoughts.

Ken *(angrily)*. Your mood is somewhat warm, Sir Knight, and shortens your remembrance, methinks.

Con. It may be so!—My mood is like the moon, subject to change; and oftentimes not fair.

Ken. This morn you bid me, ere the sun declined, fail not to meet you here. The highest peak on Cheviot's brow, long since reflected back the setting ray—

Con. Thou art right! thou art right, good Kenrick! but since then, my wits have wandered far.—Even to the very portals of my castle, the horrid apparition has pursued me—Didst thou not meet it as thou entered?

Ken *(agitated)*. Meet who?—No one hath entered here—your words are vague—I do not understand you.

Con. Good!—'Tis as I wish: thou must not understand me.—But, Kenrick, I believe some fiend, e'en in my tower, my slumbers hath annoy'd. Weary and restless through the live-long day I press'd my couch, nor could seduce soft slumber to my aching eyes. At length the day declined, and through the gloom, the melancholy song of eve in hollow murmurs stray'd: I listened to the sighing breezes, as they swept along, which gently seem'd to lull me to repose: each weary sense inhal'd the soothing balm, and sunk at last to rest.

Ken. Some sickly dream hath troubled thy repose.

Con. It was a waking dream, good Kenrick. Didst thou e'er mark, that near the entrance of my chamber, in the western tower, the harp of Lady Geraldine hung?

Ken. I do remember it well.

Con. In strong vibrations, its half-shatter'd chords loudly responded to an unseen hand.—Sudden, I woke; and springing from my bed, demanded quick, if Kenrick waited there? No answer met mine ear; but through the twilight's dubious shade, methought I saw a tall majestic form retire.

Ken. Then he it was, in sable armour clad, Caled encountered near the postern way: in haste he seemed, and of no common mien. Caled demanded parley, and, with drawn falchion, stood athwart his way—Vain request! he deigned him no reply, struck down his arm, and with gigantic stride, strode on towards the chapel east of yonder glen.

Con. In sable armour, Kenrick, didst thou say? and was his casque in raven plumage deck'd, dark as the frontlet of his ebon vest?

Ken. Not so! His massy helm did towery bear high waving plumes, blanched white as mountain snow. His visor clasped and latticed thick with gold, did from all mortal ken his visage screen.

Con. Hush! Kenrick, hush! no more my soul appall! thy words congeal the life spring in my heart.—The form that Caled saw was a fell-boding sprite, that restless flits beneath the moon's pale beam.—Vain, vain indeed, was Caled's shining blade! for none his airy footsteps can retard.

Ken. Away with these wild fantasies! his was no spectre form.—Thou knowest him not, I ween?

Con. I knew him once where Trave's dark waters swell, *(Kenrick starts.)* and own'd him there as Conrade's deadly foe; but soon the stripling felt my veteran arm soil his fair honours on the blood-stain'd sand. To thee, it were needless now to breathe his name, or say to whom the sable Knight belonged, or point to where his mouldering relics lie:—the triple secret lodges in thy breast.

Ken. Too well the tale I know!—O'er my distracted thoughts a sudden terror passes, that overpowers me.

Con. Thy mood is changed; and hasty too the means—But late thou scoff'd, in taunting strain, that I should fear dark magic spells and incantations foul—Kenrick, I like it not! my mind misgives me—and yet, methinks thou durst not.—But, *(Seizes hold of him.)* mark me, should I find thee false, or fail in ought that thy fair words and promises held to me, thy conscious soul may guess my deep designs;—but the high meed beyond thy fancy lies.

Ken *(violently agitated).* Enough! enough! No more of this, I pray!—Say, shall we pass the guard? 'tis now past midnight.

Con. What ails thee, coward? thou seem'st to startle at the passing breeze; and e'en thy shadow glancing across thy way, in thy blanch'd visage shews thy rising fears.—Shame on thee, thus to shake thy soul!—Straightway prepare us some convivial cheer; in the full cup we'll wash thy fears away, to arm thee with a fortitude like mine; and lest the sparkling beverage lacks a zest, we'll pledge the warrior in the snowy plume.

(As Conrade ceases to speak, a strange and horrid noise is heard at a distance. It advances with a loud knocking under the stage. One of the marble compartments suddenly flies open, and a gigantic figure slowly rises, bearing a flaming torch in one hand, and the other resting on the hilt of his sword: a bugle horn is suspended at his breast; his vesture shaggy, like a bear; and his whole appearance horrific. He springs forward, and addresses Kenrick.)

Spectre. Kenrick! thy time is come, the die is cast;
This hour, this waning hour, is doom'd thy last.
Thy fate, in myst'ry wrapt, I may not tell;
Nor where thy guilty soul shall henceforth dwell.
Unlike the spectre, which at dead of night,
In Macedonia, burst upon the sight
Of Brutus, and thus spoke: "We meet again—
Where wait thy legions on Phillipii's plain?"
No such thou seest in me: lo! here I come,
To free from added guilt thy hast'ning doom;
And ere the measure of thy crimes run o'er,
Permit thy crimes to scourge mankind no more.
Conrade! to thee some further time is given;
In which, repentance points the way to heaven.

E'en as I breathe thy foul detested name,
Unwonted horrors chill my airy frame.
Prepare thee quick! or soon the fading light
Shall close thine eyes in shades of endless night.
Now, Kenrick, now! the dawn's advancing ray
Bursts the dark veil of night, and chides delay.
In council deep, the ministers of fate
To seal thy final doom expectant wait.

(The spectre sounds the bugle, a band of fiends spring from the floor; he waves the torch over Kenrick, they raise him of their shields, and descend with him through the floor, followed by the Spectre. Conrade faints, and the curtain falls.)

END OF ACT II.

Act III. Scene I.

Sunrise.   Outside of Conrade's Castle. Drawbridge, Moat, &c.
Sentinel on guard before the great entrance.

(Enter Oswald from the Castle, upon the Platform.)

Osw. Good-morrow, Bertram.

Ber. Good-morrow, comrade; say, how fares our chief?

Osw. O, ill at ease! the live-long night he sighed; and ever and anon, such piteous groans burst in strong conflict from his tortured breast, that, in sooth, I bethought me he would die.

Ber. Some deeds of darkness canker his repose. 'Tis said, that he it was, aided by Kenrick, the last time Percy revelled in his tower, caused the Lord Raymond's death, by mixing in his wine a deadly weed.

Osw. I do believe it, Bertram; for he cannot rest, though twice twelve moons have circled o'er his head since Kenrick vanished, and no one e'er knew how.

Ber. Aye, he made some awful end, that's certain. But dost thou remember that time Lord Raymond went a pilgrimage to Loretto, when all his band were murdered in a forest at midnight, his treasures stolen, and himself left for dead?

Osw. I do remember it well.

Ber. This same Sir Conrade, mark me, knows it too. Poor Philip, rest his soul! in his last frantic moments, divulged the horrid secret, for he it was that overheard the Knight at his confession, and Philip never did well after it.—But softly, these are dangerous tales to tell.

Osw. Confession! why the sun had scarce tipt the top of the towers this morning, when he dispatched Caled for Father Anselmo, the old dumb hermit.

Ber. Aye, aye, he judges wisely, Oswald, dumb confessors tell no tales; and this same hermit, who lost his speech in the holy wars, by a barbed arrow being shot through his tongue, hears all, but says nothing.

Osw. Right, right, comrade!—But tell me, is it true that Earl Northumberland for tilt and tournament to-morrow, forms the lists on Alnwick's green?

Ber. It is; and there Umfranville, now the Earl of Angus, will display his skill in arms; and shortly means, 'tis said, to wed his gentle cousin, the Lady Bertha.

Osw. Aye, I remember him well; and fame speaks loudly of him; for late he conquered in the lists, Philip de Valence, Pembroke's proud Earl; the same that did betray him to his father, that time he meant to have borne away his long betrothed bride.

Ber. It was a trait'rous deed—but see, the holy hermit is approaching.

(Enter Kenrick, disguised as Anselmo. He signs to them to let down the Bridge: he crosses and enters the Castle, followed by Oswald.)

Scene II.

A Gothic Chamber in Conrade's Castle. Conrade laid upon a Couch, pale, haggard, and restless. Caled in waiting.

Con. How wears the lingering time?—No tidings yet; and now the beaming day chases far hence the sallow shades of night.—Why comes he not?—Say, what the answer sent?—Didst thou not urge the import of my need?—Speed thee again, and say, I may not wait, the aid required admits not of delay.

(As Caled approaches the door, it slowly opens, and Anselmo enters; he waves his hand to Caled, who retires.)

Con. *(rising.)* Father, all hail! I crave thy holy aid—guilt, conscious guilt, distracts my tortured breast; fed by despair, the livid pestilence consumes my soul.—In such distracted mood, Oh! can no consolation minister to ease.

(Anselmo points toward heaven.)

Con. Thinkest thou, O Father! I durst e'er presume to raise my hopes and look for mercy there? By thee untrod the wasting path of sin, thy guiltless mind can form no estimate of the dark deeds that fester in my heart. Thy hand was never raised against the traveler in the lonely wild; nor when mirth's summons sped the rosy draught, didst thou, unseen, the deadly nightshade blend, and with the cup the social pledge betray—This have I done. *(Anselmo weeps.)* Oh! spare thy tears, Anselmo—in pity spare; and list thee straight to what I would unfold. To brave Northumberland I debtor stand, for gentle

usage and fair courtesy, when first a stranger to his tower I came—
How thinkest thou, Father, I repaid his care?—Oh! do not curse me,
and I'll tell thee how—I stole a treasure when beneath his roof.
Amidst the full abundance of his house, it was the richest heaven had
bestowed. Deep in the subtle wile, to aid my purposes, beneath a
vassal's garb, I found a friend. Oh! had my life, ere that detested day,
closed its sad course; but all too true to the fell mandate given, ill-fated
Kenrick stretched his wayward hand, blended the draught, and—
(Anselmo violently agitated, falls upon the floor, and groans aloud.)

    Con. *(raising the Hermit.)* I do implore thee thy strong grief
restrain, it shakes my purpose, and unmans my soul. Oh! could I but
recall the time that's past; or lose remembrance of those horrid
scenes!—But it may not be done.—Since that terrific night, when
Kenrick's doom met, in dark mystery wrapt, its closing date, no hour
of rest my waning life has known; for then a hideous sprite did me
forewarn to sin no more, but fit me for the grave. *(Anselmo waves his
hand in derision of spectres and prophetic appearances. Conrade
points to the window.)* Seest thou, Anselmo, where yon turrets rise? in
hopeless grief, within their circling walls, a woe-worn fair her cruel
fate bewails. Twice o'er her head the summer's golden beams have
twice succeeded to stern winter's gloom, since, like a blast, a spoiler
stept between her promised hopes, and blighted all around. But stern
repentance, no, nor season's change, can animate the dust in yonder
tomb. *(He seizes hold of Anselmo in frantic agitation.)* Methinks, e'en
now, I see a shrouded shade, ghastly and pale, flit through yon misty
glen.—Sudden the airy form glides forth again, rears its lank arm, and
points to yonder grave, where, like a summer cloud, it mounts on high,
sheds balmy fragrance, and then blends in air.—*(Quits his hold of the
Hermit; but is more violently agitated.)* See, father, see, anon it re-
appears: such, on the banks of the Trave, where the proud Serra Valta
towers on high, a belted youth, with casque and snowy plume, I once
encountered—Ye horrid phantoms, hence!—in mercy, hence! nor thus
distract me!

*(He faints into Anselmo's arms. The Hermit, after a short pause,
strikes his foot forcibly upon the floor; the noise dissipates Conrade's
stupor: he then points to the quarter where Conrade's fears had
attracted him, and, smiling, waves his hand in contempt of such
imaginary apprehensions. Then collecting his looks, placing one hand*

upon his breast, and extending the other towards heaven, he bursts into tears, and looks with pity and compassion upon Conrade.)

Con. I thank thy speechless pity more than worlds can tell; and crave thy pardon for this wild alarm; but memory lords it o'er my sickly brain with fantasies of strange and horrid guise. Ere then thou leavest me, mark my fixed resolve: to-morrow's sun will set in vain to me; nor its returning beams e'er glad my sight. And when my stormy day of life is pass'd, tell noble Percy, that the dying wretch, who, like a mildew o'er the infant year, blighted the promise of his noble line, in the dark, dread arrears, gave life for life. Now fare thee well, good father! fare thee well! and in thy prayers, remember me! *(Exeunt severally.)*

Scene III.

A Hall in Northumberland's Castle.

(Enter Clifford, very tipsy.)

Clif. It is impossible to remain any—longer among these dissipated fellows. A sober, steady—man, like myself, has no chance with them. For my part, I hate drink—ing: there is something so genteel—so ungenteel in being seen in—liquor, that I always, never, am, do, persuaded, induced, to trespass upon—sobriety. Now there is that little fellow, Goliah, a shame to be seen; he is as drunk as an—owl, and as blind as a bat; and yet I could not make him sensible how—very ridiculous he looked.—I must certainly discard him from my list of acquaintances—to be certainly I shall.—Goliah, says I— *(Enter Goliah. Clifford staggers to meet him, and shakes him violently by the hand.)* My dear little friend, how do you—do? I am so glad to see you.—I was just saying to my—self, that myself, and my dear, dear friend, moonsheer Goliah, were the only two sober—gentlemen in the whole party.

Gol. I do not know vat you mean, monsieur Clayfort. I alvays vas one man sober, sair; but you are dronck, vary dronck, sair. I ave drink littel; but you ave drink moch, vary moch indeed.

Clif. My dear little fellow, I excuse you, you do not see quite—clear just now. I only drank a bumper to our noble master, one to Lord Ravenna, one to Lord—Hubert, and that made two—one to Lady

Gwynilda, another to Lady Bertha—you know I could not possibly omit drinking the ladies'—healths, sweet darling creatures; and then, by way of a finish, I had a brace of bumpers to all our noble—selves, and that made three—No man could be more moderate, I'm sure.

Gol. Vel, vel, dis is pretty doing; nobody sober but myself, for dis week past. My Lor Ravenna, and my Lo Hubert, ave turn de castel upside down.

Clif. Upside down! I told you, my dear little fellow, you were a little upon the go: you don't know, you see, which—end of you is uppermost, upon my—honor, you don't.

(Enter Ursula.)

Urs. I declare there is no such thing as living in this castle now; all is riot and uproar, from the banqueting hall to the warder's lodge. My Lord calls it jovalty and fessafetivety; but I call it uproarious. As to you, *(To Clifford.)* you may be ashamed of yourself; you amphibious fellow; you are a pretty superintender of my Lord's household, in this state of intostercation.

Clif. Intoxication!—More shame for you, Mrs. Ursula, at your time of life, to addict yourself to take liquor. I see—perfectly well how you are, you have been upon the go all this week, and now you are quite—done over.

Urs. I depicted to take liquor! You vile monster, it is yourself that is depicted to it—But I shall let my Lord know that you have seduced my character, and I take Mr. Goliah as a witness.

Gol. Yes, yes, I vil be von vitness that you seduce Mrs. Ursula.

Clif. I deny the charge—I positively deny the—charge.

Urs. You are an odoriferous fellow; and unless you procrastinate yourself upon your knees, and beg my pardon, I will tell my Lord in what a clandesterous manner you have seduced my good name, that's what I will.

Clif. My dear, good Ursula, I never said a word against you in all my life— You—know I never did.

Urs. I know you are a lazy fellow: yonder stand all the boxes, pokemantles, and luggish, belonging to my Lord Ravenna, in the warder's lodge; a whole week has relapsed since his arrival, and you have never found time to displace them in his chamber yet. But I must not waste my time in talking to you here; to-morrow will be a day of days, and I must go and make the proper derangements for the table.—O, how I long to see that fascinating youth, Lord Ravenna, at the tournament! he will look as the song says,

> Like Proserpine, the god of war,
> When driving in his hazy car.

Clif. "Like superfine, the god of war!" O, how—beautiful that will be!

Urs. Pshaw! you silly fellow, get along with you; go to bed, and try to desperate by sleep, the efficacy of intostercation—But remember this, you are all to be dressed in your new robes, or no tilting match for you to-morrow.

Gol. Indeed, monsieur Clay-fort, you had better go a bed. I go. I assure you, and Madame Ursa go; for I dare not leave her alone vid you, at present.

Clif. You dare not live alone! I don't wonder at that, my dear little fellow; but I will take care of you, do not be afraid, I will protect you with my—life; so never fear, never fear.

Gol. Vat de diable should I be afraid of, I fear no man at all, monsieur Clay-fort.

Clif. No, no, keep up your heart, don't be afraid, nothing shall hurt you whilst I—am beside you. I don't care that *(Snaps his fingers.)* for the devil himself, no, nor all the devils put together—devil take them.

(Enter Motley from a door in the back scene, dressed as the spectre that carried off Kenrick: he advances cautiously, and placing himself between Clifford and the Dwarf, speaks in a fierce manner. Ursula screams aloud.)

Mot. Pray, which of you gentlemen was inquiring for me, I heard my name thrice repeated? *(All horribly frightened.)*

Gol. Sair, vat you vant here?

Mot. *(To Clifford.)* I think it was you that called me, are you ready?

Clif. Stand off!—Don't touch me! *(He endeavours to screen himself behind the Dwarf.)* It was he that called you, not me—Stand off, I say, stand off.

Gol. Fie, for shame, monsieur Clay-fort! vat you posh me dat vay for? You know ver vel it vas yourself, dat talk about Monsieur le Diable—you know it vas; Madame Ursa can tell de same.

Urs. O dear, what an ugly monster it is! *(Aside.)* Upon the honor of a single female spinster, my dear, sweet gentleman, it was that somniferous fellow, Clifford, that did revoke your name. Thrice three times I heard him say devil, as loud as he could bawl.

Mot. Aye, I thought it was him—Come, quick, quick, quick! you have been a sad wicked fellow: confess your sins before we go, confess, I say. *(At the close of this speech, Goliah steals off.)*

Gol. Bless my art, vat monstrous ugly diable it is! and vat orrid stench of brimstone it has. *(Exit in great haste.)*

Clif. I do confess all my sins, indeed I do—Now pray stand a little that way—I am engaged with a party to-night, in the hall—excuse me leaving you. *(He attempts to get off.)*

Mot. Not so fast, not so fast! there is a party waiting for you—(he points to the ground) you understand me.

(Ursula glides off in silence.)

Clif. Mercy on me! what shall I do? what shall I do? *(Aside.)* Just then let me go and bid them farewell? I'll return in two minutes, I will indeed.

Mot. I dare not; I expect my master here every moment, he intends to have you for his supper to-night: when the castle bell tolls twelve, he will swallow you at one gulp; and if I let you escape, he will eat me in your stead.—I'll look and see if he is coming. *(Whilst Motley goes up to the door by which he entered, Clifford strides off. Motley returns.)* Ha, ha, ha! I think I am upon the square with you now, Master Clifford, *(Throws off the disguise.)* for the drubbing you gave me long since. *(Examining the dress.)* Well to be sure, this is a pretty dress enough! I warrant, poor Kenrick thought the devil had got him in real earnest, when one of the banditti (whose mid-night revels were disturbed by Sir Conrade being in the castle) carried him down into the vaults beneath the Marble Hall—But I must put this exactly where I found it, as Clifford by this time is brought to his sober senses—should he discover me with it, my word, he would give me a trimming for my new jacket. *(Exit at the door he entered at.)*

Scene IV.

A Gothic Apartment in Alnwick Castle.

(Enter Ursula, speaking as she enters.)

Urs. Now be sure that all is ready; and go and see if that recumbent fellow, Clifford, is risen yet: my Lord was inquiring for him an hour ago.—*(Enter Motley, dressed in a new suit of various colours, with blue cap and variegated feathers.)* Ha! Motley, is that you? why I declare you are so smart, I did not know you—you are quite a phenomenon.

Mot. Yes, I think I shall do some execution among the girls to-day, at least my elegant appearance will; and I shall not be the first gentleman that owes his success to the set of a cap and the cut of a doublet.

Urs. Well, I give you joy of your ominous hopes—But really, Motley, you played the devil in such defection last night, that you almost frightened me out of my wits. I declare I am quite hopuponacrack, as the doctor book says, this morning.

Mot. A what! hop-upon-a-cracket! I never heard of such a disorder in all my life; and as to doctors' books, they are all flummery. I never took either draught, pill, or bolus, and here I am, as sound in wind and limb as ever. But tell me, have you all in proper order? for the tilting match will soon begin: they were forming the lists before sunrise this morning; and you know you will have no time to arrange house affairs after.

Urs. All is properly deranged; I have only my own dress to expiate upon, and then I shall set out to the green. I intend to be the very polyanthus of perfection; so good bye to you, and mind that you pay every possible disrespect and attention to the company, good bye. *(Exit Ursula.)*

Mot. Good bye—Aye, there she goes, as kind hearted an old wench as ever lived: a little outlandish, or so, with cramped words; but she is a great scolar, reads all the hard books that fall in her way, and knows a vast deal more than we do. By this time all must be in high glee; and I always like to be first at a feast, and last at a fray: but before I go, I'll rehearse my new song that I have to sing to-night, that I may be, as Ursula says, the polyanthus of perfection. *(Motley sings.)*

The sages of old this maxim have told,
   "'Tis best to be merry and wise."
But with their permission, I'll change the position,
   And make it wise and merry.
   With nigh down derry,
   All that are wise will be merry.

The reason for why is as plain as my eye,
   As grieving all own is a folly;
Then who'd be so mad to be foolish and sad,
   When wisdom consists in being merry.
   With a high down derry,
   All that are wise must be merry.

'Tis whimpering and whining, and useless repining,
   That bleaches crop of the skull;
Whilst joke, laugh, and song, our beauties prolong,
   Provided we're wise when we're merry.
   With a high a down derry,
   Lack wisdom, and none can be merry.

(Exit.)

Scene V.

The Lists for a Tournament, the upper Tiers filled with Ladies, and the lower ones with Lords, Knights, &c. At the head, an elevated seat with a canopy overt it; and a platform, for the Fool and Dwarf to stand upon. Bagpipes heard at a distance. (Air,—"Scots, wha hae wi' Wallace bled.")

(Enter Heralds, Armour-bearers, &c. Pipers, in blue, faced with yellow, silver crescent upon the right arm, followed by Earl Northumberland, richly attired, leading in Gwynilda; Lord Hubert, now Earl of Angus, in full suit of armour, leading in Bertha, her dress white satin, surmounted by a tartan plaid. They cross the ring; Northumberland takes the elevated seat, placing Gwynilda on one hand of him, and Bertha on the other. Ursula, Motley, and Goliah,

follow, and place themselves upon the platform, by their Chief. Earl Angus bows to Northumberland and the Ladies; then advances to the wicket of the ring. His Herald takes the other side of the entrance, and sounds a challenge, thrice, upon his bugle.)

Herald. Hubert de Umfranville, Angus' noble Earl, to every valiant knight this challenge sends: On warriors' sacred word, for honour's cause, he'll throw the lance, or wield the glittering blade. Caparisoned aright, he now awaits, to prove the skill of any bold compeer.

(Flourish of Trumpets. A Knight advances from the crowd, to the center of the ring. His armour is old and defaced: no plumes on his helmet: his manner, notwithstanding, high and commanding. His visor close clasped.)

Knight. No Marshal-man at arms, I deem, there needs assert those claims that rest alone on skill; nor serves it ought to a swell warrior's fame, his large possessions and high sounding titles. Whence, or what am I, boots it not to say. Roused by thy challenge, here I ready stand, and proof of thy Lord's prowess, fearless claim.

(Flourish of trumpets. A Warrior, most splendidly attired in armour, a red cross upon his right arm, springs into the ring. He strikes his lance upon the ground; then throws his gage at the feet of him that spoke last. They tilt with their lances, till the red cross Knight breaks that of his opponent. They draw, and after a severe combat, the Knight in rusty armour is wounded, and falls. Trumpets flourish.)

Herald. By courtesy, Sir Knight, whoe'er thou art, thy name and lineage I here demand?

Hubert. By friendship's sacred bond, the Knight I claim. Together leagued, we braved the holy wars, 'mid countless perils, marked with many a wound. On Asia's plains, Ravenna's conquering name swell'd her proud echoes with his matchless deeds. To grace our lists, his sword, the warrior drew; and well has won Northumbria's applause.

(A groan of anguish from the wounded Knight. They turn towards him; when their attention is arrested by the hasty entrance of a Monk, who eagerly presses into the ring: he gazes a moment over the wounded Knight; then throws aside his mantle and discovers Anselmo. He kneels and raises the Knight in his arms, unclasps his visor, and removes his helmet; then addresses him.)

Anselmo. List thee, Sir Conrade!—For a moment hear!—The sound of consolation now awaits thee.—Oh! once again unclasp thy closing eyes.—Thou man of mighty ills, cans't thou not trace thy servant, Kenrick? *(He throws off his cowl from his head, and discover himself.)* In this woe-worn form, have watchful penance, hard and ceaseless prayer, stamp'd my wan features with so sad a change, that nought remains to guide thee to the past? *(Conrade feebly lifts his hand.)* I understand thee—brief I must be—then let my words solace thee: Lord Raymond lived, saved by my hand—thy soul is lighter by one crime, at least. An opiate of strong power, I blended in his cup; and when the subtle weed had spent its force, I sought, at midnight hour, his lonely tomb, and gave him life and liberty again. By sacred bond I held the noble youth, never to divulge the horrid secret, till twice twelve moons had pass'd o'er Alnwick's towers. In that long lapse of time, I sought him on the plains of Palestine, where, flushed with conquest, in ill-fated hour, beneath a Pagan's arm, the hero fell.

(With a wild convulsive scream, Gwynilda faints. Ravenna springs across the ring, and raises her in his arm.)

Ravenna. Thou excellence divine! behold in me, one whose fond heart's for ever link'd to thine. *(He removes his helmet, and discovers Lord Raymond.)* Awake, my fair! Thy death-like fears dispel! 'tis Raymond calls thee back to life and love.

(The Knights rise, and wave their helmets thrice; the Trumpets flourish, and Gwynilda revives.)

Rav. My destined bride, thy long lost Raymond see! nor let despair, amid the varied ills that chequer life, again exclude thy hopes of better days: myself, the inmate once of yon lone tomb, yet breathes to tell thee, that I live for thee.—*(Conrade groans.)* Kenrick! thy master needs thy utmost care; remove him hence, and minister in all that can be done to aid him: the warrior's greatest conquest is to save.—*(They bear Conrade off.)* Come then, my love, our plighted vows fulfilled, again the harp and song shall breathe around their magic influence, through Alnwick's towers.

> Whilst love and friendship in soft union join'd,
> With hallow'd bonds, our future fate shall bind.

(Curtain falls to appropriate music.)

THE END.

ST. CLAIR OF THE ISLES;

or,

The Outlaw of Barra

A Scottish Historical Melodrama

In 3 Acts

by

Elizabeth Polack

LLOYD'S MINIATURE PORTRAITS *IN KING AHASUERUS.*

Mrs. Gomersal as Queen Esther.

Mr. Freer as Haman.

Mrs. Windgrove as Queen Vashti.

Mr. Ford as Barnazabus.

Mr. Cobham as Mordecai.

Mr. Dibden Pitt as King Ahasuerus.

London Pub.d by R.LLOYD, at his Wholesale Theatrical Print Warehouse, 40,Gibson St. Waterloo Road.

Lloyd's toy theatre edition of characters from Elizabeth Polack's melodrama, *Esther, the Royal Jewess; or, The Death of Haman.* Reproduced by permission from the collection of Mr. Barry Clarke, Pollock's Toy Museum, London.

St. Clair of the Isles

In her chapter on "Women Pioneers" in *Feminism and Theatre,* Sue-Ellen Case comments on the lack of biographical information available for pre-twentieth-century women writers and concludes that "the invisibility of their biographies suppresses valuable knowledge about the experience and models of women in theatre. Though 'firsts seem to be important in dominant histories, 'first women' do not" (44). Such sentiments are especially resonant in the case of Elizabeth Polack, the first Jewish woman melodramatist in England.

Little is known of the private life of Elizabeth Polack. The dates of her birth and death are unknown, but, given the limits of her professional career (1830–1838), it is likely that she was born sometime within the first decade of the nineteenth century. It is also likely that she was a member of the Polack family of the Whitechapel district and conceivably a close relative of Joel Samuel Polack who, in 1831, emigrated to New Zealand where he lived until 1837. Between 1838–1839, after Elizabeth had established herself as a playwright in London, Joel's biographer reports that he returned to London and lived with a sister in Piccadilly.[1] While the evidence is hardly conclusive, it is possible that Elizabeth was that sister.

Elizabeth Polack is credited with the authorship of five plays:[2] *Alberti; or, The Mines of Idria, Angeline; or, The Golden Chain* (both lost), *Woman's Revenge,* and the two highly successful melodramas, *Esther, the Royal Jewess; or, The Death of Haman* and *St. Clair of the Isles; or, The Outlaw of Barra.* While the first two titles are lost, *Woman's Revenge* exists in the Lord Chamberlain's copy, licensed for production on 25 February 1832 and performed thirty times at the Royal Olympic Theatre beginning 27 February 1832.[3]

Advertised as an "entirely new burletta," *Woman's Revenge* depicts the attempts of Frank Merton, a good-natured wastrel, to gain his aunt's permission to marry the girl he loves. Unfortunately, the girl happens to be the daughter of Sir Thomas Dillon, the man who jilted the aunt, Miss Flashington, years ago and the matron exercises her "woman's revenge" by opposing the match. Through the various machinations of a servant called Fag (played by the ubiquitous actor James Vining), Frank Merton marries his sweetheart and Miss Flashington resolves her differences with Sir Thomas, who, happily, having recently lost his wife, can finally return the sentiments. Peppered with bluff country characters, the play is an innocuous mixture of wit and sentiment, most notable for the strength of the women characters who, typical of Polack's work, possess all the authority, money, and power in the play.

More significant is the "Eastern Melodrama"[4] *Esther* produced on 7 March 1835 at the Pavilion Theatre, one of the more notable theatres playing melodrama in the East End of London and one of the three that survived into the twentieth century (*English Melodrama* 54).[5] The cast featured Cobham as Mordechi, Freer as Haman, Mrs. Wingrove as Vashti, Mrs. Forde as Irene, Mrs. Henry Lewis as Esther, and, as Ahasuerus, George Dibdin Pitt, the author of the 1847 melodrama, *Sweeney Todd.* The play is filled to the brim with exoticism as the stage directions for the first scene of act one indicate:

The Grand Tent of Ahasuerus, the whole of the Stage occupied, having the appearance of a splendid Marquee, erected on golden and silver Pillars; The Draperies of white and purple. Splendid Banners, &c. A magnificent Banquet, in the Eastern style; the Vases, Cups, &c. of the most costly appearance. . . .Trumpets and Cymbals. A Grand Ballet, in which the Performers at intervals salaam to the King, and present the Guests with wine. Grand Flourish. (5)

What follows in three long acts is a fairly true account of the story of Esther, the Jewish wife of the Persian king Ahasuerus. Through her nobility of soul (as well as great physical beauty) she saves her people from the evil machinations of the villain, Haman, the king's favorite.[6] The pomp and splendor of the piece is mixed with a heavy dose of masochism in the character of the king's first wife, Vashti who, having been banished pleads with Haman in high style:

No! give me death; but save me from horrid banishment! Haman! you will not suffer your queen to plead to you in vain! *(He turns from her—she kneels to him.)* See, I am at your feet—I to whom all vast Assyria once paid homage! Let your guards pierce my heart: yes, let me die! and as the life blood flows from this lacerated bosom, I'll bless thee for thy mercy! *(Rises.)* Still you reject me? then all is lost! Irene! my slaves! will none save the wretched Vashti! Ha! see, see! my royal husband—he comes! yet nearer—see! he raises his sabre! Strike, great Ahasuerus, and let me die! here, at thy feet, thy queen implores thee—strike! He laughs as if in mockery at my prayer—now he ascends the throne! shall I not take my place there?—do you refuse your queen? Do not raise the sceptre in anger—*(Screams and falls.)*—Gods! he has struck me!—my brain is on fire!—madness! death! banishment! ha! ha! ha! *(She laughs hysterically.—Music—Haman coolly folds his Arms. Tableau.)* (13)

Two facts set *Esther* apart from other Eastern melodramas: the heroine is, in fact, the hero of the piece, and the exoticism is Jewish rather than Turkish. Both these issues culminate in the final speech of the play (usually reserved for the male hero or masculine symbol of restored order) where Esther exalts her victory as well as her people:

Blessed be this hour! happy be my king! and prosperous be the Jews of every land and clime! May the sacred tree of liberty never lose a branch in contending for religious superiority; but all be free to worship as he pleases. Let that man be for ever despised who dares interfere between his fellow man and his creed. Oh, people of my own nation, may the heart promised home you've sighed for present you golden hours of freedom; and down to posterity may the sons of Judah in every clime celebrate this time in happy Purim! (30)

A transparency descends with the word "Purim!" on it and the curtain falls, after a grand tableau.[7]

The success of this work is marked by the fact that the play was published by Duncombe in two undated editions (both believed to be printed in 1835) and again as Vol. 120 of *Lacy's Acting Edition of Plays* in 1884.[8] In one of Duncombe's editions, the author acknowledges her debt to John Farrell,[9] playwright and manager of the Pavilion Theatre, by dedicating the play to him:

Permit me to offer you a Drama which your indefatigable and liberal conduct has contributed to render more successful than my most sanguine hopes anticipated. I dedicate my *Royal Jewess* to you, as a tribute of gratitude for the attention you have bestowed on its production, and which I am proud thus publicly to acknowledge.

In *Getting into the Act,* Ellen Donkin reports that while a theatre manager's approval was necessary for any author, male or female, to get a play produced, among women, "the sense of debt appears to have extended well beyond the practicalities of editing and producing, and to have worked its way into the creative mechanism itself" (26-27).

This seems to have been the case between Polack and Farrell. But at a time when mentoring between managers and playwrights was marked by "conflict, disobedience, or adversarial behavior" (Donkin 27), such a public display of gratitude must certainly have been refreshing, and most advantageous to her career.[10]

The ethnic nature of Eastern melodrama is reprised in Miss Polack's great Gothic melodrama, *St. Clair of the Isles,* based on the 1803 novel by Elizabeth Helme,[11] and produced for three weeks beginning on 16 April 1838 at the (Royal) Victoria Theatre.[12] Here the Jewish race is replaced by a Scottish clan. Once again, the author provides the spectator with ample spectacle, clearly designed to accurately portray a national group, and a reversal of gender expectations within the dramatis personae.[13] Where *Esther* presented the audience with a female hero, *St. Clair* offers them a villainess even more fully realized than in the novel;[14] a character named Ambrosine first appears as a boy and then as St. Clair's bride; the character of St. Clair's supposed son, Randolph, and the virtual "hero" of the piece is (again, typical of Polack's oeuvre) played by a woman.[15] As even a cursory reading of the play will indicate, *St. Clair of the Isles* is not a typical "tortured heroine" melodrama.[16]

The playbill for the first performance of the play gives the following cast:

John, *Lord of Roskelyn*: Mr. Wilkins.

St. Clair Monteith, *the Outlaw Chief*: Mr. Maddocks . . . his first appearance.

Hamilton: Mr. Johnstone, his first appearance this season.

De Bourgh: Mr. Rayner, from the Pavilion Theatre

Ross: Mr. Montagne.

Randolph, *supposed son of St. Clair*: Mrs. Loveday.

Sir James Stuart, *Knight of Lorn*: Mr. Harwood.

Knight of Traquair: Mr. MacDonald.

Carnegie, *steward to Lord Roskelyn*: Mr. Loveday.

Donald, *a nice little boy, in love with Bridget*: Mr. J. Parry.[17]

M'Lellan, *retainer at the castle*: Mr. King.

1st Herald: Mr. H. Lewis.

2nd Herald: Mr. Stuart.

Officer: Mr. Boury.

Spectre of the Bodach Glas: Mr. Williamson.[18]

Lady Roskelyn: Miss Richardson.

Ambrosine, *St. Clair's wife*: Mrs. Maddocks, her first appearance here.

Bridget: Mrs. Corry, first appearance here.

Ladies: Mesdames Rose, Wilson, E. Wilson, Gray, Gilbert, Edgar, Brier, J. Brier, Young, etc.

Highlanders, Knights, Soldiers, etc. etc.: by an efficient corps of auxiliaries.

In addition, the playbill advertised the more sensational and spectacular elements of the play, much like a modern film trailer:

ACT I. GRAND TOURNAMENT: TERRIFIC COMBAT! ST. CLAIR DISCOVERED. GENERAL ATTACK.

ACT II. ST. CLAIR A PRISONER! ARRIVAL OF RANDOLPH, HAMILTON AND DE BOURG[H]. RANDOLPH'S DISCOVERY OF HIS FATHER. AFFECTING TABLEAUX.

ACT III. ST. CLAIR CONDEMNED TO DIE! DESPAIR OF RANDOLPH! PREPARATION FOR EXECUTION. ST. CLAIR ABOUT TO BE SHOT, WHEN RANDOLPH RUSHES IN AND RECEIVES THE BULLET IN HIS OWN BREAST! ARRIVAL OF THE PARDON! GATHERING OF THE CLANS!

Clearly nineteenth-century audiences were not adverse to knowing the end of a play before seeing it. It seems, rather, that the promise of a sensational climax was a greater incentive to attend a play than the surprise unraveling of the plot.

The production does not appear to have lived up to the author's expectations as the "Remarks" printed before the play suggest an inadequate cast and filthy scenery, and the play was never revived. The *Times* reviewer devotes few words to the production but what he does say is indicative of the theatrical milieu in which the play was produced:

The novelty produced for the entertainment of the holyday folks at this theatre was an Eastern spectacle entitled *The Fiend King, or the Ruby Cross and the Last of the Magi.* . . . The spectacle was preceded by a melodrama called *St. Clair of the Isles, or the Outlaw of Barra,* a good adaptation of the romance of that title, and the interlude of *Hide and Seek.* The first [play] introduced a Mr. Maddocks, whose debut was deservedly successful, and the interlude restored to the theatre that old favourite of Surrey audiences Mr. Yale, who was most rapturously received. We regret to say the house was not so crowded as might at this season naturally be expected; the audience was, however, much more orderly and good-humoured than in these holydays is generally the case, and they retired evincing unequivocal symptoms of the complete gratification which the performances of the evening had afforded them. (Tuesday, April 17, 1838)

Nothing is known about Miss Polack after the presentation of this play. Perhaps she married, came into money, or was forced to assume familial responsibilities due to the death of a relative.[19] All we know is that no play bearing her name was produced in London after *St. Clair* in 1838.

St. Clair of the Isles was published twice in the nineteenth century. First published by James Pattie (undated; the British Library gives 1840, Nicoll suggests 1838), it was reissued with minor differences in punctuation as No. 794 of Dicks' Standard Plays [1886?]. The text printed here regularizes spelling and punctuation and notes the differences between the texts.

Notes

1. *The Dictionary of National Biography* suggests that, in May 1837, Joel Polack returned to London where he published books about his travels to New Zealand and lived with a sister in Piccadilly. Eventually, however, he settled in the United States and married the widow of William Hart, whom he had met in his travels to New Zealand.

2. This attribution is based on advertisements to her published plays.

3. Both Nicoll and the *Catalogue of Additions—Plays Submitted to the Lord Chamberlain 1824–1851* attribute this play to John Howard Payne, an American playwright. This attribution is suspect however, since the manuscript and all published advertisements for the play fail to cite the author.

4. Booth notes that the Eastern play, "a melodrama with a specific or vague Eastern and highly imaginative setting, including various exotic aspects of Eastern life," is even "more romantic and relying more heavily on spectacle" than Gothic melodrama (*English Melodrama* 88).

5. In his *A History of Early Nineteenth Century Drama 1800–1850*, Nicoll remarks that the Pavilion, "celebrated for 'Newgate melodrama,' was opened, under the direction of Wyatt and Farrell, on Monday, Nov. 10, 1828. It was burned to the ground in 1856, but, rebuilt, it has continued its activities to the present day, being now the home of Yiddish drama in the East End" (226). It was located at 191–193 Whitechapel Road, in the same district as the Polack family.

6. It is interesting to note that the play appeared at a time when Jews were entering into English public life. In 1830, Jews were permitted to become Freemen of the City. In 1835, the year *Esther* was performed, Sir David Salomons, a founder of the Westminster Bank, was elected one of the two City Sheriffs. Since Salomons was a Jew, Parliament had to create a law to permit him to take office without swearing a Christian oath ("Sheriff's Declaration Act," 1835). Later that year, Parliament permitted Jews to vote without swearing a Christian oath, and in 1837, the University of London was founded to admit students irregardless of their religious beliefs. (Alderman 2–3) *The Gentleman's Magazine*

records that in May 1835, a "panoramic view of the city of Jerusalem" had been painted by Mr. Burford (3: 522) and that later in November, an "operatic drama, entitled *The Jewess* . . . was received with great enthusiasm" (4: 644).

7. Polack's *Esther* is certainly not the first English drama to treat this story but it is the first to emphasize Jewish ritual. Thomas Brereton's *Esther; or, Faith Triumphant* (a translation of Racine's *Esther*), published in 1715, and John Collett's *Esther*, printed in 1806 were both Christian interpretations of the Bible story and not performed.

8. Lloyd's *Miniature Portraits in King Ahasuerus* issued between 1830 and 1860 is a toy theatre version of the play.

9. John Farrell was no novice to Gothic melodrama or Eastern spectacle. His *The Maid of Genoa; or, The Bandit Merchant* had been produced in 1820 and *An Arab's Faith; or, The Seven Towers of Jaba* was performed in 1822. While not a writer of the first rank, Farrell had a keen eye for theatrical effect. In *The Maid of Genoa*, for example, there is a combat sequence in which the adversaries' blows are carefully timed with chords struck in the orchestra—a device which has found its way into twentieth-century film and television. See *English Melodrama* (68) for a description of the event.

10. It is quite tempting to suggest some sort of romantic liaison between the manager and the playwright but I have not been able to document any non-professional relationship between them. It is important to note that Polack exemplifies the pattern advanced by Donkin for escaping the "impostor syndrome" in which a woman writer feels completely dependent upon the manager's creative support (27). She had a play produced successfully and went on to reap the fruits of her reputation. Unlike other women authors mentioned by Donkin, Elizabeth Polack appears never to have experienced difficulty in establishing a psychological distance from her mentor because her playwriting career was never tied to a single theatre and thus never controlled by a single individual.

11. Elizabeth Helme (d. 1810) was a popular Minerva Press novelist who often portrayed women as spirited and strong-willed. Not primarily an author of Gothic fiction, she was especially successful as a writer of sentimental romances.

12. On the south bank of the Thames, the Victoria Theatre, nicknamed the "Old Vic," was the home of lurid melodramas, "a Blood Tub, the name given to a theatre staging crude melodramas at very cheap prices" (Bergan 112). The theatre, which had opened in 1818 as the Royal Coburg (named for Leopold of Saxe-Coburg), changed its name to the Royal Victoria in 1833, in honor of the fourteen-year-old princess (Rowell 27; Howard 163–164). In his *A History of Early Nineteenth-Century Drama*, Nicoll notes that the Royal Victoria "had a very deep and narrow stage (94 feet by 32 feet) and in 1820 boasted the possession of a magnificent looking-glass curtain. In 1819 it was managed by Moncrieff; under him and others it indulged in melodrama of the most startling nature; performed before audiences of the 'lowest kind'" (230). In Vol. 1 of *London Labour and the London Poor*, Henry Mayhew describes the unruly behavior of the Royal Victoria audience:

> By-and-by a youngster, who has come in late, jumps over the shoulders at the door, and doubling himself into a ball, rolls down over the heads in front, leaving a trail of commotion for each one as he passes aims a blow at the fellow. Presently a fight is sure to begin, and then every one rises from his seat whistling and shouting; three or four pairs of arms fall to, the audience waving their hands till the moving mass seems like microscopic eels in paste. But the commotion ceases suddenly on the rising of the curtain, and then the cries of 'Silence!' 'Ord-a-a-r!' 'Ord-a-a-r!' make more noise than ever. (18–19).

Rahill adds that after 1833, the Royal Victoria Theatre "touched new depths of spine-chilling melodrama" (140) but, despite the apparent popularity of blood-and-thunder spectacles, between 1834 and 1841, the Royal Victoria was only barely surviving. Theatre managers were constantly changing, established actors were scarce, and the constant threat of prosecution for trespassing on the territorial rights of the patent houses loomed high (Rowell 33–34).

13. In *Thinking About Women* (1968), Mary Ellmann suggests a number of "feminine stereotypes" that have emerged from literature. Among these are formlessness, passivity, instability, confinement, piety, materiality, spirituality, compliancy and irrationality (56–145). Elizabeth Polack explodes many of these misconceptions of femininity in her plays.

14. While the melodrama follows the novel in plot essentials, it does differ in significant details. Missing in Polack's *St. Clair* is Matilda, Randolph's sister, mistakenly betrothed to him and her mother (Lady Roskelyn) threatening to kill her rather than permit the wedding. Also absent are St. Clair's children, Phillippa, Bridget, and James, and an extended subplot chronicling Randolph's maturation. What Polack adds is a trenchant theatricality to the novel. She sharpens the villainy of Lady Roskelyn by giving her greater focus; she creates a *coup de théâtre* by revealing Randolph's parentage at a moment of intense conflict rather than during the celebratory banquet of the novel; and she provides an original moment of pathos by changing the ending of the novel and giving Randolph a heroic death.

15. It was not unusual for youths to be played by women on the nineteenth-century stage. It was not typical, however, for a transvestite youth to undergo the tests of heroism that beset young Randolph.

16. DeLamotte argues that the "isolato at the heart of the Gothic is not one of those singular individualists (Ambrosio, Melmoth, or Frankenstein), but the many Emilys, Emilias, Matildas, and Julias who stand, in their very interchangeability, for Woman—the true 'separated one' at the heart of a social order whose peculiar disorder it is to make her the fearful Other" (28). The concept of woman as a victim of the Gothic order is somewhat revised by Miss Polack.

17. The "acting and stage manager" of the Royal Victoria Theatre.

18. The 23 April playbill indicates that he was replaced by Mr. Davidge.

19. In 1840 the death of Moses Polack appears in the Whitechapel register. The previous year, Solomon Polack is listed as dead in the Kensington register. Their relationship to Elizabeth Polack is uncertain.

ST. CLAIR OF THE ISLES;

or the

OUTLAW OF BARRA

A SCOTTISH HISTORICAL MELODRAMA

Dramatis Personae

John, *Lord of Roskelyn.*
St. Clair Monteith, *the Outlaw Chief.*
Hamilton,
De Bourgh,
Ross, *His Friends.*
Randolph, *supposed Son of St. Clair.*
Sir James Stuart, *Knight of Lorn.*
Carnegie, *Steward to Lord Roskelyn.*
M'Lellen,
Donald, *Retainers at the Castle.*
1st Herald
2nd Herald
Officer
Spectre of the Bodach Glas
Lady Roskelyn
Ambrosine, St. Clair's Wife
Bridget, Lady Roskelyn's attendant
Highlanders, Knights, Soldiers, Ladies' servants &c. &c.

A supposed lapse of ten years between the first and second Acts.

STAGE DIRECTIONS.[1]

R. means (Right.) L. (Left.) C. (Center.) R.C. (Right of Center.) L.C. (Left of Center.) D.F. (Door in the Flat, or Scene running across the back of the Stage.) C.D.F. (Center Door in the Flat.) R.D.F. (Right Door in the Flat.) L.D.F. (Left Door in the Flat.) R.D. (Right Door.) L.D. (Left Door.) S.E. (Second Entrance.) U.E. (Upper Entrance.)[2]

COSTUME.

St. Clair Monteith.—Red shirt, with clasps down the front— ample green mantle—bonnet and feathers—fleshings and sandals— breast plate. *Second dress:* the same—with helmet—gauntlets—and vizor. *Third dress:* full highland costume.

Lord Roskelyn.—Tartan jacket—kilt and scarf—breast plate— bonnet and heron's plume. *Second dress:* dark chain armour— helmet and plume—fleshings and sandals.

Hamilton.—Green plaid shirt—scarf—breast plate, bonnet and heron's plume.

De Bourgh.—Blue velvet shirt, puffed with red satin—tartan scarf—bonnet and feathers—sandals.

Ross.—Dark velvet shirt—plaid scarf—bonnet and plume— fleshings and sandals.

Randolph.—Highland kilt—jacket and scarf—fleshings and sandals, bonnet and plume.

Carnegie.—Comic jacket and full trunks—plaid waistcoat and scarf—black clock stockings—black shoes—white wig.

Donald.—Green plaid jacket and scarf—white drawers—red stockings—black shoes.

M'lellan.—Highland costume.

Spectre.—Dark mantle—white wig and beard.

Knights.—Armour—helmets and plumes.

Officer.—Highland costume.

Lady Roskelyn.—Black velvet dress, trimmed with gold—plaid silk scarf, white shoes and gloves.

Ambrosine.—Crimson silk shirt, trimmed with ermine—black velvet hat and white feathers. *Second dress:* white satin—crimson silk train. *Third dress:* white muslin—plaid silk scarf—black velvet hat, blue feather.

Bridget.—Blue shirt, trimmed with plaid white body.

REMARKS

St. Clair of the Isles; or, the Outlaw of Barra

A Scottish Historical Melo-drama from the pen of a young Lady deserved attention, and therefore, utterly regardless of the "peltings of the pitiless storm," we visited the Victoria Theatre, on Easter Tuesday last. We are free to confess that we anticipated a milk and water concern, but Miss Polack, the fair authoress of *St. Clair of the Isles,* agreeably disappointed us.—The present production does her infinite credit, and although palpably taken from the novel of the same name, the incidents are so well strung together, and the interest so well preserved, that, not to award our mite of approbation to the lady would be as ungallant, as unjust. Our of consideration to her feelings, we will not criticize the performers who played in the piece, for, with the exception of a Mr. Wilkins, a Mr. Maddocks, and a Miss Richardson, the performers introduced into this melodrama, would have disgraced a barn. By the way the bills of the night announced a grand Tournament! All we can say, is, if there was one introduced on the stage, the filth and dirt of the scenery, obscured it from our vision—for we saw none. The manner in which this piece was gotten up must have sorely grieved Miss Polack, but, we believe blue stocking ladies care little about the "appliances to boot," so they do but appear before the public. "Print my book, Mr. Colbourn, in what form you like," says Lady Blessington, "but mind you do print it"— perhaps her ladyship is right, for is not the ostentatious display of the endowments of the mind less indecorous, than that of personal beauties; talents, learning and science, whether real or fictitious, cause the world to talk too much of a woman. Depend upon it that she, who is least talked of, is either the most virtuous or the most prudent, and certainly the most happy of her sex. It seems as if society was not striving to withdraw more and more the veil, which Nature has thrown over the fair sex. The flower expands with a superior brilliancy in the sun; but the sun more speedily dries up the dew, which, while covering the flower, heightens its beauty and its fragrance. Dramatic writing, is perhaps the least injurious to the sex of any. Miss Polack appears to know that poetry assists the imagination in colouring the dull realities of life with ideal beauties which man loves to do, but which woman cannot live without doing. Few of them can enter into the feelings of statesmen, warriors, and merchants, and calculate what advantages are to be derived from the revolution of a neighboring state, or from a war by sea or land, or from bankruptcies, or from dearth, which lowers the public funds, raises the price of necessities, and places, at the mercy of the speculator, both the purse and the stomach of his fellow-citizen. Novels on the other hand, teach the Art of loving, which many young Ladies have need to learn, and improve them in the still more necessary Art of exciting love, for which Nature has given them all more or less genius, and an irresistible vocation. But though we are far from recommending the *Ars amandi* which Ovid taught *Corinna* of old, in verses much resembling prose; neither do we admire the lessons in love, which the modern *Corinna* has given in a prose that aspires to the character of poetry, and with too much matter of speculation, to her fair contemporaries. It is true, that

'Tis a like sense, 'twill serve the turn as well—*Cowley.*

But Shakespeare assures us, that "Love talks with better knowledge, and knowledge with dearer love." When too much art is discoverable it only serves to put people on their guard: and if a *stupid* woman deserves pity, a *foolish* one never escapes contempt. We are not aware whether Miss Polack meditates a change in her condition, if she does, it behooves us to be upon our editorial p's and q's, for husbands of Literary ladies, invariably carry stout walking sticks. Mr. S.C. Hull, to wit—but for the present we are safe, we take a leap with old father Time, and fancy a few years hence, we hear our authoress singing

Ah, wretched virgin! what shall be my fate?
With books in plenty—but without a mate.

When the cold wings of Time, in his silent and invisible passage, begin to weave wrinkles at the external angles of the eyes of young ladies, and to freeze the freshness of their lips then it is that they are desirous of shewing that they have profited, by the lapse of years, to adorn their minds. Then it is that they obstinately dispute, like Amazons, the literary victory with some old pedant, who, at length loses all patience and, renouncing a gallantry which is of no service to him, grapples with his enemy, or attacks her at a distance with a volley of epigrams, and never forgives her, till she lies prostrate at his feet.

Phylo Dramaticus.[3]

Act I. Scene I.

An Apartment of Lord Roskelyn's.

(Enter Lord and Lady Roskelyn, L.—Music.)

Lord R. Lady of Roskelyn, I once more advise you to cease this persecution of the outlaw, St. Clair Monteith; the time is arrived for the payment of his demand on our agent and though it has pleased James of Scotland to proscribe him and his companions; we have no right to refuse his claim to his own property; you will therefore order Carnegie to satisfy St. Clair's demand.

Lady R. Never, my lord; the estate and property devolve to us by the king's will, and till he commands, they shall not be restored. If St. Clair Monteith dare impugn the mandate of King James, I shall find means to silence him.

Lord R. What says our steward, Carnegie, to this?

Lady R. I have secured him to our service; be you but firm in your refusal, and all will be our own.

(Enter Carnegie, R.)

Car. My lord and lady, there wait without, two men, craving an audience; so please ye they bear a message from Monteith the outlaw.

Lord R. Admit them, Carnegie, and see that you are at hand to witness all that passes.

Car. That will I, my lord, yet , with your favour, they failed in due respect to me, for though I told them I was your lordship's trusty steward, the ill-mannered clowns refused to duff their caps at my bidding; but I'll usher them into your lordship's presence this moment. *(Exit R.)*

Lady R. Now Roskelyn, act with firmness and decision, remember, 'tis by sanction of the king.

(Re-enter Carnegie, followed by Ross and Hamilton.)

Car. Know you in whose presence you stand, rude clowns, that ye do not move your caps?

Lord R. You come from the outlaw, St. Clair, to demand the property which he imagines he has a right to claim; say to him from me, that that same property is now mine by justice, and the king's will; therefore is your errand useless.

Ham. *(R.C.)* I understand not that; it may be the fashion at courts to rob a man of his own, but we do not so in the Isle of Barra.

Lady R. It seems you have learn'd insolence from your employer, but have a care lest the prison tower makes you fear to give your speech such license.

Ham. I fear nothing but a woman's tongue, nor did I come to parley with a woman; my answer must be brief, will St. Clair's demand be paid?

Lord R. It will not, and further mark me, if you are found here within an hour, you shall repent your daring.

Ross. *(R. Throws down his glove.)* A time of repentance will come for all, there is my gage; whoever defies me, though it were yourself, John of Roskelyn, I will answer as a man.

Lord R. Away with him, I'll bear no more. Carnegie, seize and confine these men till I give you other orders.
(Exit with Lady R., L.)

Car. Now, gentlemen, you see we are the conquerors, so follow me. *(Ross and Hamilton draw swords from under their cloaks.)* Oh! you're armed, eh? well, give me your swords.

Ross. First we'll clear a passage to the gates. Out of the way, and let us pass, or the first thrust shall be through your hypocritical body.

Car. But gentlemen, this is contempt of my authority you'll please to remember that I am private agent and confidential steward to lord and lady Roskelyn.

Ross. Will you let us pass? don't stare, but leave us a free passage, or our swords shall make one.

Car. *(aside.)* Those are a pair of desperate fellows, so my safest plan is to leave the room altogether. Gentlemen—I—that is to say— I'm gone. *(Runs out, L.)*

Ham. Now, what think'st thou of this business?

Ross. That St. Clair shall and must revenge this infamous detention of his property.

Ham. But he has not the power; remember he and Roskelyn are brothers, and although the tie is scarcely acknowledged on either side, it can never be broken.

Ross. Then by what means can he protect his property?

Ham. Have you forgotten our meeting with one of Roskelyn's vassals, who told us the young heir was on his road to the castle? by his account 'tis a shrewd boy, and nearly five years old.—He must be ours.

Ross. 'Tis a bold plan, if it could be done with safety.

Ham. We are well armed, night draws on, and our persons are unknown; the young Montrose shall be the hostage for his father's honour; and once again on the Island, even James himself dare not attack us.

Ross. But should they offer ransom for the boy, where must it be sent?

Ham. We will not part with him so easily; come, let us on, and if they ask where he will be conveyed, simply reply—to England; thus by taking the road to Barra, we shall elude pursuit.

Ross. This is about the time the cavalcade will pass;—the air of this chamber suits me not, I like a purer atmosphere.

Ham. Let us go then, act by my advice, and the prize will be ours, remember 'tis in the cause of justice, and St. Clair Monteith.
(Exit R.)

(Donald peeps in at R. side, and Carnegie at L.)

Don.. All's clear, they're gone; you may come in, master Carnegie. *(Enters R.)*

Car. *(Enters L.)* I'm glad it's all over without my being obliged to show them my authority. I say, Donald, queer doings, eh, my lad? Now who'd think his lordship and St. Clair, the outlaw, were own brothers.

Don.. But now master Carnegie, you're a man that studies such things, may be you can tell me what they mean by an outlaw?

Car. Why you see, I have something to do with the law, so I ought to know its ins and outs;—an outlaw—is—yes—as far as I know of such matters—an outlaw is—an outlaw; but his lordship only made his brother an outlaw because he wanted his fortune.—I'm in the secret, nobody else, her ladyship tells me everything; I know it all;—I keep the money, settle all her accounts—but she'll have a long account to settle somewhere else, or I'm very much mistaken.

Don.. Lord, master Carnegie, how can you do such things, an't you afraid you and her ladyship will go and settle accounts together?

Car. What's it to me? I only obey orders and get paid, that's all I care about. But our young lord Montrose is expected every hour, let's prepare to receive him, and I say, Donald, you know it's between ourselves, not a word about the money—mum of her ladyship, we know nothing, no business of ours,—come along. *(Exit R.)*

Scene II.

Interior of a Gothic Hall.—Music.—De Bourgh and four others seated at a table drinking.

(Enter St. Clair, L. U. E.)

St. C. Fill your goblets, nay, fill to the brim, this is my pledge, "May the generous prosper, and the oppressor sink into deserved infamy." *(All drink.)* 'Tis well, drink to the very dregs, for though we are outlaws we will support our liberties as men.

De B. *(R.)* And yet, St. Clair, I have never known you so peaceable inclined as you have been since James Stuart did us the favor of sending us here.

St. C. *(L.)* Perhaps it may be so;—from eighteen to twenty-one, the world plundered and laughed at me; now, though they still plunder, they tremble at my name. But I deserve it not; at the final account which priests say we all must give, let the widow I have wronged, the orphan I have oppressed, or the virgin I have betrayed, stand forth and bruit it to my face. *(Horn sounds.)* Hark! 'tis the signal of our friends' return from Roskelyn. *(Music.)*

(Enter Hamilton and Ross, L.)

St. C. Welcome, my friends, I hardly hoped to see you in so short a time, but tell me, what says Roskelyn to my just demand?

Ham. He dares deny your right to the money, and refuses to pay to your order; he further says he holds your property as his, by order of King James.

St. C. The miscreant! I will proclaim him villain even to the tyrant's face.—With the first fair wind I will away to Scotland and retrieve mine own, or die in the attempt.

Ross. Then I go with you, you shall not fall alone, nor unrevenged.

De B. *(R.)* We will all share your danger; St. Clair shall leave none of his friends behind.

St. C. Men! friends! why use the only means that can dissuade me from my purpose? the present quarrel is mine only, and I alone will meet it.

Ham. Trust me St. Clair, we have revenged thy insult; we have brought thee a noble hostage; no less than Roskelyn's heir, the young Montrose.

St. C. Impossible! why have ye done this? what is Roskelyn's child to me?

Ham. In him conclude your wealth and liberty restored; for be assured they will endeavor to regain the boy at the expense of all they have purloined from thee.

St. C. It may be so, but I will never owe the recovery of my rights to a child, even that of my direst foe. Restore him to his parents, we must not conquer by such unjust means.

Ham. *(L. C.)* Thus over officious friendship deserves to be repaid; yet hear me, if you send back the boy, our detection is certain, and would you gratify your enemies by subjecting yourself to whatever punishment their rancorous spite may assign you?

St. C. No, Hamilton, never; sooner would I live and die upon the shores of Barra; but should we detain him here till time has so altered his appearance, that in after years he be disowned as an impostor, and thrust unheeded on the world, how I shall curse the hour in which I owed my freedom to this child.

Ross. *(L.)* That can never be, for nature has stamped his birthright; he bears a red wine mark on the right arm.

St. C. That is sufficient, but more of this hereafter, tonight we will let the goblet shew our joy at your safe return.

(Music.—They go to the table, drink, and again come forward.)

De B. *(R.)* This way of life may suit you, St. Clair Monteith, but for a Frenchman of my age and gallantry to be mewed up like a monk in a cell is too much for any man's patience; I still sigh for the society of lovely women.

St. C. Women! by heaven, chevalier, when you introduce them you lose me; bring me tigers, devils, any thing but women.

Ross. Well said, St. Clair. Are you weary of a life of quiet, that you mention them, De Bourgh? if we are monks, we are merry men, we will have no mistress but the bottle, no crime but drunkenness. *(Horn sounds.)*

Ham. Strangers are entering the fortress, and see I a youth approaches; by his garb he seems one from the court of James.

De B. Perhaps a spy, be on your guard, St. Clair; we will remain apart,—he comes. *(All retire up but St. C.)*

(Music.—Enter Ambrosine as a page, carrying a casket, L.)

Amb. My business is with the chief, St. Clair Monteith, I pray you direct me to him.

St. C. I am so called, and beg to know the tidings brought by such a messenger?

Amb. Then, to be brief, I was entrusted with this casket to deliver to you from one who calls himself your friend, now residing at the Scottish court; will it please you to examine its contents, and give me some trifling memorial that your friend may know I have performed his mission faithfully.

(The others come forward—St. Clair takes the casket, and opens it.)

St. C. By heavens! my long lost jewels are restored, and here are sixty marks; in faith, good youth, you must inform me how these escaped the general wreck, also the name of him who has befriended me.

Amb. I am but a lad, chief, yet I can keep a secret like a man; be satisfied you have a right to what I bring, but your friend must choose another messenger, for it likes me not to be thus closely questioned.

St. C. Then I will ask no further; but thou comest from the court, how fares all there?

Amb. When I departed, rumours were spread that Lord Roskelyn's son had been stolen, and conveyed to England. I doubt but his mother will soon forget his loss, for the tournament commences tomorrow, which is to be graced by the noblest of the Scottish nation. But time wears, I must depart.

De B. *(L.)* In faith, young sir, I have seen some of the fairest hands in every court in Europe, but yours exceed them all. Will you not taste our wine? for though outlaws, we boast many comforts of which our enemies cannot deprive us.

Amb. I love not compliments, nor did I expect to find them at Barra.

St. C. You must excuse the chevalier, he cannot forget that he was once a courtier; but ere you leave us, promise that should you ever need assistance, you will claim it of St. Clair Monteith.

Amb. I will, for even now I am beset by foes, and may soon need thy friendship.

St. C. *(Giving her a ring.)* Take this ring, and when the hour of danger is at hand, return it with instructions how I best may serve thee.

Amb. I will not fail, and be assured the time is not far off when St. Clair will have full restitutions of his wrongs. Farewell. *(Exit* L.*)*

Ham. *(R.)* This is a strange adventure, who can have sent this mysterious youth, for never was mission done with such apparent truth and honesty. What says our chief, St. Clair?

St. C. I can but wonder, and rejoice at having a portion of my wealth restored; doubtless the boy obtained them from one who knew me while at the court of James.

Ross. *(R.)* To my thinking we have been imposed on—that youth can be no other than a spy sent by Roskelyn, and it is fortunate he left us without having seen the child, or we might have fallen into dangerous hands.

De B. *(L.)* I differ from you all; you argue the subject as men and warriors, but I consider it as an admirer of female beauty:— that seeming youth is a woman.

St. C. A woman,—oh! ridiculous! Why should a woman, and such a woman, come to the Isle of Barra?

De B. Marry, to comfort thee, and that is but charitable.

St. C. If thy surmise be true, I will journey throughout Scotland to discover her;—and the means are open. Didst thou not hear there is a tournament to be held at court, I will go there disguised—if she is of noble descent, we are sure to gain intelligence.

De B. Bring me tigers, fiends, devils—any thing but women! Oh, how I like to see a fellow brought to his senses!

Ham. I approve St. Clair's plan, and will go with him. Disguised as knights we can join the sports without fear of discovery.

St. C. Let all remain unseen except myself, De Bourgh, and Hamilton; see that the rest be assembled near the hall, that in case of danger we may have aid at hand. Now then for Scotland and the court of James! *(Exit.)*

Scene III.

A front apartment at Lord Roskelyn's.

(Music.—Enter Lady Roskelyn, followed by Carnegie, carrying a box, L.)

Lady R. You know my orders; in that box are papers and gold, all of which St. Clair the outlaw is entitled to; see they are well secured, and should Lord Roskelyn ask you aught, deny all knowledge of them. Remember Carnegie, all rests on you.

Car. I'll be careful to obey your ladyship's orders—he shall never have a single mark while Carnegie has a head on his shoulders. Perhaps your ladyship never heard how those knaves insulted me? They refused to bend to my authority!

Lady R. Secure the property where no human eye can penetrate; I go now to prepare for the tournament; when that is over, we will confer again; go instantly, and see you manage all as best may lull suspicion. *(Exit L.)*

Car. I wish this business was over; her ladyship pays me well, and so she ought. Who but such a good-natured fellow as myself would turn rogue to please her? But it's no business of mine—I'm only her aid and abettor; she'll bear the blame, not me. Now, where can I put this money?

(Enter Donald, R.)

Don.. Master Carnegie, have you any business on hand?

Car. Yes, and devilish dirty business it is, but why do you ask? I ain't wanted, am I?

Don.. Yes you are.

Car. *(aside.)* If it's his lordship it's all over—what shall I do with the money? But who wants me?

Don.. I do—only a little advice though.

Car. What, law advice? You're a sensible lad, Donald; always apply to me, you shall have my opinion for half as much as you would give any one else. Now proceed.

Don. Why you see, master Carnegie, there's a nice young woman in the castle.

Car. What's that to do with my advice?

Don. Oh! nothing, only I wanted your opinion.

Car. Well, go on, I won't charge you for waste of breath, I'll be very moderate; now what do you want to know?

Don. Whether I shall marry her now, or wait a little.

Car. You saucy knave, if I wasn't in a hurry, I'd make you repent this; but you shall pay me for loss of time, as sure as I'm confidential agent and steward to his lordship.

Don.. I'll tell you what, master Carnegie, it's my opinion you've an eye on her yourself, I'm sure I did no harm, I thought all such matters belonged to the law. *(Exit L.)*

Car. I wish this box was safe; nobody sees me now. I'll go and— *(Enter a Servant, R.)*

Ser. So please ye, three strange knights on their way to the tournament, crave an audience.

Car. Show them in. *(Exit servant, R.)* What's to be done? These knights have heard of me; perhaps they come to ask my advice on some point in the law. Can't I hide the money first?—No, here they are. *(Music.)*

(Enter St. Clair, De Bourgh, and Hamilton, dressed as Knights, St. C. wearing his vizor down, R.)

Ham. All happiness wait on the worthy Carnegie.

Car. Most noble knights, you are welcome to this part of the castle, which by leave of his lordship belongs to me. I pray ye remove your helmets, and honour me by taking some refreshment.

De B. We thank your hospitality, but are now hastening to the tournament.

Car. Aye, I see you are sportively inclined, but you will take such poor welcome as I can offer before you disclose your business. *(Calls.)* Within there, bring wine.

St. C. *(L. Looks at the box.)* Know you him whose name is on that box?

Car. Marry, that I do, and a right desperate outlaw he is. I now proceed to put his property in safety till he comes to claim it.

St. C. And should he do so, will you restore it to him?

Car. That is as her ladyship pleases to direct. *(Enter servant with wine, L.)* But come, Sir knight, the wine is at your service.

Ham. *(fills.)* Carnegie, fill to the brim and drink my pledge, or instead of the wine entering your mouth, my sword shall enter your body.

Car. You are merry, Sir knight, but let's have your pledge.

Ham. St. Clair Monteith, and confusion to his enemies. *(Carnegie lets the cup fall.)* Let no one stir, we have armed men within call, and whoever attempts to leave this room, dies upon the spot. Hark ye, Carnegie, these arrears of St. Clair must away with me to Barra, or you shall go in their stead.

Car. Patience, good sir; be not thus hard upon me. It is true that what I now hold, belongs to the chief Monteith, but I dare not pay it to strangers; if he himself were here, I could not withhold it.

St. C. *(raises his vizor, L.)* Behold I am here thou poor knave; and now what subterfuge hast thou?

Car. I tremble universally, but take your property, only give me an acknowledgment and I'll begone. *(Gives Hamilton the box.)*

St. C. *(gives him a paper.)* 'Tis here; remember this lesson, and profit by it.

Car. Marry, that will I, and when her ladyship knows what has befallen me, I shall have no reason to forget this day. *(Exit L.)*

St. C. We are thus far successful, yet should I fail to discover the mysterious youth, even this recovery of my property will be unheeded. *(Music.)*

(A Servant enters, gives St. Clair a letter with ring, and exit.)

St. C. *(reads.)* "I am beset with fools and surrounded by dangers, and now claim your promise aid. Fail not to meet me at the tournament—you will know the writer by the token."

De B. Trust me, St. Clair, 'tis as I said, our mysterious guest will appear in her true colours.

St. C. And if she does, I will protect her, even from James himself; and if I gain her friendship, 'twill be the only recompense I ask.

De B. Commend me to the friendship of a fellow like you, and a girl like her. No doubt she will prove an heiress, and if you do not free her from her enemies by making her lady of the fortress at Barra, I will proclaim you the veriest poltroon of Christendom.

St. C. De Brough, you know not what you say. Could I confer happiness and wealth upon her, I might presume to offer them, but as it is, Monteith dares not forget he is a banished man.

Ham. But may not be so for ever.—The decrees of James will not outlast his life, and is it not better that we live in calm seclusion, than to succumb beneath the Scottish tyrant?

De B. To my thinking, the pretended youth is of thy mind, and as there is no criterion for taste, she may prefer our mountains to the court. *(Trumpets sounding.)*

St. C. Hark, the sports of the tournament are about commencing; are our friends at hand?

Ham. They wait without the hall, and stand prepared to obey the signal;—our horses are ready, should instant flight be necessary.

St. C. 'Tis well, now hear me friends; let us not separate, lest in case of danger we may lack assistance; remember, we are here at peril of our lives; let us be cautious, and success will yet be ours. *(Exit R.)*

Scene IV.

An open plain, and turrets of the castle with banners. —Lord and Lady Roskelyn discovered on an elevated seat.—Knights, ladies, &c. &c. Trumpets.—1st Herald comes forward, L.

Lord R. Valiant knights and noble ladies assembled;—know that this tourney is held in honour of the Queen of Scotland, and the lady Margaret of Roskelyn. Herald, pronounce the challenge of the noble knight of Traquair. *(Trumpet sounds.)*

Her. The knight of Traquair here proclaims the beauty of the Queen of Scotland unrivaled. Should any knight dispute it, he dares him now to single combat. *(Trumpet sounds.)*

(2nd Herald advances, R.)

Her. Sir James Stuart, Knight of Lorn, proclaims the beauty of the Lady Roskelyn surpassing that of the Scottish Queen, and now defies the knight of Troquair to maintain his boast by single combat. *(Music.)*

(The knights advance, Sir James in black armour.—The Knight of Traquair throws his gauntlet, Sir James takes it up, they fight. Sir James disarms the Knight of Traquair, then takes his sword and shield, kneels and lays them at Lady Roskelyn's feet.)

Lady R. Rise, Sir Knight of Lorn, though you have chosen one unequal to compete with the beauties of our land, I thank you for having supported your claim thus nobly; and here is one who shall reward your gallantry;—behold! 'tis Ambrosine, the heiress of Kintail. *(Music. Enter Ambrosine, R.)* Maiden, approach; it is from thee our gallant knight expects his well earned recompense.

(Ambrosine seats herself next to Lady Roskelyn.)

Sir J. So please you, noble lady, I do not yet deserve your thanks—to my last breath will I maintain thy charms unrivaled. *(Trumpet orchestra, answered in pit—Music.)*[4]

(Enter St. Clair, Hamilton, and De Bourgh, over pit platform.)

Ham. *(R.)* Yonder is the lady Roskelyn presiding at the tournament, neither her beauty or her spirits seem lessened by the loss of her son. Did I not always say that woman had no heart? But behold, the sports have commenced.

De B. Monteith, where are thy eyes, man? Ambrosine, the heiress of Kintail, and our mysterious visitor, are one.

St. Clair of the Isles 249

St. C. *(aside.)* Impossible! and yet methinks the features are alike, but let us attend to her voice, for that once heard, cannot be forgotten. *(Music.)*

Lord R. Sir Stranger Knight, we greet you, but regret you were not here at the commencement of the tourney. Herald, do then again pronounce the challenge.

(2nd Herald advances L.—Trumpet sounds.)

Her. Sir James Stuart, Knight of Lorn, proclaims the beauty of the Lady Roskelyn surpassing that of the Scottish Queen, and now defies any knight to maintain his boast to the contrary, by single combat.

St. C. Nobles and knights, although unknown to ye, I claim a right to join in this day's tournament, therefore, Sir Knight of Lorn, my gage against yours, nor Queen or Danish fair directs my sword; prepare to acknowledge the charms of Lady Roskelyn surpassed by Ambrosine the highland maid, with an angel's form and a hero's spirit, and if I disarm you not, the disgrace be mine.

Sir J. Have with ye then, the lady Roskelyn's beauty yields to none.

(They fight, and St. Clair disarms Sir James. — Music.)

Sir J. *(aside.)* Vanquished, and by a stranger too, this must not be; I'll dare him again to the combat, though at the hazard of my life.

St. C. *(L.)* Enough, Sir knight, you find that queens may contend against the Highland maid in vain.

Sir J. *(R.)* Not so, I dare thee to the proof once more.

(They fight, Sir James is again disarmed.)

St. C. 'Tis well, our steels confess the charms of Ambrosine remain pre-eminent.

Sir J. Confusion! foil'd again before the noblest of the court;—once more I dare thee on.

Lord R. *(rising.)* Hold, Sir Knight of Lorn, let me revenge the foul disgrace thus heaped upon you. *(Comes forward.)* Stranger, hitherto you have borne it bravely, now to the final trial. *(Down R.)*

St. C. *(L.)* How! fight with thee, John of Roskelyn?

Lord R. What, does the foreign boaster quail to meet the lord of Roskelyn hand to hand?

St. C. Fear is a word that I have yet to learn, I am not breathed,—come on. *(Music.)*

(They fight, St. Clair disarms Lord Roskelyn.)

Lord R. *(On ground, L.)* I know not which thou'art most, whether man or devil, but thou art brave, I'll have no more of thee. Let the trumpet sound, and be the prize bestowed, the sports are ended.

Lady R. Nobles of Scotland, by the Queen's command a prize will be conferred by Ambrosine upon the knight of Lorn; and further, 'tis the Queen's will, that on this day, before the knights and nobles here assembled, she doth accept the repeated offer of his hand.

Amb. *(R. C.)* Noble lady, I have long been persecuted on this subject, and my refusals have been met with scorn or insult; therefore in presence of these noble guests, I solemnly reject the claim, and here aver that while I have reason to direct my course, I never will consent to wed the knight of Lorn.

Lady R. Rash girl, remember whose command you brave by this refusal, dare not persist, or the cloister's walls shall close on you for ever.

Amb. And if they do, their peaceful shelter will be more welcome to me then the exalted throne of Scotland; but think not I will long submit in blind obedience to tyrannic power.

Lord R. Lady, you answer well, but threats cannot avert your fate, for who will dare oppose the will of royalty.

St. C. *(advancing R.)* I dare; nay, wonder not, 'tis I, her knight will free her from a life of slavery.

Sir J. Then shall thy sword assert thy right to be the champion of my affianced bride.

St. C. Hitherto I have remained unknown, now behold the friend of Ambrosine. *(Raises his vizor.)*

Sir J. *(throws down his sword.)* St. Clair Monteith!

All. St. Clair Monteith! *(All advance.)*

Lord R. Monteith the outlaw, here? in defiance of the king's command!—you rush upon your fate.—Secure him till the pleasure of the royal James be known.

St. C. *(draws his sword.)* He dies who dares approach me. *(Chord.—Brings Ambrosine forward.)* If I go hence alive, we go together. Sir James of Lorn, you have proved noble, and I honour you. Roskelyn, farewell;—if James of Scotland wishes to chastise, I shall be found at Barra. We go, if thou canst seize on shadows, follow us. *(Exit with Ambrosine, followed by Hamilton and De Bourgh.)*

Lady R. They shall not escape—quick, let a guard secure the castle gates.

Lord R. Within there. *(Enter Soldiers.)* Soldiers! prepare; point your pieces towards the turrets, should they attempt to pass, fire at all hazards. *(Soldiers point to the turrets, St. Clair and Ambrosine appear on them.)* St. Clair Monteith, restore the Lady Ambrosine, and yield yourself a prisoner, or we shall fire.

St. C. Let no man stir, or I will hurl destruction on you. Clansmen, friends, advance to the rescue of your chief.

(Highlanders suddenly rush over pit and platform. Soldiers on stage fire.— General fight.—Tableau.)

END OF ACT I.

Notes

1. The stage directions are evidently designed to approximate the original production of the play. As the editor of the text printed by James Pattie (n.d.) suggested, "The Editor of this Work prints no Plays but those which he has seen acted. The Stage Directions are from personal observations, during the performance."

2. The text published by Dicks' Standard Plays (#794, n.d.) notes that "The Reader is supposed to be on the Stage, facing the Audience" and adds the following directions: M.D. (Middle Door); L.U.E. (Left Upper Entrance); R.U.E. (Right Upper Entrance); L.S.E. (Left Second Entrance); P.S. (Prompt Side); O.P. (Opposite Prompt).

3. This review was not printed in Dicks' text.

4. The Dicks' edition has *"Trumpet without, and is answered in the distance.—Music."*

Act II. Scene I.

Open country, barren hills at the back, at one side a gate, leading into the fortress. Ross, Hamilton, De Bourgh and others sitting at a table drinking, R. Music.

De B. Were it not for those hills we might forget we are yet outlaws, for our life has been one of plenty and content since St. Clair wedded the Lady Ambrosine.

Ham. The time has passed full swiftly, 'tis now ten years since she became mistress of the fortress, and in all that time we have been free from Roskelyn's tyranny.

De B. Marry, I had almost forgotten the knave yet lived, but I am glad his son fell into our hands, he never would have been what he is now, had he been reared by Roskelyn.

Ham. Thou'rt right; Randolph is a noble youth, and well for him he does not know his parents.

(Music. Enter St. Clair and Ambrosine from the fortress, L. U. C.)

De B. Well met St. Clair, neither you nor the lady Ambrosine seem weary of this peaceful life; for myself, my arms are rusted from want of use. Oh! for a tournament at court to let me have a breathing.

Ham. Would we could use our arms to better purpose; methinks, St. Clair, your patriotic zeal has strangely cooled of late that you do not raise an arm to save your country.

St. C. Friends, do not wrong me thus; we dare not call upon the storm to rage because we fear it not; stay yet awhile, till but the faintest ray of dawning liberty lightens this age of despotism, let but one voice be raised for freedom, let but one hand be laid upon the sword, and if St. Clair Monteith refuses to stand forth, and right his fallen country, may the fell curses of an injured people rest upon him.

Amb. 'Tis spoken like St. Clair; well might the wife of Roskelyn call thee brave, and curse the day when you rejected her.

De B. True, lady, and she had ample cause; it was St. Clair who, when her father's revenues were mortgaged, cleared them for four thousand marks; and for the lady, she would sigh for rings and ornaments, till she had drained his coffers to obtain them; marry, had'st thou wedded her, St. Clair, thy first child should have been born ready dressed for its christening.

St. C. Nay, chevalier, a truce with what is passed, my recent trials have expiated all the follies of my early years, and heaven has sent me pardon in the form of Ambrosine. Now tell me, have any of ye seen Randolph yet this morning?

Ham. He went at dawn as usual to the hills and has not yet returned.

St. C. We have kept him too long in ignorance of his birth. Randolph must no longer think himself my son, he shall quit our island, and assert his rights; but should they be denied him, should the proud gates of haughty Roskelyn refuse to open to their lawful heir, our home shall again be his.

(Randolph appears coming over the hills. R. 5 G.)

De B. See where he comes.

(Music. Enter Randolph; he shakes hands with all, then with St. Clair.)

St. C. Randolph, why hast thou stayed from home beyond the usual hour?

Ran. I climbed the hills this morning with the dawn, and as the sun glided their snowy tops, I prayed it soon might light us on to freedom; nor did I pray in vain. The hour is come. Thy country calls thee to protect and save her.

St. C. Explain. What mean'st thou.

Ran. As I returned, a stranger asked me to guide him to the dwelling of Monteith the outlaw. Tell him, said he, I come to speak of liberty. At mention of that word, I freely guided him towards the fortress.

St. C. And bravely hast thou done; where is this stranger?

Ran. He waits your pleasure.

St. C. Quick bring him hither. *(Ran. goes in the side and beckons. Enter M'Lellan.)* Approach friend, thou art welcome; now speak thy business, I am Monteith the outlaw. *(M'Lellan gives St. C. a letter. He opens it and reads.)* "Our country shall again be free, the proud court of Scotland shall bow to the barren rocks of Barra, and dread the victims of oppression; if you would hear our native hills echo the name of liberty, follow our messenger to the place of meeting." Then Scotland yet may hope; friends, joy with me that there are other swords to aid our cause, and noble hands to wield them. Haste, arm yourselves, let not our aiders in this glorious cause think that we lack the spur to urge us on to its fulfillment.

M'Lel. So please you, chieftain, you are requested to depart alone, your followers for a time must be excluded from the conference.

St. C. My followers are my friends, no word or act of mine must be unknown to them, the leader of a race of men is not to be an arbitrary tyrant; he who would govern well, must govern mildly, and is unworthy to command, if he would fetter those whom he should teach to love and honour him.

M'Lel. My orders are that we depart alone.

St. C. It shall be so; I do not fear the man who thus comes forth to urge his country's right. *(To Ran.)* Randolph, a cup of wine; our guest shall drink success to this good cause. *(Ran. gives M'Lel. wine.)*

M'Lel. Then hear my pledge: destruction to the enemies of him I serve. *(Drinks, Amb. takes back the cup.)*

Ran. *(Aside to St. C.)* Father I fear this stranger is not what he seems; I pray you not go with him.

Ham. St. Clair, be on your guard; some treachery is meant; you must refuse to join them.

St. C. How! this from one who thought my patriotic zeal had cooled?—I thank thy caution, but in this cause I must not be dictated to.

M'Lel. Chieftain, time wears. Shall Scotland rise or fall? Your world decides her fate.

St. C. Then witness, Heaven! My country shall be free; and if I never wield my sword again, I'll draw it now undaunted in her cause. *(Draws.)*

M'Lel. We must tread dangerous paths and rocky passes.

St. C. Randolph, bring me my dirk and claymore. I will not go unarmed.

Amb. St. Clair, are there none else in Scotland who bear oppression? Risk not your life for those who can defend themselves.
(Randolph brings a dirk and shield from the table, R.)

M'Lel. The dirk will be enough; you'll find a shield burthensome.
(St. Clair puts the dirk in his belt. Randolph takes his shield.)

Ran. *(aside to St. Clair.)* He does not mean you well; some danger lurks beneath this seeming kindness. Let me go with you, and should evil be intended, my presence may avert it.

St. C. I thank thee, Randolph, but it must not be. Fear not, all will be well.—Friends, to your care I leave my Ambrosine, and before another morning lights the hills, I shall return.—Till then may Heaven guard you! Now friend let's on, and may we soon behold the Court of Scotland bow to the barren rocks of Barra.

(Music.—St. Clair takes leave of Ambrosine and the others, then exit over the hills, followed by M'Lellan, R. 5 G.)

Ham. My mind misgives me still. What think you lady? 'Tis a strange occurrence.

Amb. I have no fears. St. Clair has not a foe on earth—who, then, would injure him?

Ran. A thought now strikes me. It is not too late; I'll climb the hill that overlooks the sea, and watch their movements. *(Exit R. 5 G.)*

De B. Friends, have you forgotten Roskelyn yet lives? Do not your thoughts turn to our secret enemy?

Amb. I cannot think he is so lost to honour, but see,—yonder is Randolph.

(Randolph appears on a hill at the back.)

Ran. *(looks out.)* They are now waiting on the shore; a boat bearing two men nears them; now they step into it, and leave the shore. What do I see? My father gives his dirk to one, the other raises something—can it be?—yes—a chain! Now they surround him! See, see, he's bound! Friends, 'tis as we feared, he is betrayed!—he is a prisoner. *(Jumps down.)*

Ham. Let us not lose a moment. Arm, my friends, arm, our chieftain shall be free!

Ran. Hold! I am the wretched cause of all. I led the foe towards our peaceful dwelling, and I will save my father.

De B. But surely not alone. Thou, yet so young, can never hope to conquer those whose stratagems have deceived St. Clair.

Ran. Their artifice shall be met by artifice. I will depart alone, and if he lives, I swear we will return together, or I behold my native hills no more! Yet, where can I seek him? If I but knew the dwelling of his enemies, I still might track his footsteps. Friends, is there no clue to guide me to his rescue?

Ham. *(aside to De B.)* Dare I name Roskelyn?

De B. *(aside to him.)* 'Twere better not, for should they ever meet while unknown to each other, the consequences might be fatal.

Ran. What does this silence mean, this seeming mystery?—as if you feared to trust me with the knowledge of my father's foe.

Ham. Do not mistake us, Randolph; we only fear your just resentment may extend too far. The only enemy our chieftain has is John of Roskelyn.

Ran. Enough, my friend, enough; but let the haughty lord beware, for in this cause his castle's proud security shall not protect him,—farewell—now heaven speed me to the gates of Roskelyn. *(Going.)*

Amb. Randolph, stay, there is a tie that binds you to the lord of Roskelyn, which death alone can break.

Ran. Then one of us shall rend that tie asunder; mother, do not delay me longer. I feel as if some warning voice now bade me go and free my father from the tyrant's power. Once more, I swear we will return together or I return no more. *(Exit R.)*

Amb. Ill-fated boy, you rush upon destruction; say Hamilton, De Bourgh, how can St. Clair be saved?

Ham. To my thinking, noble lady, 'twere best we follow Randolph; our swords shall never rest within their scabbards until St. Clair returns in freedom.

Amb. Thanks are too poor to speak my gratitude, soon may your chieftain add a richer recompense.

De B. His liberty is all we hope for, lady,—farewell—we'll save St. Clair Monteith, or perish with him.

(Exit De Bourgh and Hamilton, R. Ross, Ambrosine, and others into fortress, L.U.E.)

Scene II.

A front Saloon.

(Enter Carnegie, L.)

Car. I was in hopes all this business was over, but I find her ladyship is as bad as ever. I did not expect she would have trusted me again, after what happened to me ten years ago, when Monteith the outlaw took his property away. I don't like these doings, but it's no business of mine, she pays me well, and that's all I care about. Oh! here comes Donald; now he'll call me to account about Bridget; I expect her too with a message from her mistress, so between the two I shall be in a nice hobble.

(Enter Donald, R.)

Don. Well, master Carnegie, have you thought about that affair,—you know what I mean;—a man at your time of life, you ought to know better, that's all I've got to say.

Car. Then I advise you to be off, I've some law business on hand—can't attend to you now.

Don. But I've some justice business for you, that's what you hav'n't had a long time.

Car. That's a good lad, always apply to me, I'll settle it for you; let's hear the case.

Don. In the first place I'd thank you not to call me lad, that was very well former years, but it won't do now.

Car. Well, pass that over, I long to hear the law business.

Don. I accuse you of trying to inveigle the affections of a discreet young woman, what do you say to the charge?

Car. Oh! that's another affair altogether, I know nothing about young women, you want to ask me about law business, and that's all I am prepared to answer; you've been plaguing me in this way for the last ten years.

Don. Then why don't you give her up, you know she can't marry us both; don't I see you and her whispering together every now and then; do you think I'm a fool, Master Carnegie?

Car. Why there's little doubt about that, but I say, you didn't hear what we talked about, did you? *(Aside.)* If he did, it's all over with us.

Don. Then you confess your share in the plot?

Car. Eh? what do you say?

Don. Am I to have Bridget or not?

Car. *(aside.)* He's on the wrong scent, if I can keep it up we're all right. *(Aloud.)* Suppose we both ask her, and which ever she likes best shall have her.

Don. Well, that's fair, and as I live, here she comes: now, which is to speak first?

Car. Bridget coming? then you must be off.

Don. Be off, what do you mean by that? didn't you just say—

Car. Never mind what I said, will you go?

Don. I'd much rather not; here she comes, and here I'll stay.

Car. But I tell you this meeting is of the greatest consequence to me.

Don. So it is to me;—now I say, do you think I am going to stand this?

Car. Only go out while I speak to her, and I'll make her promise to marry you directly.

Don. That won't do for me—but now on second thoughts I think I may as well go.

Car. Now you talk like a sensible man; go along, and when I've settled all, I'll come to you.

Don. *(aside.)* I'll come to you first, though, old boy. I'll find your schemes out. *(Aloud.)* I'm going, Master Carnegie.

(He goes out, L. re-enters instantly, and hides at the side, unperceived by Carnegie.)

Car. Now that fool's gone, let me think of my own affairs. A likely thing that I should ask the girl to marry him, no, no, let this business be finished, and then he may do as he can, it's nothing to me, I never do any thing without I'm paid for it.

(Enter Bridget, R.)

Brid. Ah! master Carnegie, here you are, exact to the time as usual.

Car. Yes, Bridget, I'm always punctual, that's one capital thing I learnt by studying the law. Never keep people waiting; now what news have you, is he come?

Brid. Yes, he is arrived, he's such a noble-looking man; do you know I quite felt for him.

Car. Ah! you are like all the women; now think how many years I've been persuading you to take pity on me, but now there's a new face come I ain't thought of.

Don. *(aside.)* There's another one come! Oh! ain't you a nice pair of crocodiles?

Brid. Why, yes, master Carnegie, I did think of your offer some time back, and as we are not as young as we were, I have made up my mind on the subject.

Don. *(aside.)* And a pretty subject they're making of me.

Car. *(aside.)* All right, she'll have me.

Brid. Are you sure nobody can hear us?

Don. *(aside.)* Oh! quite certain.

Brid. *(in a low voice.)* I mean to have Donald.

Car. Better not, he's the greatest fool living.

Don. *(aside.)* No, I was wrong, they ain't talking of me at all.

Brid. Then who would you advise me to have? You know I'm growing older every day, I'm sure you will advise me for the best, as you are growing old yourself.

Car. *(aside.)* She needn't have mentioned that, but never mind. *(Aloud.)* Why I think—here comes her ladyship, and you hav'n't told me how the scheme is to be managed.

Brid. Listen, at midnight a boat must be waiting under the watch-tower, ready for instant flight.

Don. *(aside.)* Ain't you a nice couple? There will be somebody there you don't expect, I promise you.

Car. But tell me what the signal is to be.

Don. *(aside.)* That's just what I'm waiting to hear.

Brid. Three claps of the hand—and have all prepared.

Car. That's enough, I shall be there.

Don. *(aside.)* So shall I. *(Exit L.)*

Brid. Do you know, master Carnegie, I think her ladyship is doing very wrong.

Car. What's that to us, don't she pay us well for what we do? I tell you it's no business of ours,—but hush, here she comes.

(Enter Lady Roskelyn, L.)

Lady R. 'Tis near the appointed hour, is your prisoner arrived?

Car. So please you, my lady, he waits your pleasure.

Lady R. Let him be conducted hither.

Car. I will, my lady. *(Aside.)* Queer doings, to speak to a prisoner in her own apartment; but it's no business of mine. Come Bridget, we had better go.

Brid. But I had much rather stay.

Lady R. Leave me. I would be alone, remember the watch-tower at midnight.

Car. We will not fail to obey your ladyship. *(To Brid.)* We'll go, here's plenty of mischief brewing without us. *(Exit with Bridget, R.)*

Lady R. I scarcely hoped M'Lellan would succeed so well, or that St. Clair could fall into the snare so easily;—but he approaches, looking more noble in his prison chains, than ever did John of Roskelyn, decked in the gilded trappings of a court. *(Enter M'Lellan, followed by St. Clair in chains. To M'Lellan.)* Retire, and have a care that none approach. *(Exit M'Lellan, R.)* And is it possible that the brave St. Clair Monteith, who defies the menaces of kings, is thus defeated by a woman's art? Thou dar'st not scorn me now, thou knowest I have power; but act with prudence lest I exert it farther.

St. C. Do so at once, call in thy myrmidons, for they are worthy their employer,—but where is my brother? Where's John of Roskelyn? why does he delegate a task to you that's better suited to a hired assassin?

Lady R. He knows not of this enterprise, but fear nothing, though all is wrapped in seeming mystery, I mean you well.

St. C. Then why detain me here? Why am I bound? I never injured thee or thine; let me return to Barra—to the home which for fifteen years has sheltered me in peace, and all my wrongs, my unjust outlawry, even the disgraceful occurrence of this day, shall be forgotten.

Lady R. You sue for freedom, then;—you fear to stay a prisoner in the castle.

St. C. Lady of Roskelyn, hear me; I have dared the battle and the storm, my sword has drank the blood of Scotland's foes, I've heard the cannon's thunder spreading death around me, still I feared not; I've borne the raging of the tempest, when all was dark and desolate, save when the lightning's flash lit the wild ocean, and if I feared not in that hour of peril, think you my eye would dim, or my heart quail, before the wife of Roskelyn?

Lady R. I would not have thee look on me as one who seeks to injure thee; thou art as brave, as fearless, as when first we met; and now I look on thee, thou art scarcely changed, time has dealt well with thee,—say, do I look the same? Either the world flatters, or I retain some portion of those charms that caught thy heart, when long years since, you asked my hand.

St. C. I am no judge of beauty, or if I am, my taste has changed since then; but why prolong this interview? Does not thy pride recoil, thus to hold converse with Monteith, the outlaw?

Lady R. Cursed be the pride that made me what I am—removed me from the path that led to happiness, and robbed me of thy rightful claims and title,—my borrowed honours sit so heavily upon me, that at a word of thine, I would resign them all.

St. C. Lady, speak not of bygone days, lest the remembrance of thy guilty follies sink thee still lower in thine own esteem than thou art already fallen in mine.

Lady R. 'Tis well, reproach me,—for I deserve it at thy hands; nay, I will assist thy memory, here in this hall you paid my father's debts, in this hall too, you plighted me your faith, and I accepted it.

St. C. I'll serve thy memory further, 'twas in this hall that I rejected thee—gave back thy perjured vow, and then fled thy presence as from the guileful serpent, which coils around in seeming innocence, then at one spring plunged its poisoned venom to the heart.

Lady R. Since chains cannot restrain thy lofty bearing, accede to my conditions, and thou shalt be free at midnight.

St. C. Free, saidst thou?—and to-night.

Lady R. By midnight thou shalt quit the castle, free!

St. C. And see my home again? and join my friends, and Ambrosine?—name thy conditions, and if they do not militate against my country, I will accept them.

Lady R. I must be the partner of your flight.

St. C. I do not comprehend you.

Lady R. Then I will throw aside the mask I have worn so long,—know that I never loved the lord of Roskelyn, I now despise and loathe his very name, and will follow thee to any spot on earth, and there await, until Roskelyn's death makes us the legal heir to his possessions.

St. C. Can I have heard aright? And does such perfidy exist in woman? No, no, it cannot be I have mistaken her.

Lady R. Not so St. Clair; I still repeat that I will share thy flight, till by the death of my detested lord, you become heir of Roskelyn; decide not hastily, if you reject my offer, your fate is death.

St. C. What, and desert my wife? break my vow to her who forsook the world to share my banishment? Never! Conduct me to whatever death you will—I'll bear the direst torture thankfully, sooner than purchase liberty by crime like that.

Lady R. 'Tis well, your fate is now decided—yet I will give you further respite; at midnight expect me at the prison watch-tower, and if you then reject your freedom, I will denounce you to the Court of Scotland, and you shall meet the death of a traitor. *(Calls.)* Within there! *(Enter M'Lellan, R.)* Conduct your prisoner to his dungeon, see he is strictly guarded—*(To St. Clair.)*—and for thee, midnight brings death or liberty. *(Exit L.)*

M'Lel. Chieftain, repentance is not in my nature, or I should feel it now; I always fancied the countess look'd on you with a favourable eye, but did not think she meant you harm.

St. C. Lead to my dungeon, I seek no further parley with thee.

M'Lel. I have drunk from your wine cup, you gave me fair words and a kind welcome, which I repaid with treachery.

St. C. To what does all this lead?

M'Lel. Ensure me double the sum the countess gave me to make you her prisoner, and you shall be at liberty within an hour.

St. C. Thou despicable hireling, that would'st betray thy mistress, who shelters, feeds, and clothes thee! And for what? Does justice prompt thee? No! 'tis love of gold, of paltry gold, for which you would as gladly see me hang upon the gibbet, as open your prison doors to set me free.

M'Lel. Perhaps you're right; but her plans shall be concealed no longer from the lord of Roskelyn, for if the young Montrose yet lives, he will return one day to claim his rights. And see, his lordship comes.

St. C. Let me begone; I will not meet the base usurper, lest my accumulated wrongs make me forget the ties of blood which now unite us, and bid my chains turn weapons to avenge them. *(Exit R.)*

M'Lel. The Countess was a harsh tyrannic mistress, till her own interest made her seek my services, and she shall soon repent her confidence. St. Clair Monteith is too noble to be the dupe of one like her. *(Enter Lord Roskelyn.)*

Lord R. M'lellan here! Say, who is yon stranger passing to the watch tower?

M'Lel. So please you 'tis my lady's prisoner.

Lord R. Explain! there are no prisoners in the castle. What is your business in this apartment?

M'Lel. My lord, I am bound to secrecy, but will no longer deceive you. St. Clair Monteith was, by your lady's orders, lured from his home, and is now a prisoner within these walls.

Lord R. Amazement! Know ye her motives for so strange an act?

M'Lel. Why I should guess they are such as cannot do honour to a lady of the house of Roskelyn. They are to meet in the watch tower at midnight, where a boat is to be under the window ready for their immediate flight.

Lord R. It cannot be! Base vassal, dar'st thou cast such aspersion on thy lady's honour! What! she hold intercourse with Monteith the outlaw?

M'Lel. 'Tis even so my lord; but if you doubt my word, be at the watch tower at the appointed time, and if you find I have deceived you, I will submit to any punishment you may inflict.

Lord R. Then be it so! at twelve to-night meet me there with a body of guards. Now begone, and see my orders are obeyed.

M'Lel. Depend, my lord, I will not fail, and take my word, I'll not deceive you. *(Exit R.)*

Lord R. Can she then brave me thus, and choose for her companion in her flight the very man whom she has plundered of his rightful property?

(Enter Donald, L.)

Don. *(aside.)* His lordship here? I thought to find Bridget. Never mind, I'll go.

Lord R. Come hither, what seek ye here?

Don. *(aside.)* I've a great mind to expose her—no, I won't! I'll tell all but the name.

Lord R. Answer me, knave, what seek you here?

Don. Why your lordship must pardon me, but it ain't exactly convenient for me to tell, because, you see, if I expose her I shall expose myself, and that may bring disgrace upon you at the same time. He an't half so bad; it's all her doings.

Lord R. *(aside.)* By Heaven! this boy knows all. *(Aloud.)* Tell me, is it of thy mistress thou art speaking?

Don. She was my mistress once, but that's all over now; I'll never own her again as long as my name is Donald.

Lord R. Unhappy, perjured woman, why thus heap misery on all that love thee?.

Don. That's what I say! To think she should give up the one she ought to love, for a nobody like him.

Lord R. Then you know of their intended flight?

Don. Of course I do! didn't I stand and overhear them both? The boat will be under the watch tower, and off they go.

Lord R. By Heaven, it shall not be.

Don. What! will your lordship knock up the plan? That's what I'm trying for; only let me catch the pair of 'em, see if I won't give it 'em in style.

Lord R. I thank thy zeal, but remember, whatever be her failings, she is still thy mistress. Be ready at the given time; we meet at midnight. *(Exit, L.)*

Don. Upon my word it's very kind of his lordship, to take so much interest in my affairs, but he knows Bridget won't meet my fellow in very quick time. Won't old Carnegie be nicely caught? But I'll go and get ready—we meet at midnight. *(Exit, L.)*

Scene III.

Outside of Roskelyn Castle with folding gates.

(Enter Randolph armed, L.)

Ran. My search seems useless. I have entered every dwelling on my dreary way, yet find no trace to lead me to a knowledge of my father's fate—this castle seems to be inhabited, what if I seek admittance—yet, where may he be? Perhaps exposed to danger from which I might rescue him.—Ah! the gate opens, I'll stand aside; perhaps I may gain some clue to guide me on my way.

(He stands aside. Enter Bridget from the gates.)

Brid. What a misfortune it is to be handsome! Here I am being teased to death because I won't marry Carnegie or Donald! Now, if a nice, good-looking young man happened to come and ask me, I might think seriously on him! *(Sees Ran.)* Who can this be? I dare say he's come after me—he's very shy, so I'll speak first. *(Aloud.)* Good day, young sir! You seem very tired—will you rest a little in the castle?

Ran. Thanks for your kindness—I have walked two long days and nights and need rest.

Brid. I dare say you do; and if I might ask why are you in such haste?

Ran. I am in search of one for whom I shall not grudge a life of weariness!

Brid. *(aside.)* He's come after me, I know he has! *(Aloud.)* And you have traveled very far to find this person, I suppose?

Ran. I have, and if I am so blest that we return together, I shall not have lived in vain!

Brid. Then I suppose you are very partial to this person?

Ran. That is too cold a word—join all of love and reverence that virtue claims, for even that is poor to what I feel.

Brid. Well, set your mind at rest, for I know who you are come for.

Ran. Impossible! Does he then live?

Brid. Why, what does the boy mean?

Ran. Nay, this suspense is worse than all. Tell me, and quickly— does my father live?

Brid. Your father, boy—how can I tell? Hav'n't you come after me?

Ran. This is some mistake. My father has been lured from his home by treacherous villainy, and I am seeking him.

Brid. Then you didn't come to marry me after all? How disappointed I am! But if you like to rest for an hour, I'll take care my lady don't see you, for she never allows strangers here except to suit her own pleasure. Ah! I've a sorry life with her—I'd rather remain as I am than be the countess of Roskelyn!

Ran. The countess of Roskelyn! Is she the lady of this castle?

Brid. Yes truly; why, does that surprise you?

Ran. I have not prayed in vain—thank Heaven, my search is ended! I go no further!

Brid. Oh! but you must; if my lady sees you, she'll have you confined in the tower with the other prisoner.

Ran. What prisoner? Speak I conjure you, for something tells me my father is within these walls.

Brid. I'll tell you all I know. Three nights since M'lellan brought a stranger to the castle, my lady had an interview with him, and he has been a prisoner in the watch-tower ever since.

Ran. It must be he—and I may save him still! Say, my good girl, can I obtain admission to his prison?

Brid. *(R.)* Why I'm almost afraid. Now, if my lady was to see you, she might take you into her service.

Ran. What! I become the vassal of a tyrant! and bend to the will of that remorseless woman! Never! Sooner would I die here, on the threshold of my father's foe!

(Enter Carnegie.)

Car. *(aside.)* Hollo! what's this? As I'm living, it's Bridget talking to a young man! I'll keep out of sight, and hear what they're after.

Brid. Oh! you must not speak so of my lady—you'll never succeed in this way.

Ran. True; you are right. Let me but know I have not come in vain, and I will do all thou bid'st me.

Car. *(aside, L.)* I knew it—there's another poor fellow in her snares—she shall repent this!

Brid. Then attend to me. You must agree to all my lady proposes, and you shall know the plan of the watch-tower, then we can all escape together.

Car. *(aside.)* Oh, ho! she wants to betray us, and go off with that young fellow. Now, if I could tell my lady what's going on, she'd thank me.

(Enter Lady Roskelyn.)

Lady R. How is it girl, I find thee here? Who is this strange youth?

Brid. So please you lady, he has mistook his way, and I was directing him to the right path.

Ran. *(aside.)* Can this be her whose very name I used to shudder at? Can guilt exist in such a form as that?

Lady R. Young man, whence comest thou?

Ran. From beyond Inverness.

Lady R. Why have you left your home?

Ran. To seek justice and preferment.

Lady R. Would you be faithful to those who help you to achieve your wish?

Ran. Yes, if I loved them.

Lady R. Could'st thou love me?

Ran. To look upon you only, I could worship you.

Lady R. Wilt thou serve me?

Ran. I will do all that truth and honesty dictate, and if you need such service, lady, you shall receive it at my hands.

Lady R. 'Tis well. Bridget, conduct the youth, and follow me. See that he be attired as a page of the house of Roskelyn. *(Exit into the castle.)*

Car. *(comes forward.)* Here's a pretty situation for a man that studies the law. They will bet Monteith out of one scrape, to lead him into another. I wish I could get out of the business altogether. If I could trust the keys to anybody else, I wouldn't go near the place at all.

Brid. *(to Ran.)* Yonder is master Carnegie; he has the keys of the watch-tower; I will try and coax him to give them to me; and, if I succeed, your father shall soon be at liberty, Go now, and wait for me without. *(Exit Ran.)*

Car. *(aside.)* Ah, there she is now. I'll be bound she wants to make it up with me, after all; but I won't have her till she learns what is due to a man that studies the law.

Brid. Master Carnegie, I have been thinking that I have used you very ill in refusing to marry you. I'm sure I'd do anything to serve you; now only try me, and see if I ain't worthy of confidence as well as you.

Car. *(aside.)* Aye, I knew she'd come to her senses at last. *(Aloud.)* Now you talk like a prudent, sensible young woman, and to prove my love for you, I'll entrust you with the keys of the watch-tower—but mind, don't let them go out of your sight, as you value my head. *(Gives keys.)*

Brid. Thank you, master Carnegie; I'll only give them to those who know how to make proper use of them. *(Exit, R.)*

Car. I think I've been rather too hasty in this business. Suppose she don't marry me, after all, what a precious fool I shall have made of myself.

(Enter Hamilton and De Bourgh, L.)

Ham. *(to De B.)* Here let us pause, De Bourgh. Know you this castle?

De B. Marry, that do I. It is ten years since we entered it to claim St. Clair's revenues; and if my memory fails not, yonder is the man from whom we took them. Let us interrogate him; methinks our chieftain is in the power of Roskelyn.

Ham. Do so; by his means we may gain intelligence.

De B. *(to Car.)* Most worthy Carnegie, how fares it with thee?

Car. I thank ye, noble sirs, right well. No doubt some law business brings you hither, on which you require my advice?

Ham. 'Tis even so; but can we rely on thee?

Car. What! private business? You couldn't apply to a better person on such matters. But I'll remove all doubt most worthy sirs, by telling you the confidence her ladyship puts in me. Would you believe that through my agency the outlaw, St. Clair Monteith, is at this moment a prisoner in the castle?

Ham. St. Clair Monteith! Impossible!

Car. I marvel not at your surprise; but listen. A strange youth has also gained admittance, and I suspect they mean to escape together; all I want is to keep them apart, for if they meet what will become of me?

Ham. *(aside to De B.)* It must be Randolph. *(To Car.)* In truth, good Carnegie, there is much to fear; but say can we assist you?

Car. Marry, that can ye, sirs, if your business is not very pressing, you might do me great service in this matter.

De B. Nay, heed not us; our wish to aid this cause is greater than you imagine.

Car. If it is so, I will guide you to the watch-tower, when there, bid the guard in my name to retire, and leave you on his post; have a care that no one passes in or out till midnight except my lady.

Ham. Fear not, we'll do thy bidding faithfully.

Car. I thank ye kindly, sirs, now then, let's in.

Ham. *(to De B.)* We have succeeded beyond our utmost hopes, now let us hasten to our chieftain's rescue.

Scene IV.

Interior of a prison, with folding doors. St. Clair discovered.

St. C. Is this indeed reality? am I a prisoner in this dwelling which by right is mine, a slave to the will of her I scorned,—my wife! my friends! what must their sufferings be? 'Tis near the hour the wife of Roskelyn appointed, and what resource will then be left me?—to spare her guilt, or die a traitor's death. *(Chains heard.)* They come, perhaps to drag me forth! yet where is she?—am I again betrayed?

Ran. *(without.)* Monteith! Monteith!

St. C. That voice! methought I knew it,—no, no,—'twas but my fancy—let me prepare to meet them. *(Calls.)* Agents of hell! come on—I am prepared.

(Enter Randolph in a rich cloak, Hamilton and De Bourgh, C. D. F.)

Ham. St. Clair! we come to save or perish in your cause.
(Gives St. C. a sword.)

St. C. My friends; and Randolph too! do I indeed behold you! say, how fare my wife and friends.

De B. We left them plunged in sorrow for thy danger; but thou art found, and joy once more shall reign in the halls of Barra?

St. C. Randolph, what means that garb emblazoned with the arms of Roskelyn?

Ran. By these means only could I gain admittance; I am supposed a page in the service of the lady Roskelyn, but let my father be once more beyond these walls, and I quit this subterfuge of meanness and dishonour.

Ham. Hush! I hear footsteps!

St. C. 'Tis Roskelyn's wife,—at her signal, do you my friends come forward, and we may escape by the very means she has taken to ensure her plans; retire—she comes. *(Exit Randolph, De Bourgh, and Hamilton.)* Now I must seem obedient to her will, or we still may fail. *(Enter Lady Roskelyn, C. D. F.)*

Lady R. St. Clair, I come to know thy final answer, the guard is dismissed, and all favors our departure; say, art thou ready?

St. C. What will be my fate if I refuse to go?

Lady R. To-morrow's sun shall light thee to thy death.

St. C. Then be it so, lady, I will prepare to die.

Lady R. Yet pause, Monteith, think of thy wife, can'st thou quit the world and leave her desolate? reflect again—who is there left but thee to save his country, and make his native hills echo the welcome sounds of liberty.

St. C. Lady, forbear! I will not live upon the terms you offer; now leave me, let me not waste the few short hours that I can call mine own.

Lady R. I go! St. Clair, heed well my words, retract thy resolution, or the worst tortures my hatred can devise shall be inflicted on thee, then beware, for you have raised the spirit that never yet spared aught in its revenge.

(Clock strikes twelve.)

St. C. *(aside.)* Now to retract, and let them have the signal. *(Aloud.)* Yet hold, can nothing but instant flight ensure my safety?

Lady R. Nothing!

St. C. And the estates of Roskelyn?

Lady R. Shall be shared with thee.

St. C. I'll live then!—quick!—thy signal!

Lady R. thou wilt go with me then?

St. C. I will!—thy signal.

Lady R. To live secluded until Roskelyn's death!

St. C. Time wears!—thy signal!

(Music—Lady R. claps her hands three times.—The doors open.— Roskelyn and Soldiers rush in. Enter De Brought, Hamilton, and Randolph from one side—Carnegie, Donald, and Bridget from the other.)

Lady R. *(C.)* How's this! we are betrayed!

Lord R. You are, and thus thy plans of infamy are crushed for ever. For thee, Monteith, my sword shall speak my sense of the disgrace you would have heaped upon me.

St. C. *(R.)* John of Roskelyn, by heaven you judge me falsely, I have been lured by treachery, and though the wrongs I've borne from thee might almost sever the tie of kindred that unites us, I could not be the wretch your words imply.

Lady R. My lord, believe him not; he would have had me break the vow I made you at the altar! My page, stand forth and answer, have I not spoken truth?

Ran. *(comes forward, L. C.)* I will stand forth, false and degenerate woman! what! I thy page? I'd sooner serve the meanest reptile that crawls upon the earth!—thus do I throw aside the garb that has disgraced me, and trample on it as I would on thee. *(Throws off the cloak.)*

Lord R. *(L.)* Secure Monteith, and see the boy escape not.

(Enter Hamilton, R. U. E.)

Ham. Hold! touch him at your peril, Monteith has friends who will not yield to Roskelyn.

Lord R. Monteith, when last we met, you were the conqueror, try if thy sword is still true to thee.

(Music.—St. Clair and Lord Roskelyn fight, Hamilton and De Bourgh fight with two of Roskelyn's party. At a pause in the combat, St. Clair is secured from behind and disarmed. Randolph presents two pistols at Lord Roskelyn.)

Ran. *(rushing forward.)* Treacherous villains! was he reserved for this? Roskelyn advance, for you escape me not! The son of the brave Monteith will bitterly avenge his father's wrongs. *(Takes St. Clair's sword.)*

St. C. Randolph, I charge thee, hold! raise not thy arm against him!

Ran. Father, it cannot be!—he is thy foe, and that declares him mine. Roskelyn, if thou art not a coward, prove it now.

Lord R. Coward!—and from thee!—come on.

(Music.—Randolph and Lord Roskelyn fight, Randolph disarms him.)

Ran. The just cause has triumphed! Restore St. Clair to liberty.

Lord R. Never!—secure the boy! (Randolph draws two pistols and prevents them.) Quick, fire upon him.

St. C. No! Roskelyn! on thy life! I conjure thee!—harm not the boy! If they attempt to fire, their lord dies upon the spot.

Lord R. Obey me! fire upon him!

Ran. Thus, then, I rid my father of his foe!

St. C. *(rushes forward.)* Roskelyn forbear! Randolph! harm not the lord of Roskelyn! He is thy Father!!!

(Randolph drops the pistols.—Tableau.—The drop falls.)

END OF ACT II.

Act III. Scene I.

Outside of the fortress by moon-light, hills &c. as before.

(Music.—Enter Randolph.)

Ran. I have reached home at last, and gaze upon those hills which I have climbed so oft with him, without whom I vowed to return no more. How can I meet those friends who will expect to see us come together in freedom and in joy.

(Enter Ambrosine, Ross, &c. from the fortress, L. U. C.)

Amb. 'Tis Randolph! Welcome, my boy, a thousand welcomes. Speak of thy father, hast thou found him? does he yet live?

Ross. *(L.)* Lady we must not hope too much, Randolph is returned alone, and did he not swear?

Ran. Yes, I did swear, but could not keep my wild and ill-starr'd vow.

Amb. Then he is dead, deny it not, I read it in thy face.

Ran. *(C.)* Not so; he lives, but his hours are number'd, the lady Roskelyn has denounced him to the Scottish court, and by their orders, he is condemn'd to die.

Ross. *(L.)* Alas, I fear'd as much; but we must not despair, I'll join our friends Hamilton and De Bourgh, and at the peril of our lives we'll crave his pardon of King James.

Amb. Can I do nought to save him? must he then die, and shall we meet no more? Randolph, is there no hope of mercy? Will they not let him live?

Ran. Mercy from a Roskelyn! Rather expect it from the infuriate beast of prey, which, like him, seeks out its victim only to destroy.

Amb. I'll to the Lady Roskelyn—'tis long years since we met. Perhaps a latent glow of pity may induce her to hear my prayers and save St. Clair.

Ross. Randolph, give us thy counsel; in such a time of danger thou wert not wont to stand so calmly by. Where is thy lately boasted courage?

Ran. I have seen that which has chilled my blood with horror, and frozen the wild vengeance of my heart for ever.

Amb. Speak! what hast thou beheld?

Ran. The Bodach Glas!

Amb. The Bodach Glas!—What mean'st thou!

Ross. 'Tis the grey spectre, which is supposed to appear to the heirs of any noble Scottish house, to warn them of their approaching death. But Randolph, let this not hold upon thy fancy thus; doubtless it was some peasant whom thy fear mistook.

Ran. Not so; I saw it plainly gliding across my path in the broad moonlight; once it paused, pointed to the spires of Roskelyn and disappear'd.

Ross. But this cannot allude to thee.

Ran. Am I not Roskelyn's heir?

Ross. You know then—

Ran. Yes, I know all. But let us now endeavor to save him, whom once I proudly called my father. (Turns round.) See, day will soon dawn, and he may not see another sun.—Look! look!—'tis there again—the Bodach Glas!

(Music.—A figure wrapped in a grey mantle, with long white hair and beard, glides along the top of the hills at the back, to L. U. G.)

Amb. I see it not, Randolph, 'tis but thy fancy; there is no one near us but our friends.

Ran. It glides along, see, see!—'tis gone.

(Figure goes out.)

Ross. This folly is unworthy of one rear'd by the brave Monteith. His life is threatened, and if human aid can yet avail, nothing must be left untried to save him.

Amb. Then, heaven speed me; Randolph, friends, assist me with your prayers. I go to sue for that I dare not hope for—mercy from the wife of Roskelyn. *(Exit, R. 5 G.)*

Ross. Randolph, return to our chieftain, and bid him hope once more. Follow me friends—on, to the Court of James.

(Exeunt all but Randolph, L.)

Ran. Deluded friends, yours is a hopeless errand; their plans are taken with too much caution, for your help to avail him now. And can I do nothing to avert the evil I have caused? I guided the enemy to our peaceful dwelling. *(Muses.)* Yes, yes, there is but one resource, and I'll not shrink from it. But I'll not speak my dark resolve, lest even in this solitude some friend may loiter near, and hear my purpose. The dark prediction of the Bodach Glas shall be fulfilled; yet, I must mourn to gaze my last upon my native hills, to quit the world which seem'd to smile invitingly before me. But 'tis for him, and I regret it not. Home of my childhood—country that I love, receive my last farewell.

(Music.—As he is going slowly out, the spectre enters and meets him. Randolph stops—the spectre glides slowly across the stage.)

Ran. In heaven's name, spirit, what would'st thou?

Spec. Randolph! beware—to-morrow.

Ran. Say on, shall he be saved? *(Spectre turns and glides again. Randolph follows it.)* My fate is certain, but speak of him—I do conjure thee, speak!

(Spectre goes out. Randolph falls on the stage, scene closes over him.)

Scene II.

An apartment in the castle with folding doors.

(Enter Carnegie and Donald.)

Don. Well, Master Carnegie, how do you feel? I'll tell you one thing, I wouldn't be in your shoes for a trifle—there, now.

Car. Well, this is pretty language to a man that[1] studies the law! I do feel rather queer, but that's no business of yours; I got into the scrape myself, and now I must manage as well as I can. I never dare meet her ladyship here any more that's certain.

Don. Oh! I'm blest if you won't meet her somewhere else before long. *(Points down.)* But, I say, are you sure the execution is to be to-morrow morning?

Car. Yes, and nothing can save his life, without his friends can get a free pardon from the king.

Don. Then I wish I was one of his friends, I'd soon get one. Would not you save him if you could, eh, Master Carnegie?

Car. And suppose I would, it's too late now. He must die, poor fellow. But, I say, suppose we talk a little of our own affairs.

Don. Ah! I knew it; we never like to hear of our own bad deeds;—you are a deceitful, scheming, covetous old rascal.

Car. Hollo! hollo, is this treatment to a man who studies the law—do you suppose I'll stand it.

Don. Hold your tongue, and keep civil. I've done with you; Bridget has made up her mind to have me—and now you may hang yourself for want of better employment.

Car. She has? what, without consulting me? I won't believe it.

Don. Won't you? then here she comes, may be you'd like to ask her yourself.

Car. *(aside.)* I wonder what ill luck has sent her, just now, to remind me of the share I had in this plot, I suppose.

(Enter Bridget, R.)

Brid. Ain't you ashamed to be seen? you wicked old dealer in law, it's all your doings, you know it is.

Car. *(aside.)* There, I knew it, there will be no more peace in this house, I see. *(Aloud.)* I'd thank you, young woman, whatever you say to me, not to presume to speak with disrespect of the law.

Brid. Poor St. Clair is to die in the morning, and who ensnared him in the castle but you.

Car.. Then if I ensnared Monteith into the castle, you ensnared his son outside the gates.

Don. I say Bridget,—what's all this?

Brid. I did ask him to rest himself, and then my lady saw him, but Master Carnegie, he would never have got into the watch-tower if you hadn't given up[2] the keys.

Car. *(aside.)* The jade has me there, I must be quiet. And have you made up your mind to have this fellow instead of me?

Brid. Oh! anybody, rather than you.

Don. There now, are you satisfied? do you know I think you'd better go about your business before his lordship sees you, besides we don't want your further acquaintance.

Car. Don't insult me, young man, I'll stay as long as it suits me; you may go if you like, but I shan't stir.

Don. Oh! very well, do as you please, here comes his lordship, so we'll leave together.

Car. His lordship coming, I wouldn't see him for the world; stay, there's a good fellow, and keep him here till I'm out of the way.

Don. I'd much rather not, I always do as I'm told; come Bridget, we'll be off; master Carnegie, you'll stay as long as it suits you.

(Exit with Bridget, R.)

Car. It's all over with me,—here's a pretty scrape for a man who studies the law, I'll try to sneak out before he comes.

(Goes slowly to the side.)[3]

(Enter Lord Roskelyn, L.)

Lord R. Villain, come back.

Car. *(aside.)* That's me, it's no use; I'm a dead man. What is your lordship's pleasure?

Lord R. Answer me truly, or thy life shall pay thy disobedience, was it by thy lady's order that Monteith the outlaw was brought hither.

Car. Truly it was, my lord.

Lord R. Did he come willingly?

Car. That did he, my lord, by means of a forged letter, which, by my lady's order, I penned with this unworthy hand, praying him to join a meeting whose purpose was to fight for Scotland.

Lord. R. Who planned the meeting at the watch-tower?

Car. So please you my lord, I had her ladyship's orders for all I did.

Lord R. But the boy,—what do you know of him?

Car. Aye, with your favour 'tis a shrewd young knave, he calls himself the outlaw's son.

Lord R. Enough,—you may retire.

Car. *(aside.)* I'm all right, I never thought to get off so well, I'll make the best of my way for fear he calls me back. *(Exit, R.)*

Lord R. The wily hypocrite Monteith, imagined that if I thought he had restored my son, it would have saved him, but I'll not be thus deceived. Montrose was conveyed to England, and had he lived the ransom which I offered would have restored him long ere this.

(Enter Lady Roskelyn.)

Lady R. Roskelyn, speak—have you found the boy?

Lord R. Mean'st thou thy page?

Lord R. No, 'tis our child, 'tis Montrose, whom for ten years we mourn'd as dead.

Lord R. Do you too credit the vile falsehood?—but why should I wonder you believe the word of him, for whom you would have sacrificed honour, truth, and fame.

Lady R. No, I have proofs that he is indeed Montrose, for in his struggle to escape, his sleeve was raised, and I beheld a blood-red mark on his right arm.

Lord R. Indeed? I well remember that Montrose bore such a mark.

Lady R. He did, he did; Roskelyn, I do conjure you by the remembrance of our early happiness, forgive my errors, and restore my boy.

Lord R. I will endeavor to regain the boy, but he and I are henceforth lost to thee for ever. I have borne with thy follies, and suffer'd my judgment to be subdued by thy example, but thy reign of tyranny is over. I will no more be guided by thy will; I have been just and will be so again.

Lady R. But may I not behold my boy once more?

Lord R. It cannot be—I would not have him know his mother's crimes. I have burst the trammels that made me thy slave so long, and he shall never be another victim. Lady of Roskelyn, farewell, for now we part for ever. *(Exit.)*

Lady R. I have deserved all this, and yet the blow falls heavily upon me. It was St. Clair who bore away the child, and had he not a right to injure them who injured him? have I not been his most inveterate foe—and dare I murmur that he has taken vengeance for his wrongs?

(Enter Bridget, R.)

Brid. The lady Ambrosine craves an audience of your ladyship.

Lady R. 'Tis St. Clair's wife, why comes she here? No matter, I will see her. *(Exit Bridget.)* Perhaps she will ask his life, but she has come in vain.

(Enter Ambrosine.)

Amb. Lady of Roskelyn, I need not tell the cause that brings me here.

Lady R. You would ask the pardon of Monteith the outlaw. 'Tis ten years since, that in the presence of the Scottish nobles, you proudly spurn'd my request, so do I now treat yours.

Amb. True I did, but there was no human being's life depending on my word, as there is now on yours.

Lady R. Your husband is a traitor, and must die.

Amb. St. Clair a traitor? Who but thyself dare call him by that name? Was it for this that thee and thy proud lord usurped his title and his property, and to substantiate your vile pretensions, robbed him of his liberty, and now would take his life? Was it for this he rear'd your son in the bright path of honour, and taught him to be brave and noble as himself.

Lady R. Think you this haughty bearing will avail you now?

Amb. I had indeed forgotten the humility which the degraded outlaw's wife owes to the proud usurper of his rights. But one word more, and that will be the only boon I ever prayed for at thy hands; will you exert your influence to save St. Clair.

Lady R. If thou wilt swear that from this hour thou wilt resign Monteith for ever, so that he quit Scotland never to return, I will attempt his rescue.

Amb. He would not purchase life upon such terms; he would not live and forsake her who gave up all the world to follow him. St. Clair had rather perish here in his native land than live in freedom on a foreign shore.

Lady R. Then he must die,—there was a hope for him that you have crushed;—remember well 'tis you, not I, who have refused to save him. *(Exit, L.)*

Amb. Unhappy woman, she is still the same, here then I have no hope, my last resource is now to follow De Bourgh and Hamilton, should their entreaties fail, perhaps my prayers may yet obtain him pardon from the King. *(Exit, R.)*

(Enter Carnegie.)

Car. I've overheard every word, if her lady leaves the castle, my fortune's made again; and now the young heir is found, they will want some sensible discreet person to look after him, and they cannot find any one better suited for such a situation than I am, besides he may want a little instruction in the law,—there I shall be at home. Nobody thinks I listened, so I'll make them believe I'm in his lordship's confidence, and that he has acted by my advice.

(Donald peeps cautiously through the folding doors.)

Don. *(aside.)* An't you a conniving old rascal, but I have been listening as well as you. *(Comes forward.)* Well, Master Carnegie, you an't gone I see.

Car. Gone—no, there's queer doings going on, but you'll get nothing out of me, so don't expect to hear any thing.

Don. Why you couldn't make more fuss if the young Montrose was found.

Car. I say, you've been listening, you dog.

Don. I? I'd no more be guilty of such a mean action than you would, Master Carnegie, without I could find out that my lady was going to leave the castle.

Car. *(aside.)* I am sure he's been listening, but I'll find out. *(Aloud.)* And how did you learn all this news?

Don. His lordship tells me every thing now, and always acts by my advice, so you may pack up and be off.

Car. *(aside.)* He has told me the very thing I meant to tell him. *(Aloud.)* Are you to have any preferment in the castle?

Don. Of course; I am to instruct the young heir in every thing I know; won't he be a clever fellow if he knows all I can teach him?

Car. What will you tell him to do first?

Don. Kick you out of the house. If you teach him law, I'll teach him justice. I must go now, it's near the time of poor St. Clair Monteith's execution. I only hope one thing—

Car. What's that?

Don. That I may soon have the pleasure of seeing you in the same situation. *(Exit, R.)*

Car. Here's a situation for a man that studies the law, but it serves me right, for doing as her ladyship told me; only let me get out—out of the house, and I'll never be ensnared by a woman again, as long as I live.[4] *(Exit, R.)*

Scene III.

The stage to represent an open plain, hills at the back,—Slow Music.—An officer enters with soldiers, who arrange on L. by wings.

(Enter Lord Roskelyn.)

Lord R. Are you sure there is no alternative—must the prisoner die at the appointed hour?

Officer. He must, my lord.

Lord R. The grounds appear but slight to warrant this severity.

Officer. It appears in the charge of treason brought against him by the Lady Roskelyn, that he escaped from Barra ten years ago, but his immediate return frustrated the designs of justice; he has again returned from outlawry in defiance of the king's command, for which is punishment is death.

Lord R. He came not willingly, he was betrayed.

Officer. It may be so, my lord, but he has been condemned, and nothing can avert his fate.

(Slow Music.— Enter St. Clair, guarded, R.)

St. C. *(R.)* Roskelyn, what seek you here? your persecutions have clouded the bright sun that might have shone upon my early life, why are my last brief moments of existence to be embittered by your presence?

Lord R. *(L.)* Monteith, you know me not. I never was your foe, the wrongs you name were never caused by me.

St. C. When the dread thunderbolt bursts from that darkened heaven, be it from north or east, it will alike descend and crush the devoted head that rests beneath it.

Lord R. I have obtained a mitigation of your punishment, in consideration of your having fought for your country in early youth, you are to die a soldier's death.

St. C. Thanks even for that—now hear me, your son is safe; when I am dead, seek him in the Isle of Barra. I reared him as my own, and loved him; Roskelyn, if there is a bitterer pang than that of death, it is bursting the tie that binds me to him and Ambrosine—but this is useless now; restore him to the home he will adorn, and chide him not if he should breathe a sigh or shed a tear in memory of St. Clair.

Lord R. Would that I had the power to save thee—yet say, is there ought else that I can do to serve thee?

St. C. Delay the execution of my sentence but a short time longer; my wife and friends will surely come to receive my dying blessing—and Randolph too, I could have wished to see him ere I die, that from my hand you might receive your son. Grant me another favour, Roskelyn, 'tis the last. I know that after death my head will be fixed upon the city gate;—let it be turned towards the Isle of Barra, that even after death my sightless orbs may turn to the bright blue hills I love so well.

Officer. My lord, the hour is past.

Lord R. I will account for all—wait yet longer.

St. C. They surely know my fate, what can detain them at an hour like this?

Officer. My lord, your pardon, but I dare not delay longer.

St. C. Nor do I ask a longer respite, perhaps 'tis better that I have none around whose presence might augment my misery. Roskelyn, farewell, your present kindness has erased all memory of the past; bear my last blessing to Randolph, my wife, and friends, tell Ambrosine that my last prayer was breathed for Scotland and for her. Now I am ready.

(Officer approaches with an handkerchief.)

St. C. No, I will not close mine eyes upon the light of day until they close for ever.

Lord R. I cannot see thee die,—I will retire.

St. C. Not so, fear not, for a true Scot can die unshrinkingly.

(Soldiers form opposite St. Clair,—he kneels, R.)

Officer. Make ready!—present!!—fire!!!

(They fire.—Randolph rushes before St. Clair, receives the fire, and falls.)

St. C. *(starts up.)* Eternal powers! 'tis Randolph! Roskelyn, they son has died for me!

(Lord R. raises Randolph, in doing so, his sleeve turns up, and a red mark is seen on his right arm.)

Lord R. Behold the proof! he is indeed my long-lost son, and have I lived to see him thus restored?

(Shouts behind.—Enter Ambrosine, Hamilton, De Bourgh, &c.&c. L. U. E.)

Amb. No, we are not too late. Look friends, he lives! St. Clair! thou'rt free, behold a pardon from the king.

St. C. Look on this dying boy, dying for me,—and tell me who can think of joy or liberty, while gazing thus on him? Ill-fated boy, he has then lost his life in saving mine.

Officer *(reads the paper).* King James gives a free pardon to St. Clair Monteith; further, it is his royal will that the titles and estates hitherto unfairly held by John of Roskelyn, be now restored to St. Clair Monteith; the son of Roskelyn never having appeared to claim them, he is now the only lawful heir, henceforth the Lord of Roskelyn!

Ham. Monteith, heard you those welcome tidings? Said I not truly that you would triumph over your foes, and have your rights restored?

St. C. No more,—methinks he breathes.

Ran. Mourn not for me—oh! I am happier now than to have lived, and know I had usurped another's rights. To die in saving thee is better far than to have lived in any other cause. But ere I close my eyes for ever, let me behold my friends once more. *(All surround him.)* Let the last sound I hear on earth convince me that my death ensures his liberty.

Ham. *(R.)* Long live St. Clair Monteith, Lord of Roskelyn.

All. Huzzah!

(Slow Music.—Randolph kneels, and appears to pray, then joins the hands of Lord Roskelyn and St. Clair—then falls slowly, the others arrange in tableau as the curtain slowly descends.)

THE END.

Notes

1. Dicks edition reads "who" instead of "that."
2. Dicks has "given me the keys."
3. Dicks reads "Goes slowly to the table."
4. Dicks omits the repetition of the word "out" so that the line reads "only let me get out of the house, and I'll never be ensnared by a woman again as long as I live."

THE BOND

A Dramatic Poem

In 3 Acts

by

Catherine Gore

The Bond

Catherine Grace Frances Gore was born in 1799 in Nottinghamshire, the daughter of a wine merchant named Moody.[1] She was educated at home and exhibited "literary genius" at an early age (*The Dictionary of National Biography*, 1921–1922 ed.), producing a number of poems that were praised by Joanna Baillie but never printed.[2] On 15 February 1823 she married Captain Charles Arthur Gore who sold his commission as sub-lieutenant of the 1st life guards to support his wife. During the years that followed, Catherine raised ten children and began writing in earnest to supplement the family income. Her first novel, *Theresa Marchmont; or, the Maid of Honor* appeared in 1824, followed immediately by her first play, a closet melodrama in three acts entitled *The Bond*.

Eleven novels later in 1831, she produced two plays, *The School for Coquettes* at the Haymarket (7/14/31) and *Lords and Commons* at Drury Lane (12/20/31). While *The School for Coquettes* became her first major success and enjoyed a run of thirty-seven performances in London, *Lords and Commons* was "judged by the critics to be far superior to her first" (Adburgham 175). The following year, because her husband accepted a diplomatic position in France, the family moved to Paris where Mrs. Gore presided over Sunday literary salons at the Place Vendôme. Though she was neither beautiful nor charismatic, Mrs. Gore had a wit "unequalled by any other Englishwoman—some put it even higher than that of Madame de Stael" (Adburgham 239).[3]

Five novels later, in 1834, a melodrama, *The Queen's Champion* was produced at the Haymarket (9/10/34) and a comedy, *Modern Honour; or, The Sharper of High Life* was performed at Covent Garden (12/3/34). The following year, her comedy, *The King's Seal* caused a riot at Drury Lane (1/10/35) because it contained veiled allusions to contemporary English politics.[4] Undaunted, Mrs. Gore produced two more highly successful melodramas that year: *The Maid of Croissey; or, Theresa's Vow* at the Haymarket (7/20/35) and *King O'Neil; or, The Irish Brigade* at Covent Garden (12/9/35).[5]

In 1836 a financial crisis accelerated her output, prompting her to write eleven novels and two melodramas in three years. Of the melodramas, *Don Juan of Austria*, an adaptation of C. Delavigne's

Don Juan d'Autriche, was produced at Covent Garden (4/16/36), and *A Tale of a Tub* was performed at the Haymarket the following year (7/15/37). In 1839, a two-character farce, entitled *A Good Night's Rest; or, Two in the Morning,* appeared at the Strand[6] (8/19/39) and the next year, the closet melodrama, *Dacre of the South* was published in addition to three novels.

In 1841, the Gores returned to England and Catherine produced her best known novel, *Cecil; or, Adventures of a Coxcomb,* which she published anonymously in order to capture the public's interest in a "new writer." Thirteen novels and collections of stories later in 1844, she won the £500 prize in a comedy contest held by the Haymarket Theatre. The award winning play was *Quid pro Quo; or, The Day of Dupes* (6/18/44) which ran for five weeks despite a terrible reception from the critics and public alike.[7] Following the death of her husband in 1846, Mrs. Gore redoubled her creative energy and produced three novels a year until 1850 when an inheritance providing her with financial stability enabled her to relax the pace. Between 1850 and 1855 she wrote only three books, but when her guardian Sir John Dean Paul embezzled £20,000 from her bank account in 1855, she went back to work reissuing her 1843 novel, *The Banker's Wife,* originally dedicated to Sir John, and writing a new novel exposing the scandal, *Mammon; or, The Hardships of an Heiress.*[8]

Three more novels later in 1858, the author began to exhibit symptoms of blindness and though she retired completely from the society she loved, she continued to work at a feverish pace. Finally on 29 January 1861, Catherine Gore died at the age of sixty-one and was buried in Kensal Green cemetery, survived by only two of her ten children and over two hundred volumes of plays, novels, poems, and stories.

In *The Bond,* her first melodrama, Mrs. Gore drew upon the Faust legend, borrowing themes, motifs, and dramatic incidents from Joanna Baillie's romantic drama, *De Monfort* (1798), Monk Lewis's *One O'Clock; or, The Knight and the Wood Demon* (1807), R.C. Maturin's sensational revenge melodrama, *Bertram* (1816), and T.L. Beddoes's bloody drama, *The Bride's Tragedy* (1822). It was in this play that Gore began experimenting with the Byronic hero, whom Bonnie Anderson describes as "cold, silent, and slightly sinister" (409). In contrast to this brooding, mysterious, highly sexual—though evasive—

man, is the heroine whose goal is to transform him, and convince him that she is worthy of his attention.

In her study of "Women, Masochism, and the Gothic," *In The Name of Love,* Michelle A. Massé argues that in such a relationship, the traditional view of Gothic plots always posited the male in the dominant position:

> The Ur-plot is a terror-inflicted variant of Richardsonian courtship narrative in which an unprotected young woman in an isolated setting uncovers a sinister secret. After repeated trials and persecutions, one of two possible outcomes usually follows: the master of the house is discovered as the evil source of her tribulations and is vanquished by the poor-but-honest (and inevitably later revealed as noble) young man, who marries the woman; the master of the house, apparently the source of evil, is revealed to be more sinned against than sinning, and he marries the woman. Strangely enough, in both scenarios the narrative is shaped by the mystery the male protagonist presents and not by the drama of the supposed protagonist, the Gothic heroine" (10).

Certainly in *The Bond,* where Helen, the heroine, is much less active than Falkenstiern, her brooding husband, the traditional interpretation might appear to have a surface validity. Yet, it is Helen's suffering (a kind of masochism, in Massé's view[9]) that is both the moral and efficient cause of the play's action. Anderson suggests that the interrelationship between suffering heroine and Byronic hero actually elevates the stature of the suffering heroine:

> The heroine's attraction to this sort of hero confirms her own superiority—she and she alone can see through the mask to the true worth within. Also, only she is brave enough to risk engaging with a man who terrifies "normal" women. The dynamics of the relationship . . . are as follows: the heroine finds herself attracted by a man who seems to look down on her (as he does on all women). Against the advice of well-meaning friends and relatives, she ventures upon a relationship with him. She is braced for pain: rejection, betrayal, or cruelty at his hands. (410–411)

While Helen might suggest the traditional female stereotypes of passivity, obedience, morality, and confinement, as expressed by Mary Ellmann in her book, *Thinking About Women,* Helen also embodies what Anne Williams suggests is central to the Gothic tradition, a mythos of family (22).[10] All of her action is directed to the perpetuation of the system that ultimately robs her of her life. Yet, deeply rooted in a Christian tradition, Helen has little alternative. She has a moral imperative to provide for the eternal salvation of her child. Though governed continually by the men in the play, Helen faces the greatest dilemma. Must she obey her confessor (one moral imperative, leading to eternal salvation), or her husband (another moral imperative, leading, however, to eternal damnation)? In her attempt to reconcile her conflicting duties, she dies, another testament to Massé's assertion that "The ground of the Gothic is littered with wounded and dead wives whose husbands assure them that their injuries are self-inflicted, caused by some larger force, or negligible because of the husbands' own pain" (25).

More overtly active are the women in *Dacre of the South,* another melodrama driven by the mythos of family. Here the Byronic Falkenstiern is replaced with a young idealistic hero, obsessed with his private notions of justice and honor. Here it is the male figure who is passive and confined while the women in the play are the active forces in the attempt to protect their family. Dwinell suggests that this desire to protect the family demonstrates a significant difference in the way men and women approach moral decisions in the plays:

This difference reflects their social experiences. Women were expected to stay home and care for the family, leaving public concerns to men. It is therefore not surprising to note that most of the women in the plays define their morality from within the domestic sphere. They make their moral choices based on what is good for the maintenance of the family and what they think constitute moral choices for themselves, regardless of public opinion. The men define their morality, however, based on a more public sphere and consequently they are more concerned with how others perceive them. (45)

Anne Fiennes, Dacre's sister, and Mary, his wife, not only embody the mythos of family, they also participate in what Ellen Moers suggests is a central ideal of the Gothic, "the traveling woman: the woman who moves, who acts, who copes with vicissitude and adventure" (126). We have seen traveling women in this collection, but in other plays women have been active in concert with men.[11] Here, the women act independently, often at odds with the idealism of the hero, who often wishes to "preserve" the women from external influences. Dwinell argues that in Gore's plays, women resist the stereotype of being confined to the home and "refuse to be protected from the outside world, move outside their designated spheres into unknown and forbidden territories, and do not limit themselves to roles as doting mothers and wives" (57).

Of the women writers here represented, Mrs. Gore was the most prolific as well as the most acclaimed during her lifetime. As a novelist she was the "mistress of the silver fork school" (Adburgham 165), producing fashionable novels that depicted the love affairs, foibles, and scandals of high society with a "sharp wit and keen insight into the pretensions and absurdities of the fashionable world" (Schlueter and Schlueter 199). The only woman playwright whose work was regularly performed at Covent Garden, Drury Lane, and the Haymarket (the *major* theatres), Mrs. Gore imbued the melodrama with a sophistication that appealed to the upper classes and can be considered the earliest female practitioner of "Gentlemanly Melodrama."

Though criticized by many modern critics for "extolling the virtues of male domination and female submission" in her novels (Blain, Clements, and Grundy 443), Mrs. Gore took a very different stance regarding women in her plays. While her first dramatic effort, *The Bond* (1824), follows the more standard pattern of Gothic melodrama with a long-suffering heroine and her Byronic lover, her later plays vary the formula to include strong, noble, active women who seek to control their destinies on their own terms. While the success or failure of their attempt is ultimately in the hands of male authority, the women in these plays (especially *The Maid of Croissey, The King's Seal, King O'Neil,* and particularly *Dacre of the South*) actively and heroically, pursue their objectives, assuming an equality with men not present in the novels.[12]

The present edition of *The Bond* is based on the text published in London by John Murray, Albemarle-Street, printed by Thomas Davison, Whitefriars in 1824.[13] *Dacre of the South* is taken from the edition published in London by Richard Bentley, New Burlington Street, Publisher in Ordinary to Her Majesty, 1840.

Notes

1. The editor of *The Life of Mary Russell Mitford,* A.G.K. L'Estrange, suggests that she was the stepdaughter of Dr. Nevinson (1: 297).

2. In his chapter on Mrs. Gore in *The Silver-Fork School,* Matthew Rosa mentions other tributes to Mrs. Gore from Mary Russell Mitford and Edward Bulwer-Lytton. Mitford writes that "Miss Nevinson is a very extraordinary woman: her conversation (for I don't think very highly of her writing) is perhaps the most dazzling and brilliant that can be imagined" (119), while Bulwer-Lytton argues that, in comparison with Thackeray, Mrs. Gore "knew good society infinitely better" (117).

3. Among the regular guests was the young Coventry Patmore who fell in love with Mrs. Gore's daughter, Cecilia. Though his passion was unrequited, it did inspire him to write *The Angel in the House* (Basil Champney, *Memoirs and Correspondence of Coventry Patmore,* qtd. Adburgham 239). She was held in high regard by Mary Russell Mitford, Charles Dickens, William Beckford, Leigh Hunt, and William Thackeray who satirized her in *Punch.*

4. See *Times* 12 January 1835.

5. It was sufficiently popular to be revived twice, in 1839 and 1867.

6. Adburgham suggests that this play was written immediately following *The Bond* in 1824 (164).

7. The August 1882 issue of *The Theatre* chronicles the difficulties Mrs. Gore had with this play, not the least of which was the refusal of Madame Vestris and Charles Matthews to play the roles assigned to them. It concludes:

> "Quid pro Quo" was written with some smartness if with inferior taste. The dialogue was of the pert and punning sort, with here and there approaches to wit and humour, and oftentimes a declension into mere vulgarity. The work was not designed to be read; it did not and it does not offer any temptation to readers; on the stage it did not succeed, although Mrs. Gore claimed that her play, condemned and in a great measure unheard at its production, was afterwards repeated with "a result as brilliantly successful as the first ordeal was vexatious." Like "The Rivals," as she urged, "unfortunate in a first representation, it now succeeds in drawing crowded houses and eliciting the hearty laughter so welcome to the ears of the performers." But this seeming prosperity did not endure. No doubt the public were for a while curious on the subject, and the manager did all he could to promote the interest of the comedy and to retain it upon his stage. "Quid pro Quo" was played for some five weeks therefore, but to audiences that gradually diminished and departed, and its final representation was at length announced. So the prize comedy vanished from the stage, to which it has never since been invited to return. (74)

8. In her thesis study, "Gender Issues in the Plays of Catherine Gore," Jeanine Dwinell argues for the existence of a final melodrama entitled *The Woman of the World,* produced at the Queen's Theatre (11/13/58) under the pseudonym of "Lady Clara Cavendish" (4). While Mrs. Gore did indeed write under various pseudonyms during her lifetime, it is unlikely that this play is hers. The original from which the play was adapted was not, as Dwinell suggests, Mrs. Gore's novel, *The Woman of the World* (1838) but the serial of that name which appeared in *Reynold's Miscellany* in 1858–1859. While it is not impossible that the serial (and others that followed under the anonym of "Lady Clara Cavendish") was the work of Mrs. Gore, it is highly unlikely, even though the microform issue of Lacy's Acting Edition (#38) of the play (in the *English and American Drama of the Nineteenth Century* series) is catalogued under the names of both authors.

9. Massé suggests that the Gothic "is a pointed reminder of cultural amnesia in its insistent representation of the *process* through which a woman becomes a masochist and assigns subjectivity to another" (3). She goes on to describe the suffering characteristic of a form she calls, "Marital Gothic":

Perfect love supposedly has cast out fear, and perfect trust in another has led to the omission of anxiety. . . . Yet horror returns in the new home of the couple, conjured up by renewed denial of the heroine's identity and autonomy. The marriage that she thought would give her voice (because she would be listened to), movement (because her status would be that of an adult), and not just a room of her own but a house, proves to have none of these attributes. The husband who was originally defined by his opposition to the unjust father figure slowly merges with that figure. The heroine again finds herself mute, paralyzed, enclosed, and she must harrow the Gothic in an attempt to deal with that reality through repetition. (20)

10. Dwinell proposes that Gore's women are "determined to preserve their families at all costs" (45).

11. Usually the women are following the directive of the hero. A notable exception to this is Lady Roskelyn in *St. Clair of the Isles,* the virtual villain of the play.

12. Anderson argues that Mrs. Gore elevates "female submission to a virtue" in her novels and maintains the ideology that women are "morally inferior" to men "because of their weaker natures" (414–415). She adds that the "womanly ideology did not permit women to triumph in a man's world—instead it gave total fulfillment in a woman's world: a successful marriage, a happy family, a beautiful home, and fashionable success" (420).

13. The play was published under the authorship of "Mrs. Charles Gore." The title page bore two literary quotations which were significant to the appreciation of the play:

"Be these juggling fiends no more believed,
That palter with us in a double sense;
That keep the word of promise to our ear,
And break it to our hope."—*Macbeth.*

and

— "Is it not written, that
Whoe'er shall worship these dark Powers shall bear
Upon his brow, and fix upon his race,
A curse eternally?"—*Werner.*

THE BOND,
a
Dramatic Poem

Dramatis Personae

Falkenstiern, *a young baron of the Palatinate.*
Rothberg, *his kinsman.*
Father Michael, *his confessor.*
The four Electors of the Rhine.
Count Lahnstein.
Host.
Meinhard, *an evil spirit; disguised in the first act as a traveling*
student, in the succeeding ones habited as a German noble.
Helen, *the affianced wife of Falkenstiern.*
Child and Attendant.
Chorus of Spirits.
Chorus of Peasants.
Musicians, civil officers of the Palatinate, &c.

*The action is supposed to pass towards the end of the fourteenth
century.*

Act I. Scene I.

An Apartment in the Inn at Bonn.

(Enter Host, Falkenstiern, and Meinhard, as from a Journey.)
   Meinhard. A blazing faggot, and a sparkling flask!
Spare not despatch, good host, for the keen blast
Hath chill'd our very hearts.
   Host.   Truth, sirs, the storm
Hath spread the drifting snow too heavily
To lure forth travelers to an onward venture.
Small speed for sledge or steed in such a season
Eight hours would scantly bear ye to Cologne;

But here, safe housed from perils of the night,
Ye may defy the blast.

    Falkenstiern.   'Twere wiser, friend,
To satisfy our wants, than tediously
Discuss our evil hap.

    Host.   Your pardon, sir;
You shall be served anon. Within there—ho!
Logs to the hearth, and goblets to the board!
Will it not please ye, noble sirs, to name
Your favourite vintage? Haply strangers here
Our native Rhenish—if my countrymen—
The grape of France commands a preference—
Bourdeaux—or Rhone—or if I might presume—

    Falkenstiern. Prythee, leave prating, and provide me quickly
The choicest that thy paltry stores enclose.
Speed, babbler!

    Host.   Nay, my masters, I am gone.
(Exit Host.)

    Meinhard. You are impatient, sir: it is the wont
Of these fat knaves, who drowse away their hours,
Flagon in hand, beside their blazing ingle,
To palm their dullness on their customers,
And gather tidings of the waking world
From every hapless comer.

    Falkenstiern.   'Tis my wont
To check the insolence of prying fools.

    Meinhard. Why this is very churlishness! 'Twas thus,—
Pardon, sir traveler, for I, too, own
Habitual rules, and one is, perfect freedom
In honest speech—'twas thus erewhile you sought
By moody silence, or by brief reply,
Which I might term uncourteous, could I feel
Ruffled by boyish petulance, to silence
The social converse that I sought withal
To cheer our dreary way.

    Falkenstiern.   I am not apt
In idle parley—I am ill at ease,
And deem not that the same untoward chance
Which bids me brave the night-storm howling o'er

Yon rolling river, equally commands
That I should ope the temple of my mind
To every vulgar footstep. Art thou answer'd?

    Meinhard. With less than courtesy—but, be it so—
We part not yet—

(Enter attendants with refreshments.)

                  And may this welcome cheer,
A common bond of union 'mid mankind,
Dissolve your stern reserve. Come, pledge me, sir:
A calmer brow—a gentler heart attend you.
Tomorrow's dawn, perchance, more cheerily
May light us to Cologne. E'en now the blast,
Which yell'd erewhile with frightful violence,
Lashing the Rhine-waves like an angry ocean,
Subsideth—as a fretful infant's cries,
That sinks to sleep upon its mother's breast.
The storm is o'er:—but, come, the well fill'd board
Courts our approach.

    Falkenstiern.   I need not food tonight;
Enjoy your feast alone. Another bowl,
Another brimming bowl, to thaw the chill
Of my cold bosom, and farewell till morning.

(Drinks hastily, and exit.)

    Meinhard. Farewell! Proud man, thine hour is almost come!

(Scene closes.)

Scene II.

The ramparts of Bonn, overlooking the Rhine; the Seven Mountains seen by the light of a rising moon.

(Enter Falkenstiern, solus).

    Falkenstiern. Calm, calm and silent! the unsparing tempest
Hath pass'd into the stillness of repose!
So would it pass—the tempest of my mind,
Which slowly wears away my springs of life,
Dare I but plunge, and sleep! Ye rolling waves,
Dark with the mystery of night, arise!

Arise! and overwhelm my being! Make
The deed your own! Quench my repining soul!
Resolve it to the elements!
                                Breath! breath!
Inheritance of ill—accursed gift—
Why cling'st thou still unto thy struggling victim?
There's not a fountain of unlawful knowledge
So dark with fiendspells, nor so bitterly
Drugg'd with repentance, but my desperate soul
Would quaff its perilous waters. Spirits once
Walk'd visibly the paths of earth; but now,
Demons themselves gaze on the woes of men,
Unaiding, and unpitying!
(Enter Meinhard, and stands beside him.)
                                Get thee hence!
Why dost thou haunt my steps? Am I not free
To breathe the soothing nightwind on these banks,
But thou must thrust thy dark and unsought presence
Between my weary heart and loneliness?
'Tis with yon countless orbs, yon mountain tops
O'er which they shine, my spirit seeks communion,
Not with my fellow toilers of the dust.
Hence!
    Meinhard. Falkenstiern!
    Falkenstiern.   Ha! speak—thou know'st me not?
    Meinhard. Not she upon whose fond maternal breast
Thy spirit dawn'd in restless infancy,
Could know thee better.
    Falkenstiern.   Till this dreary morn
I never look'd upon thee.
    Meinhard.   Falkenstiern!
While yet a stripling, and unquiet thoughts,
A thirst of hidden knowledge, and a pride
Beyond thine earthly nature, bade thee seek
The practice of forbidden arts, thy tongue
Cast mockery on those things which other men
Reverence in silent awe! Thy mother, then,
Whose spirit hover'd on the verge of life,
Alone beheld in terror, and in grief,

Thy bosom's secret doubts. With gentlest prayers,
With sorrowing tenderness, she strove to check
Thy vain aspirings; and her dying words
Were—

  Falkenstiern. Peace, oh! peace, mysterious being!
Yet wherefore fear that thou couldst rend my heart
With the remembrance of her cherish'd voice:
We were alone—and from that fearful hour
None ever heard me breathe her sainted name.

  Meinhard. When from her dying hand she took the ring
Which sparkles now on thine, I stood beside thee.
When to the mighty ruler of the earth
Her faltering prayers rose up in humble love
For thee, her erring and rebellious child,
I heard them perish on her icy lips,
Seal'd by the hand of death! Yea, Falkenstiern!
When thou, too late repentant, oh! too late
Touch'd by the vain remorse of love, didst fall
Beside her shrouded form, and call on her
For pardon—pressing on her marble hand
Thy quivering lips, beating thy frantic breast,
Which mock'd the patient stillness of the dead—
I heard thy self-reviling—I beheld
Thy fruitless penitence; and had my nature
Allow'd such weakness, might have pitied thee.

  Falkenstiern. Now by my mother's grave (the holiest oath
My heart avows), I was alone—alone
Beside the bier! and thou who canst show
The secrets of my solitude, art more
Than mortal nature owns. Speak!

  Meinhard.   Thou hast said it!
I am the spirit of thy destiny!
Through all thine errors, weakness, and despair,
Thy guilty pride, thy feeble penitence,
I have been shrouded in thy bosom thoughts—
Have mark'd the vain repinings of thy spirit,
Thy wrongs, thy thirst of vengeance, and the hate
Which hath o'erwhelm'd thy proud and wounded heart;
And now I wear this frame of mortal clay

To aid thee as thou seekest. Falkenstiern!
This is thy ruling hour of fate! Tonight
Thou mayst redeem the curse that blights thy being:
Thy pilfer'd heritage—thy destined bride—
All shall be thine before this hour to-morrow,
So thou wilt swear—

    Falkenstiern.   In vain—thou speak'st in vain:
No aid can rescue now, no power redeem me
From the oppressor's gripe. Didst thou but know,
As thou affect'st, the story of my fortunes,
Thou would'st not mock me thus with idle schemes,
Or proffer'd aid.

    Meinhard.   Once more I tell thee, boy,
I have the power to give unto thy grasp
All that a father's dying malediction
Wrung from thy baffled hopes. Incredulous?
Then lend thy cold dull ear to the detail
Of galling injuries, which thou deem'st secret
Betwixt thee and revenge.

*(Meinhard seats himself carelessly on a buttress of the works, while
Falkenstiern stands near him, and betrays impatience and anger as
the narrative proceeds.)*

                        Few years have past
Since 'mid yon flaunting train of noble youths,
The rufflers of the court, none seem'd to wear
A brighter destiny than thine. A name
Graced with the laurels of succeeding ages,
Thyself its sole inheritor; a form,
A presence, worthy of its nobleness;
A sire—though haply stern, yet mainly doting
Upon thy dawning manhood;—and a mother
Even thy savage heart delights to honour!
Such were thy gifts: and last, yet dearer far
Than all, thy destined bride—their orphan ward—
Thy childhood's playmate—youth's companion—Helen,
The loving and beloved! Yet even then,
While fortune's choicest blessings wooed thy touch,
Thy wayward heart spurn'd all! By choice a rover,
The gentle ties of home and kindred pall'd

Upon thy wild and all insatiate nature.
Rarely thy treasured presence yielded joy
Unto thy father's halls: thy parents saw
Age and decay approach them as they sate
Neglected by their lonely heart; and rumor
Brought tidings of thy life's dishonoured course,
Which made it worse than lone!
       Thy mother died!
I will not say that sorrow more than years
Dug her untimely grave; but thou wilt own,
That knowledge of thy fall from virtue strew'd
Thorns on the pillow of the dying saint.
Then, Falkenstiern, 'twas then—when death had stolen
The solace of thy father's drooping heart,
The brightest link of the domestic chain
Which bound him still to earth—when thou, his child,
Who should'st have soothed the peevishness of age,
Deserted him and home for gayer scenes—
Thy noble kinsman, Rothberg, pitying
The desolation of the aged man,
Replaced thee in the duties of a son,
And by his generous self-devotion made
The dreary season of decrepitude
Smile in the sunshine of—
  Falkenstiern *(interrupting him furiously).*
His—the perfidious, silver-tongued deceiver!
Who, like the wily Hebrew, profiting
By the infirmity of age, supplanted
The absent son, bereaving me of all—
My father's blessing, mine inheritance,
And the fond love which should have better stood
Against the lies and paltry machinations
Of such a villain! He might have won the rest—
The lands:—the dross he craved, I valued not
For their own sordid price—mine heritage
He might enjoy unenvied;—but that she—
She—from whose lips such vows of faith and love,
She—from whose eyes such tears of tenderness
Awaited me at parting, should forget

All ties of future hope, of past affection,
And yield her hand unto the man I hate
As I abhor the reptiles of the earth;
It maddens me—it breathes into my soul
A thirst of vengeance rendering life a curse
Loathsome to bear!

    Meinhard *(with a careless smile).*
                  Before the sacred altar
Tomorrow at the morning hour will Helen
Be wedded with thy foe!—Tomorrow noon
The bridal revelers will meet to triumph
Within thy father's hall, whence thou, a stranger,
Alone art banish'd forth. Tomorrow eve,
The gentle bride—

    Falkenstiern.   Fiend! Sorcerer! darest thou thus
Sport with the fury of a desperate man?
I am a fool to curse thee—Speak again—
Erewhile, I met with mockery thy professions
Of power and will to aid me—Speak again—
Whate'er be the conditions of thy bond,
Thou canst not rate thy services so highly
As to provoke refusal—Speak again—
Unfold thy purpose.

    Meinhard.   'Tis the midnight hour;
And when the rays of morning waken man
To his accustom'd tasks of toil and care,
The bridal train will gather. Ere the dawn
Rothberg and thou must meet.

    Falkenstiern.   Then all is lost.
The fleetest courser of the Arab plains
Would scarcely bear me back to Falkenstiern
In twice twelve hours—

    Meinhard.   The fleetest steed that owns
Obedience to the check of mortal hand:
Nay—wherefore start?—thou art but scant of faith.
Look to the summit of the Drachenfels,
What seest thou?

    Falkenstiern.   Ha! a crescent moon, and lo!
Reflected on the river's surface, shines

The Queen of night, full orbed and bright!
    Meinhard *(raising his hand towards the Seven Mountains)*.
                        Descend!
(The Meteor appears to glide towards them, and vanishes at their feet.)
Art thou content that I am gifted far
Above thy baser nature?
    Falkenstiern.   Awful Being!
Proclaim thy will, that I may swear obedience.
Yea—bind me as thou wilt—by every tie
Human or superhuman, I am thine.
Speak—by what oath must I attest—
    Meinhard.   Not here;
The vow I shall require must not be breathed
In the open air of night:—the mystic rite
Which must cement our fellowship would rend
Yon mighty crags asunder, and dissolve
The ancient channel of the rolling Rhine!
Give me thy hand, and fear not—Thou art mine.
Hence, and with speed.
(Scene closes.)

Scene III.

A vast cavern, supported by basaltic columns, and imperfectly seen through a veil, which overhangs the foreground. A faint symphony of flutes is heard behind the scenes. Falkenstiern is seen lying senseless on the earth. He rises, and receives a talisman from the hand of Meinhard, who chants the following stanzas.

              Rise from thy trance,
                  Our charm is spoken,
              Mortal! advance—
                  Receive the token
              By which thy hand
                  O'er earth and sea
              Shall hold command
                  And mastery.

Gnome of the mine—
   Sylph of the air—
Wave-born undine—
   Hither repair!
By the dark word
   Mighty in sway,
Bow to your lord,
   Hear! and obey.

Demon of night,
   His wish fulfill!
Spirit of light,
   Bend to his will!
Imp of the flame,
   Answer his call—
Through the dread name
   Ruling ye all!

Elf of the wood—
   Hag of the wind—
Fay of the flood—
   Hither combined
Wing your dark way!
   Haste to my call,
Through the dread name
   Ruling ye all!

(Chorus of Spirits heard at a distance.)
   First Chorus. Lo! we come! thy law obeying;
Stores of glittering dross displaying
From the mine-embosom'd mountain,
From the golden sanded fountain.
   Second Chorus. Lo! we come! thy will performing,
While the ocean-billows storming
Send the Tyrian Argosy
To thy coffers of the sea!
   Third Chorus. Lo! we come! thy task fulfilling,
While the dews of night distilling,

Freshen o'er the eastern bowers
To wreath our mystic cave with flowers!
Fourth Chorus. Lo! we come! with gifts of splendor
Meet obedience here to render.
Lo! we come! with gifts of beauty,
Here to prove our fitting duty.
All. At thy summons meekly bending,
We are here! What task impending
Calls our due performance, say?
We but listen and obey.
Meinhard. Through the ambient air,
    Mocking time and place,
  We would now repair
    To our trysting-place:
  Through the starry void
    Of the realms of night,
  On plumed pinions buoy'd,
    Aid our rapid flight!
  Shell-breathed harmonies
    Cheer our dreary way,
  Till the lonely skies
    Shine with dawning day.
(A rushing of wings is heard: the Spirits encompass Meinhard and Falkenstiern, who disappear. Four Imps remain to guard the cavern.)
First Imp. He is gone, the sinful slave,
  To prepare a brother's grave:
  He is gone, in fiend-wrought mood,
  To bathe his hand in kindred blood!
  Ready implement of hell,
  He shall serve our bidding well!
Second Imp. No! upon his brow the sign
  Yet delays his destined hour;
  Adopted by the rite divine,
  He derides our master's power.
Third Imp. Though our service he may scorn,
  He hath yielded the unborn
  To our kingdom: we have won
  To demon-slavery his son;
  And through time and art, his soul

Yet may bend to our control.

Fourth Imp. Try him with riches, try him with power;
With woman's witching in Pleasure's bower.
Grant him skill of hand, and strength of limb.

Second Imp. Such lures avail not with one like him!
'Tis a peevish fool, whose pride of mind
Aspires to knowledge above his kind;
He hath wander'd in mazes of arts forbidden,
And pry'd into lore from mortals hidden.
Meteor or goblin avail not to daunt
His wandering step from the wood-wolf's haunt:
By midnight, by twilight, he watcheth the sky
To interpret his star-written destiny.

First Imp. From such vain quest
Let us urge his breast
With omen and sign,
Till his soul shall incline
To our purport and seeking.

Third Imp. See! morning is breaking.

(The four Imps join hands and sing.)

Mark! the day-dawn shining,
Lo! our hands entwining,
Thus and thus combining,
Hence o'er earth and air:
Toilsome tasks pursuing,
Discord still renewing,
Deeds of blood and ruin
Claim our patient care!

O'er the earth-world slumbering,
Bound in chains encumbering,
By tyrants far outnumbering
Yonder ocean's sands;
Freedom's ensigns waving,
Burst its bonds enslaving!
Till Rebellion raving,
Heads her death-doom'd bands.

Slander's venom arming,

Pride's presumption warming,
Beauty's blindness charming,
   Haunt the human heart:
Treason's plots inflaming,
Priestcraft's powers defaming,
Murder's weapons aiming,
   Our master's laws impart.

Shame awaits our coming,
Through the man-crowd roaming,
Sin and sorrow dooming,
   Let us work our will:
Tears of anguish falling,
Wild Repentance galling,
Crimes beyond recalling,
   Shall reward us still!

(Scene closes.)

Scene IV.

*The Interior of a Gothic Apartment in the Castle of Falkenstiern.
Helen and Father Michael are discovered. She holds a Dial on a
Pedestal.*

Helen. Thrice have I struck the hour, and still the sound
Advanceth not; the same unvarying tale
Upbraids my vain impatience.
    Father Michael.   It is late—
Retire, my child; and in the silent darkness
Of thine own chamber, seek a brief repose
From thine inquietudes. The night is dark,
And stormy was the close of day; the ways
Are steep—a weary steed—a swollen river—
A thousand accidents by flood or fell,
May have delay'd the messengers who seek
Count Falkenstiern.
    Helen.   As one who, safe on shore,
Watcheth the tempest-ridden ocean's rage,

Calmly thou canst behold and speak of peril;
But I am like the bark-tost mariner,
Proving, and shrinking from its terrors! Father,
I cannot call to mind that hour of life
In which I loved not Falkenstiern. From childhood
Our troth-plight was the charter of my love!
And now—and now—when the dread hour approaches
Which shall confirm our mutual faith for ever,
What marvel is it that my bosom waits
With equal trepidation his approach,
Or his delay?
(Storm heard without.)
     With evil omens fraught
This day hath pass'd! To my foreboding ear
Yon tempest's roar hath a prophetic voice
Awful and sad—a dire presage of ill
Hangs heavy on my heart! These stratagems,
These plots to win a noble mind from error,
I like them not—no good can come of falsehood—
None of deceit. Why cheat him with the semblance
Of all this heavy load of injury,
This measure of calamitous oppression?
Would I had never lent my aid!
 Father Michael.   My child,
When the warm pleadings of affection, when
The mandates of parental will, hard fail'd
To win the wanderer from the fatal paths
Of vice and prodigality, no means
Avail'd to save or to reclaim, unless
The iron lessons adversity!
Count Falkenstiern hath tasted in its fullness
The bitter cup of poverty—hath proved
The vanity of worldly friendships! Those
Who pluck'd the golden fruit, and wooed the shade
Of his too prosperous summer days, forsook
The barren tree in winter's nakedness
Bared to the storms of fate! He will return—
He will return with eager love to seek
The ties he held so lightly, and the home

Which wearied him of old.

Helen.   Meanwhile, alas!
What heavy hours—what perils—what privation
Hath he been doom'd to bear! My Falkenstiern!
I have slept soft—fed daintily,—while thou —
Thou, my beloved—my noble Falkenstiern!
Hast struggled with the meanest wants of nature.
Food—raiment—shelter—may have been denied
To him, the rightful lord of these proud halls.
While yet he linger'd near his former home,
I was content to bear my part among ye,
And wrong myself and him with a false show
Of having left him, like the faithless crew,
And given the love, so long, so truly his,
To one who had supplanted him in all!
But since unknown, unmark'd, beneath the shade
Of night, he left these plains; and whether urged
By indignation, grief, or direful want,
Sought refuge in some cold obscurity,
To live—perchance to die—in loneliness,
How oft have I repented—oh! how oft
Have I bewailed the coldness of my heart
Which lent itself to such deceit, and made
His path of life a desert! Falkenstiern!
Oh! Falkenstiern! who knows what dreadful act
The desperation of thy mind hath urged!
For me—*(Listening.)* Oh! Father, through the night-storm's roar
I hear the clank of the descending bridge,
A passing steed—now—he comes—oh! forth,
In pity forth, and greet him at the portal.
(Exit Father Michael.)
(After a pause, enter Rothberg: Helen goes eagerly to meet him; he looks upon her sorrowfully.)
Thou bring'st me evil tidings! Nay—but speak!
Thy mournful silence hath a voice more deadly
Than the deep knell which shakes a new made grave.
Speak, Rothberg!

Rothberg. Helen!
Helen.   Pr'ythee mock me not;

A messenger but now returned—too well
I know the tale he bore! My Falkenstiern
Hath fallen a victim to thy paltry arts.

    Rothberg. In sooth no search hath yet avail'd to trace
His path.

    Helen.   Are all the messengers return'd?

    Rothberg. One yet remains with unabated zeal,
Tracking the wanderer's course.

    Helen.   Blest be his speed!
Oh! what a precious guerdon shall await
That man's return. My gratitude shall rate
His services with true affection's price,
Unbounded ever. Rothberg! thinkest thou
Ere morning's dawn he could be here?

    Rothberg.   Dear Helen!
Pr'ythee to rest, and leave the task of watching
To one who needs not slumber. Sweet! to bed.
It is not fitting thou shouldst share my vigils,
For I have many an instrument of moment
To sign and seal this night, ere I resign
My stewardship to the rightful heir. Yet, Helen,
Tarry awhile—one moment—'tis the last
That still belongs to Friendship; for to-morrow
May Love assert his claim! I know not why,
But some strange sense of sorrow ill defined
Disquieteth my heart. I feel like one
About to venture on a lonely journey
Of length and peril; therefore, fare thee well!
And ere we part, let me remind thee, Helen—
That 'tis tonight—

    Helen.   Speak not of this!

    Rothberg.   Tonight
The year expires of Falkenstiern's probation,
Remember'st thou how, at this very hour,
His dying father with his parting breath
Sued—nay, commanded, that for one short year
I should assume the semblance of his heir,
And occupy the place, the rights, the honours
Of his discarded son; e'en to betrothment

With thee, his destined wife? I have fulfill'd
To the utmost verge the will of one whose acts
Were ever urged by nobleness and virtue.
Well have we play'd our part—for there is none,
Not one throughout the castle, but believes
Tomorrow's sun will shine upon our bridal.
The chapel is prepared, the halls are hung
With emblems of festivity and love;
And should our search reward us, and restore
Our Falkenstiern to his inheritance,
They still may serve to grace your union. Helen!
Before we part tonight, speak kindly to me!
For since thy fears arose for Falkenstiern,
Harsh doubts have seem'd to haunt thy mind—harsh words
Have breathed suspicions of thy friend. Dear Helen,
May God desert me in my dying hour
If I were urged by any baser motive
To my ungracious task!

    Helen.   Pardon, good Rothberg,
Pardon my petulance: a mind o'erwrought
By anxious fears too often scapes the bounds
Of Reason's mastery. Thou art to me
In all thy kind protecting love—a brother,
Nor less, nor more: and he shall thank thee, Rothberg.
He will be here tonight—I know it, feel it,
With a sure prescience.

    Rothberg.   Fare thee well, then, Helen!
Thy hand at parting—thus—thus: now to rest,
And angel guards watch o'er thy sleep.
(Exit Helen.)

    Rothberg *(solus).*   She's gone!
I hear her parting footsteps lightly touch
The corridor—the marble stair:—she's gone!
I feel a chill steal o'er my weary frame.
Would I could call her back, and say farewell
Once more—but once—she is so fair, so gentle,
That fear and sorrow seem to fly her presence!
The drowsy knaves, who have o'erwatch'd themselves,
Awaiting Falkenstiern's approach, are sunk

In deepest sleep; and I alone am waking
Throughout the castle. 'Tis an awful feeling
To know oneself a solitary watcher
In a mighty mansion, and I feel tonight
Oppress'd by such a consciousness!
                                    Come, idler;
On to thy task—thy weary, sickening task—
To ponder o'er the subtleties of law,
And mark the thrice-riven fetters man hath forged
To circumvent the fraud of fellow-man.
*(Seats himself by the table; takes out a casket, a string of jewels, a
picture, some scrolls, &c.)*
These gems form part of Helen's dower. Tomorrow
I will restore them. Ha! her picture, too—
A pledge of past affection—let me gaze
Upon this portrait—'tis her gentle self,
Pure as e'en now she parted hence. Sweet Helen!
Heaven grant thou mayst not live to curse the hour
In which I render'd up my charge, and gave
Thy hand unto my kinsman. *(Pauses.)*
                                    Weariness
Creeps o'er my meditations, like a mist
Stealing at evening over some lone waste.
I will remove the lamp, and sleep awhile;
The warder hath command to sound réveillée
When he shall challenge Falkenstiern's approach,
Or the return of those who seek him. Ha!
Vainly I combat with—   *(He sleeps.)*
*(A faint symphony is heard; the scene becomes gradually enlightened,
and a cloud rises in the background, from which Falkenstiern
emerges, wrapt in his cloak. He gazes around the apartment for some
minutes in silence.)*
     Falkenstiern. This is the very chamber where I last
Looked on my father's face! And is it thus—
Thus hooded in the mask of night—thus urged
And aided by the counsels of a demon,
I visit it again? 'Twas here—'twas here
I held mine infant sports; 'twas here my mother
Subdued my soul with gentle admonitions,

In happy childhood; yea, 'twas here I thought
To watch in turn a fair and joyous group
Wearing my Helena's beauty on their brows,
And chasing life's vain cares with their glad pastimes.
And now I stand a stranger here—by stealth
An inmate of these walls!

                They cast me forth,
They robb'd me of each better gift of life,
They bared me to the buffets of the world,
Leaving me homeless,—penniless.—By Heaven
The very churl who kneels to swear allegiance
To the new Lord of Falkenstiern, hath here
A better claim than I!—

                Who hath done this?
Why, Rothberg, noble Rothberg—the companion
Of my young days of innocence, the friend
Of my maturer years! But now, the worm
He trampled with malignant hate shall sting
The traitor home.
(Approaching, and gazing upon Rothberg.)
                How peacefully he sleeps!
Wearing the same clear open brow, the same
Benignant smile with which he stole upon
My youthful confidence! What holds the wretch
So tenderly within his grasp? Just God!
It is her picture!—nay, the very same,
My promised gift upon our marriage day!
This seals my doubtful purpose—

                Rothberg! wake,
Villain! awake, the avenging hour is come,
And I am here!—

    Rothberg *(waking and rising).*
                Oh! art thou come at last,
Dear Falkenstiern! why, greet me as a friend,—
Turn not away. We look'd for thee tonight.
Our preparations are achieved; to-morrow
Helen at length will gird the bride-krantz on.
    Falkenstiern. Speak not of that.
    Rothberg.   Nay, I will have so:

Long have I hoped to consecrate to-morrow
To love and joy.

    Falkenstiern. Peace! peace!

    Rothberg.   Didst thou not mark
The chapel aisle o'erhung with flowers? Tomorrow
Before the altar—

    Falkenstiern *(furiously)*. Villain, no! thou diest
Tonight! *(Stabs him: he falls.)*

    Rothberg. Now Heaven have mercy on my soul!
For I am hurt to death. Oh! Falkenstiern!
Why hast thou done this deed?

    Falkenstiern.   How!—look on me,
Look on thyself, and ask me, am I not
An alien here, in my ancestral home,
Where thou art lord of all?

    Rothberg.   Is't possible?
Have not my messengers, my letters, reach'd thee,
That still thou deem'st thyself an outcast, still
Believ'st thy rights transferr'd? Raise up my head,
The current of my life ebbs to my heart;
Yet would I fain, before its course is check'd
For ever, interchange some words of peace
And pardon with my murderer.

    Falkenstiern *(starting back)*. Oh! God!
Must that accursed word in future brand
The noble name of Falkenstiern? Say on:
If thou canst prove thou hast not injured me—
But no!—

    Rothberg. My breath of life passeth away—
Brief let me be: Oh! Falkenstiern, thy sire,
Thy friend, was guiltless of a thought that wrong'd thee.
To wean thee from companionship with those
Who fed on thy profusion, to restrain
Thine oft-repented follies, still renew'd
With deeper tinct of shame, the will was framed
Which feign'd assignment of thy rights to me.
Within yon casket lies the instrument
Which makes them thine again, on expiration
Of one short year—within yon casket lies

The marriage contract which I hoped to-morrow
Would bind our gentle Helen thine for ever!
But now the hand which should bestow her on thee
Will own no pulse of life: the heart, whose love
Was thine and hers too fondly for its peace,
Will lie—

  Falkenstiern. Oh! Rothberg, Rothberg, if thy tale
Be truth, as thy condition, and the voice
Of dire repentance waking in my bosom,
Attest—what—what am I? A murderer!
A double damn'd and blood-stain'd wretch! The sport,
The prey of fiends, here and hereafter! Rothberg,
Thine eyes turn dimly on me, yet with looks
Of gentleness—as when we two together
Walk'd through the sunshine hand in hand! I pray thee
Look not so kindly on me, for my heart
Swells e'en to bursting!
(The voice of Meinhard is heard from without.)
       Falkenstiern! the hour
Of morning steals upon the earth. Beware
Lest thou remain here for detection: so
Shall earthly punishment fall on thy deeds
Of blood and desperation.

  Falkenstiern.   Oh! thou Fiend!
Wilt thou disturb his dying moments? No!
I will not quit the dying! *(Rising proudly.)*
       Let them come!
I render to the scaffold or the wheel
This mortal frame!—the ministers of justice
Ne'er dealt a blow more righteous than the one
Which lays it in the dust!

  Meinhard *(without)*. And yet bethink thee,
Ere it be yet too late, bethink thee well
Of the dread forfeiture thy bond ensures.
Thy bond—thy bond!

  Falkenstiern. Yea—I remember now:
The first o'erwhelming consciousness of guilt
Had wrought oblivion of the dreadful past!
Methought it was a dream—a hideous dream;

But I remember now that I am seal'd,
With hell's own burning signet, from the mass
Of common criminals. I have blasphemed
The God of my salvation—have deserted
The altar where my fathers knelt in faith,
And to the powers of darkness sign'd away
Mine own—mine offspring's heritage on high:
Therefore—oh! therefore must I rather bear
The load of ignominious guilt which clogs
My frame of flesh, than in eternity
Seek—

    Rothberg *(faintly)*. Falkenstiern! the hand of Death
Already chills me with his icy grasp!
Yet ere I die, retract those fatal words:
Let not my parting soul recoil in horror
From one so fondly loved, so deeply cursed!

    Meinhard *(becomes visible)*. His words are sooth!

    Rothberg.   Almighty Father! mercy!
(Dies. Falkenstiern stands over the body in silent agony.)

    Meinhard. Why dost thou gaze upon that mass of clay
With such a peevish air of grief?

    Falkenstiern *(without hearing him)*. This evil,
Was it achieved by me? O hideous dream,
Release my 'wilder'd mind! Alas! my mother,
Thine augury of evil is fulfill'd—
I am the slave of my presumption.

    Meinhard.   Why
Griev'st thou to know thy murderous hand hath sped
His gentle soul to blessedness? He died
Even as he lived—in peaceful execution
Of virtue's duties; and was summon'd hence
To meet his just reward amid the just,
In that sweet land which thou canst never more
Aspire to reach. But lo! we trifle—come.
(A sound of approaching footsteps.)
The avengers are at hand. On—rescue! rescue!
*(The cloud envelops them, and they disappear as the domestics of
Rothberg enter the apartment, and with exclamations of horror, close
round his body. Scene closes.)*

Three years are supposed to elapse between the preceding Act and

Act II. Scene I.

An Apartment in the Castle of Falkenstiern, with an open Door leading to an inner Room. The Countess Helen enters, leading in a Band of Musicians. She points to the Door.

Helen. This is your station—and your task, to breathe
Some low-voiced strain so soft and soothingly
As to provoke the heaviness of sleep.
Let not one tuneless note be heard to jar
Upon the wakeful ear; but like a stream
Gliding with measured cadence, let the song
Float on the buoyant air! *(She enters the inner room.)*

GLEE *(sotto voce.)*
Soft, as summer moonbeams sleeping,
Soft, as evening twilight creeping,
Soft, as zephyr's faintest breath,
Steals the song; above—beneath—
Around: and list! again—again
The echo of the dying strain!
Sweet, as memory's dream of love;
Sweet, as wreaths by childhood wove;
Sweet, as fall of spring-tide showers.
Over Eden's spicy bowers.
List! around—again—again
The echo of the dying strain!

(Helen re-enters, throws them a purse, and closing the door of the inner room, departs).
    Helen.   Your task is done! *(Exit.)*
(The Four Musicians come forward.)
    First Musician. 'Tis a strange task of ours, nightly to soothe
The watchful Count by low-breathed melodies,
Himself still hidden from our sight. Is't sorrow
Or sickness keeps his mind thus restless?
    Second Musician.   Nay!

It is enough for me yon gentle lady
Pays us with golden thanks. My service here
Hath yielded heavier weight unto my purse
Than ever serenade—
    First Musician. Thus art thou still
Bent on thy heap of worldly pelf; but, pr'ythee,
Thou, to whose eye a florin wears such charms,
Dost thou not marvel that a man endow'd
With brimming coffers and broad lands, as rich
As avarice can coast—and withal
A wife so passing fair, a babe so gifted
With early beauty, should have need of music
To make his downy pillow yield repose?
Give me his lofty chamber, silken hangings,
And floors so richly cover'd that the foot
Falls on them like a snow-flake, I should need
No rocking on my dainty couch.
    Third Musician.   Ay, haply,
If still condemn'd to earn by daily toil
Thy daily bread; for labour gives a charm
To rest, unknown unto the rich and slothful.
    Fourth Musician. But this Count Falkenstiern is none of those
Who wear away their hours in indolence.
I've track'd his footsteps through the early dew;
I've seen him urge the chase with hound and horn,
When all his train were worn with weariness.
Daily I hear his courser's flying steps
With clattering speed pass by my lowly dwelling.
By Holy Mary! I would rather tenant
That sordid home, with heart as cheerful, sleep
As peaceful as my own, than this domain
With such unquiet thoughts as Falkenstiern's.
    First Musician. 'Tis said his early course of life was tainted
With deepest vice and folly; and Repentance
May be the imp that haunts his pillow.
    Third Musician.   No!
The venial prodigalities of boyhood
Rarely implant lasting remorse. Excess,
A weed o'errunning the rank soil of youth,

Leaves not a seed so deadly.

Second Musician.   I have heard
The Count is still a mourner for his kinsman,
The noble Rothberg, who, scarce three years past,
Fell by his own rash hand. They say that love—
Love for the Countess Helen, urged the deed;
For she was then upon the eve of marriage
With Falkenstiern.

First Musician. Was't here—within the castle?

Third Musician. Ev'n so:—but he was absent on some course
Of wild excess; and when the fatal tidings
Reach'd him of this unhappy act, he raved
With very madness in his grief. He could not
At his return look on the dead, nor witness
The last sad rites. The chamber door where Rothberg
Was found self-murder'd, weltering in his blood,
With solid masonry is barr'd against
All human access. And although his marriage
Was shortly solemnized with the fair cause
Of this dread mischief, from that hour the Count
Hath been absorb'd in sorrow.

Second Musician.   He hath sought
A strange companion for his consolation.
By heaven above, 'twould drive me mad to wear
A friend within my bosom such as Meinhard,
Who dogs him like his shadow!

Third Musician.   Ay—the Count
Must have some knowledge of his excellence
Beyond the penetration of my mind.
There is a smile upon his countenance
More withering than—

First Musician.   Thou hast a noble courage
Even to whisper evil of that man;
For go where'er thou wilt, in some dark corner
He lurketh—

Fourth Musician.   Like his prototype, the Evil One,
Speak of him, and he cometh.
(Enter Meinhard.)

Meinhard *(with affected deference)* Courteous sirs!

Your gentle presence is indeed most welcome.
Seek ye with gentle airs to cheat the night
Of its repose, and mar the rest of such
As worn by labours of the day, would love
Their weariness in sleep?
    Third Musician.   Our gentle presence
Waits on our master's bidding; and our task,
Now ended at his pleasure, gives us freedom
To leave the noble Meinhard to his thoughts,
Unvex'd and unmolested. *(Exeunt Musicians.)*
(Meinhard bows with ironical courtesy.)
    Meinhard.   Gone already?
Curs! idiots! slaves! go, howl for hire—pollute
The ear of youth, and enervate the mind
Of man. Ye filthy dregs of human earth,
Ye were but carrion prey to one who flies
Even at the highest game! Thus far the Count,
Encompass'd in my snares, bends to my swoop.
'Tis glorious sport to see this worm of pride
The abject slave of its own furious passions!
My ordinary lures were worthless here:
Wealth—power—indulgence in those filthy vices
Which form the vulgar criminal, with him
Had nothing weigh'd; but in his breast there dwelt
A nest of reptiles, which beneath my wing
Were warm'd to rankest venom. Pride, Revenge,
Hatred, and baffled Hope, were there! With these
I form'd a viperous coil around his heart,
With which I hold him at my bidding. Yea!
This fool of Reason —this time-mending sage—
This philosophic lover of his kind,
Is mine—at once my victim and my slave.
His children, too—Lo! peace—mine enemy!
On whom my bolts of detestation fall
Like sunshine on the ice-bound mountain top. *(Becomes invisible.)*
(Enter Father Michael and the Countess.)
    Father Michael. My daughter! grieve not thus. The rooted sorrow
Which so appalls thy tender nature wears
A promise to my hope of better feelings.

From the dark soil of grief and penitence
The flowers of grace spring glorious!

    Helen.   Holy father!
'Tis not the natural grief of one who mourns
O'er past transgressions, nor the tenderness
Of those who sorrow for departed friends:
Tears such as theirs are like the showers of spring,
Freshening the earth with verdure. Oh! but his—
My Falkenstiern's—are like the wint'ry storm
That wears no ray of promise to dispel
Its awful darkness!

                   He was gentle once—
Courteous and kind—and still his looks are fraught
With gentleness to me, save when dark thoughts
Distort his noble nature:—yet of this
It fits me not to speak.

    Father Michael. Hast thou implored
His acquiescence in—

    Helen.   Before he slept
This night—e'en while with words of tenderest love
He spake of earlier days—days long ago,
When we were first betroth'd—I urged my suit
That to our boy the rite of baptism,
The necessary sacrament of grace,
Might yield the promised heirship of salvation.
He heard me—smiled away my earnest pleading,
Which I renew'd, till, changing from his tone
Of tenderness to such a horrid gaze
As my mind pictures of the sentenced Cain,
He grasp'd my hand, and in a dreadful whisper
He said, "It was for thee —it was thy beauty
Which fix'd this curse eternally on me,
And on my guiltless child."

                   But when he saw
The tears of grief and awe his fury drew,
His own fell fast; and on his knees before me—
I cannot speak of it! *(She shudders.)* Oh! holy father!
Pray for him—pray that his bewilder'd mind
Resume a calmer tone—pray for him, father,

As I do.

    Father Michael. My unhappy child, be patient.
Thy path of life is gloomy and perplex'd:
Its thorny way—

    Meinhard *(without)*. Intolerable proser!

    Helen. Heardst thou a sound?

    Father Michael.   The stormy winds of night
Ruffling the river waves.

    Helen.   Alas! my heart,
Weary and worn with sorrow—

    Meinhard.   Hence! away!

    Father Michael *(with dignity)*.
Come with me to the altar! There, oh! there
Peace will o'ershadow thy perturbed mind
Like a descending dove, till heavenly thoughts
Wean thee from every vain solicitude.
(He leads her out, and the scene closes.)

Scene II.

The Castle of Falkenstiern—Morning. The Count and Countess are discovered seated on a terrace overlooking the Rhine. Helen's Attendant holds their Child in her arms.

    Helen. In very truth, thou lov'st him not as I do!
Look on his deep blue eyes—'tis a sweet boy:
And wears upon his cheek the very smile
With which that same proud lord, that mighty scholar,
Albert of Falkenstiern, first won the heart
Of his poor Helen. Take him to thy bosom—
Take him awhile—nay, I will have it so.
I love to see his little arms entwine
Around his father's neck. Ye are together
The two most cherish'd on this earth!

    Falkenstiern.   Dear Helen!
I am unskillful—I shall haply injure
His delicate frame. *(Replacing the child in the Attendant's arms.)*
               Bear the imp hence awhile—

He wearies me.

  Helen.   'Tis ever thus! Thou hold'st him
A very alien—

  Falkenstiern. Helen! trust me, love,
A wife's best wisdom is to spare all comment
On that which seems distasteful to her husband.
Inquire not curiously.

  Helen.   Too just reproof!
I will not urge the point again.

  Falkenstiern.   My best,
My gentlest girl! seek out some irksome task,
Enjoin some penance for my many sins
Against thy fond submission. Thou art skill'd
To sway the rod of empire, who so meekly
Thus ever bend'st thy will to mine. Oh! speak—
What proof, what evidence can I unfold
Of the deep measure of my love, save vows
Of firm fidelity, whose utterance yields
Even in itself a charm!

  Helen.   I have a boon—
Look not upon me so intently, Albert;
I dare not meet thy gaze; for my bold prayer
Savours of such presumption, as may move
Thy wrath against me.

  Falkenstiern. Never—gentle one!
He were a wretch indeed who could unloose
One angry breath against a flower too frail
To bear the west wind in its rougher mood!
Sweetest! what wouldst thou?

  Helen.   I have vainly sought
To win thy presence to the holy chapel
At the appointed hour of prayer—

  Falkenstiern.   Is this
Thy boon? Wouldst thou behold me wear
A countenance of sanctimonious dullness,
A mortified and peevish air, like his,
Thy favour'd friend, thy bosom counselor,
The ghostly father!

  Helen.   Speak not thus in mockery

Of God's appointed servant, 'tis not well!
He honours not the creed who wantonly
Casts shame upon—But why should I oppose
My feeble mind to thine? Yet, if thou lov'st me,
Kneel with me at the altar; let our prayers
Ascend together to the throne of God!

    Falkenstiern. Helen! the Fountain of all Wisdom reads
The thoughts of his poor creatures better far
Than they can utter them! If He is wise,
He knows my wants; if He is good, his power
Will aid me without seeking.

    Helen.   Wherefore, then,
Withhold the sacrifice He hath commanded?
If not in supplication, lift thy voice
In gratitude!

    Falkenstiern. The incense of a heart
Which tastes each good and perfect gift in joy,
Breathing the air, plucking the fruits of earth,
And gazing on its loveliness with feelings
Of hourly thankfulness and worship, wears
A fairer grace than any measured form
Of priest-enjoin'd devotion. Trust me, love,
A superstitious rite will nought avail
In sight of Him, who in his awful balance
Weighs human deeds.

    Helen.   My Albert! these are doctrines
Which have a specious sound; but it is written
In his appointed ordinance, that men
Shall gather to adore him openly;
And that by water and the name of Him
Who died upon the cross, our sinful nature
Shall put off its corruption in his sight.
Oh! Albert—Albert—harden not thy heart
Against thy Maker's will, lest in his wrath
He render thee, like the Egyptian king,
Incapable of grace. 'Tis Meinhard—Meinhard,
Who puts these evil pleadings in thy mouth.
Oh! what a thrill of horror chills my heart
When I behold that man's sarcastic sneer!

The voice of laughter hath a withering sound
From him.

    Falkenstiern. He is my friend.

    Helen.   He is not—no!
In this, in this alone, dare I deny
Thy better judgment. 'Tis an enemy—
A deadly enemy—who leads thee on
To the dark gates of that accurs'd domain,
The inheritance of sin! Shun him, my husband:
Avoid the dark pollution that awaits
His all-contaminating touch.
(Enter Meinhard.)

    Meinhard *(sarcastically).* All hail!
The scholar and preceptress. Gracious lady!
Lay on thy chastisements, and spare not. Wherefore
Should Falkenstiern disdain the appointed tasks
Of his fair monitress—

    Helen *(without heeding Meinhard).* My best and dearest,
Let not yon scoffer throw the mask of scorn
Upon my words. I leave thee, Falkenstiern;
And may'st thou with the gentleness of love
Reflect upon my words.   *(Exit Helen.)*
(Manent Falkenstiern and Meinhard.)

    Meinhard.   A goodly lady—
Apt in discourse, and froward in demeanour,
Like all her prating sex.

    Falkenstiern.   Dare not to cast
The venom of thy slanderous tongue on one
Who walks the earth like some immortal shape
Of blessedness. Oh! she is fairer—dearer
Than all—

    Meinhard. Uxorious and romantic! Come—
Seek we some other theme.

    Falkenstiern.   What hast thou left me
On which to rest my baffled thoughts in peace?
The magic powers which I had imaged forth
As fountains of delight, are turn'd to springs
Of bitterness! My home—my peaceful home—
Is tenanted with shapes which dog my steps

At every turn: shadows and awful sounds
Perplex its inmates. The lone forest's paths,
Where once my courser's flying steps were heard
Familiar as its echoes, now afford
No solitude to me: fantastic shows
Of beings strange, and dreadful to my nature,
Appall my heart.

    Meinhard. Yet wherefore dost thou shun
The joys of festal cheer—the sweet communion
Of friendship and good-fellowship? Whene'er
The gallants of the court, thy former friends,
Yield the gay sunshine of their sprightly presence
Unto these halls, whose hospitality
Of old was graceful in the eyes of men,
With moody silence and distemper'd looks
Thou shar'st—

    Falkenstiern. What part have I in them or theirs?
My cares—my fears—mine aspirations—all,
Are higher—deeper—more intense! A cloud
Is o'er me and around me. When the bowl
Sparkles amid my guests, I dare not pledge them:
I dare not break the seal which binds my lips
By the convivial cup. There was a time
When every foolery of wild excess
Had power upon my mind; but no pursuit
Avails me now. The source of all is open:
Wealth, useless wealth, weighs on me—power at will
Attends my call—beauty I can command,
With all her wanton, loathsome wiles. Each sport
Has lost the chance whose doubtful fortune gave
Its only charm. Without the alternation
Of hope and fear, the world becomes a blank.

    Meinhard. Thou hast a child—a lovely boy.

    Falkenstiern.   Alas!
Why dost thou thus record my misery?
He is not mine, but thine! I dare not look
Upon his beauty, nor with yearning love
Hold him to my fond heart! I dare not fix
My hopes upon his being.

Meinhard.　　　　Yet how freely
Thou gav'st the boy to my demand!
　　Falkenstiern.　　　　I gave him
Unknown—unborn: nor till the bitter hour
When his first cry smote on mine ear—a knell
Of mingled joy and anguish—did I know
The force of love within a father's heart.
No more of this!
　　Meinhard.　Wert thou not wont to prize
The laurel weed, for whose attainment man
Dyes his pure hands in blood, or wears away
The sunshine of his youth in cheerless study;
Renouncing Nature's page of bright and fair,
Where Wisdom hives her stores, and mocks the search
Which vainly seeks her footsteps through the night
Of ages? Science, with her thoughtful brow,
Held thee awhile mazed in her labyrinth.
　　Falkenstiern. Yea; but the knot, whose mere unravelment
Became a pastime, I have cleft in twain;
And like the child who scorns the tardy growth
Of nature, and with mad, impatient hand
Rifles the flower long ere maturity
Gifts it with fitting fragrance, I have look'd
Into the secrets of the bud of knowledge!
I know the emptiness of words —the show
Of the dull pedant wading through the dust
Of schools, whose best of wisdom is mere folly.
The hollow cant of vain philosophy
Is but a riddle, whose obscure solution
Is one of many toys on which we waste
The hours which Nature meant for nobler things;
Else wherefore tricks she forth her loveliness
To woo our worship?
　　Meinhard.　　　　Ay, as the fair landscape
Through which the Rhine flows at our feet!
　　Falkenstiern *(gazing on the valley beneath)*.
　　　　　　　　　　　　　　'Tis beautiful!
A thousand times, from childhood e'en till now,
Have I look'd down in pride and admiration

On this abounding stream! Prosperity,
Honour, and Power appear to guard its course.
Over its swelling breast a thousand rafts,
A thousand busy sails, unceasing spread.
There's not a vale of summer-greenery
Lending its tributary brook, but shields
In its embosom'd copse a spire-crown'd village
Sleeping in peace and shade: there's not a rock
Riseth in pride of place, but rears its crest
With massive tower and lordly portal graced;
While from its rifted sides, or sloping base,
Hang the rich clusters of the glowing vine.
'Tis glorious all! a living landscape, wrought
With all that God or man have made eternal!
  Meinhard. Ha! ha! ha! ha!
  Falkenstiern.   Hush thy disdainful sneer;
It but recoils upon thy fiendish nature
In the Creator's triumph spread around!
  Meinhard. Enthusiast! gaze—yea, gaze thy fill; behold
With swelling heart these glories of thy race!
I tell thee, I—whose glance prospective mocks
The obscuring mists of Time, that all these towers,
Which to thy circumscribed vision seem
Fashion'd as firmly as their rocky base;
I tell thee, these pride-honour'd halls, whereon
The pennons of their several tyrants flaunt
In narrow self-security, shall fall
Prone to the dust we tread. The wolf shall prowl
Amid their fallen ramparts; round their walls,
Roofless and tenantless, the bat shall flit,
Sole guardian of their mouldering solitude.
Where now the loud acclaim of festal cheer—
Where now the sparkling wine-cup and the song
Cheat the tired heart to self-oblivion—Time
Shall see the vulture rear her screaming young
Safe from the haunt of man.
  Falkenstiern.   Where then shall house
The race whose might upholds these battlements?
And what protecting hand shall guard the vassals

Whom now their power o'ershadows, as the bird
Screeneth her feeble offspring 'neath her breast?

Meinhard. What! thou too—thou, who hold'st thy mind enlighten'd
Beyond thy race and age—art thou so vain,
So blind with pride and weakness, as to deem
Oppressive tyranny protection? Thou—
Dost thou not see that this same feudal power,
This all o'erwhelming despotism which binds
Mankind in slavish vassalage, inflicts
A direr evil than it e'er repell'd?
E'en as the shadow of yon mountain-hold
Casts barrenness around, and from the cot
Sleeping beneath its influence, intercepts
The beam of day—a blessed heritage
Common to suzerain or churl—the shade
Of human power sheds darkness and despair
Upon the minds it rules!
                                          A future age
Shall see the enfranchised villains, now condemn'd
To till their tyrant's land for scanty bread,
Sitting beneath the shade of their own vines,
By the free home their industry hath won.
To distant climes their venturous barks shall bear
Domestic produce; and from distant lands
Their patient toil shall gather golden store
With greater honour than their chiefs can boast,
Who wring it forth with the strong arm of power,
By conquest, or oppression of the poor.

Falkenstiern. Thou hast a gift of eloquence to which
My dazzled ear, but unconvicted mind,
Yield no reply. From the first age of earth
Men have been doom'd to seek and bear the yoke
Of fellow-men—raised by superior wisdom—
By skill of hand—by strength or bravery,
To lordly eminence; and as the soul
Bent still on noblest objects must attain
Ennobled powers and firmer texture, these
Can boast attainments which the vulgar herd

Rarely achieve. In that enlighten'd age
Which thou foredoom'st, although baronial pride
Abate beneath the chilling touch of Time;
Although the patriarchs of the forest, fell'd,
Give space for baser shrubs to bourgeon forth,
Some still will tower above the rest. The earth
Must still unfold beneath the eye of heaven
Mountain and vale on its unequal breast,
And man must bend to his ennobled fellow —

    Meinhard. Who, spite the emblazon'd shield, the herald's lie,
The ermined pride of pomp, is basely prone
To the same vulgar accidents—disease,
Slumber, and death—as his poor follower!
Lo! to the grave they bear with solemn pomp
Departed majesty! The graven 'scutcheon—
The sable-waving plume—the pompous style
Proclaim'd with empty pageant o'er the bier—
The muffled music pealing through the aisle—
The mantled mourners—all, in measured state,
Mock the pale sleeper's nothingness! Pass o'er
One year—descend into the vault, and lift
The gorgeous coffin-lid; there shalt thou see
The same most loathsome triumph of decay—
The mouldering flesh and creeping worm, that fill
The pauper's lonely grave! Yea, Falkenstiern,
Those lordly sires thou boast'st—

    Falkenstiern.   Demon! traducer!
Pollute not thou the ashes of my fathers!
Their deeds are writ on History's scroll, amid
The heroes of their country! and though now
Their name must perish like a wither'd leaf
Blighted by thy temptation, and my sin;
Yet, like a mighty time-wreck, it shall float
Above the waters of oblivion! Men,
In those thy vaunted days of general freedom,
When blood shall have effaced each ancient charter,
And factious anarchy and civil war
Have swept away the landmarks of the earth,
Men still will turn, with retrospective pride,

Unto the records of the great and good;
And the dim spirits of the mighty dead
Shall sway them from the tomb.
                              Look on the past:
Assyria—Greece—and Rome in later days—
Each hath her page of warning. Freedom—lured
From straw-roof'd huts to marble palaces,
Betray'd by luxury to vice—forgets
To guard her rights; while foreign conquests made
Some laurel'd victor a domestic tyrant.
Then comes oppression, by rebellion crush'd;
Then faction's grosses tyranny. These—these
Are the same watchwords through succeeding ages!
Happy the land whose uneventful records
Afford no lesson to mankind!

Meinhard.   How now?
How now? Whence spring these novel charms
In the cold dullness of a world resign'd
To its own dark abuses? I have mark'd
Of old, thy kindling eye, and faltering voice,
Wake e'en to inspiration in the pleading
Of human rights.

Falkenstiern. In visionary days,
When good and perfect were not words but things
Unto my buoyant hopes. I have outlived
My trust in human nature.

Meinhard.   Verily,
Thou breathest here the stagnant air of home,
Till every better energy of manhood
Relaxeth to decay. The distaff now
Becomes thy feeble humour more—

Falkenstiern.   Not so:
By my dead father's will, on penalty
Of forfeiture, I must endure to dwell
In mine ancestral home, save when my country
Needs the poor aid of such an arm as mine.

Meinhard. Then rouse thee from thy slumb'rous lethargy—
Waken the dormant vigour of thy mind:
War is declared—war!

Falkenstiern.   Like a bird of prey,
Thou snift'st the carnage.
Meinhard.   Ay—'tis my vocation!
It once was thine. The sword that hangs inglorious
In rust of peace upon thy castle wall,
Once seem'd thy fitting toy of sport. Time was,
That at the trumpet's summons thou would'st start
Like a fierce charger to the field.
Falkenstiern.   Then—then
These hands had not been stain'd with midnight murder!
Pride—fear of shame—hope of distinction—all
That steels the mind to heroism, is now
A dream to me; I have a stake beyond
Such empty visions.
Meinhard.   Thou wilt then disdain
The charge of leader of the Rhenish forces
Against the proud invaders of thy country,
Which the Electors have conferr'd on thee?
Falkenstiern. No! I will forth, and meet them like a man!
While yet I wear this breathing form, no stain
That blood can wash away shall soil the name
Of Falkenstiern! When will these tidings reach
The castle?
Meinhard. Even now the courier's steed
Echoes with heavy tramp from yonder drawbridge.
Come, let us meet him: we must hence to-night.
On Arnheim's plains the chiefs assemble: there
New scenes, now hopes, will rouse thee, as of old.
A brief farewell unto thy gentle dame,
Then to the field of honour!
Falkenstiern.   Art thou bound
On the same quest?
Meinhard.   I shall attend thy steps.
But come—they seek thee.
(Scene closes.)

Scene III.

The Apartment of the Countess in the Castle of Falkenstiern. The Count and Countess.

Helen. And must thou hence to-night?
Falkenstiern.   E'en so, my Helen.
Helen. Ah! no—thou'lt surely tarry till to-morrow—
At my entreaty, till to-morrow night—
To-morrow noon—nay, at the dawn of morning
Thou canst be gone, so thou wilt stay to-night.
I have a thousand parting words to speak;
A thousand quarrels —yet that's not the word—
A thousand playful differences, in which
To sue for pardon. Thou wilt stay to-night:—
Say so—and bless me with the sound!
Falkenstiern.   Dear Helen,
Thou would'st not have thy Falkenstiern a laggard
In honour's cause, and at his country's call?
Helen. No! I would have thee ever foremost—ever
Hear thy name hail'd—yet wherefore speak I thus,
When my heart quails ev'n at the sound and sight
Of these dread preparations? Oh! my husband,
That plumed helm, which well beseems thy brow;
That mailed vesture, mantling o'er thy breast,
Thy Helen's happiest refuge,—they are hateful
Unto the eye of tenderness! My husband,
Forgive me that I hang about thee thus—
Forgive me, Falkenstiern; for never more
May I entreat, or thou bestow forgiveness.
Falkenstiern. Sweet Helen! calm these fears. The enemy
Presents no formidable show against us:
If prosperous days await us, we shall need
Small care and brief encounter to disperse
Their petty forces.
Helen.   Oh! not so—not so.
'Twas but this morning we were prophesying
A long and bloody war. Thou hast but changed
The tale to fit thy purpose.

Falkenstiern.   Rouse thy firmness:
Embitter not the gloomy hour of parting
By such anticipations. Trust me, love,
I shall be with thee ere the golden autumn
Shines on our vintage feast.
      Helen.   Thou'lt write to me?
      Falkenstiern. Surely:—but, Helen, should the chance of war
Command my silence, let not apprehensions
Perplex thy gentle mind.
      Helen.   Sorrow and fear
Heed no command. My Falkenstiern! I fell
That for the last dear time I hold this hand
Warm with the pulse of life; or thou or I
Shall be among the silent and the dead
When peace returns; therefore if—
      Falkenstiern.   My beloved!
      Helen. If I have ever anger'd thee—if ever
A word—a look of mine hath wounded thee,
Pardon me.
      Falkenstiern. Be our fond forgiveness mutual.
We part not here, my Helen; I have yet
A final counsel, and 'tis one of moment,
To breathe for thine observance. Summon hither
The holy father.
      Helen.   In the oratory
He offers prayers for thee and for our country.
      Falkenstiern. 'Tis well! we'll meet him there; my parting words
Shall then await thee. *(Leads her out.)*

Act III. Scene I.

The Plains of Arnheim. Falkenstiern is discovered reading in his Tent at midnight.

Falkenstiern *(throws away his book).*
Away!—cold truths that sternly picture forth
The mind of man, I'll none of ye: too much
Such subtleties have steel'd my breast of old.
No! let me feed my meditations here!
(He takes out a picture of the Countess.)
These looks of love and loveliness—in them
I read the smiling tale of early years—
In them, my scroll of destiny unfolds;
And all the past, and all the future, form
One mournful lesson for the present hour.
Oh! Helen—Helen—little dost thou deem
On what a precipice of guilt and grief
We tread together! While I linger'd near her,
Striving to walk the path of earth like one
Versed in its vulgar usances, nor knowing
An interest beyond its daily forms,
How wearily the hours pall'd on my mind!
But now—in absence—from the hour we parted
My heart hath been with her! The home I held
With loathing and contempt hath now become
Mine anxious care, the haven of my hope!
For when I turn'd to gaze on it afar,
Sleeping amid its wooded screen, beneath
The gray light of the early morn, I felt
As though some dire mischance o'erhung its walls,
Like a dark thunder-cloud. I feel—I feel
Than an impending stroke of fate forbids
That we should meet again.
                              Yet have I gain'd
One step to peace by absence: the dark shade
That haunts my steps hath here deserted me.
(Meinhard suddenly stands beside him.)
Curse of my life! what would'st thou?

Meinhard.   Sweet discourse
And gentle parley with my learned pupil,
My treasured friend.
    Falkenstiern.   Insulting fiend!
    Meinhard.   Why thus—
Thus ever runs the graceless speech of man!
Still have I served thee with my best intent,
Forestall'd thy wishes, saved thee with my presence
From the cold blank of solitude, while thou—
    Falkenstiern. Would I had power to drive thee from my sight,
And rescue my torn heart from the remembrance
Of the dread past!
    Meinhard.   Thou would'st but wish me back.
Thou art so courteous—so urbane—so noble—
Beneficent to all mankind—
    Falkenstiern.   Be silent,
And leave me to my thoughts.
    Meinhard.   Good Falkenstiern,
Too well I know the value of my counsels
To spare them thee in such an hour. To-morrow
The toil of war commences. Dost thou hear
The armourer's clang o'erpowering the challenge
And measured step of distant sentinels,
Who watch, like me, to guard thee from surprise?
Yet fear not, Falkenstiern; in the dark hour,
When flashing steel and roaring fire pursue thee,
Blench not.
    Falkenstiern. To me, infernal hound! such caution?
Who ever mark'd the eye of Falkenstiern
Shrink in the hour of peril?
    Meinhard.   Ay, of old
Thou wert indifferent valiant, while the heat
Of ardent youth, the calm of innocence,
Nerved thy proud arm. Those days are over now.
But though the stain of murder weigh like lead
Upon thy heart—though Rothberg's dying groans
Pour in thine ears the note of trepidation,—
Fear not, thou bear'st a charmed life—already
The talisman secures success and safety.

Falkenstiern. God! must this last poor triumph be denied me?
Must the fond effort of my arm be check'd
By this foul taunt?
     Begone! thou loathsome scoffer!
Thou hast awoke a spirit in my mind
Which spurns thy fetters! I will yet be free!
In God's own name—by His redeeming power
Who died upon the cross—hence from my sight!
Pollute my heart no longer with thy presence:
Thus do I cast thee off!
(Throwing away the talisman, which he draws from his vest.)
     Thus I fling from me
The wages of my sin! This be my trust.
(Lays his hand on his sword.)
  Meinhard. Bravely thou mouth'st thine anger: I have yet
A debt unpaid. The Bond—audacious fool!
The Bond shall aid the sweetness of revenge.
Farewell! proud Falkenstiern! we meet again.
(Meinhard disappears.)
  Falkenstiern. He's gone, and I am free! Oh, happy hour!
I feel as if my tide of fate had turn'd
From its dark stormy wretchedness, to all
Its sunny hopes of youth, as spring bursts forth
Glowing and beauteous from the gloomy breast
Of winter! I am free—free as the winds—
Free as the eagle, which o'erlooking all
The clamours of the world, soars on direct
To the bright source of glory. Still this arm
May win from Fame—*(Starting and shuddering.)*
     Oh, righteous Heaven! in vain,
In vain have I unmanacled my soul!
The withering sneer with which he parted hence—
His vows of vengeance unfulfill'd—I read,
I read his fatal purpose. In his grasp
I see my struggling child—my wife:—great God,
Protect their innocence—protect my home!
Alas! my bow—my murder'd boy!
(He falls senseless, and the scene closes.)

Scene II.

A Village on the frontier of the Palatinate; a triumphal Arch is erected; Garlands are hung at the Doors, and Peasants are waiting with Baskets of Flowers to scatter at the Feet of Falkenstiern, who is expected to pass on his return at the head of his victorious Army.

Chorus of Peasants. Cheerily, cheerily lead the song,
    They come in triumph, in peace they come;
Strew the green laurel their path along,
    And welcome your valiant defenders home.
Hurrah! for the Rhine chief, whose gallant sword
    Still waved them on o'er the field of blood;
Through terror and time, let his name be the word
    To hallow the brave, and to honour the good.
Hurrah! for the victors who rescued our land
    From the braggart invader now cold in the grave;
Hurrah! for the chief, at whose noble command
    They were first to subdue, and yet foremost to save.
We have tears for the slain, but they fall not to-day;
    Let us hush the cold sigh, and our sorrow restrain,
While we welcome the brave and strew flowers in their way
    Who restore us to peace and contentment again.
    Female Peasant. Fritz! are they near?
    Fritz.   Seest thou the rising dust
That darkens yonder copse?
    Second Peasant.   Hark! how the wind
At intervals brings sounds of music, soften'd
By distance; louder now—how cheeringly
It sounds.
(Martial music heard at a distance.)
    Fritz. Ay, as we hear it—mingled
With shouts of joyous triumph. Didst thou know
Its piercing harshness on the battle-field,
Thou'dst think it less enlivening.
    Female Peasant.   Falkenstiern
Holds it, I guess—
(A body of the Civil Guards of the Elector Palatine enter.)
          But who are these?

Officer of the Guard.   Good friends!
Ye are assembled here to greet the entrance
Of the victorious army?
     Peasant.   Yes; to welcome
Our noble general, and his gallant train.
     Officer. In which, no doubt, many among ye count
Sons—husbands—brothers?
     Peasant.   Why, our loyal village
Hath lent its contribution. Those who trust
To find such dear ones living 'mid the ranks
Of our brave army, have been off since day,
To meet them sooner. *(Music sounds again.)*
     Female Peasant. Hark! they come—they come!
     Officer. My friends, no mirth—no music—no acclaim
Of love and gratitude must greet the Count:
Disperse your merry bands, tear down your garlands.
     Peasant. How! rend away the emblems of our joy
At the success of our loved countrymen?
Good masters, get ye gone—what would ye here—
Who, strangers as ye are, presume to dictate
To those who little need your presence? Off!
Or we may—
     Officer. Peace! in the Elector's name:
We bear his warrant of arrest, to stop
Count Falkenstiern upon the frontier.
     Female Peasant.   What—
Arrest our general! How—on what suspicion?
     Officer. The very foulest that could stain the name
Of man! The murder of his wife and child!
     Peasant. Out, slanderer!
     Second Peasant.   'Tis the sorry jest of one
Who seeks to mar our preparations.
     Officer.   No!
'Tis a most fatal truth.
     Peasant.   Take heed, base liar!
Lest for your calumny ye find yourselves
Acquainted with the waters of our lake,
We need but little urging to the labour
Of sending ye—

(Officer produces a parchment.)

Officer.   Look on our warrant.

Peasant.   Lo!
It bears the Elector's signature and seal.

Second Peasant. Of murder? 'tis impossible! So good,
So brave a man.   *(Music and a peal of bells heard.)*
                    Hark! they are near. Too late
Thy mandate came to check our merriment.
(Enter Falkenstiern through the Archway, followed by a brilliant retinue, guards, &c.)

Falkenstiern. Thanks, my kind countrymen, thanks—
thanks to all:
So warm a greeting, such heart-cheering welcome
Unto our fatherland, effaces all
Remembrance of our labours in its cause.
A cup of wine, I pray ye, gentle friends,
That I may drink prosperity and peace
Unto your village.

Officer.   General! 'tis with feelings
Of deepest sorrow—

Female Peasant. Heed him not, my lord;
He comes, with yonder ruffian band, to mar
Our promised day of joy with lying tales,
And slanderous mention of thy noble name.

Officer. Alfred, Count Falkenstiern; I here arrest you
Upon the Elector's mandate, on suspicion
Of murder.

Falkenstiern. This is ill-timed mummery.
Murder—of whom?

One of Falkenstiern's Suite. Command us, sir, to seize
This insolent, and his unmanner'd crew!

Officer. Be pleased to look upon our warrant: there
Our exculpation stands.
(Gives the scroll to Falkenstiern, who looks over it with astonishment and horror.)

Falkenstiern.   'Tis even so!
Ha! do mine eyes deceive me? of my wife—
My child! Am I indeed bereaved
Of all, at one dark blow! Accursed fiend!

This is the fatal measure of thy vengeance.
(Throws himself on the ground.)
Down, Falkenstiern, down to the earth, as low
As sorrow and repentance—Oh! my wife—
My gentle, unoffending Helen! thou—
Art thou become my Victim!

    Peasant.   Let us home:
This is an awful sight—we but augment
His grief by observation. *(Exeunt Villagers.)*

    Officer *(approaching Falkenstiern).* Noble Count;
We must reluctantly demand the weapon
Which—

    One of the Count's Followers.

          No! by Heaven you shall not! Never
Shall the base hand of such a slave as thou
Receive the sword of Falkenstiern.

    Falkenstiern *(rising with dignity).* Good Lahnstein!
Bend to the law of Fate as I do.
(Unbuckling and delivering his sword.)
                  There!
Take thou my sword:—thus I surrender it
Unto the Prince, in whose just cause its worth
Hath been too often tried.
(Murmurs among the soldiers.)
                Silence, my friends!
None who love Falkenstiern will dare obstruct
The special cause of justice.

    Officer.   To Count Lahnstein
You are required to delegate your charge
As leader of the army, which will follow
Its primal destination. You, Sir Count,
Must with us to the place of trial.

    Falkenstiern.   Whither?

    Officer. To Marensbourg—a prisoner of state
Within the guard of Hesse's noble Landgrave,
Till the convoked Elector's shall assemble
To sit in judgment on thee.

    Falkenstiern.   Mine accuser
Should be some person well accredited,

That they proceed against a loyal subject
With measures so severe and summary.

Officer. His name is yet unknown.

Second Officer.   Sir, we delay
Too long our journey.

Falkenstiern.

              On—to my dungeon.

(Loud murmurs and groans among the soldiery.)

                              Friends!
Comrades! fellow countrymen! rebel not
Against your laws—your prince. I must awhile
Resign a charge most precious to my heart,
And bear mine ignominious shame as firmly
As I have borne the flush of conquest. Time
Will rescue me from this most foul suspicion:
Meantime think of me as a sorrowing friend,
And let obedience to your general,
My friend in arms and comrade, noble Lahnstein,
Be my best pledge of safety. Fare ye well!
And as ye love me, go in peace and quiet;
Nor by mis-timed resistance aggravate
My present sorrow!

(Turning to the Officers) Now—for Marensbourg.

(Scene closes with a slow march.)

Scene III.

The Castle of Marensbourg. An Apartment with strongly grated Windows. Falkenstiern in Fetters stands watching the setting Sun.

Falkenstiern. The day is done: the yellow evening light
Steals soft and gracious e'en o'er these cold walls.
Oh! could I see it once again illuming
My home, as oft of old, when she—the loved—
The lost one—sat beside me, overlooking
Yon mighty stream, with looks of gentleness,
Like a fair lily bending on its stem.
The earth is o'er that cheek—the dew of death

Hangs on that brow, so warm with life and love
When last it lay upon my bosom. Helen!
Where art thou now? Oh! Helen, could I gaze
Once more upon thy beaming countenance—
Hold thee again unto mine aching bosom—
Hear thy faint voice—the music ever dearest
Unto mine ear—I could endure to stand
Against Affliction's tide. Mine own beloved!
Had I been near to soothe thy dying hour—
To soothe—Great Heaven! she died abhorring me!
(A symphony is heard, and a magic show is seen in the back-ground of a garden adorned with the fairest fruit and flowers, with groups of female figures reposing by the side of fountains. Meinhard, disguised as an Egyptian sorcerer, points towards them, while the following Chorus is heard.)

> Think not of the silent tone,
> > Think not of the wither'd brow
> Of the lost and lovely one—
> > Other charms await thee now.
> Other cheeks more soft and pure,
> > Other smiles more fond and fair,
> Wait thy wishes to allure
> > 'Mid the Daughters of the Air!

Falkenstiern. Away, false vision! hence fantastic fools!
Think ye the bloom of youthful loveliness,
Though brighter in its hues than Heaven's own arch;
Think ye the graceful form, the practiced step
Of wantonness, hath power upon a heart
Which once hath proved the warmth of pure affection?
Hence! with your vain allurements—
    Meinhard.   Gaze again!
Yon glowing bowers—
    Falkenstiern.   I will not. There is none,
Not one of beauty's daughters but would seem
An Ethiop to mine eye, while I retain
Remembrance of my Helen! Sweet remembrance!
That like a saintly image haunts my breast,

Hallowing the temple with its holiness.

(The show changes to a tangled wood. A clashing of cymbals is heard, mingled with shouts of laughter. A crowd of Bacchants enter, leading a ram wreathed with flowers. They sprinkle the earth with libations.)

Chorus. Pour the wine-cup fresh and high,
    Gird it with a rosy wreath;
Mirth and frolic cradled lie
    Its ruby waves beneath.
Soft oblivion lurketh there,
    Joyous dreams, and sweet repose;
Pain and sorrow, fear and care,
    Vanish as it flows.

Meinhard. Wilt thou exchange thy prison's dreary space,
Thy meagre fare, and doubtful destiny,
For joys like these?

Falkenstiern.   Leave me in peace—I shun
Companionship with thee and thine. A heart
Tortured with sorrow seeks not consolation
In the mere joys of sense.

(The scene changes to a lonely valley, bright with sunshine. A river is seen gliding through its rocky banks, and a herd of antelopes is grazing in its pastures.)

Meinhard. Yon shadowy bower, yon silent stream
Gliding like some mysterious dream;
Yon valley, where the insect's wing
O'er herb and floweret wandering,
Disturbs alone its breathless peace,
Might bid thy vain repinings cease!
Would'st thou be free, to tread once more,
Through thicket, vale, and winding shore?

Falkenstiern. Ill dost thou read the human mind, to deem
That solitude could soothe a wretch like me!
There—in the lonely hush of Nature's rest,
Reflected from the purity around,
I should behold my crimes glass'd like a mirror.
'Tis from myself I ask deliverance now:
If thou hast mercy, hide me in the crowd
Unseen, unknown.

(Scene changes to the square of a magnificent city, adorned with lofty palaces, domes, and towers, seen by moonlight.)

Chorus of Spirits. We will bear thee far away
     To a land of loveliness;
     Distant kingdoms, fair and gay,
       Yet thy rescued fate may bless.
     There are cities where thy race
       May be run, unharmed and free;
     In high degree, and pride of place,
       Beyond thy former destiny!

Meinhard. Bestow the pledge I ask, and thou art safe
Beyond all human power.

Falkenstiern.   No! I will seek
No aid but Patience and Humility
Against my doom. I know thee now, dark fiend!
By thy false show of truth and candour. God!
In thy great mercy strike this wretch to dust,
And vindicate the justice of thy cause.

(The magic show changes to the Oratory in the Castle of Falkenstiern. Helen, with her child in her arms, beckons him towards her. Falkenstiern rushes wildly to clasp her in his arms; and the show vanishes amid yells and shouts of fiendish laughter. Scene closes.)

Scene IV.

The Trial of Falkenstiern. The Königsssthul. The four Electors of the Rhine are seated in front, a space being left opposite for the Prisoner. The Nobles of the Palatinate occupy the background. Officers with wands, Heralds, Secretary, &c.&c.

Elector Palatine. Is all the Court assembled?

Officer of the Court.   All:—the prisoner
Waits in the hall of audience.

Elector Palatine.   Summon him.

(Voices are heard without, crying, "Room for the prisoner, room for Count Falkenstiern." He enters, guarded, clad in deep mourning, and stands fronting the Judges, his looks fixed on the ground.)

Elector Palatine. Count Falkenstiern! lift up thine eyes. Behold

In these, the assembled magnates of the land,
At once thy peers and judges: it is fitting
That thou should'st know them, here convoked by virtue
Of an especial mandate from His Holiness.
The charge—which aims at no less than thy life—
Itself of nature in these latter days
Most happily a marvel. Thy great name
And station in this land, demand a trial
As strictly true unto the ends of justice
As might await the meanest churl accused
Of deeds so lawless. By my noble brethren
I am deputed with authority
To set forth the brief seeming of this matter:—
    Sir Count! the charge on which thou art arraign'd.
On accusation of a holy father,
Noted among us for his piety
And gentle execution of all duties
Pertaining to a Christian priest—is this:
That thou didst cause, by certain incantations,
Certain unlawful dealings and enchantments,
Whereof the form and nature rests a mystery,
The murder of thy wife and child!—a deed
Not only tasking the most awful rigour
Of civil law, but by its aggravation
In the manner of the act, craving the judgment
Of sovereign Rome itself.
          Count Falkenstiern!
There are those here amongst us bound to thee
By ties of kindred—others who have dwelt
With thee through years of fellowship and love;
And many more, from whom thy recent service
Done in the public cause, hath won respect,
Effacing the wild courses of thy youth.
For me, beneath whose rule thy span of life
Hath worn away, I have still look'd on thee
As a young brother of my house, and held
Thine honour precious as mine own. E'en now
I gaze upon thee as thou stand'st before me,
Where I had fondly hoped to tender thee

A grateful nation's thanks, till in my bosom
The holy character of thine accuser
Scarce weighs a feather in the scale against thee.
Yet are we bound impartially to listen
Ere we distribute our award. Come forth!
Come forth, oh! holy father, and relate
The grounds of this proceeding.
(Father Michael comes forward, and stands opposite to Falkenstiern,
who on perceiving him shudders, and averts his head.)

Father Michael.   Noble lords!
Full well I feel that in a graceless light
I stand as the accuser of this man,
Rich as he is in the regards of those
Assembled here to judge between us. Heaven—
Heaven who sees all—alone can tell how truly
My heart hath mourn'd o'er his iniquities,
Nor ever cherish'd one malicious thought
'Gainst him or his. But it is written there,
Where human laws must pay their first obedience,
That whoso worshippeth the Powers of Darkness
Shall be exterminated utterly:
Therefore, I dare not bury in my bosom
The evil which I know—the more than evil
Which I suspect of yonder Falkenstiern.
Sirs!—It is known to many that I held
Appointment in the household of Count Rothberg.
He died! and of the manner of his death
Ye have heard rumours, which my recent knowledge
Leads me to hold most false and slanderous.
Upon this dread event, the Lady Helen,
The ward of the deceased, the affianced wife
Of Falkenstiern, and from her infancy
My cherish'd pupil, claim'd me for her service;
And like a friend and father in the Lord
I sojourn'd in her dwelling. Falkenstiern,
From his first marriage hour, with cold disdain,
With starts of pride and petty insults, strove
To fright me from my task, and in my absence
Estrange the mind of his unhappy lady

From Christian tenets and observances.
My faith, my duty to the God I serve,
Taught me humility to brook injustice;
Therefore with prayers and patient love I met
His hatred and contempt, nor once refrain'd
From my appointed duties. 'Twas his wont
To signify the loathing which he bore me
By interchange of taunts and scurrile jests
Against the doctrines of the Christian church
With the companion of his looser hours—
One Meinhard—who by flight alone hath 'scaped
Participation in this trial.
(Falkenstiern exhibits tokens of deep suffering.)
                              In time
A son was born to Falkenstiern. I sought,
E'en from the moment of his birth, permission,
By ministration of baptismal rites,
To wash away the innate stains that soil
A frail inheritor of sin. In vain
The gentle mother join'd my prayers with all
The soft persuasion of the sweetest nature
That ever triumph'd o'er the bonds of Satan.
Our zeal was term'd officious by the Count,
Who bade me, as I valued life and peace,
Desist from my entreaty; and by Meinhard
The holy Sacrament, whose glorious aid
Opes the bright gates of life eternal, met
With terms of blasphemous derision which
Would soil my lips i' the record.
                              Years pass'd on—
And the young boy, whose brow was doom'd the bear
The honours of the house of Falkenstiern,
Remain'd an alien from that nobler House
Whose heritage is open unto all.
At length the way-cry rose, and Falkenstiern
Raised the proud banner of his sires amid
The chieftains of the land: within his castle
Women and aged men alone remain'd.
What was his parting benediction to

The wife and child he loved? "Beware," he said,
"Beware, lest weak credulity should lead thee
To bring our boy to the baptismal font:
So surely as thou seek'st to celebrate
That rite, his life and thine are forfeited."
I heard his valediction, and resolved
To win her from obedience to commands
So deadly to salvation. 'Twas a fault,
Perchance, to urge the passions of a wife
Against an absent husband—but 'twas one
Of erring zeal. I soon concerted measures,
Aided by pious brethren of my order,
In secrecy and silence of the night,
To minister within a vaulted chapel,
Framed in some hour of peril 'neath the castle,
The sacrament of baptism. We met!—
Look to the Count, my lords! Mark how he bears
The mere recital of what follow'd.
    Falkenstiern *(approaching him)*. Father!
Delay not—pause not—tell me how they died!
    Father Michael. There, as we knelt before the altar, rose
A lurid flame from out the earth, with sounds
Of horrid and unearthly dissonance.
Meinhard, amid the clamour, stood amongst us!
'Twere vain my trembling lips should strive to paint
The countenance he wore, when, in defiance
Of his dark presence, boldly I renew'd
The ceremony of grace. He laid his hand
Upon the hapless child, and sudden darkness
Spread through the torch-lit vault! When we renew'd
The failing light, Meinhard had vanish'd. Death
Had smote the babe, who lay a shapeless mass
Of foul corruption in its mothers arms,
From whose sacred mind each better sense had fled.
    Falkenstiern. But thou didst comfort her—with gentleness
Soothing her in her sorrow? Holy Father!
Say—did she struggle with the heavy load
Of her affliction?
    Father Michael. On the fatal night,

Of that dark day she died! And ere her soul
Fled to the judgment-seat of its Creator,
A moment of returning sanity
Enabled her to send one sad farewell
Unto the absent Falkenstiern.
(Turning to the Count, who listens with breathless emotion.)
                              My lord!
With the bold truth of one who knows no guile,
I now deliver thee her dying words:
"Tell my unhappy husband, that the woman
He sacrificed, in death forgave the deed!
And bade him, if he ever held her dear,
Desist from practice of those lawless arts
Forbidden by the word of God—through which
His noble hand hath been betray'd to sin,
Even in the murder of his wife and child."
(Falkenstiern throws himself on a bench, exhausted.)
My gracious lords! who have unwillingly
Lend audience to my tale, pray ye acquit me
Of groundless and malicious calumny:
To evidence my truth, my holy brethren,
And the attendants of the Countess Helen,
Await your future pleasure.

    The Elector of Cologne. Father Michael!
Heaven grant that one of thy great sanctity
Be not in this accusal urged beyond
A fitting zeal. Say! on what grounds, beyond
The dreams of a bewilder'd woman, rests
Thy knowledge of Count Falkenstiern's consent
And pre-admission in the dreadful deed?
Can any witness yield us evidence
Of bond or compact 'twixt the prisoner
And the open murderer?

    Father Michael. Your Highness knows
That dark confederates in a deed of blood
Bare not their plots unto the eye of day.
Meinhard was still the friend and chosen inmate
Of Falkenstiern; yet doth the Count deny
All knowledge of his dwelling—station—name—

Which might enable us to touch the culprit
With the strong arm of Justice.
    Elector Palatine.   'Tis enough!
Count Falkenstiern, we look with earnest trust
Unto thy refutation of this charge.
Stand forth: and God accord thee grace to clear
Thy noble name from these foul imputations!
*(Falkenstiern rises and comes forward: at first with an air of deep
dejection and indifference; but in the course of his defense he resumes
and appearance of his former pride and energy.)*
    Falkenstiern. There was a time, my lords! when he who stands
Before ye, like the meanest criminal,
To plead for life and death, had scorn'd defense
Beyond the brief denial of an act
Abhorrent to his nature: for methinks
A Falkenstiern who boldly cries, "Not guilty!"
Hath some poor claim to credence in this land.
But now—though guiltless of this great offense—
Guiltless of any willful injury
Against a child, a wife I loved so well,
Yet can I not confront this proud assemble
With the clear open brow of innocence;
Nor freely claim that quittance at your hands,
Which I must win by patiently unfolding
The tale of mine affliction. Good my lords—
(For there are some among ye whom I know—
I feel—must look with most indignant scorn
On mine accuser), let me first proclaim,
That from my very soul I pardon all
Yon Friar's suspicions. He had cause of doubt,
Which render'd fitting to the eye of faith
This public question of the fact.
                        My lords!
I stand accused of murder!—'tis a word
Whose very utterance appalls my heart:
And for the deed—the hellish act itself—
May the great God who hears me pour upon me
Before your eyes his heaviest bolts of wrath,
If I would not redeem with my own life

The lives I am accused of having ta'en!
Each sin of human growth may be retraced
To some dire motive. A mere love of bloodshed
Aims not the dagger's point, nor drugs the chalice
Of the common'st bravo. Hatred—or Revenge—
Or Fear—or sordid lust of gain, suffice
To urge the assassin's work of slaughter. Say—
Which of all thee could instigate the crime
With which ye would infect my life? The lady
Whose timeless death hath roused such dark suspicion,
Was known among ye for her gracious gifts.
When last I stood among ye, 'twas the day
That our great Emperor, whom may God preserve!
Received his crown from the Electoral Powers:
Amid his noble train, in pride of place
Fitting our ancient name, I led my Helen,
The fairest of your highborn dames, who gazed
In envy of her beauty. Like a star
She rose amid surrounding clouds!
                                        What triumph
Beat in my bounding heart to hear the praise,
The whisper'd love, the fervent blessings lavish'd
Upon her as she pass'd! There was not one—
Not one among the throngs that day assembled,
But would have forfeited fame—fortune—life—
To hold her to his heart in weddeth faith;
And I—and I, who loved her—I, whose truth
Had been from childhood pledged her own; who saw her
Not only thus amid the pageant's pomp
Holding her jewel'd state with fitting pride,
But in the fond recesses of a home
Dear as the Eden of a sinless world,
Pressing her child—my child—unto a bosom
Whose love was only ours—I to betray her
Unto the murderer's grasp!—Oh! gracious God!
Is it in man to have the heart to do it?
And for my boy—the first-born of my love,—
Meed bud of such a flower!—the future heir
Of a long line of spotless ancestry,

Whose name must now lie perish'd in my grave,
Why should I seek his murder? I appeal
Against such accusation to the heart
Of every father here!
*(Murmurs of approbation and encouragement are heard through the
assembly.)*

The Elector Palatine. Peace in the court!
Count Falkenstiern, from these unseemly murmurs
It grieves me to entreat thou augur not
Too surely of acquittal. Thou hast yet
Simply denied the act:—now to the point.
Whence sprang the dying counsels of thy wife?
Whence sprang thy parting admonitions? Whence
Thy fellowship with that dark man of sin,
Whose absence leaves thee to atone for both?
Thou pausest. Sir! take heed: on thy reply
Hang life and death.

Falkenstiern. If the unmeasured ravings
Of one distraught avail as testimony,
Justice is throned upon a tottering base.
For my communion with that loathed being
Whose flight redeems him from the bonds of Justice,
That man—whose very name sends through my heart
A thrill more icy than the bolt of Death—
In that I do avow my crime—in that
I merit all the lawful chastisements
In peril of whose pains I stand—in that
My sin and misery are blent in one!
For through his damning influence have I heap'd
The burning flames of endless punishment
Upon—

The Elector of Cologne *(interposing).*
Sir Falkenstiern! you are not call'd
To criminate yourself by a confession
Of wrongs that stand not in your accusation.

Falkenstiern. Your caution is humane. I speak of this,
But that ye all may know I should disdain
To plead for such a toy as life—gift
Ever of doubtful worth; and to a man

Branded with public shame—domestic grief—
And deep anguish of a heart bereft
Of all—alas! of all—a very curse!
But that to one sear'd with the burning trace
Of guilt, Eternity hath deeper shades
Than Time, however gloomy, can unfold.
Yea! I do ask my life! do humbly crave
For mercy, if ye still deny me justice!
If any act, my forefathers' or mine,
Gracing the name of Falkenstiern, hath claim
Upon my country's gratitude, on that
I rest for mitigation of your sentence.
If ye suspect my pleading urged by dread
Of pain—by any recreant fear—in pity
Try me with tortures—bind me to the wheel—
Or bare me to incision of your weapons
To the very verge of life—I shall not shrink:
But while my quivering flesh writhes 'neath the steel,
Mark how I'll smile in mute contempt.
                                  But death!
But death! My lords! I sue for banishment.
That I have intercommuned with a man
Leagued with the powers of darkness, shows presumption
Beyond the nature of a child of clay;
But were we now placed front to front, my hand
Should fell the murderer to the earth, who stole,
Like a foul kite, to my defenseless nest,
And at one swoop, in his remorseless talons
Bore every blessing of my life away!
Is it my crime that I was far away,
Serving your bidding with my heart's best blood?
If we can prove by living witnesses
My dark participation or fore-knowledge
Of this accursed deed, then pour on me
Your execrations and most bitter sentence:
If not—again I sue for banishment.
Oh! what have I to do among ye more?
My home is desert:—all hath pass'd away
Which bound me to the loved domestic hearth,

Now cold and desolate!

                   I see among ye
The noble knight of Oppenheim, to whom
The law bequeaths in heirship my possessions.
Here do I willingly surrender all;
I would be poor in fortunes as in peace.
My lords! I wait your sentence!

(Falkenstiern returns to his seat. The Electors retire to the background; while an urn is carried round to receive the votes, and is afterwards placed in the hands of the Elector Palatine, who dictates to the secretary in dumb show. While he is writing, the following Chorus is faintly heard from below.)

    Chorus of Spirits. Falkenstiern! thine hour is come—
      The scaffold waits—the axe is bright:
  On—to thine infernal home;
      On—to realms of endless night!
  Lo! thy master waits thy doom—
      Yelling fiends thy path prepare
  Through eternity of gloom.
      Falkenstiern! despair—despair!

  Would'st thou yet thy life prolong?
      Would'st thou 'scape this bitter hour?
  Join thee in our magic song,
      Bow thee to our master's power!
  Yet, oh! yet delay not:—speak
      One little word, and thou art free!
  We will bear thee hence to wreak
      Vengeance on thine enemy!

  Silent still?—Seest thou the crowd
      Spurning thy cold and mangled form?
  No peace pall thy limbs must shroud,
      To veil the triumph of the worm:
  Bared to the shrieking bird of prey—
      Bared to the rabble's mockery—
  The deathsman shall that form display
      Upon the loathsome gallows tree!

Silent still?—bethink thee well—
　　Thine hours to final judgment roll;
Think of the unfathom'd gulf of Hell
　　Which yawns to seize thy forfeit soul.
Silent still?—one moment more,
　　And thou art lost eternally:—
'Tis done—'tis done!—our task is o'er—
　　Falkenstiern! despair, and die!

(The Electors resume their seats, except the Elector Palatine.)

Elector Palatine. Albert of Falkenstiern! rise, and receive
The sentence of the Court.
　　　　　　　　　　Thou art convicted,
Upon thine own confession, of experience
In arts forbidden by the sacred law
Through which we seek redemption.
　　　　　　　　　　　　We have found
No evidence to prove thee surely guilty
Of the imputed crime of murder; therefore
Thy country here acquits thee, by my voice,
Of the dark stain of blood, which would demand
Blood for its expiation. Take thy sword!
It is the sole possession which the Court
Hereafter leaves thee:—to the state thy lands
And heritage are forfeited. Go forth
To banishment! nor upon pain of death
Henceforth be seen within the empire's bounds.

(Falkenstiern kneels, and receives his sword from the Elector Palatine.)

Falkenstiern. 'Tis done! and I am now a lonely blot
Upon the face of nature!—doom'd to bear
My sorrow in some distant clime, where never
The voice of mine own country shall renew
This degradation. O'er the desert earth
I am a lost and charter'd wanderer!
And like a solitary vessel, braving
Upon the ocean's dread immensity
Tempest and thunder-cloud, my lonely heart
Must wrestle with the storms of fate. The world
Is all before me: with this sword and Hope—

Hope! whose bright arch of promise still o'erhangs
The clouds of Memory, I will oppose
The ills of life—the wrath of Destiny!

THE END.[1]

Notes

1. The printed text reads "END OF THE FIRST PART." If Mrs. Gore had planned to imitate Goethe's *Faust* and compose a two-part drama, each part complete in itself, no second part of *The Bond* was ever published.

DACRE OF THE SOUTH;

or,

The Olden Time

A Drama

In 5 Acts

by

Catherine Gore

The Royal Coburg Theatre, later renamed the Royal Victoria Theatre—the home of spectacular melodrama.

DACRE OF THE SOUTH

The following essay was written by Mrs. Gore and published with the play in an attempt to emphasize the historical accuracy of her drama.[1] The play is dedicated, "as a token of sincere admiration" to "the author of *Vathek*," William Beckford (1759–1844), a wealthy writer of Gothic and exotic fiction, whose own life was filled with scandal and eccentricity.[2] Whether or not Mrs. Gore sought to draw parallels between the men's "antisocial" behavior (Beckford's guilt was never proven, though—as in Dacre's case—it was clear that his accusers were more interested in his wealth than his morality), both men were shining examples of the Gothic ideal.[3]

NOTE.

The fate of Thomas Fynes or Fiennes, Lord Dacre of the South, is related by various historians,—Hollinshed, Stowe, Godwin, Camden, Dugdale, &c.

The details of his fate contained in Hollinshed's Chronicles, have been followed, with very slight variations, in the foregoing play. His condemnation, which (according to Hale's *Pleas of the Crown*,) established a severe precedent in English law, occurred on the 27th of June, 1542, before Lord Audley de Walden, as High Steward, with nine other peers, to constitute a court; and two days afterwards, being St. Peter's day, he was hanged at Tyburn, and buried in the church of St. Sepulchre. At eleven o'clock, on the day appointed for the execution, his lordship was delivered in the usual form to the Sheriffs of London; when, just as they were quitting the Tower, a gentleman belonging to the household of the High Steward brought a respite, which the populace (who were strongly inclined in his favour) expected would prove final. Yet at two o'clock of the same day, he was again brought forth, and executed! Historians agree that the severity of his sentence originated in the rapacity of the King's courtiers, who hoped to profit by the confiscation of his estates; and certain notes compiled by Sampson Lennard (who, in the succeeding reign, became the husband of his daughter Margaret,) expressly point out two Privy Councillors as having stimulated the rigour of the court and the obduracy of the King.

Lord Dacre was but twenty-four years of age when he suffered death, and a young man of exceeding promise. By his lady (Lady Mary Neville, daughter to the Earl of Abergavenny, by Mary, daughter of Edward Stafford, Duke of

Buckingham,) he left two sons and one daughter, who were restored in blood and honours in the first year of Queen Elizabeth.

Fine portraits of Thomas Fiennes, Lord Dacre, and of his lady, by Holbein, exist in the family collection of Sir Thomas Barrett Lennard, Bart. The house of Dacre, Dacres, or D'Acre, is of great antiquity; dating its nobility to the feats of an ancestor distinguished at the siege of Acre, in the first Crusade. In the reign of Henry VIII, it was divided into two branches, the Lords Dacre of the South and North. Lord Dacre of the North, (mentioned in the Lay of the Last Minstrel,) was Warden of the West Marshes, and impeached for high treason; and it is remarkable that among all the state trials during that fatal reign, he was the only prisoner of note honourably acquitted. To the Lords Dacre of the South belonged Dacre Castle, Hurstmonceux Castle, the Manors of Gilsland, Graystock, &c. The fine ruins of Hurstmonceux Castle still attest its former splendours.

Notes

1. While it is difficult to ascertain her private politics during this period, Mrs. Gore's calling attention to the youthful Queen Elizabeth as the arbiter of justice and reason (where men had previously failed), restoring Dacre's children to their "blood and honours" is particularly resonant in the early days of young Victoria's reign.

2. Beckford, a married man, had been caught *in flagrante* with a lad named William Courtney and ostracized by polite society. In the later years of his life, his few intimate friends included Catherine Gore.

3. Both men lived in Gothic splendor: Dacre, in Hurstmonceux Castle, Beckford, in a magnificent romantic "ruin" with a Great Tower called Fonthill Abbey.

Dacre of the South

Dramatis Personae

Lord Dacre of the South.
Earl of Abergavenny, *his father-in-law.*
Lord Audley de Walden, *Chancellor and High Steward to Henry VIII.*
Sir Nicholas Pelham, *Sheriff of Sussex.*
Hubert Pelham, *his Nephew.*
Sir Walter Mansel, *affianced to the sister of Lord Dacre.*
Masters Poyntz, Roydon, Chenies, Frowds, *friends of Dacre.*
Mark, *an old Seneschal of Lord Dacre.*
Dick Sumner, *Pelham's Park-keeper.*
Lieutenant of the tower.
Secretary to Lord Audley.
Privy Councils, Courtiers, Guests.
Serving Men, Pages, Javelin Men, Yeomen of the Guard.

The Lady Mary, *wife to Lord Dacre.*
Lady Anne Fiennes, *his sister.*
Madge Sumner.

Time—Reign of Henry VIII.

Act I. Scene I.

A chamber in Hurstmonceux Castle, adorned with armoury. In the background, tables for shovel-board, &c.

(Enter Mark, and two serving men.)
    Mark. Is all in order for the banqueting?—
    First Man. All, Master Seneschal! Fresh rushes spread

O'erstrewn with spicy herbs;—the tables set,—
The bossy flagons ready for their frothing
From a fresh broach of Gascony!—

    Second Man.   The feast
Reeks from our vaulted kitchen with a steam
Might fill a hungry man! The lordly haunch,
The goodly chine, fat capons, cygnets, quails,
Sweat i' the basting; while a garnish'd boar's head
Grins in the midst!—It makes a fellow's lips
Run o'er, to talk on't.

    Mark.   It were well, Sir knave,
Thy lips and tongue ran less. Mark me!—To-night
The Pelhams and their mates pledge with my lord
A wassail cup of amity. I charge ye,
Upon your zeal, give these proud men no pretext
To call the Castle wanting in its welcome.

    Second Man.   Old Nicholas a guest at Hurstmonceux?
Methinks—*(A horn sounds.)*

    Mark. How now?—

    First Man.   It is my noble lord
Home from the hawking.

    Second Man.   Or some smell-feast neighbour
Seeking to scan our cheer—

    Mark.   Leave prating, Sirrah!
Look out, there!—To the hall! *(Exeunt Men.)*
(Looking out.)   Now, by the rood!
The bearings of the noble house of Neville.
My lady's sire, the venerable Earl!—
(Re-enter serving men, showing in the Earl of Abergavenny and his train.)
My gracious lord! *(With reverence.)*   Welcome to Hurstmonceux!

    Aberg. Old Mark?—Still at thy post?—

    Mark *(bowing)*.   There to remain
Till palsy shake the wand from my old hand!
(Abergavenny signs to his train to retire. Exeunt.)

    Aberg. My daughter and her lord, yon knaves inform me
Are still a-field?—'Tis well!—Should the wind serve
I'll join their sport to-morrow.

    Mark.   Good, my Lord,

The o'er night promise chimes not ever with
The morn's observance. We've a banquet toward
Will make the roofs ring and the torches blaze
Far into a midnight. The old Knight of Laughton
And Master Pelham are our guests.

Aberg.   I'm glad on't!
There ran ill-blood of old betwixt your lord
And old Sir Nicholas.—Heaven's mercy keep him
From foes so potent as these vauntful Pelhams!—

Mark. Foes, my good Lord?—They're now staunch friends—
sworn brothers!—

Aberg. Tut, man!—Such bitter feuds ne'er ended yet
In friendship worth the trusting. *(Bugles heard.)*
                    Ha! my daughter!
*(Enter from hawking, Lord Dacre and his Lady, Hubert Pelham,
Poyntz, Roydon, Frowds, Chenies, and attendants. The Lady kneels to
Abergavenny.)*

Aberg. *(raising her.)* Rise, dearest! *(To her Lord.)*
                    Dacre! a fond father's blessing
Is earn'd thee by this wench's sunny looks.
The Pe'nsey breezes, girl, have fix'd the hues
Of health upon thy cheek.

Lady.   Say rather, Sir,
The cheer of happy hours.

Aberg.   Long rest thy so!
(Lord D. brings forward Hubert, and presents him.)

Dacre. I pray ye, know our neighbour, Master Pelham,
Or let me say—our *friend!*—

Aberg.   Your father, Sir,
Was comrade with me in the Irish wars.
Friendship should be a thing of heritance. *(Takes his hand.)*

Dacre *(to his Lady).* Mary! our children lack their grandsire's
blessing.
Why are they absent? *(To Aberg.)* I've a boy, my Lord,
Would crave so much love of ye, as his parents
Hold due unto yourself. *(To his wife, leading her out.)*
              Go!—bring him hither.—
(Exit Lady.)

(Hubert, Poyntz, Roydon, Frowds, and Chenies retire to the background, settle to the tables, and play in dumb show.)

Aberg. Dacre!—I find thee girt with troops of friends,
And rural pastimes. I had hop'd ere this
Thou'dst weary of this homely country life?—

Dacre. Duty and choice entwine the two-fold chain
That anchors me to home. Each passing hour,
Big with its special bus'ness, leaves no lapse
For weariness to seize on.

Aberg. *(contemptuously.)* Duty, Sir!

Dacre. 'Tis meet my Lord, you courtiers of Whitehall
Scorn the poor claims of rural suzerainty:
Our hodden grey shows coarse beside the gloss
Of three pil'd velvet or gay paduasoy;—
Yet is there, solid service in't!

Aberg. I grant ye!
Doff we the cap to your stout Sussex yeoman,
The bulwark of the coast! But Heaven's high will
Hath loftier duties for the legislator
Of England and her millions, than mere thrift
For South Down flocks, and garnering of harvests!—
The true-born English squire, with his old hall,
And hospitality, and hoarded cheer,—
His heart and door still open,—still of oak,—
Forms a brave emblem of the land we love!—
—Lord Dacre of the South hath sterner virtues
Carv'd by the hand of history on his blazon!
To achieve their knightly nobleness, your sires
Pledg'd their own worth and valour!—'Tis for *you*
Redeeming these, to make their honours *yours*,
Or a great name becomes a great reproach.

Dacre. You're serious, Sir!—

Aberg. As fits a serious theme!—

Dacre. Sir, I but parried with a wanton jest
A charge I deem'd mere pleasantry. Take now
A graver answer from my inmost soul!
You do upbraid me that I thus abide
In my ancestral home,—sullen,—obscure,—
Spurning both court and city!—I reply,

Such is my pleasure,—such my mission's law!—
Deem not mere vulgar lust of rule inspires
My love of these fair fields,—these brave retainers:
'Tis that my soul derives a godlike strength
From faithful stewardship in the trust I hold.
The sun that riseth on this castle, hears
No murmurs wrung from wrong'd or grieving hearts.
Happy, and happy-making, 'tis my joy
To render back to man the gifts vouchsaf'd
By God himself.
          My people are content!
The village glebe yields them their labour's price;—
The village green rebounds with their glad sports;—
The village echoes catch their lightsome songs;—
The village church shelters their grateful pray'r!—
Is not *this* something to be proud of?
    Aberg.   *Much!—*
But amplify your sphere of usefulness,
Unto the patriot's vast and fruitful task,
And you may prove, with wider scope of virtue,
A blessing to your country and mankind!
The State—
    Dacre *(impatiently).*   The State's grown a mere *name*
The King's the state!—The King—that fickle tyrant!—
The King, whom God had given us in his wrath,
To fill our land with blood,—our homes with tears,—
Making our English court a Golgotha,
And the degrade name of British honour
A by-word to the nations!—
    Aberg. *(ominously.)*   Sir, I pray ye
Restrain yourself! *(Looks toward the players.)*
    Dacre.   Nay! 'tis a privilege
We rustics have, that near our honest hearths
No hireling plays the spy. What I dare show
To Heav'n in thought, I dare show man in word.
    Aberg. You are too bold!—
    Dacre.   Father, I do beseech ye
Pardon my warmth!—Obedient to your will,
Four years ago, I was a cringing courtier.

For young Prince Edward, at the sponsal font,
I did due service;—nay, some twelvemonth since
Rode forth appointed by the King's good grace,
To welcome home his royal bride! My Lord,
There were two names united in that bond
Might well have kept it sacred;—*two*, my Lord—
A woman's name, and England's!—*Both* were mocked!—
The Lady Anne of Cleves, a prince's daughter,
Cast off, dishonour'd by the wanton King;—
And I, Lord Dacre of the South, (whom now
You twitted with the honours of his race,)
Sham'd as accomplice in a shameless act!—
    Aberg. My Lord!—
    Dacre. Such was the meed vouchsaf'd me by this man,
This King—this HENRY!
    Aberg.   Good, my Lord!—
    Dacre.   No fear!—
There are none here but friends.
    Aberg.   Not e'en thy friends
Should hear thee thus arraign the Lord's Anointed!
That, man!—accuse the King's vindictiveness,
Yet thus defy his vengeance?—
    Dacre.   Vengeance, Sir,
Is for the King of Kings! Let Justice shine
The milder attribute of earthly crowns!
    Aberg. To Heaven alone belongs the right to dictate
To royal ones. Leave thus the King to Heaven.
    Dacre. I will,—I do;—and therefore shun his presence!
If he have stript the land of its old laws,—
Its ancient faith,—its rich and fair endowments,—
And above all, its trust in kingly virtue,—
Lo! Conscience hath a snaky scourge, whose stings
Not e'en a regal mantle holds at bay.
But for myself, enough of courtiership!—
For me,—no dallying with this king of fagots,—
This torturer of women's fears,—this prince
Whose faithful servants yield him at the block
Their heart's blood up in sacrifice!—For me,
Henceforth,—free air,—my homely hearth,—and peace!—

Aberg. E'en these were forfeited, should envious tongues
Echoing thy reckless words, proclaim thee traitor!—
I *pray* thee be less rash!—
    Dacre.   What!—Be a slave?—
Crush every fervent impulse of my soul
Under my own free roof?—Shout with the crowd,
(That clowns may emulate my loyal zeal,)
"God save King Henry!"—Then, with grinding teeth,
The whisper'd curse—the curse that mounts to Heav'n
Louder than fifty thousand brazen voices,
Clamouring the golden virtues of a throne!—
Say!—speak!—what plea should prompt an honest heart
To such a degenerate patience?
(Lord Abergavenny suddenly brings forward the Lady Mary and her children, who have entered during the foregoing speech, and places them before Lord Dacre.)
    Aberg.   These, my Lord!
This woman's and these infants' happiness!
You owe it me that the dear child I gave ye
To be as dear a wife, be not cast forth
A traitor's widow on a loathing world!—
(To the child.)   Go to your father, boy! Hang on his neck!
And bid him prize the life that guards your own.
(Lord D. embraces the children, and encircles his wife with his arm.)
    Dacre. No more, my Lord! "He who hath wife and children,
Gives hostages to Fortune!" Lo! henceforth
The jade is mistress o'er me!—Dearest wife!
Let these fond tears, which I would fain repress,
Lest they should shame me in thy sight, attest
How dearly I am sworn to thee and thine.—
So judge me He whose judgment errs not!
(Releases his wife and looks round towards the rest.)
                  Pelham!
We make no stranger of ye, in thus yielding
Our household babble to your scrutiny?
Pardon us, Sir!—anon we shall be merry,
And worthier of your gentle company!—
    Hubert. Needs it excuse that you distinguish me
With a friend's privilege? *(Pressing his hand.)*

Dacre.   We but await
The tidings that our good High Sheriff's train
Hath reach'd the drawbridge, for the batteries
To speak our welcome.
(Exeunt Poyntz, Roydon, Frowds, Chenies, &c.)
    Hubert.   Sir, you honour us
Too dearly!
    Dacre. 'Tis your due to be *twice* honour'd:
As noble guests, and foes redeem'd to friendship!
Your leave! — We go to fit our state to grace ye,
And straight are here again. *(Going.)*
    Hubert.   No ceremony.
Use me as you have call'd me—like a friend!—
(Exeunt Lord Dacre, Lady, Abergavenny, and attendants. Hubert traverses the stage with impetuosity.)
    Hubert. 'Twas time they went:—my patience was nigh spent!—
Is't not enough I vail my pride to him,—
The traitor whom my passion's restless impulse
Would fain call brother,—but my swelling soul
Must in submissive silence sanction thus
His accusations 'gainst the King, whose favours
Prosper our house with still increasing grace?—
Let Dacre look to't!—The old knight, my kinsman,
Will tender him anon my loyal suit
For his fair sister's hand. Then, let him look to't!
The Lady Anne becomes my bride, and Laughton
Allied, for life and death, with Hurstmonceux,
Or to Whitehall the tokens of his treason!—*(Looks out.)*
Lo! in good time she comes, to tranquilize
My soul's impatience!—Oh! what conscious joy
Stirreth the atmosphere encircling round
The gentle form we love,—forewarning us,
Like harmonies that herald angel guests!
(Enter Lady Anne, attended by a Page.)
Lady!
    Anne. So soon return'd?
    Hubert.   So *soon?*—
    Anne.   I pr'ythee
What sport a-field?—Did I not well t'abjure

The hawks to-day?—Nay, speak, Sir! you're not wont
To be thus silent when I deign to question.

Hubert.   Lady! 'tis now my turn for questioning;
And on thine answer hang such worlds of joy
As may not brook suspense.—Oh! fair as Heaven!—
Like Heav'n be true,—like Heav'n be merciful—
In audience of my prayer.

Anne.   So earnest, Sir?—
Are you the same wild playmate, who last night
Toy'd with my nephew in the sagittary
'Till none could swear which was the greater boy?—
You are grown wondrous grave!—I've heard it said
A night will turn men's heads from black to white:—
A night hath wrought a mightier marvel *here!*—

Hubert.   Heav'n keep those sportive smiles upon thy lip,—
Heav'n keep that raven gloss upon thy locks,—
Heav'n keep—

Anne.   Amen!—Is this a benison?—
Would you perchance usurp the chaplain's place
Here in the castle?

Hubert.   Lady Anne, beseech thee
For once be earnest!—Nay, for once, sweet love,
Yield me this gentle hand.—

Anne *(drawing up).*   Speak ye in sooth, Sir?

Hubert.   In sooth! in true and fervent courtship!—Hear me!—
Nay, shrink not thus: I'd but prepare thy thoughts
For the demand wherewith my noble kinsman
This night must greet thy brother.

Anne.   Not a word, Sir!
Nay, not a syllable!—I was to blame
Not to divine and check this fruitless project.
'Tis not too late.—No more on't!—I entreat ye
Forgive me but for having heard thus much,
Which you may wish unsaid.

Hubert *(fervently).*   Never!—My suit
Is open to all ears and eyes. I court
The *world* as witness *(Tenderly.)* while I swear by all
It holds of great and gracious, I had rather
Call thee my own that the most gorgeous throne

Dazzling the vulgar eye! Oh! hear me, love!—
(Kneels, and tries to take her hand.)
Be not thus coy.—Snatch not thy hands away!—
One—one, at least,—as hostage for thy heart!—
Thus let me seize my captive!—
    Anne *(with dignity.)*   Rise, Sir—rise!
The sister of your friend—ne'er to be *more*
Than your friend's sister—*(mark me!)*—pray ye, rise!
    Hubert *(starting up).*   Thou saidst?
    Anne.   I said—
    Hubert.   Speak out—that thou wouldst never
Be mine?—
    Anne.   I urg'd it in more courteous phrase:
I said I *might* not!—
    Hubert.   Who shall dare prevent it?—
What hateful obstacle?—
    Anne.   My hand and heart
Affianc'd to another!—
    Hubert.   For *his* sake
Do not say that:—say anything but that!
Say that thy heart, like these embattled towers,
Scorns in its strength all threat of mortal conquest;—
Say thy vocation leads thee to the cloister;—
Say what thou wilt, but that another woos thee
With happier chance than mine!—
    Anne.   Sir, ere I knew you,
Ere I knew aught, save a fond father's will,
My hand was given in trothplight to his ward!
    Hubert. To Mansel?—to his ward?—Why, this is glorious!
Oh! just desert!—How?—have I moved my kinsman,
O'erlooking feuds of former years,—o'erlooking
His grade as Henry's representative,—
O'erlooking state and station, pride and place,
To come here suing, cap in hand, like some
Merchant of Chepe, or franklin of the marsh
That counts his grazing beeves by tens and scores—
For what?—To court the cleaving ignominy
Of this rejection!—Lady Anne! one word;—
Think better of my suit!—

Anne.   Sir, I already
Think *worse* of one who thus presumes to raise
His voice against a woman.
    Hubert.   Pardon,—pardon!—
The waves, that warring winds toss up and down,
Harass'd to frenzy, cannot tame their hoarseness
To the small murmurs of their summer voice:
Yet I'll speak gently, so thou'lt gently hear.
    Anne. I cannot!—I have said it.—Be advis'd.—
I *love* young Walter Mansel!—In that word
Be answer'd.—Ere the forest leaves shall fall,
I'm pledg'd to be his wife.—Think all unsaid
I've heard to-day.—I know no suitor in ye,—
Dream none, desire none:—be henceforth, as even
The *friend* of me and mine! *(Exit.)*
    Hubert *(furiously).*   Their fellest foe,
If there be truth on earth, or hate in hell!—
That I, of iron nature—I, a man
Fashioned for manly deeds,—of high resolve,—
Implacable resentment,—should thus fall
Into a snare to cozen boys!—They saw it:
Fostered with fiendish joy my growing passion;
Then, gaily jesting round their household heart,
Cried, "Thus and thus the fool shall play his part,
And thus we'll spurn him!"—Oh! Revenge, revenge!
Bring but our pride once more on equal ground,
And leave no human eye the right to glare
Triumphantly on mine!—*(Chambers.)*—And hark! the signal—
The train of old Sir Nicholas approacheth.—
How to accost him?—How reveal all this?
Yet I must speak—must warn him to desist
From our projected overtures!—Great God!
One hour for patience!—one proud silent hour,
And *then*—a LIFE'S REVENGE! *(Exit.)*

Scene II.

A Gothic Hall, adorned with hunting trophies; the music-gallery filled with minstrels. A banquet. The guests standing. Attendants bring forward a table richly spread, and seats.

(Enter, in front, Lord Dacre, Mark, and serving-man.)

    Dacre *(to guests).* Good cheer and welcome! *(To Mark.)*
      On your lady's entrance
Give signal to the music.—Lo! she comes!—
(Enter the Lady Mary, led by Sir Nicholas Pelham; Lady Anne, led by Sir Walter Mansel; Hubert, Poyntz, Roydon, Frowds, Chenies, &c).

    Dacre *(to Sir Nich.)* Thrice welcome, worthiest neighbour!
Oft be that cheering word renewed between us,
And thou receive it graciously as now!
Ne'er did I feel more proud to play the host.—
A health! *(They bring a goblet.)*
      Lo! be this cup a font of peace
To consecrate the faith of new born friendship.

    Sir Nich. You make a stranger of me, good my Lord,
By too much courtesy!

    Dacre *(to the guests).* Sit, Sirs, beseech ye!— *(All sit.)*
(Hubert lingers in front.)

    Hubert *(as he is about to sit).* How my soul thrills at
    these hypocrisies!—
To sit at meat, a blessing on one's lips,
With those on whom we burn to fling a curse!—
It was to move me that she took his hand.
Let me not seem to note the insult! *(Sits.)*

    Dacre.   Ho!
The gleemen there!—a loud and jocund rebeck—!

GLEE AND CHORUS.

      'Tis a very merry thing,
      When blending voice and string,
      Sweet harmonies do bring
           Together;
      Ho! masters, while we sing,

Deep healths to the King!
Fill your cups, take your fling,
        Together, together;
And clink, while you drink
        Together!

'Tis a very merry sight,
When torches blazing bright,
Glid the roofs with their light
        Together;
Ho! masters, if to night
We yield ye sweet delight,
Fill your cups, do us right
        Together, together;
And clink, while your drink
        Together!

'Tis a very merry sound,
When echoing roofs rebound,
As the clanging harps ring round
        Together;
Ho! masters, beat the ground,
Let no sober knave be found,
Fill your cups, pledge around,
        Together, together;
And clink, while you drink
        Together!

Sir Nich. I' faith, well sung!—
Mansel.   I crave your Lordship's leave
To thank your minstrels for the lighsomeness
Their strain hath taught my spirits.
(Unclasps a jewel and sends it by a page to the gallery; then drinks.)
                Health and good speed
To them and to their art!—
Hubert *(tauntingly).* A royal patron
Could not have king'd it better!
Mansel *(tauntingly).*   Would, fair Sir,
Some kings I wot of, king'd it half so gently!

The gracious arts of peace need cherishing
From bumpkin knights, like me, since at the court
No stave holds good, save penitential psalms,
Chanted to cheer sad women to the scaffold!—
Honour to "De profundis!"—but we rustics
Love a less doleful strain!

    Anne *(aside to Mansel).*   I pray ye, peace!
Why thwart him with this captious bickering?

    Mansel. I'll curb my thoughts for no man!—

    Anne.   For no *man!*
But when a woman sues—

    Mansel.   A woman, sweet,
Pledg'd to become a soldier's bride, should learn
A spirit that beseems her more than patience.

    Anne. I've done! Would thou couldst say as much!

    Dacre *(addressing Sir Nich).*   Sir Sheriff,
I have a noble haunch here, courts thy tasting.—
Thou'lt own anon the bucks of Hurstmonceux
Maintain their old renown, as first in fame
Of Sussex,—nay, of any English forest,
Save the King's chase at Richmond.—Ho! what ho!
A trencher here!

    Sir Nich. *(coldly.)* I've ate of it already.

    Dacre. Well, Sir?—

    Sir Nich.   The ven'son's good! but—

    Mansel.   Good?—I grant ye!—
Why, so is any ven'son! *(Half aside.)* Ill befall
Such churlish praise! I love th' outspoken man
Who fees and gives God thanks; nor would disparage
With stony brow and meanly grudging mind
The viands of his host.

    Hubert *(ironically).* Most courteous Sir!
Forgive us!—A poor Downsman's appetite
Shrinks from the unctuous herds of Pe'nsey level!—
Flavour's our mark of merit:—grosser senses
Are easier satisfied. *(To Lord D.)* Our Crowhurst hills,
Whose aromatic herbage scents the channel
Far off at sea, yield purer pasturage
Than sweltering marshes fed by brackish brooks.

The deer degen'rate there.

 Dacre *(earnestly).*   *There,*—but not *here!*—
Mine are of highest race. So long ago
As Wolsey's time, whene'er the Cardinal
Had guests of note, his token reach'd my grandsire,
Craving a gift of ven'son from our herd,—
The far-fam'd bucks of Hurstmonceux!

 Hubert *(with scorn).*   The Cardinal
Profess'd a churchman's taste,—fat benefices;
Match'd with rank ven'son!—

 Mansel.   While the presbyters
Of sober Luther, conjugating priests,
Prefer the dainty does of Laughton Park!—

 Sir Nich. Sir, you are bitter!

 Dacre.   Mansel! we are met
For festive purpose. Themes thus roughly urg'd
Become discourtesy! Our good High Sheriff
(To whom elsewhere, we tender due respect,)
Will cede so slight a point?—

 Sir Nich. *(with violence.)* No, as I live!—
The honour of my land's concern'd in't!—No!
The Laughton ven'son 'gainst all herds in Sussex!—
My hand and glove upon't!—*(Strikes the table.)*
(A murmur among the guests.)

 Dacre.   Nay,—here's Ashburnham,
Shelley, and Poyntz, take up the challenge!—

 First Guest.   Ay,—
And I!

 Second Guest. And I!

 Sir Nich.   E'en, as ye list, my masters!
I fling down fifty nobles on the issue,
To back my boast!—The King's Comptroller, Sirs,
Or whosoe'er ye hold elect of palate,
Adjudge the cause!—

 All. Done!—

 Dacre.   To a wedding feast
'Twas my intent to bid ye, ere we parted.—
There be our wager sped.

 Sir Nich.   'Tis well!—Your day?

Dacre.   The feast of good St. John!

Sir Nich.   I'll make a note on't:
My keepers shall be warn'd.—I promise ye
A stag of ten, whose haunch may grace your board,
And branching antlers, yonder trophies.

Mansel.   Sir,
We've butting things enough from Laughton, here,
Already!—

Hubert *(aside)*.   I shall find a time to thank ye
For these fair greetings, Sir.

Mansel *(aside)*.   Whene'er you will!

(Lord Dacre entreats Sir Nicholas, who has risen, and is preparing for departure.)

Dacre.   No, not to-night! You ride not forth to-night!
We've couches spread for all your train. Beseech ye!—
My good old sire, the Earl (forc'd to forego
The banquet, by mere weariness of travel,)
Will scarce forgive me should he miss to-morrow
Our promised guests.—I do entreat ye, tarry!—
The night is dark,—the ways are perilous!—

Sir Nich.   Not lawlessly, I trust; since my road lies
Solely athwart your lands and mine.

Mansel.   At least
The weather, Sir, is neither yours nor his
To answer for?—The moon's not up these two hours.

Dacre.   Come, come!—another cup!—another carol!—

Sir Nich.   Not one!—My pastime's done, my task to do.
I've duty on my hand. I ride to Lewes
On the King's errand.

Dacre.   Nay! that alters all.
(To Hubert.)   You, Master Pelham, are not charg'd in this?
You will remain with us?—

Hubert.   My uncle's years
May not abide a night-ride, unattended.
I crave your pardon, I must forth with him.

(Exeunt Sir Nicholas, Lord Dacre and Lady, Lady Anne, guests, &c. Hubert as he is going, calls aside his Page.)

Hubert *(hurriedly to Page)*. Find some pretense for loitering in
the hall —

Take note of all shall chance on our departure;—
And when the banquet breaks, hie after us,
And to *my* ear alone report your tidings.—

    Page *(aside).* 'Tis well, Sir!
    Hubert.   See't be done with care and caution.
(Exit.)
(Page retires among the attendants. Mansel, Poyntz, Roydon, Frowds, Chenies, &c. come forward.)

    Mansel. So! Let us breathe again!—
    Poyntz.   You were too fierce
Upon the heir of Laughton!—
    Mansel.   I've a quarrel
With that same Pelham, scarcely may abide
These love-feasts!
    Poyntz.   Think ye old Sir Nicholas
Will hold his wager?
    Roydon.   Else the knight were sham'd!—
    Poyntz. He may shame *us* i' the sequel!
    Mansel.   'Twere rare sport
To put a scoff upon this vaunting Sheriff!
A stratagem!—Draw near!—*(Whispers.)* What if we lift
One of his vaunted bucks of Laughton Park,—
Serve it, as Dacre's, at the feast,—and win
His condemnation?—
    Poyntz.   A right merry jest!—
    Mansel. The night is fair, the distance short to pass;—
The Sheriff and his people absent:—Come!—
A cup, Sirs, to our enterprise!—What ho!
Wine here!—*(Wine brought; they fill and drink.)*
        "A health to all night foresters!"
Thrice hath the game a zest when, in the taking,
We bring down buck and forest-laws together!—
(Re-enter Lord Dacre.)
Lo! in the nick of time, (with his moist lip
Fresh from the stirrup cup,) our honoured brother!—
Dacre! there's sport i' the wind!—We've sworn to fetch
The pride of Pelham's herd to Hurstmonceux,
And pass his ven'son on him as your own.
    Poyntz. Come! pledge us to our frolic!—

All. Ha! ha! ha! *(They drink.)*

Poyntz. The old man's beard shall wag for't!

Dacre. He deserves

Some such requital for his churlishness,

In marring thus our welcome. *(Dacre drinks.)*

Sirs! I'm *for* ye!

Though breaking parks be somewhat of the wildest

For a staid greybeard, for this once, i' faith,

I'll be a ruffler with ye!—*(Throws away the goblet.)*

All. Bravely said!—

Mansel. Afield!—another health,—and then afield!

Your chorus, Sirs, your chorus!

All. Ho! masters beat the ground,

Let no sober knave be found,

Fill your cups, pledge around

Together, together;

And clink, while you drink

Together!

(Exeunt shouting.)

END OF ACT I.

Act II. Scene I.

Exterior of an old Keeper's lodge at Laughton Park. Night. Lights within.

(Enter from the lodge, Dick and Madge, wrangling.)

Madge.   I'll not believe a word on't!—Roysterer!
'Tis some carouse that calls thee forth!—

Dick *(buckling on his belt)*.   Hard duty,
Nor more nor less.

Madge.   Never was wasteful truant
Wanting in words to sanction his outgoings:
I say again 'tis some carouse! —

Dick.   Beshrew thee!
Art thou a mother, yet dost grudge thy children
My labour's hire?—A double fee awaits
My double watch.

Madge.   Thou hadst not known the need
Of double fees and midnight deer-keeping,
Hadst thou contented thee at Hurstmonceux!
Were not our people vassals on the land?—
Was not the Baron's self my foster-brother?—

Dick.   Wilt please thee hold thy prating?—

Madge.   Marry, no!—
(Hubert's horn without.)   Ho! Lodge!

Dick *(presenting his piece)*.   Who goes? The word —

Madge.   Dolt! art thou mad?
'Tis Master Pelham!
(Opens the door to Hubert.)

Dick.   Sir, I crave forgiveness.

Hubert.   No time for dallying words!—*(To Dick.)*
          Art armed?—art ready
For fray or fence?—*(Madge screams.)* Leave fooling woman!—Ho!
Art ready, knave, I say?—

Dick *(saluting)*.   Ready!—

Hubert.   How many
Keepers and verderers serve with ye?

Dick.   Some five,
Stout men and true, wait but my bugle call

To rally round me!

Hubert.   Wind your horn! —

Madge.   A fray! *(Whimpers.)*

The Lord's great goodness keep us!—here's a bout!

Hubert.   Away with ye!—This is no time for whining! —

(Dick pushes her into the lodge.)

(Enter five keepers, armed. Hubert addresses them.)

To-night the Parks of Laughton will be broken.

Lord Dacre and his mates are pledg'd to do't!—

Know ye their persons?

Dick.   As we know your own, Sir!

(Bating disguise or mask!)

Hubert.   Sir Walter Mansel,—

Wouldst recognize him?—

Dick.   Ay, among a thousand!

'Tis the young soldier knight, who's plighted with

The gentle Lady Anne.

Hubert *(hastily)*. What's that to thee

Or me, so he infringe the laws?—

Dick.   Nay, Sir—

Hubert. Bring me that knight—that skulking midnight poach-

er,—

A prisoner to the Sheriff's bench to-morrow,

And ten rose nobles be thy meed!—

All.   *Ten nobles!*

Dick.   That's something like!—

All.   We'll warrant him for *that!*

Dick.   And for the Baron, Sir?—

Hubert.   Take him or leave him,

No matter!—

Madge *(listening behind)*. As I live, 'tis my good Lord

They threaten!—

Hubert.   An hour hence, at the moon's rising,

By the low western wall, they'll force an entrance:

A bow-shot thence, stands an old oak,—

All.   We know it!

Dick.   The wizard's oak, that flings its hoary arms

Over the brook, as though they bless'd the waters!

The deer oft herd there, Sir, o' summer nights.

Hubert. Thither repair, and wait me!—I'll but arm,
And join ye straight. *(Exit.)*

Dick. A knight turn deer-stealer?—
A lord break park?—'Tis time the keeper's fee
Were rais'd, since poaching's grown so fair a calling!

All. On, to the wizard's oak, and take our ground!—
(Exeunt.)

Madge *(stealing out).* They're off at last! A mischief light on
'em!—
That my young lord should fall into their springe!—
The western wall?—I'll warn him, though I die for't!
'Tis but to skirt the cliffs, hid in their shadow,
There lie in wait—*(Muffles her head in her dress.)*
And when they leap the wall—
(As she is going out, re-enter Hubert.)

Hubert. I had forgotten,—*(Meets her.)*—Ha! What's here! A
scout
In woman's gear!

Madge *(uncovering).* No! as I hope for mercy!—
'Tis I, fair Sir—'tis your head keeper's wife.

Hubert. What errand art thou forth on!—Speak!

Madge *(frightened).* Good Sir!

Hubert *(seizing her).* Tell me what mischief's in thee, or I'll
shake it
Forth from thy soul, like grain from chaff!

Madge. Good sooth, Sir!
I did not dare abide here thus alone,
And had a thought to join the verderers
And share my husband's watch.—

Hubert. Go to! thou durst not!
Thou liest!—There's plotting in thy face!—In with thee!
Thou'rt for the enemy!
(Pushes her into the lodge, and locks the door.)
Safe bind, safe find!—

Madge *(within).* Oh! Lord,—good Lord!

Hubert. Ay! get thee to thy pray'rs,
Thou'st need of pardon! *(Draws his sword exultingly.)*
Mansel!—Walter Mansel!—
Look to thyself!—*Thou*— towering still above me,

Triumphant in her smiles,—proud with the pride
Of being loved by *her*,—thine hour is come!—
Lo! groveling at my feet, I'll see thee lie,
And spurn thee like a dog!—The good green turf—
The moonlight for our witness—God of vengeance,
Be with me in the struggle!—

                    On!—away!—*(Exit.)*

Scene II.

A wooded glen, in the centre of which, an old oak tree. Dick and the five keepers discovered lying wait among the rocks and bushes.

    First Keeper *(coming forward).*
        Who goes? Did ye hear nought?
    Dick.   A cricket chirping
In the long grass!—
    First Keeper.   I swear, I thought I heard—
    Dick.   A linnet rustling in its nest!—Why, Ned,
You start at straws to-night—What's in the wind?
    First Keeper. Ay! *what* in sooth!—No good thing that I wot of.
As we came past the ruin'd chapel, where
King Hal o'erthrew the altar stone, to shame
Our lady's image carv'd upon't, *(Raises his cap.)* there came
A dismal shriek from the dismantled pile!—
    Dick. Some screech-owl, on the watch for midnight mice,
As we for midnight prowlers!
    First Keeper.   Hark! again—*(They listen.)*
    Dick. I only heard the distant ocean's swell,
Breaking with measur'd fall on Pe'nsey beach.
    Second Keeper *(from the Cliffs).* Some one approaches!
    First Keeper. Quick! your matchlocks prim'd!—
(A whistle. Dick answers it. Enter Hubert hurriedly.)
    Hubert. Haste to the western wall! the hour hath struck!
Their inbreak is at hand. Follow me, friends!
But calm and cautious, till we're fast upon them.
    Dick. *Then*—for St. George and England!—
    Hubert.   Mark my pledge,—

Ten nobles on his head!—

Dick. The knight shall swing for't.

Hubert. Follow me!—On!

All. Ho! Follow—follow—follow!

(Exeunt cautiously. A pause. Poyntz drops from the cliffs, and beckons down the rest.)

Poyntz. All's quiet here!—Down with ye!—down!

(Lord Dacre, Sir Walter Mansel, Roydon, Frowds, Chenies, drop down.)

All. Victoria!

Mansel. Not a breath moving!—not a foot astir —
The caitiff-keepers, in Sheriff's absence,
Have taken leave to take a good night's snooze!—

(They laugh.)

Dacre *(looking round)*. A goodly spot, and purpos'd as for ambush.
But where's the herd we came for?—

Mansel. From the cliffs
Each nook of the wide park was manifest
As though at noon;—but not a head of deer!—

Dacre. We should have kept the wall and lower ground
As 'twas first purpos'd.

Mansel *(heated with wine)*. Lo!—the lady moon
Smiles on her votaries as she'd play the rival
With sunny day. *(Kneels and speaks with much emphasis.)*
Queen of freebooting men!
Cheer'd by thine auspices, I dedicate
Henceforth my cross-bow to free-forestry!

Dacre. A truce, man, to thy mummeries —Thou'lt draw
The keepers to the spot!

Mansel *(wildly)*. *Who'll* help me raise
A beacon of dry boughs on yonder hill,
To grace this blessed eve of May, as May
Was grac'd in merry England, ere the curfew
Knoll'd o'er its conquer'd ground?—By Heavens! the blaze
Would scare the deer from covert!—

Dacre. Scare the *keepers,*—
And bring them on us ere the buck be ta'en.—
Nearer the lodge the game lies. Faith, I'll on

And reconnoitre!—*(Going.)*
    Mansel.   How?—Park company?—
(Lays hold of him sportively.)
Good sooth, we'll hunt together!—Thou'st some plot
To flout us!—Thou'st engross both game and glory!—
(Dacre escapes him.)
By Heavens he's off!—Dacre, I say!—What, Dacre!
Follow him—give him chase!—I warrant me,
That in the Baron's track we mark the deer—
Ho!—Dacre!—caitiff!—recreant!—follow me!—
(Exeunt.)

Scene III.

Exterior of the lodge.

(Enter Dacre as escaping.)
    Dacre. Ha! ha! ha! ha!—I've given the knaves the slip.
(Takes off his cap.)
Thus flush'd with wine, how wooingly the night air
Blows on my fever'd brow! Free winds of Heaven
I envy ye your pure and sweeping course!
(Looks round.)
Where have I sheltered me? *(Starts.)* 'Tis passing strange!
E'en such a scene as this hath often mingled
With shrieks and omens in my evil dreams!
My mind appears to mock me, with a show
Of things that have been, or may be, and not
The present place and passing hour!—Methinks
I dream again! Or is it wine deludes
My failing senses? So the wilder'd boatsman
Borne on some giddy current, scarce may swear
If in his barque or in the flying shores
The motion be! *(Turns towards the lodge.)* Ha! watchers here?—
    Madge *(throwing open an upper window).* Help,— help!
    Dacre. What voice is this?
    Madge.   Good stranger! if your Christian
Unbar the door and let me forth!—

Dacre *(trying it).* 'Tis fast!

Madge *(crying).* Alack!

Dacre. Why, Madge, hast thou forgot me, girl,
Thy foster-brother?—Dacre?—

Madge. My good Lord?
Sweet Heav'n be thank'd that in its mercy sent ye!—

Dacre *(aside).* What means the jade?—

Madge. They're lying wait for ye!
Away, away!—five armed and deadly ruffians
Led by my husband.—Fly, my gracious Lord;
A traitor's price is set upon your head
By Master Hubert!—

Dacre. Nay! thou'rt dreaming, Madge!
Pelham is jogging on his way to Lewes!—

Madge. He's hardly out of earshot.—Fly, my Lord!—
You're among enemies,—you're marked for death.

Dacre. If this be true, as thy scar'd looks avouch—
(A discharge of arquebuses.)
Ha! an alarm, in sooth!—*(Draws.)* Why, to it then! —

Madge. There will be murder done! —
(Enter Poyntz disordered.)

Poyntz.[1] Fly, fly, my Lord!
The Sheriff's people are upon us!—Twice
We've driven them back towards the river. Fly!

Dacre. Fly?— Hath our jest prov'd earnest? —

Poyntz. Grievous earnest!
Blood hath been spilt already.—Ere they rally,
We must have pass'd the precincts!
On!—away!
(Exeunt.)
(A second discharge. Shouts without. Mansel and Hubert fence across the stage. Mansel falls;—Hubert stands over him.)

Hubert. This for the faithful servant thou hast slain!—
This for the life whose hopes thy suit hath wither'd—
(As he is about to strike, Roydon, Chenies, and Frowds rush in, struggling with keepers. A general fray. Madge shrieks and closes the window. Lord Dacre and Poyntz rush in, and with their party, drive off the keepers and Hubert.)

Dacre. Ha! Mansel wounded?—

Mansel *(faintly).*   'Twas a well-earn'd blow;
One of the keepers hath a deadly hurt,
Struck by my arm!—
    Poyntz.   They will return anon,
With succours from the house. Quick! bear him off.
    Dacre *(assisting to raise him).*
Thus!—gently!—have a care!—Now towards the castle:
Reach but my land, and he is safe.—Come on!
They dare not beard the lion in his den!
(Exeunt bearing Sir Walter Mansel.)

Scene IV

Hurstmonceux Castle by moonlight. The drawbridge up. Horn at a distance. Warder appears on the battlements.

(Enter Poyntz disordered.)
    Poyntz.   Warder! the drawbridge! Speed! there's life and
    death on't!
(Enter Lord Dacre and his companions, bearing Sir Walter Mansel on a litter of branches. Drawbridge descends.)
    Dacre. They're fast upon us!—Haste!
(They cross. Exeunt into the castle. As the drawbridge rises, Hubert and his men arrive, and form a tableau.)
    Hubert *(furious).* Baffled? Derided?
(With solemn emphasis.)
Hail haughty towers, hail and farewell! Already
My curse hath prosper'd! O'er your battlements
Death waves his ghastly banner! Blood-stain'd house!
Lo! I devote thee to th' avenging laws
Whose ruthless will shall judge 'twixt thee and me!

END OF ACT II.

Notes

1. No speaker is indicated in the published text.

Act III. Scene I.

A Chamber in Hurstmonceux Castle. Sir Walter Mansel wounded, on a couch; Page attending. Near him, Lady Anne. The Lady Mary watching at a window.

Anne. Thou'rt easier now?—

Mansel.   I did not say so, sweet!—

Anne. Thy looks spake for thee—In thine eyes there shines
A light o'erfilm'd till now.—Thou'rt better!—

Mansel.   Am I?—
I' faith it *shall* be so!—*(Takes her hand.)*

Lady.   Still, Dacre comes not!—
My spirit wearies for him;—what detains him?—

Anne. A swollen ford,—his pacing nag at fault!—

Lady. A swollen ford,—i' the midst of summer drought!—
Was it a swollen ford or a lamed steed
Detain'd him on that fatal night?—Behold
(Points to Mansel.)
What chanced our friend, and *might* have chanced my husband!
(Comes forward.)

Anne. That luckless sortie was a mad exploit,
Done in the heat of wine!—Dacre rode forth
To-day, in sober morning's thoughtful light.
Ere midnight, trust me, he'll be here in safety.
(Goes to the window.)
'Tis evening yet!—The curfew hath not toll'd!—
The circling bats are scarce a-flit,—the drawbridge
Still down, and—Ha!—I spy a coming horseman!
It is—it *is* my brother!—His tir'd horse
Scarce bears him over.— Lo! the chains are drawn—
The bridge is up.—

Lady.   And Dacre safe!—Thank Heav'n!—
My home's no home to *me* when he's away!—
Dear are my babes,—but dear that they are *his*.
Dear is my father,—for he pledg'd his child
To be the wife of Dacre!—Heav'n itself
Seems mightiest to my lowly veneration
When to the throne of thrones I kneel beside him,

And in one prayer our blending praise ascends.

Mansel. Thus ever be the code of wifehood fram'd!—

Anne.   So shall not *mine*, Sir truant, should mad pranks,
Such as have laid thee here, allure *thee* forth
From thine own wedded home!—

Mansel.   From *thee* and home,
What pow'r shall tempt me!—

Lady.   Ha! my husband's Page!
(Enter Page. Going towards him.)   What cheer?—

Page. My Lord entreats the Lady Anne
Will grant him instant audience.

Lady.   Witless boy!—
To *me* thine errand ran,— 'twas *me* he ask'd for!

Page. Madame, your pardon!—'Twas the Lady Anne
His worship nam'd—

Anne.   How's this?

Page *(aside to Anne).*   He bad me pray thee
Haste to his oriel chamber.

Lady.   Something moves him!
Something's amiss!—Have I displeas'd my Lord?—

Anne *(to Page).* Say I'll be with him quickly.
(Exit Page.)

Lady *(leading her).*   Nay!—but go!
What keeps thee?—To the oriel chamber, sister!—
And when thy counsel's done, tell him there's one
Sits trembling here, waiting his summons.—Go!—

Anne. Ay!—to return, and bring him to thy presence—
Trust me, I'll chide him for this frowardness!—
(Exit. Scene closes.)

Scene II.

An oriel chamber.

(Enter Lord Dacre, followed by Page.)

Dacre. She'll come you say?

Page.   My gracious Lord, behold her!—
(Enter Lady Anne.)

Dacre *(to Page).* Leave us!

(Exit Page.)

Anne *(aside).*   His looks are strangely wild and haggard.

(Lord Dacre advances anxiously towards her.)

Dacre. Sister!—I'd fain,—*(Takes her hand and stops short.)*
                 How fares it with our friend?

What cheer with Mansel?

Anne.   Fie! is *this* your mystery?

Do all these solemn preparations end
Simply in— "How is it with Walter Mansel?"—

Dacre. My words have import in them! Once again,
How fares he?—

Anne.   Well!—But thou, dear brother, thou
Art labouring with some strange distemperature!
What ails thee?—

Dacre.   Thou wilt learn it all too soon!

Anne. Thou'rt suffering then in sooth?

(Takes his hand.)

Dacre.   Sick to the soul!—
The man whom Mansel struck in yon affray,
Died yesternight!—

Anne *(eagerly).* But 'twas not of his *wound?*—
It was some old hereditary ill!—
Or he was ag'd — he died not of his wound!—

Dacre. His days were in their prime!—The blow struck home.

Anne. Belike he was a husband too?—a father?—

(Dacre signs affirmatively.)

     (Wildly.) And Mansel struck his death-blow!—Walter Mansel!—
There's blood upon the threshold of our house,—
And vengeance will repay't!—Blood must have blood!
You said he'd wife and children?—God forgive us!—
In the dread scroll, where truth hath words of fire,
'Tis written—*"Life for life!"*—And Mansel slew him!

Dacre. Be not thus mov'd, dear sister!—

Anne.   In that death
A whole life's peace lies slain!—The man I lov'd
Was one might challenge the assembled world
To cast a stain upon his blameless life.—
I'll wed no homicide!—

Dacre.   Be calm, beseech thee!—

Anne.   Sacred shall be the word my father pledg'd!—
No other man shall claim my maiden vows;—
But in some love religious house I'll kneel
My life away,—beseeching Heav'n to pardon
The crime that made that widow and those orphans.

Dacre. Thou mayst have *cause* to kneel.—Show some compassion
Towards a falling man!—The warrant's out
May bring the friend we love—*(Pauses.)*

Anne *(alarmed).*   I—hear—thee, brother!—

Dacre. Unto a death of shame!—

Anne *(faltering).*   It *should* be so!—
Yet might the law be merciful!—The deed
Was done in heat of blood.—No malice in't
More than impels the soldier's hand to smite
His country's foe:—more than uplifts the arm
Of any living mortal, mov'd to strike
In self-defense!—*(Sinking.)* I'm—very faint, good brother,
Thine arm,—thine arm!—*(Hides her face.)*

Dacre *(supporting her).*   Be patient—be compos'd!
The worst is doubtful still.—

Anne *(solemnly).*   No!—past all hope!—
A deed of violence deals a twofold curse:—
The life that's ta'en demands a life's atonement.—
Better had Mansel fall'n with him he slew!—

Dacre. The law may view the act with milder judgment.
What proof hath Pelham that the deed was done
By *him?*—Can the High Sheriff *swear* it?—Nay,
Can *I?*—I know't by hearsay,—so doth he!—
Let them bring witnesses!—

Anne *(eagerly).*   Hath *Pelham,* then,
Control in this?

Dacre.   Sir Nicholas, as Sheriff,
Issues the warrant of the peace.

Anne.   Then Heav'n
Have mercy on our friend! The bitterest feud
Instinct with mortal murder, is less deadly
Than the intensity of hate betwixt

Mansel and Pelham!—He must die!—

Dacre. Thy *heart*
Suggests these terrors!—

Anne. No,—my *reason!*—Rivals
In war—love—fortunes,—scarce a week hath past
Since Hubert's wooing, laugh'd to scorn by me,
Renew'd their enmity.

Dacre. Ha!—for thy hand
Pelham was suitor?—

Anne. A bold, vaunting suitor,
Threat'ning unsparing vengeance on his rival!

Dacre. Pelham's a man of ruthless nature, barren
Of gen'rous impulses.—Curs'd be the hour
That drew us to that spot!—*(Walks, musing.)*

Anne *(wildly).* To die so young!—
With all the honours of his race around him—
Men's love embalming his career,—men's hopes
Invested in its promise!—Well!—the grave—
The grave hath a prompt solace for despair!—
'Tis but to *die,* and end it!—

Dacre *(stopping suddenly).* Die!—Sweet sister!—
(Takes her hand in his, and intently regards her—)
We twain grew up alone in the wide world!
Orphans in childhood,—we have lov'd each other
As men love home in exile.—Thou hast seem'd
A being wrought by Nature in her bounty
To soothe my ruggedness with mild assuagement,—
To rouse my youth to nobler aspirations,—
To make my life a comfort and a joy!—
I'm pledged to *thee* as never brother yet
Was pledg'd to sister!—Whom hast thou beside
To soothe thee, or to succour?—Whom beside
To guard thy helpless youth?—*(Falters.)*—I'd fain be firm—
But dwelling on these charities,—my soul
Melts to a woman's weakness.—Bear with me!—

Anne. Brother!—

Dacre. Not yet!—I must be heard awhile!—
I must first *prove* thy claims far far beyond
All common sympathies of love fraternal!—

Ere I avow my purpose,—(mark me, sister,)
Of taking Mansel's fault upon myself—

    Anne. With its dread penalties?—Thou dar'st not think
So meanly of him as conceive his sanction!—

    Dacre. He is my friend,—my childhood's earliest friend!—
As near to brother as may be, not claiming
The bond of kindred blood:—say!—would a brother
Refuse such service from his father's son?—

    Anne. Ay!—if it brought such peril.—

    Dacre.   Nay!—the peril
Deadly to Mansel, loses half its sting
Transferr'd to *me.*—*I* am not Pelham's rival,—
Not e'en his foe!—A baron of the realm—
High in estate,—the King courts my allegiance,—
Thrusting his favours on me past desert
And past desiring!—The Lord Abergavenny
Hath his regard.—My friends surround the throne.—
Think ye that, to avenge a brawling hind
Slain in a night fray, henry would arraign
Lord Dacre of the South?—E'en were he hostile,—
Mine is no cause for shrieval courts, controll'd
By royal frowns!—My peers—*my peers* must judge me!—
But blench not, love!—'twill never reach so far.
'Tis but a word or two, said i' the ears
Of their high Justiceships, our country quorum,
And all's forgot!—Mansel still unsuspected
And I acquit,—as lords will ever be
Till even-handed Justice hold once more
The scales of England!—

    Anne.   This must *not* be so!—
This paltering with the law is most unlawful!—
I will not hear on't!—

    Dacre.   Spare thy remonstrances!—
My plans are fix'd;—before to-morrow's noon,
My project will have prosper'd!—Let my wife
Know no suspicion!—To *her* gentle nature,
The slightest cloud that dims the summer sky
Seems thunder-charg'd!—Pr'ythee be careful o'er her!
There'll come a time hereafter for the tale,

Beside our winter hearth, when all's o'erpast
Of this disastrous chance, save consecration
Of masses to the slain, and benefits
Heap'd on his sad survivors.—What dost gaze on
Thus earnestly?—

    Anne.   Methought I heard a sound—
    Dacre.   The warder's call, telling the hour of night!—
    Anne.   No—no!—
    Dacre.   Thou were not wont to have these tremors!—
Be calm!—

    Anne.   There—*there* again!—I swear I heard it!—
    Dacre.   Heard what?—
    Anne.   Alas!—
(Enter Page hurriedly.)

    Page.   My Lord!—an armed force
Rides at the gate!—The warder bad me warn ye!—

    Dacre.   An armed *force,* quotha?—Go to!—The darkness
Hath magnified into a warlike squadron
Some wand'ring pilgrim or benighted horseman
Seeking our hospitality!—
(Exit Lady Anne.)

    Page.   My Lord!
He prays you arm yourself.—The thing is earnest!—
(Enter Mark.)

    Dacre.   Earnest in sooth!—See if my poor old servant
Be not affrighted from his bed!—

    Mark.   My Lord—
Our men-at-arms are lock'd in sleep;—the warder
Craves leave to give th' alarm!—

    Dacre.   Not for his life!—
What?—Scare thy gentle lady, to appease
The terrors of a fool whose brains are dizzied
By a too copious night-draught?—
(Re-enter Lady Anne; her hair disordered.)

    Anne.   From the watch-tower
I've look'd upon them!—

    Dacre.   Well?—
    Anne.   A company
Of twenty men or more, compact and fierce,

With serried javelins and bright partisans
Reflected by the intermingling glare
Of torches borne aloft!—

    Dacre.   Ha!—This looks serious!—
'Tis the High Sheriff and his guard!—*(To Page.)*—Quick, boy!
Go warn my squire—hie to the armourer—
Let all be up and stirring!—but no tumult—
No vain resistance.—Go!—*(Exit Page.)*

                              Sweet sister,—pr'ythee
Detain my wife from knowledge of these straits.—
Bid her to rest.—Her chamber's far remote.—
Deceive her to tranquillity.—For *thee*
I do resign thee to thy soul's high courage!—
Be but thyself!—*(Exit hastily.)*
(Enter first serving man.)

    First Serving Man. Where, *where's* my Lord?—
    Anne.   How now?
    First Serving Man. The host without demand admittance!—
    Anne *(with dignity).*   *Well,* Sir?—
Let them demand it!—Are these castle walls
So slight, that we must tamely yield an entrance
To the first loud, marauding, band of ruffians
Comes clamouring to the gate?—

    First Serving Man.   Lady!—they hold
The warrant of the law,—In the King's name
They come,—

    Anne. Hie to my brother,—to the armoury;—
'Tis Dacre's self who must decide on this,—
Nay, I will with thee!—*(Alarum rung.)*

               Ha!—it is too late!—
They've forced a way,—they come!—

               Great Heav'n protect us!—

(Exeunt.)

Scene III.

The Gothic Hall, lined with javelin men, holding torches. Sir Nicholas Pelham, bearing a scroll. Lord Dacre, Mark, Serving-men, Pages.

Sir Nich.   Your warder's a right surly one, my Lord!—
I was denied admittance.—
Dacre.   Midnight, Sir,
Is an unseemly hour for neighbours' greetings!—
Sir Nich.   As neither friend nor neighbour stand I here,—
But as the servant of the King!—My Lord!
'Tis rumour'd that within these walls you harbour
Certain rude men,—notorious brawlers,—foes
To the King's peace.—
Dacre.   These walls, Sir, are capacious!—
When, in my grandsire's time, the threats of France
Bristled our Sussex coast with loyal spears
Prompt for defense, this castle's garrison
Number'd three thousand soldiers of our vassals.—
Sir Nich.   Your lordship keeps strict *record* of your service!—
Dacre.   I would but show that the same roof which shelter'd
Three thousand loyal soldiers for the State,
Might well contain a straggler, more or less,
Unreckon'd on by *me.*—
Sir Nich.   An urgent motive
For the search-warrant issued by the King
To take and seize these malefactors.—Pray ye
Give orders that your people yield me passage,—
Opposing no impediment or hindrance
To its strict execution.
(To his men.)   Search the castle!—
Let not a nook escape ye!—
Dacre *(to the men).*   Hold!—*(To Sir Nich.)* Sir Sheriff!
'Tis not so long since you were entertained
With hospitable welcome in this hall,
As to forget that I have gentle inmates
Unapt to meet disturbance.—
Sir Nich.   Their condition
Will be respected!—*(To the men.)* Go!—

Dacre.   Yet one word more.—
I would fain learn—(my house's privilege
Invaded thus)—the *intent* of your pursuit?
          Sir Nich.   One that not e'en the loyal dedication
Of thrice three thousand soldiers to the King,
Would buy to silence!—To detect a murderer,
And yield him to the laws.—
          Dacre.   Still, inexplicit!—
          Sir Nich.   In the King's name, then,—*(Unfolds the scroll.)*
                              I demand surrender
Of one who, in your lordship's company,
Did on the eve of May, feloniously
Kill and destroy a park-keeper of mine,
Fast by the lodge of Hillingsly—
          Dacre *(interrupting).*   Sir Sheriff!—
I answer for that crime!—
          Sir Nich.   My Lord! my Lord!—
You sport beside a dark and dread abyss!—
Think twice ere ye thus brave me—
          Dacre.   Twice, or thrice,—
And still my purpose is unchang'd!—*I answer*
For that man's death unto the laws!—
          Sir Nich. *(eagerly.)*   Reflect!—
Your name is stainless,—one of high accompt
In the land's annals.—Pause!—
          Dacre.   For the third time
I say, I answer for the homicide!—
          Sir Nich.   The law defines it—*murder!*—
          Dacre.   Whatsoe'er
Ye term the act,—I answer for't.
          Sir Nich. *(taking him aside.)* Your grandsire
Fought by my side in many a valiant field,—
Sat by my side at many a festal board,—
I'll not hear this!—
(To his men.)   Go!—execute your warrant.—
          Dacre *(stops them).* *Who'll* dare to sack my house, when on the
threshold
I thus surrender to the claims of justice
The man ye seek?—*(To Sir Nich.)* Is't you, Sir, who would give

So strange a sample of the course of law?—
So mad a precedent?—*(To the men.)*—Stir at your peril!—

Sir Nich.   Your blood be on your head!—Your sword, my Lord!

Dacre *(unbuckling it)*. Not long, I trust, to bide out of my keeping.—
England hath too much need of faithful friends
To spare a blade so true!—*(Surrenders his sword.)*
(Mark throws himself weeping at Dacre's feet.)

Mark.   My good young Lord!—
This must not be!—'tis sin,—'tis sacrilege!—
These men shall trample on my hoary hairs
Ere I will see you borne a prisoner
From the unsullied dwelling of your fathers.—

Dacre.   Old man,—old worthiest friend!—
(Stoops over him.)

Mark.   Your infancy
Was pass'd in these poor arms,—they'll find strength yet
To grapple with the first who dares to lay
His hand upon my master!—

Dacre *(raising him)*. Fear not, fear not!—
I've good assurance that this seeming peril
Will pass and be forgotten.—Nay,—I pray ye—
Prove your affection by submissiveness.
(To Sir Nich.) Now?—whither are we bound?—

Sir Nich.   To Hastings Castle;
There to abide the King's award.—

Dacre.   *To night?—*

Sir Nich.   Your lordship's vassals ill would brook the shame
To-morrow's dawn must yield.—We'll forth to-night!
(Enter the Lady Anne, endeavoring the keep back Dacre's wife and children.)

(Lady's voice without.)   My Lord!—my Lord! *(Enters.)*

Anne.   Distract him not, sweet sister;
Shake not his courage with your tears.—Forbear.—
Pray ye, forbear!—
(The Lady Mary bursts in, a child in her hand, and rushes to Lord Dacre. Exit Anne.)

Lady.   What means, what means this clamour,—
What means this dread array?—a prisoner?—*Thou?—*

They dare not.— *Who* shall touch thee?—*who* unclasp
This dear embrace?—*(To the child.)* Cling to thy father! cling,
And challenge yonder men to snatch him from us!—

    Dacre. Be comforted!—'Tis a mere form:—to-morrow
Will see me here again—unscath'd—unsham'd!—

    Lady. Once past this threshold's safety,—thou nor I
Can guess what forms of law may touch thy life.—
The land is stain'd with blood,—the King is ruthless!—
I swear thou *shalt* not go,— thou *shalt* not leave me.

    Dacre *(to Mark).* Bear her away!—her anguish tortures me!—
(Enter Sir Walter Mansel, supported by Poyntz and Roydon; Lady Anne following.)

    Mansel. Dacre!—They generous purpose hath transpired!
Was it well done, my Lord, thus to o'erwhelm
With nobleness and service past redemption,
Thine unsuspecting friends?

    Dacre.   Away—away!—

    Mansel *(to Sir Nich.)* Sir—we're your prisoners! In our surrender
We claim our friend's enlargement.

    Sir Nich. *(sternly.)*   'Tis too late!—

    All. How mean ye, Sir?—

    Sir Nich.   On his own self-accusal,
In presence of these men and of his household—
Lord Dacre stands committed.—England's laws
Must judge betwixt his guilt and yours!—

    Mansel.   Yet hear me—

    Sir Nich. Reserve your eloquence, your plight may need it!
(To his men.) Escort them hence!—*(Javelin men surround them.)*
(Lord Dacre stands in the midst, supporting his lady, the child clinging to his knees. Mark beside him, clasping his hands.)

    Dacre *(to his lady).* Good angels guard thee, love!—
Fear not for me!—
Mary!—look up!—*(Perceives that she has fainted, and places her in the arms of Lady Anne.)* Now,—while she's thus unconscious,
Away! *(A murmur among his household; they advance; Dacre signs them back.)* No rescue, Sirs!—my own wild will
Hath brought this peril on me. *(To Sir Nich.)*— Pray ye, on!

END OF ACT III.

Act IV. Scene I.

A chamber in the Earl of Abergavenny's house, at Westminster.

(Enter Abergavenny and Mark.)

Aberg. My daughter absent still? Alas!

Mark. This moment
Your lordship's barge hath touch'd the garden stair.—
My lady's train alighteth.—

Aberg. From the Tower
She comes,—her duty's daily pilgrimage,—
Fostering the grief that feedeth on her life,
By solacing the captive hours of Dacre!

Mark. A prisoner,—dishonoured as a felon,—
And yet his innocence avouch'd of all!

Aberg. Consorting with the guilty, we incur
The penalties that brand their lawlessness.
The Tower hath clos'd her jarring gates upon him.—
The Tower,—whose soil—a mass of human ashes—
Still thirsts for human blood, nor lacks libation!

Mark. E'en as King Henry's craving courtiers thirst
For gold and gear of those whom foul attainder
Strips of their lives and fortunes at the block!—

Aberg. Take heed, old man!—Such words are dangerous!
(Enter the Lady Mary.)
My child!—

Lady. My father! *(They embrace.)*
Oh! in that dear word
Abides as much of comfort as a soul
So lost as mine dare cherish! *(Kneels.)* Bless me, father!

Aberg. Blessings be on thy head—and heavenly mercy
Confirm the benediction to thy soul!

Lady. Amen! *(Rises.)* If ever woman lack'd sustainment
From divine aid, 'tis *I!*—

Aberg. Say, dearest—say!
What tidings of thy lord?—

Lady. His spirit's strength
Riseth with each probation;—full of trust
In the law's equity, and the strong aidance

Of sympathizing friends.

  Aberg.   No mortal aidance
May reach so lost a cause!—

  Lady.   While I am near him,
His soul is calm. But when our parting hour
Consigns him once again to solitude,—
Him,—in whose frame the quick'ning pulse of life
Beats so responsive to the joys of others,—
Him,—to whose breast earth's sunshine and free air
Impart such rapturous sense of ecstasy,—
His spirit sinks within that silent cell
Haunted by spectres of the Past and Future;—
The Past, with its sweet, sad, reproachful smile,
The Future, with averted face, still pointing
To a dishonour'd grave!—

  Aberg.   *The grave!*

  Lady.   Oh! father!—
That word,—that thought—have pity on us, father!
Go to the King.—Fall on thy bended knees.—
Tell him how blest a life of love and peace
This heavy chance hath blighted.—Plead for us!—
Thou art too cold—too calm!—There is yet time!—

  Aberg. He must abide his trial.

  Lady.   Wherefore *must* he?—
The King's word is our law!—

  Aberg.   It doth confirm
The law, but cannot shake its dread foundations.
Dacre must bide his trial.—

  Lady.   In thy words
There breathes such marble coldness as the tomb
Strikes to a living heart.—Thou hast no soul
For intercession!—

  Aberg. From Whitehall, e'en now,
I come.—I've cring'd in Henry's antechambers
Mid grooms and pursuivants,—petitioning
His servants' servants, to procure me access
Where England's peers have charter'd right to enter.—

  Lady. And they denied it?—Speak!—

  Aberg.   A paltry bribe

Enforced my privilege!—Yon venal court
Hath not a door but keys of gold will loosen.

Lady.   Thou'st seen him then?—Ay?—Thou hast seen the
King,—
The King gave patient ear to thee?—Say on!—Speak!—

Aberg.   He gave ear,—cold, sullen, callous ear!—
No bursts of passion, as I've seen him use
T' appall some pale petitioner,—no oaths.—
He listen'd as a man whose inward purpose
Is clench'd with iron.—

Lady *(faintly).*   Well!—when all was said?—

Aberg.   He answer'd, (in a tone intense and fearful
As the fell tiger's growl when cower'd to spring,)
That I,—the husband of a traitor's daughter,—
Had aptly wed my daughter to a traitor!—

Lady.   That was mere wantonness of scorn,—no threat!
What said he more?—

Aberg. *(solemnly.)* That the same axe o'er rusted
With the black blood of Hapless Buckingham
Thirsted anew for Dacre's! *(Supports her.)* My poor child,
Born of a race foredoom'd,—doom'd to give birth
To one no less unhappy,—pardon me
That I must wound thee thus!—'Tis fit thou know
The worst!—

Lady *(resuming her energy).* There is *no* worst while hope re-
mains.
The threats of Kings are *breath,* like other men's,
Which after-words may cancel.—

Aberg.   Henry's threats
Have rarely lack'd fulfillment!—To his ear
Some enemy, with base and festering tongue,
Hath borne the tale of Dacre's wild contempts!—

Lady.   Some *enemy?*—He'd none,—no enemy!—
His cordial nature,—pure as lands that breed
No reptile race,—defied their growth!—He'd none!

Aberg.   He stood too high to be unmark'd of envy.—
The wrath of kings, as of the skies above them,
Deals on the loftiest mark its bolt of death.
Henry was eager for a fault in Dacre;

And when a royal arm is nerv'd to strike,
Never yet lack'd there parasites to whet
The sword of vengeance in a monarch's hand.—

  Lady. And this is all the comfort thou canst yield me!

  Aberg. Thou speak'st as I were cold in Dacre's cause!—
Hold'st thou for nought the bitter ashes scattered
By his sad plight upon thy father's head?—
Heaven knows how dearly I have lov'd thy lord!

  Lady. *Have* lov'd!—oh! talk not this,—as he were numbered
With things we have surviv'd—the senseless dead—
The bootless past!—*Have* lov'd?—Oh! love him still!
And bid him live, and bid thy child be happy!—
Though Henry's heart be callous to thy pray'r,
Hast thou no portion in the Nation's councils?—
No voice?—Is privilege so little worth,
That one of England's proudest Baron bows
Poorly submissive to a king whose laws
Are writ in blood,—death-warrants,—dooms,—attainders?
Whose sceptre is the axe,—whose minister
The executioner,—whose saving grace
A baptism of blood?—Be it not said
The House of Neville was so king-ridden
By this bad man!—

  Aberg.   Daughter!—

  Lady.   That name might teach thee
A kindlier glow—

  Aberg.   One chance befriends us yet!
Audley de Walden, the High Chancellor,
(A man in whose great mind justice and mercy,
Like Isaac's twinborn wrestling in the womb,
Contend for mastery,) is to preside
At Dacre's trial. From his wise suggestion
May rise some mitigating plea.—We'll seek him.—
It is the hour he quits the court.—Attend me!
Forbear all rash remonstrance!—
(About to lead her out.)   Ho! within!
(Enter two serving-men.)
Go! warn my bargemen to the landing-stair,
And wait upon our escort.—*(Exeunt.)*

Scene II.

Closet of the Chancellor. A table with parchments; two Chairs of State. Lord Audley discovered writing, Secretary attending. First and Second Privy Councillors in front,—four others in the background.

Audley *(giving papers)*. This, by express to Greenwich—to the King!—*(Secretary bows. Shouts without.)*
What shouts are these?
    Sec.   The populace escorting
The Earl of Essex to the Tower.
    Audley.   'Tis well
The King had left Whitehall,—or Cromwell's cause
Would gain small credit by their demonstrations. *(Exit Sec.)*
(Turning towards the Privy Councillors.)
Your pardon, Sirs!—These anxious times impose
Such labour on his Grace's faithful servants,
That the small courtesies of life are missed.
Your pardon?—Hath the council sat to-day?
    First Priv. Coun.   Touching this matter of the young Lord Dacre.
    Audley.   Why, what imports the council in't?—The prisoner,
Arraign'd on high impeachment, waits his trial
Before the King's commission!—
    First Priv. Coun.   Good, my Lord,
'Twas by his Majesty's express disposing.
The trial of the prisoner must be follow'd
By speedy execution.
    Audley.   *Must* it so?—
What?—Ere a note of "Guilty" be recorded,
Do ye prejudge his cause?
    Second Priv. Coun.   His cause is naught—
His Majesty hath so expounded it!
The act was *murder;*—and a felon peer
Dies like a felon pauper:—'tis the law!—
    Audley.   When *prov'd* a felon and a murderer
Before the searching inquest of his country.
    First Priv. Coun.   Ay, *prov'd,* as Thomas Fiennes this day will be!—
    Audley.   Too much of exultation, Sir, methinks,

In such a tone applied to such a grief!—
There's strong appeal to human charity
In frailties of the young.—A man less vers'd
Than I in your high merits, might conceive
You found a triumph in Lord Dacre's doom.—

    First Priv. Coun. I *do,*—my Lord!—pray ye believe, I do!—
Were I to see his head fall at the block,
'Twould wake no mercy in me.—I should say
"So perish the King's enemies!"

    Audley *(surprised).*   *The King's?*—
Lord Dacre's crime, Sir, was mere rash consorting
With loose companions, who, in tide of revel,
Made forth to steal a deer:—(no flagrant matter,—
A thing of mulct and fine,—a very nothing
To breed a stir for!)—but by luckless chance
Riot ensued,—a fray,—a fatal blow;—
Convicting thus a noble of the realm
Within a penal stature.—This is all, Sirs!—
Would *ev'ry* felon's cause brought argument
So weighty to the royal clemency!—

    First Priv. Coun. Ay!—*were* this all—

    Audley.   Pr'ythee, what knowst thou *more?*
That the estates of our young heritor
Lie in the sunniest landlight of the realm?
That Dacre of the South hath castles,—parks,—
Manors,—rich plate and lordly hangings,—apt
For the poor human worms that creep and fatten
On confiscation?—Fie!—there's something loathly
In preying on the reliques of a victim
Thus by anticipation—Fie, I say!

    First Priv. Coun. I scarcely read your lordship's mood to-day.
Yet if my ignorance might so presume,
I'd say Lord Audley's shrewd sagacity
Was dimmed by favour tow'rds a *traitor's* cause,
Or by a miracle!—

    Audley.   Call him not a TRAITOR!—
I'd have that hateful word so set apart
In the land's language, with especial shame
To paint the wretch disloyal to his King,—

That not another human fault might share
The heinousness of such an imputation!—

Second Priv. Coun. In this, as in all else, Lord Audley binds
Wisdom and Virtue link in link;—and yet,
We must repeat, there's treason in this man!

Audley. Upon what proof, Sir?—

Second Priv. Coun.   On the word of one
In birth and means his scarcely less than equal,—
Who waits without your lordship's gracious pleasure.

Audley. Let him appear!—*(Exit First Privy Councilor.)*
(Aside.)   There's malice in their zeal:—
Or the strong lust of spoil (which hath dissevered
The lands of England, once inalienable
From sire to son, till scarce a manor knows
To name its owner,) spies new forfeitures
And paves their way with treachery!—
(Re-enter First Privy Councilor, showing in Hubert.)
                              Ha! your errand!

Hubert *(giving a scroll)*. The finding of the jury, good my Lord,
With summary of proof and special verdict
Recorded on Lord Dacre's four companions.

Audley *(reads hastily)*. "GUILTY!"—the sentence "DEATH!"—Our
trusty Sheriff
Loseth no time, methinks!—

Hubert.   My kinsman's duties
Press for instruction of the royal pleasure
Touching their execution.—

Audley.   How!—So hasty?—

Hubert. Immediate death's the sentence.

Audley *(to Privy Councillors)*.   A brief respite
Might yield these wretched men some saving grace
From evidence adduced on Dacre's trial.—

Hubert *(eagerly)*. My Lord!—the land's tranquillity is periled
By ev'ry hour they breathe!—The common mind
Is sorely wrought upon.—The people murmur:—
The murder'd man was of their own condition:—
Their fellowship is not as *ours*, which sees
A comrade torn from out its ranks, and closes
Listless and dumb over the vacant space.

In *their* strong hearts both love and hate attain
A giant growth. An injury done to *them*
Must be aton'd. Were favour but surmis'd
Towards these titled ruffians, discontent
Might grow to disaffection,—tumult,—treason.—

    Audley. How, Sir?—The King's good shire of Sussex show
So bad a spirit?—Hath the Sheriff's hand
No stronger hold on its subordination?—
This must be look'd to!—

    First Priv. Coun.   Lo! the fatal fruit
Of Dacre's lawless precepts and example!—

    Audley *(to Hubert).* Of which we call on *you,* Sir, for the proof!—
Be brief!—

    Hubert. Nay, wherefore tax *my* single voice
With accusation?—

    Second Priv. Coun. Sir!—without evasion
Deliver here what to ourselves ye trusted
To bear to the King's ear!—

    Hubert *(hurriedly).*   That in his castle
Of Hurstmonceux, like some unruly Baron
Of times more turbulent, Dacre hath assembled
A company of wild and lawless men,
Marring the country's peace with loud excesses,—
Deriding the King's government and person,—
Arraigning all things royal or religious,—
And seeking—

(Enter Secretary, conducting the Earl of Abergavenny and his daughter, veiled.)

    Sec. *(to Lord Audley.)*   Good, my Lord—

    Audley *(to Hubert).*   A moment's patience!
(Goes to receive Lord Abergavenny. Lady unveils.)

    Aberg. Presuming on old memories of friendship,
I bring an humble suitor to your Grace!

    Audley. Would that some happier prompting had procured me
So sweet a guest!—*(Takes her hand.)*—Sit, gentle lady!

    Lady *(attempting to kneel).*   Nay, Sir,
It is my knee must greet ye!
(Exit Sec.)

    Audley.   Pray ye rise,

And take your place beside us. By God's will,
You're come to hear,—ay!—and belike to answer,
Strange pleading 'gainst your lord!—There are some here
Pretend that by disloyal exhortations
He doth pervert his vassals from allegiance
Unto their sovereign lord;—enkindling thus
Rebellion in the land.
    Lady *(starting up)*. *Who* dares assert it?—
If ever England had a son devoted,
Life,—spirit,—fortunes, to her welfare,—nay,
If ever human heart throbb'd with affection
For home and fatherland,—'tis Dacre's!— Show me
The arch-detractor, who, in his misfortunes,
Hath heap'd this shame upon his head!—
    Audley *(pointing to Hubert)*.   Behold him!
Pelham of Laughton.
    Lady *(with energy)*.   *You*, Sir!—*you*, who shar'd
Our hospitality,—sat by our hearth,—
Clasp'd hand in hand with us, in seeming friendship,—
You, Sir,—of gentle lineage and estate,—
You, to turn eaves'-dropper, and play the spy,
Like some poor lackey!—Oh! I pity ye—
That have this fair exterior,—yet so lack
The inward graces of a gentleman!—
    Audley *(to the privy Councillors)*. You hear, Sirs?
    First Priv. Coun. Ay, my Lord!—a woman's railing,
But no *disproof!*—
    Lady.   What proof is it ye seek?—
What single hour of Dacre's life gives colour
To such impeachment?—At what time of day
Answer'd he grudgingly the royal summons
For impost,—levy,—tax,—benevolence?—
Money or men o'er which he held control,
Were more the King's than *his!*—
(Lowers her tone.)   I blush to be
So poor an advocate:—but trust me, Sirs,
There's not a voice among our people,—not
A man of mark (saving yon Judas there),
Among our worthies,—but proclaims as loudly

The innocence of Dacre of the South!—

(Enter Secretary, two Vergers, and two Macers, bearing the Seals, &c.)

Sec. My Lord! th'assembled court awaits your presence,
All is prepar'd.

Audley. 'Tis surely not till noon
The trial should come on?—

First Priv. Coun.   Mid-day hath struck!—
We wait but to escort your lordship!—

Audley *(to the Lady).*   Madam!
Comfort be with ye!—Should it please ye bide
The issue here (where tidings good or evil
Will promptlier reach ye)—

Lady.   Oh! my gracious Lord!—
Let me attend ye, forth.—Find some poor nook
Where mine own ears will teach the fearful lesson
it may be mine to learn!—

Aberg.   Thou'lt not have strength
To wrestle with the hearing.—

Lady.   Trust me,—trust me!

Audley *(as he is going, aside to Abergavenny).*
Dispose of her discreetly. Fear the worst.
Black witness hath been borne, and Dacre's fortunes
Weigh down his cause to *death!*— Heav'n's peace be with her!
(To Hubert, as he is going.) For you, Sir, I have words in private!—
On!—

(Exit Audley, in procession with Vergers, Macers, Privy Councillors, Hubert, Secretary, &c.)

Aberg. *(to his daughter.)* Pr'ithee, let's home!

Lady *(wildly).*   Henceforth I have *no* home.
I read my husband's sentence in his looks!—
My home's where Dacre is,—the Tower to-day,—
The grave to-morrow.—Nay, deny it not!—

Aberg. My child, my child!—

Lady.   Bring me to where he is—
Let me behold him;—let me hear him plead
Against these chafferers in blood;—or dread
The desperation of a grief like mine!—

Aberg. Be calm—

Lady.   So thou content my pray'r!—

Aberg.   Then forth—

I have thy promise?—

Lady.   To my Lord,—to Dacre!

(Exeunt.)

Scene III.

Westminster Hall. Yeomen of the Guard ranged in line on either side, keeping back a crowd of spectators.—In the centre, a tribunal, consisting of Peers and Privy Councillors, seated at a long table; Lord Audley presiding as High Steward. Secretaries, Vergers, Macers, Ushers, Criers, Advocates, &c.&c.

Audley. Summon the prisoner!—

Crier.   Ho! Thomas Fiennes,—

Lord Dacre of the South and peer of England,

Come into court!—

(Enter Lord Dacre preceded by two Yeomen of the Guard, and followed by the Lieutenant of the Tower. A Verger marshals him to the left of the table. A murmur is heard among the spectators.)

First Spect. A goodly gentleman!—

Second Spect.   A noble bearing!—

Crier. Silence in court!—The Lord High Steward ariseth.

Audley. My Lord!—you're summoned here to be instructed

In the finding of a court specially called

By the King's pleasure.—With all diligence

These gentlemen, his Councillors, have heard

The deposition of your witnesses,—

The pleading of your counsel.—The result

Accredits fatally the dread arraignment

Preferr'd by the King's Advocate.—My Lord!—

Ere we proceed to judgment, I invite ye

To show some mitigating plea wherefore

Sentence of death be not recorded.—Speak!—

(Enter, among the crowd, Abergavenny and the Lady.)

Dacre. Is such the vaunted wisdom of your laws?—

Is this your equity?—Am I denounced

On a vague charge, by secret witnesses?—
Confront these slanderers with me face to face—
Or bid me not attempt their refutation.—

    Audley. The evidence hath been maturely weigh'd:
So stands the law, by the King's grace propounded,
By parliament confirm'd.—You know th' arraignment.

    Dacre. The charge is "MURDER!"—I reply—"NOT GUILTY!"—
But in a cause pre-judged, pre-sentenced thus,—
What purports my defense?—

    First Priv. Coun.   The court hath heard
Its witnesses substantiate a confession
Made freely by your Lordship—

    Dacre *(sorrowfully).*   My *confession!*—

    First Priv. Coun. Such self-incrimination brings with it
A weight most mighty!—

    Dacre.   Ay! to willing minds!—
If there be none among ye present here
Who can conceive the warmth of self-devotion
Impelling friend for *friend* to put in peril
His life and fortunes,—I have more compassion
For you and yours, than for the plight I stand in!
(A murmur of approbation among the spectators.)
Vain was my purpose:—ye have ta'en your victim!
But let your laws which doomed the life of Mansel,
Protect at least my plea of innocence!—

    First Priv. Coun. My Lord! the court's solemnity admits
No trifling with its records:—your confession
Is in our minutes duly noted!—

    Dacre.   Sir!
To a tribunal more august—more solemn
I lift my hand as guiltless.
               GOD OF HEAVEN!
Hear me and judge me,—or incline the hearts
Within thy rule and governance, to justice!—

    First Priv. Coun. He doth blaspheme the King!

    Dacre.   *Thou* dost blaspheme
The King of Kings,—thou,—who wouldst desecrate
The throne, which is His temple, with a crime.—

    Spectators. A noble gentleman!—

Crier. Silence in court—

Audley. Your Lordship's presence at the scene of bloodshed
Is incontestable!—

Dacre *(contemptuously).* Ay!—*Who* attests it?—
The victim?—

Audley. Most sufficient witnesses,
Upon whose word—

Lady *(bursting through the guard.)* My Lord!—we have a wit-
ness,
A living witness,—an unquestion'd witness,—
Will prove his *absence!*—

First Priv. Coun. Some accomplice!—

Lady. No!—
The widow of the dead.—Ye will not surely
Refute the victim's widow?—Oh! my Lords—
If ye've no faith in human virtue, do not
Deny its frailties.—Would *revenge* so sleep
As screen the murderer of her husband?—

First Priv. Coun. Ay,—
If lucre tempted her!—

Lady *(with energy).* It tempts *thyself!*—
The crime of Dacre's writ in the broad lands
Ye hunger for, not in th' offended law.
Were he as poor of pelf as thou of soul
He had been free to range the world, as thou
To wreak these persecutions on his head!—

First Priv. Coun. What makes this woman here?
(To Vergers.) Remove her.

Dacre *(taking her into his arms).* Nay!—
She shall offend no further! *(To the court.)* Lo! your sentence!
Defense were waste of words,—my cause is judg'd.—

Sec *(aside to Audley, giving a paper).* My gracious Lord,—
dispatches from the King.
*(During the following speech, Audley casts his eye over the paper,
communicates with the tribunal, and the Privy Councillors
unanimously hold up their left hands.)*

Dacre *(to his Lady).* Exert thy fortitude,—all hope is past!—

Lady *(weeping distractedly).* Oh! no—oh! sport not thus with
destiny!

Think of thy wife,—thy children!—In *thy* being
Our welfare hath its life,—and dies with thee!

    Crier.   Silence in court!—The Lord High Steward ariseth.

    Audley.   The finding of the court is "GUILTY!"

    Spectators.   How?—

    Audley.   Its sentence—"DEATH!"—

    Dacre *(looking up).*   Hear him, avenging Heav'n!
Of this, as of all else, absolve my soul!—

    Audley.   The pleasure of the King is that the prisoner
Be from this Hall conducted to the Tower,—
Thence—to the block!—

    Dacre.   Oh! wise and righteous sentence
Disposing of a human life, as 'twere
A trinket granted by the breath of Kings
To be resum'd at will!—
(To the Court.)   Your jurisprudence
Hath lessons still to learn, and to forget!
Oh! be they taught by the triumphant cry
Of an enfranchis'd nation, giving thanks
For a renewal of its ancient charters.—
Justice is for the FREE!—The hoary heads
A despot's foot hath trampled, forfeit thence
Their god-like gifts of mind,—as dungeon damps
Quench the pure light of Truth!—
(A murmur.)   All is not lost!—
A day will come when Britain's reeking soil,
Wet with the blood of martyrs, shall send forth
An emblem for the worship of mankind!—
Why,—why—withhold a victim more or less
Whose death may fertilize that glorious growth?
Lo! on that day, the spirits of the just
Shall hover o'er the triumph of the land
And bless the sufferings that avail'd her cause!—
(Murmur renewed.)

    Audley.   Break up the Court.
(To the Lieutenant of the Tower.) Conduct the prisoner forth!
(Lieutenant of the Tower approaches, and attempts to disengage Lord Dacre from the arms of his wife.)

    Lady.   No, ne'er to part again till *death!*—You'd not

Divide us on the eve of such a day?—*(Struggles.)*

Audley *(to Aberg).* My Lord!—I do beseech ye, claim your daughter—
These struggles serve to aggravate her griefs!—

Aberg. *(tearing her away.)* My miserable child!—Resist not!—
(As Dacre is marched off under guard of Yeomen and Lieutenant of the Tower, the Lady escapes from her father, and drags herself on her knees after Lord Dacre.)

Lady. No!—
Oh! no,—they shall not part us,—never,—never!

END OF ACT IV.

Act V. Scene I.

Closet of the Lord Chancellor.

(Enter Lord Audley, and seats himself at the table, Lady Anne Fiennes following him; Secretary intercepting her at the door.)

    Sec. Lady, it may not be:—make me not seem
Regardless of your tears.—His lordship's hour
Of audience hath expir'd.—
    Anne *(putting him aside).*   I came not, Sir,
To sue for pity, but to claim a right!—
Will the King's delegate withhold a *right?*—
    Audley *(looking round).* So peremptory?—*(To Sec.)* Say! what
suitor's this?—
    Sec. The noble sister of Lord Dacre!—
    Anne.   Ay,
My Lord,—his *sister;*—with a holier title
Henceforth invested,—Walter Mansel's widow:—
Wife for an hour,—widow for evermore!—
The rigour of your laws hath sacrificed
The lover of my youth.—Take heed, take heed,
Another victim reek not on your altars;—
Or, when the axe falls on my noble brother,—
My brave, my glorious Dacre,—Heav'n itself
May deal its retributions on a land
Defil'd by deeds so ruthless!—
    Audley.   May its mercy
Grant you the grace of resignation!—
    Anne.   How,—
Resign myself to yield the young, the good,
The happy—to a death of shame?—My Lord,—
Patience becomes a crime where tyrants reign!—
I could but be resign'd were Dacre's doom
An act of justice.—
    Audley.   Lady, the decree
Of an august tribunal of the land—
    Anne *(impatiently, taking a paper from her bosom).*
I have a paper here, which I'd fain read—

But 'twere as though the voices of the dead
Spake in my ears again.—*(To Sec.)* Pray ye, Sir, take it!
'Twas writ by Mansel in his dying hour,—
Sign'd by his sad companions.—They are gone
To their accompt, my Lord,—gone to confront
A Judge whom not e'en crime would dare accost
With falsehood on its lips.—

   Sec. *(having looked over the paper.)*   An attestation,
That when the fatal blow was struck, Lord Dacre
Was absent from the spot.

   Audley.   The plea is naught:
Our laws expressly hold that fellowship
Pending a lawless act, incriminates
The whole assemblage.

   Anne *(sternly).* Sir, no human law
Hath the forethoughted wisdom to contemplate
All shades of circumstance.—This stands alone!—
For justice sake, beseech you, then, recite
Unto the King these words of dying men:—
Tell him four human lives are gone already,
To avenge that single death,—*four* happy lives;—
Tell him, among our vaunted English nobles,
Not one so towardly—so full of promise—
As Dacre.—Tell him how our grandsire serv'd him
In field and council.—He should know't, methinks;—
But kings have memory only for their wrongs,
None for our virtues.—Tell him, in the wars
Of Lancaster, the substance of our house—
Its blood,—its breath,—were lavish'd on his cause.
And should his hard heart falter,—*then,* my Lord,
Bid him take all,—wealth, honours, fiefs, endowments,—
But leave us *life,*— leave us my brother's *life,*—
And we will kneel, as for an act of mercy!—

   Audley. Are you *advis'd* in this?
   Anne.   Advis'd by love
Past all computing of mere worldly dross!—

   Audley. Lord Dacre (think ye), might be mov'd to tender
Such an alternative?—

   Anne. My brother?—Never!—

He'd scorn a life was bought and bargain'd for,
Like some poor abject thing of merchandise.—
But why consult him?—Oh! my Lord, my Lord,—
You've access to the King,—you've influence, courage,
Authority:—*decree* this, and 'tis done.—
Do not turn from me,—do not!—Clinging thus
Unto thy knees, new hopes revive my soul!—
That venerable brow brings back to me
My sainted grandsire's presence. Good my Lord!
'Tis anguish makes me wild and petulant.
But now, I was a merry thoughtless girl,—
Sunshine around me;—not a care or fear
Had touch'd my soul;—and lo! this withering curse
Fell on me in the brightness of my joy
Making my springtime, winter.—Pity me!—
    Audley *(moved).* Ay!—from my heart of hearts!—
    Anne.   Hast thou a daughter?—
Such as my grief is, hers might be.—King Henry
Dooms to the block to-day who yesternight
Drank of his cup of gladness.—Thine own child
May plead as *I* am pleading!—
    Audley.   Gentle lady,—
My good intent is yours;—but count not rashly
Upon my power.—The signatures I hold,
Back'd by your earnest eloquence, *might* move
The King.—At noon, his Grace will reach Whitehall;
Await his coming forth:—*I* will be there
To second ye.—
    Anne.   Alas! my gracious Lord,—
Two hours ere noon, my brother dies:—so runs
The warrant.
    Audley.   Fear not!—a brief power of respite
Rests with my office.—Go in peace. *(Leads her out.)*
                            I pray ye—
Warn not the prisoner—'twere a cruel kindness
To shake life's parting sands with fruitless hope.
    Anne. And should *no* respite come?
    Audley.   Address your pray'rs
To Heav'n:—my purpose will have fail'd.

Anne *(about to kneel).*   My Lord!

Audley. No thanks;—as yet my zeal hath nought avail'd ye!
At noon.—*Remember!*—
(Exit Anne.)   Now, to Henry's feet!—
THOU! by whose mighty will the prophet's hand
Wrung forth from Horeb's rock the living waters,
Be with me in my pleading!—GOD of mercy!
Prosper my intercession with the King!
(Exit.)

Scene II.

A paved court in the Tower of London. At the further extremity, an archway, through which a train of ecclesiastics, bearing a silver cross, is seen departing. In front a dungeon, with a grated door; near it, a stone bench. The archway guarded by Yeomen.

(Enter from the dungeon, the Lieutenant of the Tower, followed by Lord Dacre, habited in mourning.)

Dacre. Thanks!—'twas a peevish thought,—a captive's dream!
I wish'd, in my last day of earthly thralldom,
To look unshackled on the glorious sun,
And breathe the summer atmosphere.—I thank thee!
(Looks round.)
I'm happier here.—Yon chamber weigh'd me down
With its chill vault-like vapours.—

Lieut.   Noble Sir!—
Your soul's at ease:—the comforts of the church
Have breathed a balmier influence on your spirit.
The smiles shed on ye by yon shriving priests
As on a son that honour'd them,—reveal
The worthiness of your condition.—Sir!
Were words of gladness for a day like this,
I'd say, "be of good cheer!—'tis *well* with thee!"

Dacre. Thou wouldst say ill!—Exulting thoughts are not
For erring man upon his day of doom!
For *thee* I've other communing.—I pr'ythee,
When the rude crowd press jestingly, anon,

To gaze on my remains,—(for press they *will*—
The lord that dies a felon's death must meet
Each ignominious scorn that waits a felon!)—
Shouldst thou amid the city throng detect,
By their grave looks and simpler form of raiment,
Some stragglers from my lands of Hurstmonceux,
Come on a pilgrimage of love to look
Upon their master,—let the knaves draw near.—
They lov'd me well, good souls!—no common bond
Of vassalship united us;—their faces,
Were as the faces of familiar friends
When I went forth amidst them.—Let them come!

  Lieut. Your wishes shall be laws to me.—
  Dacre.   Among them,
There may be one,—if grief have not bow'd down
His hoary head,—will ask to press my hand.
(Sad comfort for his age, that clay-cold hand!)
Pr'ythee indulge him:—'tis the truest creature!—
In infancy he tended me;—in manhood
His love was more a father's than an hireling's.
It used to grieve me that he would not live
To bless my manhood.—Lo! he hath survived
To weep upon my grave.—Thou'lt see him cared for?—

  Lieut. As 'twere a *friend,* my Lord!—Th' ascending sun
Warns me a sadder duty is at hand.
'Twas at this hour, methinks,—

  Dacre.   My wife!—my child!—
Think ye because I nam'd them not, their coming
Was absent one sick moment from my soul?—

(Enter, through the archway, the Earl of Abergavenny.)

  Dacre *(greeting him).* Faithful unto thy trust!
  Aberg. *(embracing him.)*   Alas!
  Dacre.   My *wife?*—

  Aberg. Grief hath so wreck'd her poor distracted spirit
That scarce a trace remains of happier days.
No word escapes her lips,—no tear her eyes;—
But like the calm following some midnight storm,
A deadly stillness shows the tempest's force:
Thy voice perchance may wake some touch of reason.

(Enter the Lady Mary, in mourning, led by her little son, haggard but calm.)

Child. It is my father!—See!—*(Exit Lieut.)*

Lady. Thou hast no father!—

(Abergavenny takes her hand and leads her forward.)

Aberg. Behold! 'tis Dacre.—

Lady *(having examined him intently).* Ay! in sooth in sooth,
It *is* my husband.—Truant!—what hath kept thee
So long away?—Come—let us rest awhile.

(Draws him to the stone bench, and sits beside him.)

My heart's so weary.—*(Looks round.)* How is this?—what means
This place,—this dreary place?—

Aberg. Alas! her reason
Is lost, unless relieving tears restore her!—

Lady. Oh! how unlike the home we used to dwell in.
No flowers,—no happy faces!—

Dacre *(with solemn earnestness).* Blessed wife!
Look firmly upon *mine!*—This is the Tower—
A prison—Queens have died in it ere now!—
And *I* must die here, Mary!—(Dost thou mark me?)
Dacre, whom thou so lov'st, must perish here,
By shameful death.

Lady *(wildly).* Ay!—Dacre,—but not *thou!*

(Abergavenny retires with the child weeping to the background.)

Dacre. Dost thou remember nothing of a grief
Fell on us in the fullness of our joy?—

Lady. I do!—Was't not a trial?—Thou wert with me,
And we beheld a murderer judg'd to death.—
It was a direful sight!—

Dacre. A direr still
Will chance anon:—the executioner
Must take the life so dear to thee.—Thy husband
Dies in an hour,—Mary—thy husband *dies!*—
This kiss, love, is a parting one.

Lady *(vacantly).* I know it!—
I was brought hither for a last farewell.—
But what that word farewell imports, I know not.
Thou look'st so sad—so stern,—and all around
So gloomy—Press me nearer to thy side!—

I'm full of fears, beloved,—I'm full of fears.
My heart throbs as't would burst—What means all this?
    Dacre. Listen!—
(He takes her hand; she looks anxiously into his face.)
                  There'll come a time hereafter, love,
When all thou hear'st this day,—this heavy day,—
Will, like a strain of recollected music,
Steal back into thy soul!—I'd fain have had
Some parting pledge to give thee,—some poor token
Of our last interview. They've ta'en all from me!—
Yet one thing stays within my rifled casket,
Worthless in common eyes, beyond all price
In those of wedded love.—
(Takes two tresses of hair from his bosom.)
                    Behold! dost thou
Remember this?—'Tis the first tress of hair
Shred from our first-born's head:—soft silken tress,
Fair as the hopes that smil'd upon his birth!—
(Kisses it.)
How pale thy cheek was when thou gav'st it me—
Young mother of an hour,—and when I thank'd thee,
How pour'd thy tears down!—
(She clasps her hands, bewildered.)
                  Here's another braid,—
Thy own bright hair,—thy maiden gift to me!—
The flowers it binds fell from thy bosom, love,
(Was it an omen?)—on thy marriage-day.—
They're wither'd now.—I've worn them next my heart
As I've worn thee!—When our young son shall grow
To manhood—give him these,—a sad bequeathment
From his lost father.—Bid him look on them
Whene'er he'd call to mind the sacredness
Of woman's love.—For in this parting hour,
Mary, when all earth's vanities are past,
These still retain an empire's worth,—attesting
Th' eternal treasure of thy tenderness!—
(She falls weeping on his neck.)
Tears?—let me kiss them off—my own—my wife!
(Abergavenny places the child by her side.)

Lady. Oh! Dacre, Dacre!—why hast thou recall'd me
To the overwhelming tide of agony
Now rushing on my soul.—Yes! we must part—
There's scarce a moment in our life of love
Left to us now.—
(Weeps on his shoulder.)
(Re-enter Lieutenant of the Tower, conducting six Privy Councillors.)
Lieut.   My Lord!—a deputation
From the King's grace.—These noble gentlemen
Have special message for your privacy.—
(Dacre consigns his wife to the arms of her father.)
Dacre. I yield her to your charge:—be careful o'er her.
I will rejoin ye yonder;—bear her in.
*(Points to the dungeon. Exeunt, through the grated door, Abergaven-
ny, Lady, and child.)*
Now, Sirs,—your pleasure?—
(Exit Lieut.)
First Priv. Coun.   From our Lord, the King!—
His Majesty, out of his gracious mercy,
Compassionating the dire extremity
You stand in, signifies by *us* an act
Of royal clemency.
Dacre.   Of *clemency?*
First Priv. Coun. If, by the full confession of your guilt
You ratify the justice of your sentence,
Our sovereign lord hath purpose to commute
To forfeiture of peerage and estate
The penalty of death!—
Dacre.   Confess my *guilt?*—
Ye surely mock me, Sirs.—Is good renown
So little worth, as to be bought and sold
For a poor shred of parchment, or a birthright
Of paltry acres?—Oh! ye deeply wrong
The King ye serve, to talk of such conditions.
Second Priv. Coun. We talk of *death,* my Lord!—*no* thing to
mock at!—
A death of shame,—which you may thus escape.
Dacre. Rather a *death,* Sir, than a *life* of shame!—
The honour of my name's a heritage

I owe unsullied to my children's children
As by my sires it was bequeath'd to *me!*—
Those poor estates, too, *(Ironically.)* which ye rate so highly,
Are derivations to my son,—a child
So dear to me, that e'en his mother seems
More precious when he's smiling in her arms!—
You'll say—(for ye are men of little scruple!)
That, whether Dacre live or die, the King
Will seize on his possessions.—Sirs!—*I* look
Beyond the passing time.—The King is aged.
A young and hopeful prince succeeds.—(God save him!)
And youth and innocence upon the throne
Foreshow a reign of mercy.—I appeal
To *him* and to posterity for justice!—
Revel who may in Dacre's forfeit lands,
My children will hereafter sit beneath
The trees this hand hath planted.—

                       Tell King Henry
Such was my answer!—

    Second Priv. Coun. Be advis'd, my Lord!—
He who rejects the proffer'd means of grace
Is a self-seeking murderer.—

    Dacre.   Thrice guilty
Is he who slays the honour of a name
Unstain'd for ages!—Pray ye, Sirs, relieve me
From thought of worldly cares at such a time.
(Enter Lady Anne, wildly.)
Sweet sister,—

    Anne. Ha! no respite yet—*no* respite?—
The black array of death around the gates?—
(Dacre embracing her.—To the Privy Councillors.)
My Lords, my Lords! ye see what dear demands
Press on life's closing hour.—Respect my griefs.—

    First Priv. Coun. Once more, rash man, reflect!—

    Dacre.   I have.—Once more,
I say to ye, I am prepar'd for death.—

    First Priv. Coun. You have pronounced your doom.
(Exeunt Privy Councillors, two by two. Dacre accompanies them a few paces.)

Anne *(aside).*   The hours wear on!—
No respite!—Still, to the last fatal moment
There's hope—there's hope.—
(Dacre returns.)   Brother, dear, best of brothers!
Too long I've linger'd from thee:—there was one
Whose parting hours had claims on me.
     Dacre.   My friend!—
Whose early dreams of human love and virtue
Have vanish'd, dewlike, in the morning sun.—
How many yesterdays have thus exhal'd
And brought no morrow:—not a trace—a deed—
To prove the excellence time was maturing
Deep in their silent soul.—Oh! at this hour,
If in my breast one vain regret abide,
'Tis to bequeath no token to the future
Of what I might have been.—
     Anne.   Oh! brother,—brother!
     Dacre.   Dear Mansel!—Thou wert with him in his end—
How died he?—
     Anne.   As a sinful man *should* die,—
Humble, but hopeful:—his whole soul intent
On saving *thee.—(Roll of muffled drum.)*   What means that horrid
sound?
     Dacre.   This is no scene for hearts like thine.—Retire!—
     Anne.   Desert thee?—Never!—
     Dacre.   'Tis no *woman's* duty.—
*(Roll of muffled drum repeated. Re-enter Lieutenant of the Tower.
Lady Anne flies to him and seizes his arm.)*
     Anne.   A message from Lord Audley!—is't not so?—
You come to bring a respite?—
     Lieut.   Gentle lady,
I pray ye, hasten from this fatal spot!   *(Takes her hand.)*
     Anne *(struggling).*   No, no!—There'll be a messenger anon!—
A respite's on the road—'tis *pledged*— 'tis *promis'd!*—
Thou'lt wait its coming?—Ay, thou'lt *wait!*— Man,—man!—
What boots to thee a minute more or less?—
*(Roll of muffled drum repeated. Enter a train of javelin men, and line
the court; vergers, ushers, &c. last the Sheriffs of London.)*
     First Sheriff.   In the King's name!—

　　　　　　　　　　　　　　Deliver to our hands
The body of Sir Thomas Fiennes, Lord Dacre,
That execution may be done on him,
According to the sentence of the law.—
God save King Henry!—
(Roll of muffled drum repeated.)

    Lieut. *(to Dacre.)* Sir! the hour hath struck.
(Lady Anne clings wildly to Dacre.)

    Anne. Monsters!—Ye will not take him from my arms
When I thus *swear* to ye, by all that's holy
In Heav'n or earth, a respite is at hand?—

    Dacre. Sweet sister, spare thyself and me!—The cup
Decreed me must be drain'd unto the lees—
Farewell!—
(Embraces her. Funeral bell sounds, and continues at intervals.)
　　　　　　　　Be to my wife and babes as true
As thou hast been to *me.*
(To the Sheriffs.)— I wait your will!—
(Anne frantic in front, while Dacre takes his place in the procession between two ecclesiastics, followed by the Sheriffs. The javelin-men lead the way. Chanting heard at a distance.)

    Anne. Not ye?—oh! agony,—oh! tardy wretch,
That loiterest by the way,—'twill be too late!—
(As the bell sounds, she buries her face in her hands on one knee. The procession moves slowly. When Lord Dacre has disappeared through the archway, the choristers chant "De Profundis." Lady Mary and her children rush from the dungeon.)

    Lady. Where is my husband?— *(A minute gun.)*
　　　　　　　　　　　　Ha! that maddening sound!
Where—where is Dacre?—

    Anne.　　　　With the King of Kings!—
Gone,—MURDERED!—
(Snatches the children, and presses her hands on their heads.)
　　　　　　　　Orphans!—to your knees, and pray!—

(The curtain falls.)

Appendix A

THE OLD OAK CHEST

or,

The Smuggler's Son & Robber's Daughter

A Melo Drama

In 2 Acts

THE ONLY EDITION CORRECTLY MARKED BY PERMISSION
FROM THE PROMPTER'S BOOK.
To which is added,
A DESCRIPTION OF THE COSTUMES-CAST OF CHARACTERS
THE WHOLE OF THE STAGE BUSINESS
SITUATIONS-ENTRANCES-EXITS-PROPERTIES, AND
DIRECTIONS.
AS PERFORMED AT THE
LONDON THEATRES

EMBELLISHED WITH A PORTRAIT OF MR. DAVIDGE, AS
TINOCO.

LONDON:
PRINTED AND PUBLISHED BY JOHN DUNCOMBE
10, MIDDLE ROW, HOLBORN

DRAMATIS PERSONAE

Count Lanfranco	Mr. Montgomery
Almanza	Mr. Gale
Henrico di Rosalva	Mr. Rowbotham
Nicholas de Lasso	Mr. Porteus
Paulo de Lasso	Mr. E. L. Lewis
Tinoco de Lasso	Mr. Davidge
Rodolph	Mr. Mortimer
Shabrico	Mr. Elsgood
Rufus	Mr. J. George
Conrade	Mr. Saunders
Memmo	Mr. Smith
Pietro	Mr. H. George
Adriana	Miss Watson
Roda	Mrs. Davidge
Florian	Master Meyers

Scene—Mountainous part of Spain near the Coast.

Time—that of Representation.

COSTUME:

Lanfranco—Spanish shape with cloak; russet boots; black hat and plumes; gauntlets and sword; large cloak for disguise.

Almanza—Purple tunic; tights and boots; sword, &c. large cloak over; bandage, slouch hat, and stick.

Henrico—Blue tunic; tights; boots and spurs; hat and plumes; sword, large cloak.

Tinoco—Red jacket; braces; grey tights, shoes and belt—2nd dress, Friar's gown and beads—3rd, Old woman's dress, mob cap, & stick

Paulo—Light grey tunic; tights; boots, and round cap.

Rodolph—Flesh arm and legs; bear skin over his shoulders; large boots; belt.

Nicholas—Hatcher's dress.

Shabrico—Heavy robber's shape, breast plate, flesh arms and legs; gauntlets, boots, belt; black hat and plumes, large cloak.

Rufus—Similar to Shabrico's—not so good—2nd, a skeleton dress.

Smugglers—Like Nicholas. Robbers—Various Robber's dresses.

THE OLD OAK CHEST

Act I. Scene I.

A Romantic Country, with the Entrance of a Cave—On the left a Tree, to which is attached this Inscription—"Ten Thousand Ducats Reward for the proscribed Almanza."— On the opposite side a bramble bush.

(Music.— Adriana appears at the mouth of the Cave, and cautiously advances.)

Adriana. All is silent—not a breath disturbs the leaves—the veil of twilight dims all around—surely my dear Almanza may venture forth! What a day of horror have we passed in the constant fear of being discovered. *(Sees inscription.)* Ah! that proscription! that fatal proscription! doubtless the whole country is placarded with the same. Almanza must not see it—it will urge him to madness—I must persuade him 'tis as yet too light to venture forth without the bandage o'er his brow. Yes, still must the disguise of the blind and aged mendicant conceal the brave Almanza—still as his daughter must his wretched wife bear taunts of every rude kind.

(Almanza appears at the Cave's mouth.)

Almanza. Adriana! is all safe?

Adr. My love, no, I hear a rustling among the bushes, concealment is again requisite. *(Music.—They conceal, and Tinoco crawls yawning, from the bush..)*

Tino. Well, the saints be praised, I've had a famous nap. Egad, I was cooped in my cupboard like an owl in an ivy-bush, watching my prey, who I expect ere long will sally forth from yonder cave. Well, Tinoco, honest Tinoco, thou art allowed to be the adroitest lad at cheating the people, of all Iberia—now if thou canst but smuggle the grand prize thou hast in view into our depot in these mountains, it will prove the richest cargo countrabanded thou ever conveyed safely into port. Ah, my brother appears! Well, my little crotchet, how are you?

(Enter Paulo, L. H. U. S.)

Paulo. What, Tinoco! rough and rare, Tinoco; how are you?

Tino. Cheerly, cheerly, but where stroll you at this the hour of eve—come you here in hopes of meeting with your gentle brother?

Paulo. No, truly, I come in hopes of meeting my angelic Roda: she has been to the town to-day, and I would fain see her sheltered in her father's cot.

Tino. Aye, that way your wishes bend—now give me a good keg of brandy—that's a special medicine, and makes my voice so strong: every one to his calling; you prefer the peaceful vocation of wine dresser, while I glory in the hair-breadth escapes and dangers attached to the life of a smuggler: good—every one to his calling.

Paulo.	Give me a cottage in a vale.
Tino.	Give me a vessel in full sail!
Paulo.	Give me a calm and tranquil soul!
Tino.	Give me a breeze and flowing bowl.
Paulo.	With a tink-a-ting ting, when at evening I stray,
	While Philomel warbles so sweet on the spray.
Tino.	With a tink-a-ting ting; when the docks are at rest,
	This is the warbler that pleases me best.

(Producing brandy key.)

Paulo.	Give me companions free from follow.
Tino.	Give me a set of dogs that's jolly.
Paulo.	Give me contentment, lasting joys,
	With a ting-a-ting ting &c.
Tino.	Give me bustle, fun, and noise,
	With a ting-a-ting ting &c.

Tino. Well, one word more and I'm off. Wilt thou meet us at the head quarters in the forest? I shall have a prize with me, or I am much mistaken.

Paulo. A prize! what do you mean?

Tino. The Count Almanza, a rich prize too—ten thousand ducats, boy.

Paulo. How! would you, Tinoco, close the doors of a prison upon him who set thy father free from one. But say, is the brave Almanza in thy power?

Tino. No! but he will ere midnight, I take it; for which purpose have I toiled since the burning of his castle, at which, if I mistake not, thou wert present, and ran away by the light of the flames, without rendering the least assistance: where was thy gratitude then little Paulo?

Paulo. Oh! my deeds will best speak for themselves.

Tino. And so will mine, for I swear to use every stratagem to secure Almanza; while the last four-and-twenty hours I've been a Jew, a Smuggler, a fat Friar, and an old woman . . . but I'll entrap him.

Paulo. Not if I can help it. But we'll meet again at midnight; but remember, the pass-word is . . .

Tino. Almanza! *(They retire 2nd E. L. H.)*

(Adriana re-enters from Cave.)

Adr. All is silent. Now we may in safety venture forth. Come forth Almanza!

(Almanza enters from Cavern.)

Alma. Is it not yet dark, my love?

Adr. No! though the clouds of evening are gathering fast. I pray you keep the bandage o'er thy brow—we are near the town, and many persons are abroad; caution is necessary for the persecuted wandered.

Alma. Persecuted! basely persecuted!

Adr. Think not of it—conscious rectitude must bear thee up till we escape thy enemy's persecution.

Alma. Escape! wretch that I am to cherish such a thought! madness ruled the hour when I fled prison—but 'tis not yet too late, at my Sovereign's feet I'll seek for justice and mercy; that resolution formed, Almanza is himself again—*(Throws bandage away.)*

Adr. Nay, then, behold the cruel malice of thy foes!—ere thou couldst gain thy Sovereign's presence, enemies will shroud thee in the iron grasp of death. No, Almanza! thou must still skulk, day by day, in caves and darksome holes.

Alma. Thou art my only advisor, my only friend—do as thou wilt.

Adr. Let me then replace the bandage o'er thy brow—*(She ties on the bandage.)* Come, Almanza! cheerly, cheerly—I'll warrant all shall yet be well—this way! this way!

(As they are retiring, Tinoco is heard singing—they halt and listen.)

SONG. *(Tinoco, in the distance.)*

There was a lass of Arrogan,
   No such lass as she;
Of wit, and wealth, and paragon—
   Lovers she had three:
The first was a lawyer bluff.
The second a churchman gruff—
The third a jolly young sailor, who'd never take a huff;
He wooed her and sued her wherever she mov'd,
Faint heart by fair lady was never approv'd.

Alma. The rudeness of the song bespeaks some muleteer, or market peasant, from whom we may obtain some useful information.

(Song continued as Tinoco draws near.)

Now says this lass of Arrogan,
   True as true could be—
My brass you reckon the paragon,
   Nought you care for me.
The lawyer look big and bluff,
The churchman he answer'd gruff—
But the jolly young sailor would never take a huff
He wooed her and sued her wherever she mov'd,
Faint heart by fair lady was never approv'd.

(Tinoco enters whilst singing the last verse.)

Adr. Pray you, Signor?—

Tino. Pray! aye, that I do—on Saint days.

Adr. Can'st thou set us in the way to Cordova? we would fain seek a lodging there, for we are wondrous weary.

Tino. The town is full of troops; Lanfranco himself is there; each avenue is guarded—for Lanfranco has a suspicion that the proscribed General will attempt to pass the town to-night.

Alma. Needs there so much precaution for a man, alone, defenseless and unarmed.

Tino. Go to, go to! you know but little of him, or you would not ask that question. The whole nation, if they dared, wou'd rise in his defense, seeing Lanfranco, his inveterate enemy, has been his chief accuser; however, the Governor will take care there shall be no rescue—he will make sure work, depend—if Almanza pops his head into the town to-night, I'll wager mine they pop it off tomorrow.

(Adriana, with an exclamation of alarm, faints, and falls in Almanza's arms.)

Alma. Adriana, my wife—my child, I mean: see, she's faint with weariness—in yonder crag is water—fetch it, stranger—in mercy fetch it?

Tino. Pshaw, Signior! water won't do—give her a drop out of this keg—special good brandy.

Alma. Nay, nay, water would be best.

Tino. Aye, mixed with brandy—that's what I always take when I feel myself faint.

Adr. *(reviving.)* Whither shall we go? which way shall we turn? cruel, thoughtless man! you've removed the bandage.

Tino. What, is the Signior troubled with a weakness in his eyes?

Alm. Yes, yes, yes.

Tino. More's the pity—now I am near sighted: for all I stand so close to you, I swear I can't discern one single feature in thy father's face.

Adr. Then we are safe! we are safe!

Tino. Safe! I don't think one's safe in these mountains after night-fall—it's old Nick's wolf-walk, my little lamb; however if you will share my humble resting-place I can assure you a safe and certain asylum till tomorrow; come, follow me, and you shall be heartily welcome.

Alma. *(crosses to L. H.)* Thank you, friend—thank you.

Adr. *(aside to Almanza.)* Do not follow him! marked you not those dreadful weapons in his belt?

Tino. Why do you hesitate! why, zounds! you could not be more alarmed were you the proscribed General.—Alarmed! hold, hold! I do him wrong—Almanza was never alarmed; were he here, thus would he argue:—"I may be better off by taking this honest Lad's advice—should I go farther, I may, perchance, fare worse." Then I should say to him, just as I now do to you—"Brave Almanza! there are hearts in Spain so devoted to your interest, they would shed their best blood to protect you:— follow me, General," I should say to him, "and I will lead you to a place in which you may deride pursuit and bid defiance to your enemies;" then I should present him with a brace of pistols; *(Gives him a brace of pistols.)* take care of them, they are loaded with ball; and I should conclude by saying—"Almanza, if I betray, or fail in aught I've promised, then shoot me through the head at once, and rid the world of a deceitful villain."

Alma. Enough! — lead on!

(Music.—They depart L. H.)

Scene II.

Skirts of the Forest, at night-fall.

(Enter Paulo and Roda R. H.)

Roda. I pray you, Paulo, what detained my father in your vineyard yester-even?

Paulo. We were discoursing on love and marriage—and he said, when a young man, like me, had a snug little cottage to shelter a wife, and means to support her in it, he was either a fool or a knave not to seek one.

Roda.. Well, how like you his advice?

Paulo. So well, that I set out this evening, resolved to offer myself to the first female I should meet with, which is Roda, and I am sure she will not refuse me.

Roda.. You know my heart—yet ere I yield a full consent, I have something to reveal that hangs heavy here.

Paulo. And I have something to communicate that I much fear to impart; but, mark me Roda, should what I now confess cause me the misery of losing them swear that the secret never shall escape thy breast.

Roda. I claim an equal oath—the life of one dearer than my own hangs on it. *(They kneel and swear.)*

Paulo. Roda, you have ever supposed me to be the son of the deceased peasant, Luco; alas! he was only my mother's brother. My father is a smuggler—a most notorious smuggler.

Roda.. Oh, heavens! and do you think so much of that, Paulo! I see we must part—and still I'm bound to tell thee. You take my father for a simple honest woodman—but, alas he is a robber—a most notorious robber.

Paulo. Heavens and earth! a robber!

(Distant thunder is heard.)

Roda. Paulo, do not cast me from you—I am no partner in my parent's crimes, my Paulo.

Paulo. Come to my heart, dear girl, alike in sorrow and in joy—henceforth our fates are one! nay my girl, do not weep,—*(Embracing.)*

Roda. Oh, Paulo! my happiness is now complete, to think the smuggler's son still loves the robber's daughter; but 'tis now time we part—a storm is gathering, and I dare not ask you to my father's cottage—he is too harsh and stern to bid you welcome.

Paulo. Some one approaches—we now must separate! heaven guard my love—good night.

(They retire—Roda, R. H.—Paulo, L. H. The darkness continues to increase.)
(Enter Shabrico and Rufus.)

Shab. Who was that crossed me, e'en now?

Rufus. The peasant, Paulo—a harmless hind, who courts the woodman Rodolph's daughter!

Shab. Rodolph's daughter! and why was that daughter hither brought?

Rufus. She'll not stay long—Rodolph means to marry her off, and send her hence without delay.

Shab. She never shall go hence!

Rufus. Psha, Captain! we are safe enough for her—she's not long been here, and takes her father for what he seems to be, a woodman, and honest woodman—I tell you, Captain, she's a mere child.

Shab. I'll not trust to that. She must to the castle—and as she pleases me, she lives or dies.

Rufus. As you please, Captain—but it must be done unknown to Rodolph; for though a very savage to all human nature else, he loves his daughter as the apple of his eye, and terrible would be his wrath, were he to suspect us.

Shab. Right! Is he acquainted with the secret pass leading from the Old Oak Chest in his cottage to the castle?

Rufus. No! it has not been opened since he joined us.

Shab. Good! through that, the first time Rodolph is abroad, let the girl be conveyed. Look to it quickly.

Rufus. I will; I'll examine the pass to-night.

Shab. Be thine the task to bear away our prize: but night approaches—Lanfranco will soon be here—say, are our disguises ready?

Rufus. Aye—but what need of them—hardy souls, like us, would rather use the dagger's point.

Shab. Shallow fool! would not the cry of blood, so frequent spilt, call forth the cognizance of government, and lead them to our safe retreat, here in the forest. Countenanced by Count Lanfranco, whose sole inheritance it and the castle is—and whilst we aid his daring acts of villainy, and let him share our plunder, safely we may live, robbing whom we list—murder whom we list. Hark! I hear footsteps! give the signal Rufus.— *(He whistles—the signal is answered.)*

Lanfranco *(without).* Shabrico!

Shab. Here!

Lan. Any one else?

Rufus. Yes, Rufus!

(Enter Lanfranco.)

Lan. All's right.

Shab. You are late, my Lord.

Lan. Yes; I was detained in town by information most unwelcome—most infernal.

Shab. Indeed! How so?

Lan. Almanza's friends have gained a pardon for him which every moment is expected to arrive. But mark me, Almanza or the pardon must be mine to night; he still is lurking in the mountains I am convinced, for each pass is too well guarded to admit of escape.

Shab. It is wonderful; repeatedly have we had him within our very grasp, and still he has eluded us.

Rufus. It strikes me, Captain, that audacious smuggler, Nicholas de Lasso, favours him.

Shab. I have thought so too, Rufus; for the night Almanza's castle was in flames, many of his band were there.

Rufus. Aye, and when we sought for plunder, all worth taking had been carried off.

Shab. Except his wife, whom I seized according to your Lordship's orders, when a hand of Iron felled me to the earth, and carried off my prey, crying, "Thus I pay my debt of gratitude to brave Almanza."

Lan. And suffered you this, and yet not seized on them?

Shab. Hold, hold, my Lord! you know not whom we have to deal with; they are men of desperate manner,—like ourselves, lawless and bold, we hold no intercourse but fear each other—but since they dare to throw the gauntlet down, why we'll oppose them; nay, blood to blood—we'll ferret out the General if he burrows with these smugglers; this night we'll about it.

Lan. Hark! heard you not distant voices borne upon the breeze? Let us disperse; at the castle meet the gang, and there settle our proceedings.

Shab. Hold, my Lord, we must not part without disguise—to-night you must be one of us, and play a forest spectre. Rufus! our midnight habits. *(Rufus procures from L. H. a skeleton dress and masks, two cloaks, and a dark lantern—Lanfranco disguises.)*
(Enter Henrico di Rosalvo, L. H.)

Henrico. What a day of perplexities has this proved to me: anxious to deliver the precious pacquet with which I am entrusted, to Lanfranco, the governor, I have with my impatience exhausted my poor horse, and a second time bewildered myself in the endless mazes of an impervious wood, where every step I tread seems to plunge me into further difficulties. *(Thunder reverberates.)* Hark! heard I not a distant roll of thunder? there wants nothing but a storm in this delightful situation to add to my felicity.—Ah! surely yonder gleams a light—some cottage in the wood, perchance; no, it moves; some husbandman returning from the labours of the day. Hollo! it stops, and now again it's lost amongst the trees. Maybe, 'tis some vapour of earth, engendered o'er marshy grounds, luring the ill-fated traveler to sure destruction. I see it plainer than before, and through the trees can now discover a figure wrapt in black bearing a lamp—doubtless some holy friar on a midnight visit to some sick or dying penitent. Hollo, reverend father, hollo! stay this speed,—in charity assist a lost, a care-worn traveler, to regain his way.—Hollo! hollo! *(Exit, R. H.)*

Scene III.

Exterior of Rodolph's Cottage.

(Enter Lanfranco, 1st E. R. H.)

Lan. Still am I pursued! Curses light on the wretch that dares to trace my footsteps! It is none of the castle gang, or they would have answered when I gave the signal—nor can it be a peasant hind, for he had fled affrighted from the path; but this intruder presses boldly on, and calls on me aloud to await his coming; I dare not enter Rodolph's cottage, lest he should haunt me there. Ah! here he is again.

(Enter Henrico, 1st E. R. H.)

Hen. At length I've o'ertaken you. *(Lanfranco darkens the lantern, covers himself with the cloak and steals off, L. H.)* Gone! vanished! melted into air! my every nerve is thrilled with horror—I am the victim of some magical illusion; worn with fatigue, my limbs refuse to bear me, so beneath some spreading tree must I await the approach of morn. Yet, merciful powers! should Almanza's pardon be too late! Oh, no! tomorrow it shall be delivered. *(Roda sings within.)*

> The lilies quite content remained
> And blessed the peaceful valley.

Hen. Ha! a female voice! some cottage must be near, for the sounds issued from this spot—'tis here! *(He knocks at the door.)* All is silent—not a breath can I now hear—they fear to open the door at this lone hour—perhaps some solitary female; *(Knocks again.)* Open the door, I beseech you, give shelter to a luckless traveler, benighted in this dreary forest, and quite exhausted with fatigue.

Rodol. *(appears at window.)* From whence come?

Hen. From the mountains.

Rodol. You've been hunting, I surmise?

Hen. Yes, all day long—lost my way.

Rodol. Are your companions near?

Hen. Why that question? No, many miles behind.

Rodol. Stop a moment, I'll come down to you. *(He disappears from the window and enters.)* Roda, bring hither a light. *(Roda entering with a light,* *starts on beholding Henrico, whom Rodolph surveys from top to toe.)* Well, I believe you may come in—it's fortunate you've found this cottage—'tis the only one in the forest, and as it seems inclined to be a stormy night, why you're in luck, methinks.

Hen. That's as it may happen, friend.

Rodol. Hem! well, come in or let it alone, just as you list; I shan't stand debating with you in the cold; *(Rain.)*—the rain begins to patter; so good night.

Hen. Nay, nay, I must along with you.

Rodol. Well, come in, we'll render you as comfortable as we can.

Hen. You shall not, my friend, repent your courtesy.

Rodol. Hem! that's as it may happen, friend.

(Rodolph conducts him into the cottage.)

Roda.. What evil star could guide this stranger hither to plunge my father my wretched father still in guilt; his habit bespeaks him rich, and Rodolph viewed him with a greedy eye. Ye saints above! should danger threaten, inspire the humble Roda with power and fortitude to save him.

Rodol. *(re-appearing at the door.)* Roda, what do you in the forest at this late hour? Come in, and make the door fast.

Roda.. I obey you, father. *(She follows into the Cottage.)*

(Enter Lanfranco.)

Lan. So, my pursuer has obtained a lodging for the night in Rodolph's cottage—he might as well have rested in a lion's den. He wears the habit of a courier—would that I could catch his face.—*(Looking through the window.)* What do I see! Henrico di Rosalva, the messenger from the court who bears Almanza's pardon! was ever bird snared so completely! I'll wait till he's at rest—then obtain his papers—the pardon shall be my reward—Rosalva's death and thou Almanza, once the rival of my love and power, shall on a public scaffold wash away my hatred with thy blood. *(He withdraws into the forest.)*

Scene IV.

Interior of Rodolph's Cottage, with the Old Oak Chest.—Window—fire—staircase, with doors beneath and above it.—A clock in flats—iron candlesticks—two stools, table, &c.&c.

(Music.—Rodolph and Roda setting bread and cheese on a table, with Henrico discovered—Rodolph directs Roda off for something to drink, 1st E. R. H.)

Hen. I am certain that I heard some one at the door.

Rodol. No such thing—no one inhabits this cottage but myself.— *(Roda re-enters with jug, which she places on the table.)*

Hen. You have good courage, friend.

Rodol. Courage, for what? I have lived in the forest these six years, and I never saw any thing in it worse than myself.

Hen. I believe you! But say, were you abroad to-night?

Rodol. I abroad?

(Roda is approaching to whisper "Henrico," when Rodolph draws his dagger and steps between them.)

Roda.. Father! tell the stranger supper's ready.

Rodol. Tell him yourself—you are not tongue-tied. I abroad, Cavalier! oh no, never after night-fall.

Roda.. May it please you, Cavalier, to partake of our homely fare?

Rodol. Homely fare, girl! the Cavalier can't expect dainties in a wood-man's cottage.

Hen. Nor do I wish it.—Hunger makes the homeliest fare a banquet.

Roda. I pray you, Cavalier, sit down—you are truly welcome. Father's words are oft uncourteous, but yet his heart is kind. Indeed, indeed, sir, my father is not what he seems to be.

Hen. Right, damsel, your father is not what is to be.

Rodol. Come, come, stint your prating, and to supper.

(They sit down and eat.—In the interim, Rufus is seen to lift up the lid of the Oak Chest, in the disguise of a Skeleton.)

Roda. But come, Signior, don't spare the jug—we can replenish it.

(Rufus lets the lid of the Chest fall suddenly—all are alarmed.)

Roda.. What noise was that?

Hen. It sounded near at hand!—as if the lid of yonder chest quick closed.

Rodol. That's impossible, sir, the lock has rusted within the socket; it never yet has been opened by me. The noise must have come from without—some bough, perchance, snapped by the passing wind.

Roda.. From without!

Hen. Why do you tremble?—what have you to fear?

Rodol. Fear! nothing but her own shadow.

(A knocking is heard without.)

Roda.. Ah! again—again! If it should be—

(Approaching Henrico.)

Hen. A what?

Rodol. *(interposing between them.)* A what? why a bat, Signior. They see the light in the cottage, and hit against the window. *(He pushes Roda outside.)* The simple wench is scared out of her very life at a bat.

Roda.. The very truth.—I am indeed, father; for the bats of our forest seldom fasten on a traveler but he bleeds to death.

Hen. If that's the case, I e'en shall guard against such visitors. Should anything approach me in the night. I have fire-arms, and I shall use them.—Your forest bats will find no easy prey in me, friend.

Roda.. *(taking candlestick.)* But come, Cavalier, it draws near midnight—you needs must want repose,—let me light you to your chamber. This way, Signior.

Rodol. No, give me the light.—I'll see the stranger to his bed—'tis nought but straw, but 'tis the best we have to offer, therefore excuse is needless.

(Music.—Roda beckons Henrico, as if she has something to communicate.— Rodolpho observes, and stamps for Henrico, who turns, and they ascend the staircase—open the door, and cross the gallery at back, L.H. As they withdraw the light disappears. The storm is heard howling without).

Roda.. I trust my presence in the cottage will preserve the hapless stranger. Methinks my father would never harm him;—but should any of his terrible companions call, I would not answer for the stranger's life.—Pray, Heaven, the storm may keep them far away. *(She seats herself at table.)* The Saints protect me! how the storm increases.—I am weary, and would fain seek rest. It's very strange! I am always dreaming of the Old Oak Chest! last night, methought, I had raised the lid, when from the yawning gulf within, a skeleton arose and cried "avenge my murder!" Oh, dear! I do not like to be alone at this dreary hour. The Old Oak Chest is just at hand, and I could almost fancy I heard a noise within it! *(Going to staircase.)*—Father! father! are you coming, father?—*(Rufus starts from the chest.)* Ah! the spectre!—so I saw it in my dream!—Save me, father!—save me!

Rufus *(seizing her).* Another word, and I plunge this dagger to your heart! Silence, and descend. *(Grasping her in his arms, he conveys her into the chest, and descends with her. Rodolph is seen crossing the gallery—he descends.)*

Rodol. Simple wench! what means those cries? — The storm is passing fast away —here, take the light, and to bed. *(Missing her.)*—Not here!—my mind misgives me.—*(Runs and tries door.)* All is fast—all must be safe within, Ha! another shriek!—perhaps she is in her chamber.—Roda! Roda! — my child—answer me—where art thou? *(He rushes off— Lanfranco gains admittance through the window.)*

Lan. At length, I've gained an entrance. Rodolph could, or would not, hear me—much I suspect that coarse fidelity.—No matter, to him alone I shall not trust—I have iron souls without that shall effect my purpose with Rosalvo. Ha! here comes the woodman.

(Re-enter Rodolph.)

Rodol. In vain I search—she's no where to be found.—Ha! the Governor here! — the mystery stands confessed.

Lan. How now, woodman Rodolph?

Rodol. How now, Governor Lanfranco?

Lan. Methinks you come full slowly to my bidding.

Rodol. And methinks you come full quickly without a bidding. How came, and what brought you here?

Lan. What, art thou mad?

Rodol. *(seizing him.)* Yes, and beware, lest I should bite thee. Where's my child?—I know you have taken her hence.—I heard her screams for help! Restore her—restore her innocent to me, or, by Hell, I'll bring thee and thy fell associates to the scaffold.

Lan. Villain! reptile!—darest thee threaten? then meet thy death.

(Music.—A desperate combat ensues.—Rodolph is at length disarmed, and is about to perish by Lanfranco's sword, when Henrico hastily descending stops the uplifted weapon.— Picture, and end of first act.)

Act II. Scene I.

Smugglers Cave—3rd and 4th Groves[1]—set Rocks (3rd E. R. H.) Pole, (2nd E. R. H.)

(De Lasso and Band discovered. Tinoco and Paulo, R. H. drinking.)

Chorus. Round, round, round,
Round goes the juice of the vine,
Round, round, round,
Round goes the liquor divine!
    With troubles and bubbles then let the world see,
    From troubles and bubbles they'll never be free—
    Success to brave Neptune, the son of the sea.

    Paulo. Here's a fig for dull Care,
With his silent grey hair—
His maxim the bottle shall save.

    Tinoco. Drink then to me,
For the trade is now free,
And the smuggler that's daring and brave.

    Omnes *(spoken as the Band drink).* Success to free trade!
Chorus. Round, round &c.

Lasso. Cheerly, cheerly, my friends! give way to merriment, nor look open us with a doubtful eye.

Adr. Alas! my father's blind!

Tino. Hum! none so blind as those who won't see.

Lasso. Silence! Tinoco. Fear not, we are no midnight plunderers.

Tino. Stick to the truth, good father,—we are midnight plunderers— ergo the revenue. What then?—why we plunder the revenue—the revenue plunder the subjects—the subjects plunder one another. All the world, more or less, live by plunder.

Paulo. Now stay thy clapper, if thou canst, and be more respectful to thy father's theme.

Lasso. You might as well attempt to stay the flowing wave—it is ever in his guise thus to be prating like a magpie.

Tino. Why, thou would'st not have calves head at table without tongue, father of mine.

Lasso. No, but there seems a lack of brains on this occasion, son of mine.

Tino. Aye, now I'm dished.

Lasso. Go to, for a merry knave. Our habitation, stranger, is rude, our manners rough and blunt—yet here you'll find sincerity, and that's a treasure seldom to be met with upon the smooth and smiling surface of a treacherous world. But come, Tinoco, fill up the stranger's cup, and let's give way to merriment.

Tino. It will be well if it alarms not our neighbours in Lanfranco's castle.

Alma. Lanfranco's?

Adr. Are we then so near?

Lasso. Are, our cavern west extends beneath it; but we have nought to fear from those who make it their retreat, they are on their nightly prowl ere this.—*(Gong is heard, 1st E. L. H.)*—Danger is near—out and see. *(Music.—Exit a Smuggler, 1st E. L. H. and re-enters.)*

Smug. Captain, be on your guard—the entrance to our cavern is discovered: a band of ruffians e'en now are disputing which first shall search the cave.

Lasso. Know ye the object of their search?

Smug. To secure the person of Almanza.

Lasso *(pointing to Almanza).* The person of Almanza is secure.

Alma. Betrayed! caught in the tolls! away then disguise—*(Throws off cloak.)* Behold the man they seek, fearless and firm, resolved to die as he has lived and conquered; by the sword I have lived, and by the sword I'll die—Come on, then! the man who takes me gains ten thousand ducats, but I'll have ten thousand drops of blood first. Come on then, I say.

Adr. *(throwing off disguise.)* First thro' thine Adriana's bleeding bosom must they strike at thine. Oh, hear the pleadings of his wretched wife—have mercy—save him—save him! *(Kneels.)*

Lasso. Fear not, dear lady—who is there of De Lasso's band that would betray the brave Almanza for twice ten thousand ducats?

Omnes. None.

Alma. Generous fellows! to what do I owe this zeal?

Lasso. Gratitude! remember ye the hardy smuggler your late father doomed to death when judge of Aragon?

Alma. Right well.

Lasso. Remember too, that you in pity to his wretched family, bribed his jailer, opened his dungeon door, and gave him life and liberty. From that hour myself, my sons, nay more, the band I lead, have been devoted to thy interest: thy castle, when in flames, we rifled, but to secure its treasure to thy use.

Adr. Alas! our greatest treasure on that fatal night was lost to us for ever.

Paulo. Dear lady, hope for the best—hear a tale of joy.

Tino. Stay thy clapper if thou canst, and be more respectful to thy father's theme: in plain speaking, hold thy tongue.

Lasso. In as plain speaking, hold your tongue, On board a vessel which awaits your coming on a lake hard by, thy riches are conveyed; the closing night shall see you safe on board—myself and these trust-worthy fellows shall pilot you afar, and leave you in whatever clime best suits your wishes.

(Enter Smuggler, 1st E. L. H.)

Smug. Captain, the Intruders gain upon us.

Lasso. Mislead them for a few moments to gain us time. Clear the cavern.

(Music.—Smuggler withdraws as before—the tables, stool &c. taken off—a trap door is raised at back.)

Lasso. Bring on the secret escape. *(They bring on the long pole, to which cleats are affixed, serving as a ladder.)* Lady, you and the General must here remain till night—descend; *(Pointing to U. E. R. H. of cave.)* What ho! a torch there.

(Music.—Smuggler gives a torch—Adriana and Almanza descend trap at back, De Lasso follows them.)

Tino. Now my lads, for my disguise. *(Exit Smuggler 2nd E. R. H. and re-enter, bringing a bag of disguises—Tinoco lays hold of one.)*— Psha! that's my old woman's gown—a famous habit for smuggling—I meant my hermit's gown; *(They help him on with it.)* Now then, off in a whiff. *(Music.—Exeunt Smugglers up pole.)* Why do you linger Paulo?

Paulo. I tremble, Tinoco, for you.

Tino. Tremble for me! why that's more than I do for myself; there's nothing on earth I fear.

Paulo. But an exciseman.

Tino. Don't mention it—away with you.

(Music.—Exit Paulo up pole, which is taken up after him.— Tinoco places a cross on rock piece, 3rd E. R. H. and a large book, and kneels before it.)

Shabrico *(without 1st E. L. H.).* Wait without and guard the entrance.

(Enter Shabrico with Conrade, and two Robbers.)

Con. By the light, we are right.

Shab. By the light, we are wrong. This seems the habitation of some holy man—behold him even now at his devotions.

Con. Let us examine him—the cloak of sanctity hides many a knave.

Shab. We crave your blessing, holy father.

Tino. May the blessings of the power you serve light on you.—*(Aside.)* and that's old Nick.—But come you thus early to confession?

Shab. No, but we shall bring you to confession ere we part. Who and what are you?

Tino. Oh the unrighteous sinners! not to know Father Lorenzo, the mountain hermit.

Shab. Well then, Father Lorenzo, inform us truly, or by my soul we'll broil thee on a gridiron like thy namesake, who were those we heard conversing as we entered?

Tino. Conversing! Oh, bless thine ears, it was my poor feeble voice reading a prayer.

Con. Nay, nay, father, we heard several voices.

Tino. Like enough, like enough, my sons: there are echoes all around.

Shab. Without there!—Music.

(Enter Four Robbers with torches, 1st E. L. H.)

Shab. Search the cave. *(Exeunt, U. E. R. H.)* And so you live here alone, do you?

Tino. Alone, I trust I am surrounded by good spirits.

Con. Good spirits, father! Ha, ha, ha! give us proof, father—give us proof.

Tino. Proof! the spirits here, my sons, are above proof; they float around invisible to sinful eyes.

Shab. Cease, cease your canting. *(Re-enter Robbers, U. E. R. H.)* Saw ye ought to justify suspicions?

Pietro. Nothing, noble Captain.

Shab. Then we may as well retire.

Tino. *(aside.)* A good riddance, say I.

Shab. And yet I could swear, among the sounds that drew us hither, I heard a woman's voice.

Con. I thought so too.

Tino. *(aside.)* It was the Lady Adriana's. A woman's voice!

Shab. Come, no equivocation, or by my soul you die!

Tino. Well, well, you did heard a woman's voice—it was an aged woman at confession; poor Dame Jugget, the peddler's wife of Astroga.

Shab. Well, well, produce her and we are satisfied.

Tino. I will, I will: but pray don't frighten her—she's a poor timid creature—I dare say she has crept into some corner—she has only stept to yonder fire to cook a little broth to comfort me.

Con. Ha, ha, ha! there's an arch hypocrite, can't do without an old woman to comfort him. Ha, ha, ha! bring her hither!

Tino. Well, well, I will, my friends, but pray don't frighten her. Why Jugget, I say, Jugget, Jugget!—*(Music. Exits, 2nd E. R. H.)*

Omnes. Jugget, Jugget, Jugget!

Shab. Suppose we take this Jugget to the castle, we are in want of a cook, in place of her Rufus sent post haste to the other world before her time.—What say you?

Con. With all my heart.—We are weary of being lickspits.

Shab. Call her, lads—call her.

Omnes. Jugget! Jugget! I say.

Tino. *(without, 2nd E. R. H.)* What say ye? the cavaliers want me? I'll attend on them in a minute.—Coming, coming, my masters.

Con. Here she comes! why, what a blazing visage!

Pietro. Red as a cherry.

Con. Cheery brandy, you mean. Why, Captain, she'll save us firing! she'll cook by the heat of her own countenance—But here she comes!— *(Music.)*

(Enter Tinoco disguised as Dame Jugget, 2nd E. R. H. with a stick and basket.)

Tino. Who wants Dame Jugget? what's your pleasure, worthy masters?

Shab. Father Lorenzo informs us you are an excellent cook.

Tino. Ha, ha, ha! he were a false lying knave who said otherwise.— Cook! aye, from a mutton kidney to a whole ox.

Shab. You are the very woman we want—so away with her, lads, to the castle.

Tino. *(shaking stick at them.)* What? stand off, stand off! You villains— I may chance to crack a knave's sconce.

Shab. At her, lads! at her! don't be conquered by an old woman! at her, I say— *(Music— A scuffle ensues.—Tinoco beats the Robbers off, 1st E. L. H.)*

Scene II.

A Dungeon in Lanfranco's Castle—2nd Groves.

(Enter Henrico, L. H.)

Hen. In vain do I pace my dungeon—in vain examine the walls, no outlet offers—hope itself expires—the ruffians who attend me I have tried to bribe; but they remain inflexible. Accursed Lanfranco! and thou ill-starred Almanza! thy fate is involved with mine—*(Chains are heard rattling without.)* Ah, they come! the bloodhounds come! they warn me to prepare! then, mercy heaven! on earth I hope for none. *(He kneels.)*

(Enter two Robbers, R. H.)

Memmo. You know our errand?

Hen. I read at once my doom.—Can nothing move your flinty hearts?

Both. Nothing!

Memmo. Had you not have known Lanfranco, you might have lived—but, as it is, you die.—*(They are about to seize him.)*

Hen. Not without a struggle then.—*(Throwing both on the ground.)*

Memmo. Then a leaden pill shall settle all.—*(Draws a pistol, and is about to fire, when Lasso enters up trap, 2nd R. E. and fires at the Robbers, which kills one, who staggers off R. H.)*

Lasso. Damme, but I've settled you!—*(The other Robber is about to escape, when Almanza enters, and throws him to the ground.—Adriana screams without, and rushes on from trap.)*

Adr. Almanza, forbear!

Hen. Almanza here! astonishing!

Alma. *(embracing him.)* Henrico di Rosalva!

Adr. Nay, this is not time for explanation—let us escape this accursed place.

Lasso. Indeed, my Lady, I knew not my store-house was connected with this dungeon.—*(Robber attempts to escape—Lasso seizes him, and presents pistol at him.)* I've settled your companion—and now damme, but I'll settle you.

Memmo. Spare my life!

Lasso. On one condition: know you of any secret pass, by which we may escape these vaults?

Memmo. I do! one leading to the cottage of Rodolph, the woodman.

Lasso. Conduct us there in safety, and you are free.—*(Music.—Robber points the way—Lasso takes chains and binds them round his arm and the Robber's.)* Hold, my friend! we move together. *(He presents pistol at Memmo, and all follow Memmo off 2nd E. R. H.)*

Scene III.

Kitchen in Lanfranco's Castle—three Groves—transparent fireplace (L. H. U. E.)—couch, and cloak hanging on it—A doe on table.

(Music.—Enter Shabrico and Robbers, 1st E. R. H. laughing.)

Shab. A sturdy old beldame, i'faith, and well suited to our purpose.

Con. Damn her! she's driven my nose to the other side of my face.—By your leave we must cut her throat.

Shab. At your peril, rascals, touch her; if she dresses a dinner as well as she has dressed thee, I shall have no occasion to find fault with her.

Con. Stand aside! here she comes!

(Enter Tinoco, dressed as Dame Jugget, 1st E. R. H.)

Tino. Stand out of the way, varlets! out of the way, I say.

Shab. Now, then, beldame! know you your vocation?

Tino. Yes, and please you, I'm to cook for you.

Con. Yes—you're to provide for us all.

Tino. Well, I'll do my best endeavors to provide for you all, I will—*(Aside.)* you d—d rascals, I will.

Shab. Yonder's a young doe to dress for supper—see that it pleases me.

Tino. *(going up to table.)* What, this, my master? where be the fuel to roast it by?

Con. In the forest.

Tino. Em—Balaam couldn't speak, and so the ass spoke for him. In the forest, sir, jackanapes—*(Going.)* then in the forest I can help myself, you know.

Con. No, you don't though.

Shab. No! you stir not hence till the day of death.

Tino. That's a day you'll not live to see, Mr. Goodman Bellswagger—*(Aside.)* you'll be dancing on nothing long before that.

Con. What's that you say?

Tino. Wha—what's that? why, I say that you have saved me a dance for nothing—for, had I gone to the forest—

Con. You'd have found plenty of wood, ready cut.

Shab. Away to the forest—and see that she has what she needs! begone, I say!

(Music.—Exeunt all the Robbers but Conrad and Shabrico. Tinoco retires up.)

Shab. Where's Lanfranco?

Con. In the west tower, examining Rosalva's prayers.

Shab. I shall join him thither! bring one of the best flagons the castle affords.

Con. We have some excellent abroach—warranted from the cellar of a priest.

Shab. Aye, aye!—leave the church alone for good living.

(Exeunt Shabrico and Conrad, 1st E. R. H.—Tinoco gives the doe two or three thumps with his stick.)

Tino. A pretty nest of hornets thou has got into, little Tinoco—this school will certainly finish thy honest education; ergo, may it not finish thee, my boy, by exiling thee to the honours of a wooden sign-post, where thou mayst swing for the edification of thy brother sinners.— But, mum—here come my worthy associates.—*(Takes up spit—wipes it with apron.)*

(Enter four Robbers, 1st E. R. H. with a litter of green boughs, which they put down.)

Con. Here's fuel—and now, I suppose, you'll let us have a little peace!

Tino. Peace, quota! nobody has any peace where I am.

Con. I believe you.

Tino. What! call you this fuel? green boughs and rubbish!

Con. D—n her, we've worked her now! let her make fire of it if she can.

Tino. Why, it's full of sap, like your own stupid heads: there—there, there, away with it.

Con. May we be roasted over green boughs if we do.

Tino. I say, take it away.

Con. I say we won't.

Tino. You won't.

Omnes. No!

Tino. The damme if I don't make you.

(Music.—Seizes the split and drives them three times round the place, when Rufus enters, 1st E. L. H. with Roda in his arms, in his skeleton dress and mask—he places Roda on the couch.)

Tino. *(starting.)* Why, who the devil have we here?

Rufus. How now? what means this infernal roaring? Don't you know me, comrades?

Con. Know you? we scarcely know ourselves.

Rufus. Who's the new comer? she seems a rare one.

Con. Oh, a tid-bit of the Captain's own choosing.—She'd let you know who she is anon.

Rufus. There's another tid-bit of the Captain's own choosing. Harkee, old fiery face, look to the damsel.

Tino. Look—why I can't, for looking at you.

Rufus. Oh, you don't like my appearance; you must know, we wear these masks at night to scare away intruders. *(Throws mask aside.)*

Tino. Aye, aye, thou need'st not wear a mask for that purpose, friend, for thy face is ugly enough to scare the devil.

Rufus. What means you by that, you old pole cat?

(Music.—Tinoco seizes him by the throat, shakes him violently, and throws him on the ground—Robbers stand laughing.)

Tino. Dare you, dare you, villain, take advantage of my weakness!

Rufus *(recovering himself).* D—n your weakness; it doesn't lay in your arms, I'll swear: I shall never be able to sing again, for by the lord, she's cracked my windpipe.

Con. Come, for the present pass it by, when time shall serve, we'll pay her off. *(Drawing a dagger across his throat.)*

Rufus. You speak my mind; but now I must to Shabrico, and inform him of our prize.

(Exeunt subaltern Robbers, L. H.)

Rufus *(to Tinoco).* Hark, you old beldame, look to that wench—and mark, she eats her supper with the Captain to-night.

Roda. Oh, no, no! the saints protect me! no, sir.

Rufus. Why zounds, girl, don't you look so like a corpse—I said you were to eat your supper with the Captain to-night. I didn't say he was to eat you for supper.

Tino. You dog, I'll supper you.

Rufus. Good bye, old iron fist.

Tino. Farewell, master scare babe.

(Exit Rufus, L. H.)

Roda. She seems a terrible old woman, yet I must implore her protection—it's the only chance I have left.—*(Kneels.)* Good dame, kind dame, a most unhappy girl, thus at your feet, implores your pity and protection. Perhaps you have a child!

Tino. Perhaps I have—twenty—aye, and a great many more.

Roda. Then you can feel for me; torn from my parent's arms, from an innocent and peaceful home; just too, as I was going to be married!

Tino. Aye, now do I feel for you.

Roda. Oh, Paulo, Paulo! what will become of Paulo!

Tino. *(aside.)* As I live, my brother's destined bride!—Oh, here's a pretty addition to the work already cut out.

Roda. Oh, I see you pity me, save me from this dreadful Captain and his gang! keep close to me all day, and don't let them separate us all night. Oh Paulo, Paulo! why are you not here to protect me?

Tino. Pshaw, pshaw! don't make such a fuss about Paulo—if he were here he couldn't do nothing more than I can; he's a poor silken lacquey—a twanger of catgut—a poor dirty, sturdy, sniveling knave.

Roda. How—'tis false—and you are—

Tino. His brother.

Roda. What, Tinoco! yes, it is Tinoco, and Roda's safe. *(Embracing.)* Roda's safe!

Tino. Yes, as safe as a lamb in the den of a wolf.—What's to be done?

Roda. Now, Tinoco, you know you are used to smuggling, can't you contrive the smuggle me out of this castle?

Tino. Ah, by the Lord, a thought strikes me; should I find means to get thee conveyed out of this castle, hast though courage to make thy way in the lake among the mountains, and sounding on its banks this whistle, hither lead those that answer it.

Roda. Put me to the trial—I have courage enough for anything. *(Takes whistle.)*

Tino. Enough—then help me with yon doe.

(Music.—They place the doe on the couch—Robbers laugh without.)

Roda. Ah, they're coming, Tinoco; quick, quick!

Tino. Now then, give me your hat.—*(He places it on the head of the doe.)*—Now, then, your outer garment.—*(He places cloak over the doe.)*

Roda. Anything else, Tinoco?

Tino. Now, then, creep in amongst these green boughs, and lay as an owl in daylight.

(Music.—Roda lays on the litter and Tinoco covers her over with the boughs. Enter Shabrico and Robbers, laughing and singing.)

Tino. Cease your villainous noise—cease your noise, I say.—*(Running up against Shabrico.)*—I crave thy pardon, noble prince, I knew not it was thee.

Shab. What have we here—a beauty? By my soul, a sleeping one.— *(Approaching the couch on which the doe is placed, when he is stopped by Tinoco.)*

Tino. Hold, hold! let her rest awhile—terror and fatigue have weighed down her eyelids; pray thee don't disturb the fair one, and be you witness all, I swear the female form on yonder couch shall grace my humble master's table—nay, his bed, if he thinks fit, before the coming day.

Shab. Your hand in the bargain.—But how is it the fire so sickly gleams—where are the preparations for the revel?

Tino. *(aside.)* Now's my time or never.—Let yonder pile of reeking boughs answer at once thy question—the knaves have brought it here in pure despite, to gain me thy displeasure; think you I can make a fire of wet grass? roast venison by a waterfall!—If thou art disappointed of thy dainty fare, lay not the blame to Jugget.

Shab. Go, bear it back to the forest—bring dry and proper fuel; let not your petty enmities disturb my peace. Why are my orders not obeyed? Begone, I say.

Con. Well, if we must, we must.—*(The Robbers retire, bearing with them the boughs, in which Roda is concealed.)*

Tino. Bravely said, noble Captain—I can't help laughing to think you've made the varlets do exactly what you wanted—ha, ha, ha! *(Exit, R. H.)*

Lan. *(without, 2nd E. L. H.)* Shabrico, be on thy guard—*(He enters.)* Rodolph has broken his dungeon, and, like a madman, ranges the castle, calling for his child. Why was she brought here, in defiance to my orders?

Shab. To please Shabrico—here his will is law.

Lan. Presumptuous villain! one whom I could crush— *(Drawing.)*

Shab. Ha, say'st thou so?

(A combat ensues—Shabrico is disarmed.)

Shab. Hold! I've been to blame—the wine has misled me.

Lan. Then we are friends.

Rodol. *(without 1st E. R. H.)* Where's my child; I'll raise the earth—nay, hell itself, but I will find her.—*(He enters.)* Oh, Roda, Roda! where art thou?

Shab. Behold! *(Points to couch, to which Rodolph advances.)* approach her not, presumptuous minion.— Your Roda! she's my Roda—Count Lanfranco's Roda—any man's Roda, when I am weary of her.

Rodol. Never! thou knowest not the heart of Rodolph; innocent she lived, and innocent she dies.—*(Stabs the doe.)* Now, villains, for thy heart's blood.—*(Beats them off L. H.)*

(Tino pursued by Robbers rushes on, R. H.—seizing a red hot poker, he beats them off, L. H.)

Scene IV.

(Enter Tinoco, 1st E. L. H. hastily, as Jugget.)

Tino. Oh, d—n these petticoats! I could have fought till I had killed half the rascals, but these infernal petticoats wouldn't let me move.—Here they come, and here I go.—*(Attempts to run, but stumbles.)* Oh, if ever I command an army, I'll put all my soldiers into petticoats, then they must fight—I'll be burnt if they can run. What shall I do? ah, a cottage! then in I go, without a pursuit. *(Exit into Cottage.)*
(Music.—Enter Paulo, with Florian.)

Paulo. Ill-fated Almanza—destruction encircles you—the mountains are covered o'er with troops; if I could but gain the lake, and convey this infant to his mother. What do I hear? clashing of swords—Rodolph's cottage must now afford a shelter.—*(Music. Exeunt into Cottage.)*
(Enter Rodolph, 1st E. L. H.)

Rodol. I have disarmed the villains—despair has made me more than man—the forest now must yield me shelter. *(Music.—He rushes off, 1st E. R. H.)*
(Enter Lanfranco and Robbers, 1st E. L. H.)

Lan. He has taken refuge in the cottage.

Shab. Force the door.

Con. 'Tis firmly barred within.

Shab. Round to the back—there we shall find an easy entrance. *(Exeunt, 2nd E. R. H.)*

Scene V.

Interior of the Cottage.—(The 5th Scene of the 1st Act repeated.) Paulo and Child discovered.

Paulo. Horror and confusion! the cottage is deserted—where shall I hide the child? ah, yon chest!

Tino. *(starting from Old Oak Chest.)* It's occupied already—cease thy surprise—what's thy purpose here?

Paulo. To save Almanza's child.—*(Crash without.)* Ah, they come! Tinoco, hast thou not one idea left?

Tino. No, they're all scared away.—*(Clock goes "Cuckoo!")* Ah, yon clock! I shall respect a Cuckoo, even though I should be married.—*(He conceals Child in Clock-case, and hides himself in the Chest.)*
(Enter Lanfranco and three Robbers from door, 3rd E. R. H.)

Lan. Paulo here! what, ho—a torch!—*(It is brought to him.)* fire the cottage—who shall prevent me?

Tino. *(rushing from Chest.)* Tinoco de Lasso, the Smuggler's son!
(A struggle takes place—the torch is forcibly taken from Lanfranco by Tinoco.)

Paulo. And Paulo de Lasso, the Smuggler's son!

Lan. Seize them!

(Roda enters at door, followed by Rodolph, who interposes—Roda whistles, and which she tears from Tinoco's neck—it is answered, and Nicholas de Lasso, Almanza, Adriana, and Smugglers rush on.)

Lan. Ha! 'tis the proscribed General, Almanza! he is my prisoner.

Hen. *(rushing forward.)* Behold his pardon!

Lan. Ha! eternal curses! still will I have revenge!

(A general conflict ensues—Lanfranco and his party are overpowered—he is struck to the earth—Paulo rushes to the Clock, and brings forward the Child.)—

TABLEAU.

FINIS

Disposition of the Characters when the Curtain falls.

Almanza

Paulo   Lanfranco

Roda   Tinoco

O. P.   CURTAIN.   P. S.

Notes

1. Here and below, the reference to "Grove" (or "groove") suggests the placement of scenery on-stage according to the tracks made in the stage floor parallel with the proscenium opening to accommodate moveable wings. Typically, the first set of tracks or grooves would lie closest to the audience, the fourth, farthest upstage.

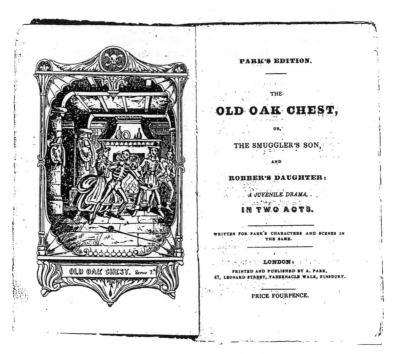

The title page from Park's toy theatre edition of *The Old Oak Chest* by Jane Scott. Reproduced by permission from the collection of Mr. Barry Clarke, Pollock's Toy Museum, London.

Appendix B

Glossary

The following is a list of foreign and archaic words found throughout the plays in this anthology.

Abroach. Broached, pierced, in a condition for letting out or yielding liquor; on tap.

Accompt. Account.

Adamantine. Unyielding; resembling the hardness or luster of a diamond.

Aidance. Assistance, aid; a means of help.

Alnwick Castle. One of the principal seats of the Percy family, earls of Northumberland, situated on the south side of the river Aln, and believed to have been built in Roman times, though no part of the original structure remains. Originally constructed of wood, stone walls were added to the triangular castle before 1157. Once the edifice was purchased by Henry de Percy in 1309, the shape and structure of the buildings (now extending over seven acres) were strengthened and modified to include seven semi-circular towers. Work continued on the structure through the eighteenth century when Robert Adam was called in to decorate Alnwick in a Gothic style. In 1854, the castle was refurbished in an Italianate style by Anthony Salvin.

Arquebuses. Plural variant spelling of harquebus, a matchlock gun invented in the fifteenth century, heavy, though portable, and usually fired from a support.

Attaint. Infected; affected with sickness, passion etc.; overcome with heat, weariness, or fatigue.

Beeves. Cattle.

Belike. Probably, perhaps.

Benignant. Serene, calm, mild, favorable.

Blazon. Coat of arms.

Bride-krantz. The style of hair, usually worn by brides, arranging the hair in a circle around the head; plaits.

Broach. To pierce, or tap, a cask in order to draw the contents; also a pointed implement or tool.

Butting. Striking or shoving with the head or horns.

Caitiff. Coward; despicable wretch.

Capacious. Capable of containing a great amount.

Captious. Inclined to stress faults and raise objections.

Certainment. Certainly; of course.

Cheviot. The principal peak (2676 feet) of a range of border mountains from which they take their name; according to old ballads, the celebrated battle of Chevy-Chase took place here.

Chine. A cut of meat including all or part of the backbone.

Claymore. A two-handed sword with a double-edged blade, used by Scottish Highlanders in the sixteenth century.

Compassionating. Pitying.

Conglobe. To form into a round, compact mass; conglobate.

Dirdum. Grumbling, blame.

Dirk. A dagger.

Drachenfels. Dragon rock (from the German).

Dumby. Dummy.

Etui case. A small decorative case for needles, toilet articles, etc.

Falchion. A broad-bladed, slightly curved sword from medieval times.

Fen. A low land covered with water; a swamp.

Freebooter. One who goes about in search of plunder; pirate, plunderer.

Freebooting. Acting as a freebooter; the name for such activity.

Frontlet. A decorative band or ribbon worn across the forehead; a cloth or bandage containing medicine.

Froward. Perverse; willfully contrary; hard to handle.

Gascony. Wine from the Gascogne region in France.

Gauds. Ornaments, trinkets.

Glebe. A plot of cultivated land; land belonging, or yielding revenue, to a parish church or ecclesiastical benefice.

Guerdon. A reward or recompense.

Hap. Luck or chance; an occurrence or accident.

Hatcher's dress. The attire of a thief, plotter, or covert planner; the costume of one who works with chickens.

Hodden. Hand-loomed, coarse woolen cloth.

Hopuponacrack. A malapropism for hypochondriac.

Horeb's rock. The mountain where, according to the Bible, the Commandments were given to Moses.

Hurstmonceux Castle. Built in 1440 by Sir Roger de Fiennes, Treasurer to the Household of Henry VI and a veteran of Agincourt, it was constructed of red brick with stone facings and considered the most *regular* of English castles. It featured seven principal and four spiral staircases in addition to a bakehouse, a dairy, a brewery, a distillery, a confectionery, a chapel, and various offices. The building was dismantled in 1770 by its owner, Reverend Robert Hare, who used many of the furnishings to equip a smaller Hurstmonceux House, a Georgian mansion he constructed on the edge of the property.

Ingle. Fire in a fireplace; fireplace.

Intercommuned. Talked over; discussed.

Königssstuhl. Throne; literally, royal chair (from the German).

Laggard. One who lags or lingers; the state of being dilatory.

Landgrave. In Germany, a count having jurisdiction over a territory and having under him several inferior counts; later, the title given to certain German princes.

Limb. To pull limb from limb, to dismember.

List. To listen (to); to like or desire; to choose.

Lour. To become dark, gloomy, threatening; frown.

Lustihood. Lustiness; vigor.

Meed. A reward or recompense.

Mulct. Penalty; fine.

Murrain. A pestilence or plague affecting domestic animals or plants.

Noddle. The head.

Oriel chamber. A small private apartment attached to a hall, usually a room with a large bay window, projecting from a wall and supported by a bracket.

Paduasoy. A corded silk fabric; a garment made from it.

Palatinate. The domain of a feudal lord or palatine.

Palatine. A feudal lord having sovereign power within his domains.

Palter. To behave insincerely; to lie or trick; to bargain with; to act carelessly.

Pantouffles. Indoor slippers or loose shoes; also applied to out-door overshoes or galoshes and to all manner of Oriental and non-European slippers, sandals, etc.; also spelled pantofles.

Pennons. Long triangular streamers attached to the head of a lance; pennants.

Phiz. Face, countenance, expression or aspect of face; physiognomy.

Pokemantles. Malapropism for portmanteaux, large traveling bags.

Polyanthus. Blooming flower, primrose; a kind of narcissus with small white or yellow petals.

Pont la Trave. In her "Notes" to *The Lay of the Minstrel's Daughter*, Margaret Harvey finds reference to Pont la Trave and Serra Valta in the travel journals of Augustus Von Kotzebue. Near Valcimara, between Serra Valta and Pont la Trave lies the grave of a Spanish Countess, murdered by her own courier and two accomplices. Immediately following the murder, the trio were taken and quartered alive, their mutilated bodies left to hang on the surrounding trees. At midnight, three bloodstained ghosts rise from beneath the trees and extend their arms in supplication toward a hovering majestic female spirit dressed in white. Unable to secure her absolution, the three ghosts burn and crackle with fire until the last stroke of midnight, and the female spirit transforms into a rosy cloud, shedding a soft pink tint over the mountain peaks.

Pulter. Poultry, fowl; more commonly spelled pultre.

Pursuivants. Officers of arms ranking below heralds, but with similar duties.

Rebeck. An ancient, bowed three-stringed musical instrument with a pear-shaped body and slender neck.

Rencontre. A hostile meeting or contest; combat. Also, a casual meeting.

Rifted. Burst open; divided; penetrated.

Ruffler. One in a disturbed state of mind.

Rushes. Tufted marsh plants, with cylindrical stems used in plaiting mats.

Sagittary. A centaur with a bow.

Sally port. A gateway permitting the passage of a large number of people at the same time; a back door.

Scurrile. Vulgar, obscene, coarse; scurrilous.

'Scutcheon. A shield on which armorial bearings are displayed; escutcheon.

Seneschal. An agent or steward in charge of a lord's estate.

Shagreen. Untanned leather with an abrasive surface, prepared from the hide of a horse.

Shrieval. Belonging, or relating to a sheriff.

Shriving. Freeing from guilt; confessing one's sins.

Sponsal. Pertaining to marriage; wedded, wedding.

Springe. A trap for catching small game; something that is designed to spring.

Thrice-riven. Split or divided into three parts.

Tokay. A naturally sweet wine from the area around Tokaj, Hungary.

Towardly. Docile; propitious; promising.

Trencher. A wooden platter for serving food.

Trothplight. Betrothal; that which is associated with an engagement to be married.

Troublous. Turbulent; unsettled; restless.

Tyrian Argosy. Fleet of merchant ships from Tyre, a Phoenician city known as a center of commerce.

Undine. Supernatural female being, imagined as inhabiting the water; a nymph; also exhibiting the qualities thereof.

Usance. Use; custom or habit.

Vail. To be of use or profit; avail.

Venturous. Hazardous; venturesome.

Verderers. English judicial officers in charge of the King's forests.

Vesture. Clothing, apparel; something that covers like a garment; as a verb, to clothe.

Vociferatious. Malapropism for vociferous: clamorous; speaking noisily.

Ween. To think; suppose; expect, hope, intend.

Wight. Any living being, creature; a human being; a supernatural being, witch or sprite.

Yarrow Streens. Village on the Yarrow Water near the Scottish border.

Appendix C

British Women Melodramatists 1790–1843[1]

(All the known plays of each author are listed below.
Dates are first performances unless otherwise noted)

Joanna Baillie (1762–1851)

A Series of Plays: in which it is attempted to delineate the stronger passions of the mind. Each passion being the subject of a tragedy and a comedy (published 1798):

    Count Basil: A Tragedy

    The Tryal: A Comedy

    De Monfort: A Tragedy (4/29/1800)

A Series of Plays (published 1802):

    The Election (6/7/1817)

    Ethwald

    The Second Marriage

Miscellaneous Plays (published 1804):

    Rayner

    The Country Inn

Constantine Paleologus (10/10/1808 Liverpool; revised by Thomas John Dibdin as *Constantine and Valeria*, 6/23/1817 London)

The Family Legend (1/29/1810 Edinburgh; 4/29/1815 London)

A Series of Plays (published 1812):

    Orra

    The Dream

    The Siege

    The Beacon (2/9/1815 Edinburgh)

The Martyr (published 1826)

The Bride (published 1828)

Dramas (published 1836):

    The Martyr

    The Bride

    Romiero

    The Alienated Manor

    Henriquez (3/19/1836)

    The Separation (2/24/1836)

    The Stripling

    The Phantom

    Enthusiasm

    Witchcraft

The Homicide
The Match
Mary Devens Balfour (fl. 1810–1820)
    Kathleen O'Neil. A Grand National Melodrama (published 1814)
Caroline Boaden (fl. 1825–1835)
    Quite Correct (7/30/1825)
    Fatality (9/1/1829)
    William Thompson; or, Which is He? (9/11/1829)
    The First of April (8/31/1830)
    A Duel in Richelieu's Time (7/9/1832)
    Don Pedro the Cruel and Don Manuel the Cobbler (published 1839)
Miss Burke (fl. 1793)
    The Ward of the Castle (10/24/1793)
Mary Emma Ebsworth (1794–1881)
    The Two Brothers of Pisa (published 1828)
    Payable at Sight; or, The Chaste Salute
    The Sculptor of Florence
Mrs. B. E. Florance (fl. 1843)
    The Bohemian Bandit (4/6/1843)
Mary Goldsmith (fl. 1800–1810)
    She Lives! or, The Generous Brother (1803)
    Angelina; or Wolcot Castle (1804)
Catherine Grace Frances (Moody) Gore (1799–1861)
    The Bond (published 1824)
    The School for Coquettes (7/14/1831)
    Lords and Commons (12/20/1831)
    The Queen's Champion (9/10/1834)
    Modern Honour; or, The Sharper of High Life (12/3/1834)
    The King's Seal (1/10/1835)
    The Maid of Croissey; or, Theresa's Vow (7/20/1835)
    King O'Neil; or, The Irish Brigade (12/9/1835)
    Don John of Austria (4/16/1836)
    A Tale of a Tub (7/15/1837)
    A Good Night's Rest; or, Two in the Morning (8/19/1839)
    Dacre of the South; or, The Olden Time (published 1840)
    Quid pro Quo; or, The Day of Dupes (6/18/1844)
Elizabeth Gunning (1769–1823)
    The Wife with Two Husbands (a translation of Pixérécourt's play of the same title, published 1803)
Anna Maria Hall (1800–1881)
    The French Refugee (2/20/1837)
    Mabel's Curse (3/27/1837)
    The Groves of Blarney (4/16/1838)

    Chester Fair (5/27/1844)

    Juniper Jack; or, My Aunt's Hobby (6/16/1845)

Margaret Harvey (fl. 1814–1822)

    Raymond de Percy; or, The Tenant of the Tomb (1822 Sunderland)

Elizabeth Helme (d. 1816)

    Cortez (published 1800)

    Pizarro (published 1800)

Felicia Dorothea Hemans (1793–1835)

    Procida; or, The Vespers of Palermo (10/23/1823)

    The Siege of Valencia (published 1823)

    The American Forest Girl (published 1825)

    Bernard del Carpio (published 1825)

Isabel Hill (1800–1842)

    The Poet's Child (published 1820)

    The First of May (10/10/1829)

    Brian, the Probationer; or, The Red Hand (published 1842)

Fanny Holcroft (d. 1844)

    The Theatrical Recorder (published 1805):

        Philip the Second (translated from Alfieri)

        From Bad to Worse (from Calderon)

        Emilia Galotti (from Lessing)

        Fortune Mends (from Calderon)

        Minna von Barnhelm (from Lessing)

        The Baron (from Moratin)

        Rosamond (from Weisse)

    The Goldsmith (8/23/1827)

H. Saint A. Kitching (fl. 1830s)

    Moral Plays (published 1832):

        The Fate of Ivan

        Keep Your Temper; or, Know Whom You Marry

        Miss Betsy Bull; or, The Johnnies in Spain

Mme. Laurent (fl. 1830s) in collaboration with W. O. Oxberry

    The Truand Chief; or, The Provost of Paris (published 1839)

Elizabeth Horner Leckie (d. 1856)

    The Power of Conscience (published 1841)

    The Hebrew Boy (published 1842)

    The Guardian (published 1843)

Harriet Lee (1757–1851)

    The New Peerage; or, Our Eyes May Deceive Us (11/10/1787)

    The Mysterious Marriage; or, The Heirship of Roselva (published 1798)

    The Three Strangers (12/10/1825)

Sophia Lee (1750–1824)
The Chapter of Accidents (8/5/1780)
Almeyda: Queen of Granada (4/20/1796)
The Assignation (1/28/1807)
Elizabeth (Wright) Macaulay (1786?–1837)
Marmion, a melo-drama (published 1811)
Mary Russell Mitford (1787–1855)
Julian (3/15/1823)
The Foscari (11/4/1826)
Dramatic Scenes (published 1827)
Rienzi (10/9/1828)
Inez de Castro (1831)
Charles I (7/2/1834)
Sadak and Kalascade (4/20/1835)
Mrs. Morton (fl. 1831)
The Gypsey Father (5/31/1831)
Elizabeth Planché (1796–1846)
The Welsh Girl (12/16/1833)
The Sledge Driver (6/19/1834)
Ivan Daniloff; or, The Russian Mandate (11/16/1835)
A Handsome Husband (2/15/1836)
The Ransom (6/9/1836)
A Pleasant Neighbour (10/20/1836)
A Hasty Conclusion (4/19/1838)
Elizabeth Polack (fl. 1830–1840)
Woman's Revenge (2/27/1832)
Esther, the Royal Jewess; or, The Death of Haman (3/9/1835)
St. Clair of the Isles; or, The Outlaw of Barra (4/16/1838)
Alberti; or, The Mines of Idria
Angeline; or, The Golden Chain
Anna Maria Porter (1780–1832)
The Fair Fugitives (5/16/1803)
Switzerland (2/15/1819)
Catherine Frances Malone Raymond (fl. 1843)
The Devil's Share (1843 Liverpool)
The Two Sisters; or, The Ghost's Legacy (9/28/1843 Liverpool)
Mariette; or, The Reward (10/24/1843 Liverpool)
Mrs. Robertson (fl. 1800s)
Ellinda; or, The Abbey of St. Aubert (published 1800)
Jane Marie Scott (fl. 1806–1822)
The Rout (11/17/1806)
Tempest Terrific (11/17/1806)
Vision in the Holy Land; or, Godfrey of Bouillon's Dream (11/17/1806)

Battle in the Shadow (1/12/1807)

Rural Visitors; or, Singularity (1/12/1807)

Spectrology of Ghosts (1/12/1807)

Successful Cruize; or, Nobody's Coming to Woo (11/14/1807)

Ulthona the Sorceress (11/14/1807)

The Magistrate (2/15/1808)

The Red Robber; or, The Statue in the Woods (12/3/1808)

The Bashaw; or, Midnight Adventures of Three Spaniards (1/23/1809)

Mother Whitecap; or, Hey Up the Chimney (2/27/1809)

The Necromancer; or, The Golden Key (12/11/1809)

Mary, the Maid of the Inn; or, The Bough of Yew (12/27/1809)

Two Misers of Smyrna; or, Mufti's Tomb (3/8/1810)

Disappointments; or, Love in Castile (12/3/1810)

The Magic Pipe; or, Dancing Mad (12/3/1810)

The Lowland Romp (12/27/1810)

The Animated Effigy (2/12/1811)

The Poison Tree; or, Harlequin in Java (11/4/1811)

The Vizier's Son, the Merchant's Daughter, and the Ugly Woman of Bagdad (12/16/1811)

Il Giorno Felice; or, The Happy Day (2/24/1812)

Asgard, the Daemon Hunter; or, Le Diable a La Chasse (11/17/1812)

Love, Honor, and Obey (12/7/1812)

Davy Jones's Locker; or, Black-eyed Susan (12/23/1812)

The Forest Knight; or, The King Bewildered (2/4/1813)

Love in the City (3/8/1813)

Raykisnah the Outcast; or, The Hallow Tree (11/22/1813)

The Magician; or, The Enchanted Bird (12/23/1813)

Whackham and Windham; or, The Wrangling Lawyers (1/24/1814)

The Inscription; or, The Indian Hunters (2/28/1814)

Eccentricities; or, Mistakes at Madrid (12/26/1814)

The Gipsy Girl (1/9/1815)

Harlequin Rasselas; or, The Happy Valley (2/9/1815)

The Summer House (2/16/1815)

The Conjurer; or, Blaise in Amaze (10/30/1815)

The Old Oak Chest; or, The Smuggler's Sons and the Robber's Daughter (2/5/1816)

Stratagems; or, The Lost Treasure (3/4/1816)

The Dinner of Madelon (12/16/1816)

Camilla the Amazon; or, The Mountain Robber (2/6/1817)

The Lord of the Castle (10/13/1817)

Widow's Tears (10/23/1817)

The Row of Ballynavogue; or, The Lily of Lismore (11/27/1817)

The Fortunate Youth (1/5/1818)

The Two Spanish Valets; or, Lie Upon Lie (11/2/1818)
Fairy Legends; or, The Moon-light Night (12/7/1818)
The Fire Goblin and the Three Charcoal Burners (12/26/1818)
The Half-Pay Officer; or, Love and Honor (1/18/1819)
Mariana Starke (fl. 1780–1800)
The Sword of Peace; or, A Voyage of Love (8/9/1788)
The British Orphan (4/7/1790 Camberwell)
The Widow of Malabar (5/5/1790 Camberwell)
The Tournament . . . "Imitated from the Celebrated German Drama entitled *Agnes Bernauer*" (published 1800)
Anna Swanwick (fl. 1840s)
The Maid of Orleans (adapted from Schiller's play, published 1843)
Caroline Symmons (fl. 1800)
The Sicilian Captive (published 1800)
Anne Trelawney (fl. 1830s)
Mary Stuart (published 1838)
Mrs. Barbarina Wilmot (later Brand, Baroness Dacre) (1767–1854)
Ina (4/22/1815)
Dramas, Translations, and Occasional Poems (published 1821)
Sophia Woodrooffe (fl. 1826–1847)
Four Dramatic Poems (published 1826):
    Buondelmonte
    The Zingari
    Cleanthes
    The Count of Flora
A Sovereign Remedy (7/1/1847)
Mrs. Edwin Yarnold (fl. 1830s)
Marie Antoinette; or, The Queen's Lover (10/5/1835)
Elizabeth Yorke, Countess of Hardwicke (1763–1858)
The Court of Oberon; or, The Three Wishes (published 1831)

Notes

1. Included in this list are all British women writers who have written at least one Gothic melodrama between 1790 and 1843.

Bibliography

Adburgham, Alison. *Silver Fork Society: Fashionable Life and Literature from 1814 to 1840*. London: Constable, 1983.

Alderman, Geoffrey. *London Jewry and London Politics 1889–1986*. London and New York: Routledge, 1989.

Anderson, Bonnie. "The Writings of Catherine Gore." *Journal of Popular Culture* 10 (Fall 1976): 404–423.

Anderson, Bonnie D., and Judith P. Zinsser. *A History of Their Own: Women in Europe from Prehistory to the Present*. 2 vols. New York: Harper & Row, 1988.

Aston, Elaine. *An Introduction to Feminism and Theatre*. London and New York: Routledge, 1995.

Austin, Gayle. *Feminist Theories for Dramatic Criticism*. Ann Arbor: The University of Michigan Press, 1990.

Bailey, J. O. *British Plays of the Nineteenth Century: An Anthology to Illustrate the Evolution of the Drama*. New York: The Odyssey Press, Inc., 1966.

Balderston, Katharine C., ed. *Thraliana: The Diary of Mrs. Hester Lynch Thrale (Later Mrs. Piozzi) 1776–1809*. 2nd ed. 2 vols. Oxford: Clarendon Press, 1951.

Bergan, Ronald. *The Great Theatres of London: An Illustrated Companion*. With a Foreword by Anthony Hopkins. San Francisco: Chronicle Books, 1987.

Blain, Virginia, Patricia Clements, and Isobel Grundy. *The Feminist Companion to Literature in English*. London: B.T. Batsford, Ltd., 1990.

Blakey, Dorothy, Ph.D. *The Minerva Press 1790–1820*. London: Oxford University Press for the Bibliographic Society, 1939.

Booth, Michael R. *English Melodrama*. London: Herbert Jenkins, 1965.

_____. *Prefaces to English Nineteenth-Century Theatre*. Manchester: Manchester University Press, n.d.

_____, ed. *The Lights o' London and Other Victorian Plays*. The World's Classics, ed. by Michael Cordner, Peter Holland, and Martin Wiggins. Oxford and New York: Oxford University Press, 1995.

Brockett, Oscar G. *History of the Theatre*. 6th ed. Boston: Allyn and Bacon, 1991.

Burke, Miss. *Songs, Duets, Choruses, &c. in "The Ward of the Castle," A Comic Opera in Two Acts, Performed at the Theatre Royal, Covent Garden*. London: T. Cadell, 1793.

Carlson, Marvin. *Theories of the Theatre: A Historical and Critical Survey, from the Greeks to the Present*. Ithaca and London: Cornell University Press, 1984.

Case, Sue-Ellen. *Feminism and Theatre*. New Directions in Theatre Series, ed. Julian Hilton. Houndmills, Basingstoke, Hampshire and London: The Macmillan Press Ltd., 1988.

Catalogue of Additions: Plays Submitted to the Lord Chamberlain 1824–1851. Additional Manuscripts 42865–43038. London: The Trustees of the British Museum, 1964.

Cerberus (pseud.). *The Theatrical Inquisitor and Monthly Mirror*. 16 vols. London: C. Chapple, 1812–1820.

Colman, George, the elder. *Polly Honeycomb*, in *The London Stage; A Collection of the Most Reputed Tragedies, Comedies, Operas, Melo-Dramas, Farces, and Interludes*. Vol. 2. London: Sherwood, Jones, and Co., n.d.

Cook, Dutton. "The Prize Comedy." *The Theatre*, 1 August 1882, 65–74.

Corfe, Tom. *Sunderland: A Short History*. Newcastle upon Tyne: Frank Graham, 1973.

Cox, Jeffrey N., ed. *Seven Gothic Dramas 1789–1825*. Athens: Ohio University Press, 1992.

Davis, Gwenn, and Beverly A. Joyce. *Drama by Women to 1900: A Bibliography of American and British Writers*. London: Mansell, 1992.

Davis, Tracy C. *Actresses as Working Women: Their Social Identity in Victorian Britain*. London: Routledge, 1991.

DeLamotte, Eugenia C. *Perils of the Night: A Feminist Study of Nineteenth-Century Gothic*. New York, Oxford: Oxford University Press, 1990.

Dolan, Jill. *The Feminist Spectator as Critic*. Ann Arbor: The University of Michigan Press, 1991.

Donkin, Ellen. *Getting into the Act: Women Playwrights in London 1776–1829*. London: Routledge, 1995.

The Drama; or, Theatrical Pocket Magazine. 7 vols. London: T. and J. Elvey, 1821–1825.

Dwinell, Jeanine. "Gender Issues in the Plays of Catherine Gore." Thesis. Florida State University, 1993.

Dye, William S., Jr. *A Study of Melodrama in England from 1800–1840*. State College, Pennsylvania: The Nittany Printing & Publishing Company, 1919.

Ellmann, Mary. *Thinking About Women*. San Diego: Harcourt Brace Jovanovich, Publishers, A Harvest/HBJ Book, 1968.

L'Estrange, A.G.K., ed. *The Life of Mary Russell Mitford*. Vol. 1. London: Richard Bentley, 1870.

Evans, Bertrand. *Gothic Drama from Walpole to Shelley*. Berkeley and Los Angeles: University of California Press, 1947.

Fairclough, Peter, ed. *Three Gothic Novels*. With an Introductory Essay by Mario Praz. London: Penguin Books, 1986.

Ferguson, Moira. *First Feminists: British Women Writers 1578–1799*. Bloomington: Indiana University Press, 1985.

"Fine Arts: Panorama of Jerusalem." *The Gentleman's Magazine* 3 New Series (January–June 1935): 522.

Fiske, Roger. *English Theatre Music in the Eighteenth Century,* 2nd ed. Oxford: Oxford University Press, 1986.

Forman, W. Courthope. "The Story of the Adelphi Theatre." *Notes and Queries* 158 no. 24 (June 1930): 419.

Genest, John, ed. *Some Account of the English Stage from the Restoration in 1660 to 1830.* 10 vols. Bath: n.p., 1832; reprint, Burt Franklin Research & Source Work Series 93. New York: Burt Franklin, n.d.

Harvey, Margaret. *The Lay of the Minstrel's Daughter.* Newcastle upon Tyne: J. Marshall, 1814.

Helme, Elizabeth. *St. Clair of the Isles.* London: Frederick Warne & Co., 1867.

Howard, Diana. *London Theatres and Music Halls 1850–1950.* London: The Library Association, 1970.

Hume, Robert D. "Gothic Versus Romantic: A Revaluation of the Gothic Novel," *PMLA* 84 (1969): 282–90.

Kendrick, Walter. *The Thrill of Fear: 250 Years of Scary Entertainment.* New York: Grove Weidenfeld, 1991.

Kenrick, Thomas. *The British Stage, and Literary Cabinet.* 6 vols. London: J. Chappell, 1817–1822.

Kilgarriff, Michael, ed. *The Golden Age of Melodrama.* London: Wolfe Publishing Limited, 1974.

Knight, G. Wilson. "Gothic [The Gothic Play]." In *The English Gothic Novel: A Miscellany in Four Volumes. Volume 4: Collateral Gothic 2.* Edited, with Introduction and Notes, by Thomas Meade Harwell. Salzburg: Institut für Anglistik und Amerikanistik Universität Salzburg, 1986.

Lévy, Maurice. *Le Roman "Gothique" Anglais 1764–1824.* Toulouse: Association des Publications de la Faculté des Lettres et Sciences Humaines de Toulouse, n.d.

Lewis, Matthew Gregory ["Monk"]. *The Castle Spectre, in The New English Drama, with Prefatory Remarks, Biographical Sketches, and Notes, Critical and Explanatory; Being the Only Edition Existing which Is Faithfully Marked with the Stage Business, and Stage Directions, As Performed at the Theatres Royal.* Ed. by W. Oxberry, Comedian. Vol. 4. London: W. Simpkin, and R. Marshall, 1819.

MacAndrew, Elizabeth. *The Gothic Tradition in Fiction.* New York: Columbia University Press, 1979.

MacCarthy, B.G. *The Female Pen: Women Writers and Novelists 1621–1818.* With a Preface by Janet Todd. New York: New York University Press, 1994.

Macqueen-Pope, W. Ladies First: *The Story of Woman's Conquest of the British Stage.* London: W.H. Allen, 1952.

Massé, Michelle A. *In The Name of Love: Women, Masochism, and the Gothic*. Ithaca and London: Cornell University Press, 1992.

Mayhew, Henry. *London Labour and the London Poor*. Vol. 1, *The London Street Folk*. London: George Woodfall and Son, 1851.

Mishra, Vijay. *The Gothic Sublime*. Albany: The State University of New York Press, 1994.

Moers, Ellen. *Literary Women*. New York: Oxford University Press, 1985.

Mullin, Donald. *Victorian Plays: A Record of Significant Productions on the London Stage, 1837–1901*. New York: Greenwood Press, 1987.

Mulvey, Laura. *Visual and Other Pleasures*. Language, Discourse, Society Series, eds. Stephen Heath, Colin MacCabe, and Denise Riley. Houndmills, Basingstoke, Hampshire and London: The Macmillan Press Ltd., 1989.

Nelson, Alfred L., and Gilbert B. Cross, eds. *The Adelphi Calendar Project 1806–1850: Sans Pareil Theatre 1806–1819/Adelphi Theatre 1819–1850*. The London Stage 1800–1900: A Documentary Record and Calendar of Performances, No. 1. Westport: Greenwood Press, 1990.

The New Female Instructor; or, Young Woman's Guide to Domestic Happiness. London: Thomas Kelley, 1834; reprint, London: Rosters Ltd., 1988.

Nicoll, Allardyce. *A History of English Drama 1660–1900*. Vol. 3, *Late Eighteenth Century Drama 1750–1800*. Cambridge: Cambridge University Press, 1979.

――――――――――. *A History of Early Nineteenth Century Drama 1800–1850*. 2 vols. New York: The Macmillan Company, 1930.

"Our Library Table." Review of *Dacre of the South; or The Olden Time*, by Mrs. Gore. *Athenaeum* 688 (January 1841): 13–14.

Pevsner, Nikolaus. *County Durham*. 2nd ed. The Buildings of England Series. Revised by Elizabeth Williamson. London: Penguin Books, 1990.

Pevsner, Nikolaus, and Ian Richmond. *Northumberland*. 2nd ed. The Buildings of England Series. Revised by John Grundy, Grace McCombie, Peter Ryder, Humphrey Welfare. London: Penguin Books, 1992.

Planché, J. R. *The Recollections and Reflections of James Robinson Planché*. 2 vols. London: Tinsley Bros., 1872.

Playbills: Covent Garden 1793–96.

Playbills: Olympic Theatre 1832–1834.

Playbills: Sunderland Theatre 1801–1853.

Playbills: Victoria Theatre 1834–1840.

Punter, David. *The Literature of Terror: A History of Gothic Fictions from 1765 to the Present Day*. London and New York: Longmans, 1980.

Rahill, Frank. *The World of Melodrama*. University Park and London: The Pennsylvania State University Press, 1967.

Ranger, Paul. *Terror and Pity Reign in Every Breast: Gothic Drama in the London Patent Theatres, 1750–1820.* London: The Society for Theatre Research, 1991.

Recording Britain. Vol. 4. Edited with notes by Arnold Palmer. London: Oxford University Press, 1949.

Review of *St. Clair of the Isles,* by Elizabeth Polack. Royal Victoria Theatre. *The Times,* 17 April, 1838.

Review of *The Ward of the Castle,* by Miss Burke. Covent Garden Theatre. *The Times,* 25 October, 1793.

Richards, Sandra. *The Rise of the English Actress.* New York: St. Martin's Press, 1993.

Rosa, Matthew Whiting. *The Silver-Fork School: Novels of Fashion Preceding "Vanity Fair."* New York: Columbia University Press, 1936.

Rowell, George. *The Old Vic Theatre: A History.* Cambridge: Cambridge University Press, 1993.

Schlueter, Paul, and June Schlueter, eds. *An Encyclopedia of British Women Writers.* New York and London: Garland Publishing, Inc., 1988. S.v. "Catherine Grace Frances Moody Gore," by Cynthia Merrill.

Scullion, Adrienne, ed. *Female Playwrights of the Nineteenth Century.* The Everyman Library. London: J. M. Dent, 1996.

Sedgwick, Eve Kosofsky. *The Coherence of Gothic Conventions.* Rev. ed. New York: Arno Press, 1980.

Sheridan, Richard B. *The Rivals,* in *The New English Drama, with Prefatory Remarks, Biographical Sketches, and Notes, Critical and Explanatory; Being the Only Edition Existing which Is Faithfully Marked with the Stage Business, and Stage Directions, As Performed at the Theatres Royal.* Ed. by W. Oxberry, Comedian. Vol. 1. London: W. Simpkin, and R. Marshall, 1819.

Showalter, Elaine. "Feminist Criticism in the Wilderness." *Critical Inquiry* 8 (1981): 179–205.

Spender, Dale. *Mothers of the Novel: 100 Good Women Writers before Jane Austen.* London: Pandora, 1986.

Stephen, Sir Leslie, and Sir Sidney Lee, eds. *The Dictionary of National Biography,* 1921–1922 edition.

Summers, Montague. *The Gothic Quest: A History of the Gothic Novel.* New York: Russell & Russell, Inc., 1964.

"Theatrical Register: Drury Lane." *The Gentleman's Magazine* 4 New Series (July–December 1835): 644.

Todd, Janet, ed. *Dictionary of British Women Writers.* London: Routledge, 1990.

_____. *Women's Friendship in Literature.* New York: Columbia University Press, 1980.

Tompkins, J. M. S. *The Popular Novel in England 1770–1800*. Lincoln: University of Nebraska Press, 1961.

Varma, Devendra P. *The Gothic Flame Being a History of the GOTHIC NOVEL in England: Its Origins, Efflorescence, Disintegration, and Residuary Influences*. Metuchen, N.J., & London: The Scarecrow Press, Inc., 1987.

The Victoria: An Original Pollock's Toy Theatre with Cinderella & R. L. Stevenson's Essay, Penny Plain, Twopence Coloured. London: Pollock's Toy Theatres, 1972.

Ward, Geoff, ed. *Romantic Literature from 1790 to 1830*. Bloomsbury Guides to English Literature. London: Bloomsbury Publishing Ltd., 1993.

Williams, Anne. *Art of Darkness: A Poetics of Gothic*. Chicago and London: The University of Chicago Press, 1995.

Wilt, Judith. *Ghosts of the Gothic: Austin, Eliot, & Lawrence*. Princeton: Princeton University Press, 1980.

Winter, Kari J. *Subjects of Slavery, Agents of Change: Women and Power in Gothic Novels and Slave Narratives, 1790–1865*. Athens and London: The University of Georgia Press, 1992.

Wolstenholme, Susan. *Gothic (Re)Visions: Writing Women as Readers*. Albany: State University of New York Press, 1993.